'ın excellent biography, which captures the real Lenin – part intellectual professor, part ruthless and dogmatic politician.'

Geoffrey Swain, University of the West of England

'A fascinating book about a gigantic historical figure. Christopher Read is an accomplished scholar and superb writer who has produced a first-rate study that is courageous, original in its insights, and deeply humane.'

Daniel Orlovsky, Southern Methodist University

Vladimir Il'ich Ulyanov, known as Lenin was an enigmatic leader, a resolute and audacious politician who had an immense impact on twentieth-century world history. Lenin's life and career have been at the centre of much ideological debate for many decades. The post-Soviet era has seen a revived interest and re-evaluation of the Russian Revolution and Lenin's legacy.

This new biography gives a fresh and original account of Lenin's personal life and political career. Christopher Read draws on a broad range of primary and secondary sources, including material made available in the *glasnost* and post-Soviet eras. Focal points of this study are Lenin's revolutionary ascetic personality; how he exploited culture, education and propaganda; his relationship to Marxism; his changing class analysis of Russia; and his 'populist' instincts.

This biography is an excellent and reliable introduction to one of the key figures of the Russian Revolution and post-Tsarist Russia.

Christopher Read is Professor of Modern European History at the University of Warwick. He is author of *From Tsar to Soviets: The Russian People and Their Revolution, 1917–21* (1996), *Culture and Power in Revolutionary Russia* (1990) and *The Making and Breaking of the Soviet System* (2001).

ROUTLEDGE HISTORICAL BIOGRAPHIES

SERIES EDITOR: ROBERT PEARCE

Routledge Historical Biographies provide engaging, readable and academically credible biographies written from an explicitly historical perspective. These concise and accessible accounts will bring important historical figures to life for students and general readers alike.

In the same series:

Bismarck by Edgar Feuchtwanger
Churchill by Robert Pearce
Gladstone by Michael Partridge
Henry VII by Sean Cunningham
Henry VIII by Lucy Wooding
Hitler by Martyn Housden
Jinnah by Sikander Hayat
Martin Luther King Jr. by Peter J. Ling
Mary Queen of Scots by Retha Warnicke
Martin Luther by Michael Mullet
Mao by Michael Lynch
Mussolini by Peter Neville
Nehru by Ben Zachariah
Emmeline Pankhurst by Paula Bartley
Richard III by Ann Kettle
Franklin D. Roosevelt by Stuart Kidd
Stalin by Geoffrey Roberts
Trotsky by Ian Thatcher
Mary Tudor by Judith Richards

LENIN
A REVOLUTIONARY LIFE

Christopher Read

Routledge
Taylor & Francis Group

LONDON AND NEW YORK

First published 2005
by Routledge
2 Park Square, Milton Park, Abingdon, Oxon OX14 4RN

Simultaneously published in the USA and Canada
by Routledge
270 Madison Ave., New York, NY 10016

Transferred to Digital Printing 2008

Routledge is an imprint of the Taylor & Francis Group

© 2005 Christopher Read

Typeset in Garamond and ScalaSans by Taylor & Francis Books
Printed and bound in Great Britain by
TJI Digital, Padstow, Cornwall

British Library Cataloguing in Publication Data
A catalogue record for this book is available from the British Library

Library of Congress Cataloging in Publication Data
Read, Christopher, 1946–
    Lenin : a revolutionary life / by Christopher Read.-- 1st ed.
        p. cm. -- (Routledge historical biographies)
    Includes bibliographical references and index.
    1. Lenin, Vladimir Il'ich, 1870-1924--Juvenile literature.
2. Revolutionaries--Soviet Union--Biography--Juvenile literature.
3. Heads of state--Soviet Union--Biography--Juvenile literature.
4. Soviet Union--Politics and government--1917-1936--Juvenile
literature. I. Title. II. Series.
    DK254.L455R43 2005
    947.084'1'092--dc22

                                                    2004026081

ISBN 10: 0-415-20648-0 (hbk)
ISBN 10: 0-415-20649-9 (pbk)
ISBN 13: 978-0-415-20648-8 (hbk)
ISBN 13: 978-0-415-20649-5 (pbk)

Contents

LIST OF PLATES   vi
ACKNOWLEDGEMENTS   vii
CHRONOLOGY   ix

Introduction   1

1 Choosing revolution   4

2 Laying the foundations of Leninism (1896–1902)   29

3 Constructing Leninism   63

4 Imperialism, war and revolution   106

5 From the Finland station to the Winter Palace   142

6 From classroom to laboratory – early experiments   184

7 Revolutionary war   205

8 Re-evaluation, succession and testament   256

Conclusion: Lenin lived! Lenin lives! Lenin will live
forever!   283

NOTES   292
FURTHER READING   300
INDEX   303

PLATES

(between pages 180 and 181)

1   The Ulyanov family in Simbirsk, 1879, Vladimin is bottom right
2   Lenin as a university student, 1891
3   Lenin and the Petersburg League of Struggle, 1895. Lenin is in the centre seated behind the table
4   Forged passport, 1917
5   Lenin sitting at his desk, c. 1921
6   Lenin, Krupskaya and children on a bench, 1922
7   Lenin in a wheelchair, 1923
8   Crowd at Lenin's funeral, 1924. The cult begins
9   Lenin's work goes on – *Pravda* editors at work (Bukharin and Maria Ulyanova, Lenin's sister), 1925

ACKNOWLEDGEMENTS

Many people have helped me understand something of Lenin and develop my ideas about him, especially colleagues, visitors and students in the History Department of the University of Warwick and at the Centre for Russian and East European Studies in Birmingham. I am deeply indebted to them all. While my ideas differ from theirs (and theirs differ from each other) two people I initially met as my teachers have exerted a lasting influence over the subsequent decades. James White, at Glasgow, opened up what were, for me, hidden aspects of the Russian Revolution and the creative differences we have had since continue to stimulate. The influence of the late Leonard Schapiro also looms large over this study. His sharply critical but well-founded and path-breaking studies remain a model of liberal scholarship.

This volume was initially commissioned by Heather McCallum who has since left Routledge. She did, however, have a decisive influence on its emergence. When I signed up to write it I was attracted by two aspects above all: the challenge, for a temperamentally and unfashionably structuralist historian like myself, of writing about an individual and secondly the fact that no up-to-date one-volume scholarly study of Lenin's life had been published for nearly two decades. However, the ink had hardly dried on the contract when I attended a study day in London for college students studying the Russian Revolution. During a break between lectures I was leaning on the imposing lectern in the hallowed Victorian lecture theatre of the Royal Institution. I turned to my two friends and fellow speakers asking them about the progress of their current research. Beryl Williams replied that she was in the throes of completing her one-volume biography of Lenin. Robert Service said he was nearing completion of his one-volume life of Lenin which was complementary to his three-volume political biography. Beryl's excellent book came out some months later and Bob's heavyweight tome went on to win prizes and appear in many 'book of the year' lists in the cultural journals. In the meantime, knowing by then that James White was also working on his biography of Lenin, I went back to Heather and pointed out that, apart from mine, there were at least three other *Lenin*s in preparation. Was it worth continuing? 'Why ever not?', she replied.

'There are sixteen Gladstones out there being written.' Only the reader will judge whether she was right to encourage me.

Since Heather's departure Vicky Peters has been a friendly, supportive and patient editor. I am, above all, indebted to Robert Pearce, the series editor, for very helpful and detailed comments on the first draft and also to Dan Orlovsky and Geoff Swain who have made many pertinent, penetrating, helpful, positive and supportive observations on the typescript. Despite all their efforts to put me right there will still be errors and misunderstandings. These are entirely my responsibility.

CHRONOLOGY

Year	Lenin's Life	Russian Events	World Events
1870	born in Simbirsk (10/22 April)		
1871			Germany unified; German Empire proclaimed
1877–8			Russo–Turkish War
1881		Tsar Alexander II assassinated	
1886	father dies; Alexander Ulyanov arrested for terrorist offences; takes school leaving exams and enters Kazan University		
1887	Alexander Ulyanov executed (May); expelled from university		
1892	awarded first-class degree in law from University of St Petersburg		
1893	first pamphlet published		
1895	first foreign journey; returns to help found League of Struggle for the Emancipation of the Working Class; first arrest (December)		
1896	spends the year in prison		
1897	exiled to Shushenskoe in Siberia		
1898	marries Nadezhda Krupskaya	Russian Social Democratic Labour Party founded in Minsk	

Year	Lenin's Life	Russian Events	World Events
1899	*Development of Capitalism in Russia* published		
1900	returns from Siberia (January) and leaves for western Europe (July); lives in Munich	first issue of *Iskra* published; *Liberation* movement, later Constitutional Democratic Party (Kadets), set up	
1901	Krupskaya joins Lenin; pseudonym 'Lenin' used for first time	Socialist Revolutionary (SR) Party founded	
1902	*What is to be Done?* published		
1903	with Krupskaya moves to London and later Geneva	Second Party Congress held in Brussels and London	
1904	*One Step Forward: Two Steps Back* published		Russo–Japanese War begins
1905	*Two Tactics of Social Democracy in the Democratic Revolution* published; returns to Russia (November); goes into hiding (December)	revolution in Russia; Bloody Sunday (January); October Manifesto; Moscow Uprising (December)	Treaty of Portsmouth ends Russo–Japanese War
1906	remains in hiding making frequent forays into Russia from Finland	Duma system set up; First Duma elected	
1907	leaves Finland and returns to western Europe (December)	Second Duma disbanded; Third Duma elected on limited franchise	
1908	with Krupskaya settles in Geneva		

Year	Lenin's Life	Russian Events	World Events
1909	*Materialism and Empiriocriticism* published; with Krupskaya moves to Paris; meets Inessa Armand		
1911		Prime Minister Stolypin assassinated	
1912	with Krupskaya moves to Poland	Prague Conference of Bolsheviks; *Pravda* first published; Fourth Duma elected	First Balkan War
1913			Second Balkan War
1914	with Krupskaya leaves Poland for Switzerland		First World War begins; Second Socialist International hopelessly split over war
1915			Zimmerwald Conference
1916	completes *Imperialism: The Highest Stage of Capitalism: A Popular Outline*; first published in truncated version in 1917	Brusilov offensive	Kienthal Conference; battles of Somme, Jutland and Verdun
1917	returns to Russia and proclaims his *April Theses*; flees to Finland after July Days; writes *State and Revolution*; takes part in October Revolution; becomes head of the new Soviet state	February Revolution; July Days; Kornilov affair; October Revolution proclaims soviet power; Constituent Assembly elected	United States enters First World War

Year	Lenin's Life	Russian Events	World Events
1918	Lenin, and Soviet government, move to Moscow Kremlin; writes *Immediate Tasks of the Soviet Government* (March) signalling shift to 'iron discipline'	Constituent Assembly disbanded; Civil War flares up (July)	Treaty of Brest-Litovsk ends war on eastern front (March); armistice on western front (November)
1919		Civil War at its peak	Communist International (Comintern) founded; Versailles Conference (Russia excluded)
1920		Whites virtually defeated; war with Poland; Tambov Uprising	
1921	dominates Tenth Party Congress; NEP adopted	Tenth Party Congress; Kronstadt Uprising	
1922	suffers first stroke (May) and second in December	Stalin appointed General Secretary of Communist Party	
1923	composes the various elements of his so-called Last Testament; last article, 'Better Fewer but Better', is written (March); suffers third stroke	Soviet Union (USSR) formally established	
1924	dies (21 January)		

INTRODUCTION

Lenin would undoubtedly have considered the current moment in world history to be profoundly counter-revolutionary. The task of presenting the life of a revolutionary to such a world is a complicated one. Writing about Victor Serge, the Russo-Belgian writer and activist who was one of Lenin's greatest admirers and a fellow Bolshevik, Susan Sontag brilliantly expounded the problem: 'English-speaking readers of Serge today have to think themselves back to a time when most people accepted that the course of their lives would be determined by history rather than psychology, by public rather than private crises.'[1] The present generation may be in for a shock as history strikes back after its much-vaunted 'end' in the 1990s. However, the current conjuncture does have one advantage for understanding Lenin. Revolution, in Lenin's early years, appeared as distant and improbable a prospect as it does today. In his time, as today, the world was thought to be post-revolutionary, the main revolution being that of France in 1789. In fact, the world of Lenin's youth turned out to be pre-revolutionary (in the case of Russia) and heading for self-destruction by means of the First World War (in the case of Europe in general). Maybe the same is true today. Whether it is or not, the experience of Lenin, his strengths and weaknesses, his triumphs and tragic mistakes, still provide a fund of experience from which we can learn. There are ideas that can still stimulate. There are other ideas which turned out to be sterile, even dangerous, from which we can learn what to avoid.

With this in mind the aim of the present study is to try to understand Lenin. Not to justify him, but to understand. To that end the emphasis is on what Lenin himself said and did rather than what others said about him. There is no shortage of material. The so-called *Collected Works* (actually incomplete) amount to 47 volumes of around 500 pages each in the English edition, 55 volumes in the most recent Russian edition. The amount written about him is exponentially greater. Almost all comments about Lenin come from someone with an axe to grind. The greatest distorters of Lenin's actions and ideas originate from two groups – his admirers and his detractors. There has been no third group of any size. Lenin's ability to wreck the closest of friendships for political reasons left a trail of emotional, angry debris out of which many memoirs of the 'Lenin I knew' genre were written. Former allies claimed that they discerned the later dictator in the younger man. As often as not, with notable exceptions like Trotsky, their writings of earlier times show no hint of this deep, prescient, perception. Admirers, too, have patched over his faults. The finest single guide to Lenin's life, particularly before October, the memoirs of his wife Nadezhda Krupskaya, steer clear of political issues. They, along with the memoirs of other members of his family, do, however, paint a convincing picture of the positive aspects of Lenin's personality and of his (limited) life and interests outside politics. But the source material remains problematic, though massive. Should one write about Lenin through the eyes of his admirers or his opponents? This offers historians a choice: follow the outlines of the interpretation offered by one group or the other. Select Lenin the affable genius or Lenin the irascible tyrant. Can one, should one, avoid those stereotypes?

The path chosen in this account is to look at Lenin's own words at the time as much as possible. His supposedly minor articles and letters are the most prominent source used. Next in priority are comments made about him close to the time. Krupskaya's memoirs have, perforce, been used extensively to fill in the personal and emotional colours of Lenin's life. In a relatively short study it has been a question of leaving massive amounts of material out. Nonetheless, the central focus on Lenin, his works and deeds, has, it is to be hoped, presented a fresh picture of Lenin resulting in a less melodramatic and caricatural view of his personality than that emanating from his committed friends and enemies.

For the benefit of the anticipated readership quotations from Lenin have been referenced to English language editions. References to these and to two other frequently used sources have been abbreviated and inserted into the text in square brackets. The sources and abbreviation conventions are: Lenin's *Collected Works*, 47 vols (Moscow, 1960–70) (English edition) appear as 'CW' followed by volume and page number to give, for example, '[CW 27 113]'. A similar format has been used for the three-volume *Selected Works* (Moscow, 1963–4) to produce, for example, '[SW 2 419]'. Where possible all Lenin quotations have been given to this set as it is relatively accessible for the potential users of the book. Two other one-volume sources have also been referenced in this way. They are Nadezhda Krupskaya's *Memories of Lenin* (London, 1970) which appears as, for example, '[Krupskaya 157]', the number, of course, being the page number; and, the best chronology of Lenin's life, G. and H. Weber's *Lenin: Life and Works* (London and Basingstoke, 1980) which appears as, for example, '[Weber 80]'. In the many quotations from Lenin all emphases, unless otherwise stated, come from the original texts. Interpolations in square brackets are authorial amendments.

Unless otherwise stated the dates in the text conform to conventional western dates. However, mainly for Russian events in 1917 I have used the Old Style calendar, which, up to its abolition at the end of January 1918, was twelve days behind the western calendar in the nineteenth century and thirteen behind in the twentieth. This is done primarily to keep the February Revolution in February and the October Revolution in October. Use of the Old Style calendar is signified by '(OS)' after the date. Transliteration follows Library of Congress guidelines with some variants so that names end in the more familiar 'y' rather than 'ii'.

1

CHOOSING REVOLUTION

Lenin was not born, Lenin was constructed. The child who was to become Lenin, Vladimir Il'ich Ulyanov, was born on 22 April 1870. He was the fourth child of a moderately prosperous, upwardly mobile teacher and public official, Ilya Nikolaevich Ulyanov (1831–86) and his wife Maria Alexandrovna Ulyanova (1835–1916) whose maiden name had been Maria Blank. At the time, the family was living in the deeply provincial town of Simbirsk on the Volga, a place which came to bear the name of Ulyanovsk in honour of their son. Ilya and Maria were not from the Simbirsk region. Ilya's family was based in Astrakhan, at the mouth of the Volga, and his life was spent in large towns along Russia's greatest river. He and Maria married and lived in Penza, where Ilya taught mathematics and physics before moving to Nizhnii-Novgorod. Maria was already pregnant with Vladimir when they moved to Simbirsk to allow Ilya to take up a prestigious post as an inspector of primary schools.

FAMILY BACKGROUND: THE ETHNIC, SOCIAL AND CULTURAL INHERITANCE

At the time of Vladimir Ulyanov's birth, the European world was already becoming deeply obsessed with national and racial identity. Nothing could better show the contradictions of such thinking than Vladimir's own background. While, to the outside world, Lenin appeared to be a symbol of Russianness in the twentieth century, like so many major national figures, the purity of his Russianness was much diluted. A great deal of research has been conducted into Lenin's family background since access to former Soviet sources became easier in the 1980s. As a result we have a clearer idea of the ethnic and social mix which he inherited. Going back to his great-grandparents, Russian, Jewish, Swedish, German and possibly Kalmyk influences can be discovered. One might say Lenin's first revolutionary act was to be born an internationalist! In fact one could argue that the fusion of Russia's two ancient groups, Slavonic and Tatar, plus an addition of Jewishness and western European influences, was the ultimate expression of a truer hybrid Russianness.

The ethnic mix came mainly from the side of his mother, Maria Alexandrovna. Her father Alexander had been born Srul (Israel) Blank. He and his brother, Abel, who took the name Dmitrii, had been officially baptized into the Orthodox church in 1820, probably as a convenience to facilitate their professional careers. As Jews they could avoid all discriminatory measures through baptism. Their father Moishe Blank had himself been a non-practising Jew who also converted to Christianity after his wife died. Moishe Blank had been a very active small trader and merchant living in the largely Jewish town of Starokonstantinov in Volhynia province in western Russia. His sons Abel and Srul had settled in St Petersburg in pursuit of their medical careers. Maria Blank's own mother, Anna Ivanovna Groschopf, provided the German and Swedish ingredients. Her father, Johann Groschopf, was German; his wife, Anna Estedt, Lenin's great-grandmother, was Swedish. The family increasingly assimilated through the generations though Maria Alexandrovna and her mother retained Lutheran connections, despite being officially Orthodox. Maria Blank's family circumstances changed when her mother died in 1838 when Maria Alexandrovna was only three years old. To help look after his six children Alexander turned to his wife's sister, Ekaterina von Essen, to help him and they set up a household together. Apparently with her money they purchased a country estate at Kokushkino, near Kazan, where Maria Alexandrovna was brought up as the child of a landowner.

The provenance of Lenin's father Ilya was less complicated. His background was overwhelmingly Russian. The exception to this was Ilya's mother. Even her name is disputed, some sources calling her Anna, others Alexandra. According to Ulyanov family lore she was of 'Tatar' origin. Exactly what her precise ethnic background was is unknown. Most sources say she was a Kalmyk, that is a member of a small Buddhist people. Others suggest she may have belonged to a Muslim ethnic group. However, nothing has yet been found to prove that she was non-Russian, though the family assumption that she was not is powerful circumstantial evidence.

There has also been controversy about the social circumstances of Lenin's father's family. Soviet sources almost invariably stated that Ilya's father, Nikolai, was originally a serf. Western writers have largely contested this, pointing to Nikolai's substantial urban house in Astrakhan and his trade as a tailor to disprove the assertion. No one, however, disputes that Nikolai's own father, Vasili Nikitich Ulianov, was a serf. It is not improbable that Nikolai was born a serf but achieved freedom allowing him to establish himself as a modestly secure urban artisan.

Arguments about Lenin's background, whether it be his Jewish relatives or the social status of his grandfather, were minor elements of the East–West ideological conflict which arose out of the Russian Revolution. For the Soviets, the leader's links to the ordinary population had to be emphasized. For western historians his links to the landowning class were occasion for much polemical writing. The Soviet authorities also tended to underemphasize Lenin's Jewish connections. Some westerners claimed this was because of Soviet anti-semitism. It was equally likely to have been Soviet caution in not wanting anti-Soviet, anti-semitic elements inside and outside Russia to make play with the facts of his background, not least in the 1930s when fascism and Nazism were equating communism with the Jewish conspiracy.

Of course, the key question is, does Lenin's background matter? At the genetic level we are not yet in a position to say that any of Lenin's characteristics and physical attributes were related to particular sources. For example, he died young, as did many of his family members, and he suffered, as we shall see, certain persistent illnesses including the sclerosis that led to his eventually fatal strokes. In the crudely materialistic atmosphere of the Soviet Union in the 1920s, it was even decided to preserve Lenin's brain for research and it was gruesomely sliced up for microscopic examination, the slides still being in existence today. However, nothing significant has emerged from such lines of enquiry. One day perhaps, the genetic roots of his mental abilities and other characteristics will be better known but all efforts so far have been fruitless. Lenin's ethnic background, in itself, is not particularly important. What is much more significant and easier to trace is his cultural heritage. The gradual social rise from serfdom to hereditary nobility on his father's side and the professional intelligentsia background of his mother, going back to her grandfather, Johann, who was a notary, plus the immediate small landowner milieu in which Maria grew up, created an active, energetic, cultured environment in which Vladimir Ulyanov was to develop. In order to examine this we can best look at his family upbringing.

THE ULYANOV FAMILY

The first point to make is that in the life of the young Vladimir, known as Volodya within the family, there was no sign of the developing Lenin. Volodya's childhood seems to have been entirely conventional for the circles in which he lived. The family seems to have been a happy one. Indeed, Lenin remained close to his surviving family members throughout his life. The Ulyanovs spent a great deal of time together. The children played with one another. There were visits to friends and family. In particular, there were summer trips to the Kokushkino estate where they all enjoyed country pursuits: long walks; an increasing knowledge of nature and its cycles; and, eventually, the art of hunting which became one of Volodya's passions as he grew up. The family lived the life of landowners, keeping themselves socially separate from the peasants. Romantic fables that Volodya used to take peasants to one side and chat about their conditions had no basis in fact.

That did not, however, mean Volodya and the rest of the family were indifferent to the plight of the peasantry, far from it. It is hard to pinpoint anything resembling a family political consciousness in the 1870s and early 1880s but there are signs that Lenin's father, Ilya, was aware of the plight of the people and attempted to do something about it. In the tradition of so-called 'repentant nobles' and the early radical intelligentsia that sprang from it, Ilya was touched by the widespread sentiment that the raw inequalities of Russian society were immoral and needed to be reduced. In Ilya's case he saw it as his mission to bring education to a wider and wider circle of the people and, as an inspector of schools, to ensure its quality was high. This did not mean that Ilya was in any sense a revolutionary. He was a loyal member of the government bureaucracy and was pleased to accept promotions up the official table of ranks including, in 1874, the attainment of hereditary nobility. He attended local official functions and wore his medals of honour with pride. Rather than associating with any revolutionary tradition, he belonged to the much more widespread group of 'small deeds' liberals who believed that grand revolutionary gestures were pointless. Instead they worked quietly and determinedly within the system to make as many real improvements in people's lives as they could.

In many ways, the atmosphere in which Ilya and his generation had been brought up was reflected in this moderation. Prior to the Crimean War (1854–6) there had been three decades of complacent immobility, reigned over by Nicholas I. The stifling and unproductive atmosphere of his reign was based on two aspects. First, it had been sparked off by fear arising from the minor threat to the autocracy posed by the Decembrist uprising in 1825. Second, the massive pride in Russia's great achievement of defeating Napoleon in 1812 and reaching Paris in 1814 lasted well beyond its sell-by date. The ensuing lack of progress was brought into focus by the disasters of the Crimean War. By chance, Nicholas died in the middle of the conflict in 1855. His successor, though no radical, realised change was necessary and, in 1861, promulgated Russia's greatest reform of the age, the abolition of serfdom. Further reforms followed. The judiciary was reformed and trial by jury introduced. Military service became more humane. Most relevant to the small deeds liberals, however, was the establishment of more systematized local authorities which looked after a growing range of local problems and amenities. Roads, bridges, agricultural improvement and other minor works came under their control.

For Ilya Ulyanov, increased local responsibilities for primary education opened up the pathways of his career. He was able to throw himself into his life of service believing that the better he served the peasants the better he served his sovereign and his country. The Ulyanovs were themselves a cultured family and middle-class accomplishments like watercolouring and music, including singing and playing musical instruments, were part of family life. Volodya became a passable piano player but gave up when he was ten years old. The children themselves were successful learners. Alexander won himself a coveted place to study science at one of Russia's best universities, St Petersburg. Although higher education was out of the question at that time for most women, the Ulyanov sisters, Maria, Anna and Olga, were also intelligent and accomplished.

Like Alexander, Volodya shone at school. At the end of his secondary school he was given a glowing report by his headmaster and achieved top marks in almost all his subjects. It is from this school report, copies of which were prominently displayed in Lenin museums around the country in Soviet times, that we have the best summary of Volodya's intellect and personality:

> Quite talented, invariably diligent, prompt and reliable, Ulyanov was first in all his classes, and upon graduation was awarded a gold medal as the most meritorious pupil in achievement, growth and conduct. There is not a single instance on record, either in school or outside of it, of Ulyanov evoking by word or deed any adverse opinion from the authorities and teachers of the school.

It is somewhat ironic that the reference goes on to say that 'The guiding principles of his upbringing were religion and rational discipline.' The latter had already begun to strangle the former. Visitors to Soviet museums who had good eyesight, since it was never emphasized officially, could discern another irony in the report. The signature of the headmaster who wrote it was that of Fyodor Kerensky, the father of Alexander, Prime Minister of the Provisional Government and arch-rival of Lenin in 1917. Alexander Kerensky, however, was yet to be born so the two men never met but the odds that the two dominant figures on opposite sides of the Revolution should come from the same provincial backwater, were enormous. The families, nonetheless, were acquainted and headmaster Kerensky, perhaps from friendship plus a desire to please an influential official, made great efforts to get Volodya into a university.

In the improving atmosphere of reform and relative toleration – many Jews, for instance, looked back on the 1860s and 1870s as a relative golden age – the reign of the 'Tsar-Liberator' changed the atmosphere for mild reformers like Ilya. The brutal conclusion of the years of moderate optimism came about as revolutionary terrorists closed in on the tsar and, after three years of serious attempts, finally succeeded in killing him in March 1881. For many, the small deeds strategy was reinforced by the assassination because, rather than achieve its goal of liberating Russia from tyranny, it brought about a massive wave of sympathy for the autocracy and provided the context for a more reactionary regime led by Alexander III and his chief adviser Konstantin Pobedonostsev to succeed the reforming tsar. It could be argued that, in the long term, the return to a stifling, anti-democratic police state undermined the autocracy more successfully than any revolutionary movement, but that was not apparent at the time. Instead, opportunities for small deeds were increasingly circumscribed.

Not all observers believed the assassination was a failure. Among those who believed that the point was to continue with classic terrorism was a small group of students at St Petersburg University, including Alexander Ulyanov. They vowed to attempt to assassinate Alexander III. When the plot was discovered Alexander tried to take the blame on himself and protect his fellow conspirators. His noble gesture failed to save them. He also refused to renounce his act, standing by it even though he might have escaped the death sentence which was eventually passed on him. Alexander's heroic stoicism was especially painful in the face of his mother's pleas and his knowledge of the grief and suffering it would bring to the rest of his loving family, which had already suffered the great blow of Ilya's death in January 1886.

Alexander's arrest, trial and execution in 1887, while an apparently routine punishment for a potential regicide, was a turning point in Russia's history. The impact turned the Ulyanov family inside out, pushing them further into increasing hostility to the autocracy. All the members were deeply affected, but none took the execution to heart more than Volodya. While, up to that point, Volodya's life had been normal and showed no signs of revolutionary tendencies, the arrest and execution of Alexander changed all that. In 1886, Lenin began to form in the soul of Volodya.

LENIN: THE FIRST INFLUENCES

Although hard information is sparse and what we have tends to be hagiographical, it seems that Alexander had become something of a role model for his younger brother. Through hard, academic work Alexander had succeeded in getting to university, no mean feat at a time when there were only some ten thousand university students in the whole Russian Empire. His fate raised the question: what had driven him to sacrifice his own life, so young and so full of promise? Providing an answer seems to have caused a pall of seriousness to fall over the often light-hearted life of the family. Apparently for the first time, the young Volodya began to wrestle with the complex questions of political and social justice and the responsibility of the individual to right wrongs which led him to follow Alexander down the revolutionary path.

Initially, Volodya appears to have become aware of the hidden political side of Alexander's personality through contact with some of his books from his Petersburg lodgings. Details are especially sketchy and Soviet commentators went to great lengths to date Lenin's first acquaintance with Marxism from this point and to present it as a road to Damascus. A much-quoted saying attributed to Lenin by his sister even implied that Lenin was already an embryonic Marxist. On hearing of his brother's fate Lenin is said to have remarked 'We will not go that way'. In Soviet interpretations the phrase was meant to imply that he rejected the path of revolutionary terror. But it is completely incredible that Volodya had already formed a core Leninist political consciousness as the story is meant to demonstrate. If he did say such a thing at the time, and, like so much from these crucial years of Lenin's life we cannot be certain, it could have had a variety of meanings, most obviously that giving away one's life so easily was wrong, that one should live on to fight and fight again. Indeed, Lenin's later life shows his great anxiety not to be captured at crucial moments so he could do precisely that.

Far from shunning revolutionary populism it is almost certain that Volodya, before Lenin was fully formed, did fall precisely under the influence of that creed which focused on idealization of the ordinary working person and stressed the corruption of the elite and the duty of enlightened intellectuals to lead the liberation of the labouring masses. Many populists believed that the peasant commune, the *mir*, and the co-operative workshop, the *artel'*, were potential building blocks of a future socialist society. In the late 1880s there was no other radical movement of any size in Russia. Although Marxism, under the influence of George Plekhanov (1856–1918), was separating itself out from populism, its influence was still very small and largely confined to Russians living abroad. After all, it was Plekhanov himself who joked, when he and Pavel Axel'rod and other founders of Russian Marxism went for a boat trip on Lake Geneva, that if they were to drown it would be the end of Russian Marxism. That being said, it should, however, be remembered that Marx had great influence on the populists and it was in 1879 that one of them had written to him putting a question with which he wrestled for the remainder of his life. The question was: could Russia bypass capitalism and go straight to the construction of a socialist society from its semi-feudal base? After much thought and prevarication Marx replied, in the Preface to an 1882 translation of *The Communist Manifesto*, that Russia could go straight to socialism provided the revolution occurred relatively soon and that the advanced capitalist countries of western Europe also underwent socialist revolutions and assisted the weaker Russian proletariat and working peasantry. It is not, therefore, surprising that Alexander had some Marxist texts in his library.

However, it was not Marx who made the greatest impact on Volodya. The didactic novel *What is to be Done? Tales of the New People* (1864), written by the academic economist Nikolai Chernyshevsky (1828–89), had a greater effect. Although much maligned by critics for its unlikely plot – including a love-triangle in which everyone tries to give way to everyone else – and its wooden, caricatural characterizations, it was the Bible of a young generation of students and became a founding text of populism. The attraction was the radical communal lifestyle of the main characters. They lived together and shared everything in the manner of 'new people' living out, before Nietzsche coined the phrase, the revaluation of all values. The crudely money-grubbing market and property-oriented values of contemporary Russian society were rejected in favour of science, reason and modernity. Sexual double standards and the subjection of women were totally rejected. In a peculiar coda, omitted from most English translations of the novel until it was restored in 1989,[1] Chernyshevsky portrays a vision of a futuristic building, based on London's Crystal Palace, a great wonder of the age, as a temple of free love and the free life. Perhaps the most influential character, and one whose influence in turning Volodya into Lenin is almost universally recognized, was Rakhmetov. He distinguished himself by trying to make himself as tough as possible to serve the revolution. To do this he spent time with the boat-haulers of the Volga, a breed of tough outcasts who pulled Volga barges upstream. The work was hard and badly paid but they had the reputation as the toughest people in Russia. Ilya Repin painted a memorable portrait of them and they were also idealized and immortalized in 'The Song of the Volga Boatmen'. Rakhmetov is also depicted sleeping on a bed of nails to help him overcome pain. Rakhmetov became a symbol and heroic role-model for many Russians and it is often suggested that Lenin's 'fanaticism', in the eyes of his critics, or 'revolutionary determination' for his supporters, derived from Rakhmetov.

Sergei Nechaev, a real-life Rakhmetov in some respects, is also frequently brought into the explanation at this point. Nechaev wrote a text entitled *Catechism of a Revolutionary* in which he urged the would-be revolutionary to cast off all regular social ties and devote him- or herself entirely to revolution. Nechaev was a controversial figure in 1870s Russia as was his association with one of the leading revolutionaries of the age, Mikhail Bakunin (1814–76). At one time Bakunin was thought to be the author of the *Catechism*. Nechaev's extreme vision of a revolutionary as an outcast who was infused only with the single passion of revolution is often pointed to as a paradigm for Lenin's later supposed fanaticism. However, there is no evidence that the *Catechism* had any major influence on Lenin; nor, as we shall see, did he live his life according to its precepts.

The influence of Bakunin himself is harder to assess. Terrorists of the late nineteenth century, including Alexander Ulyanov, were highly influenced by Bakunin's ideas, especially his principle that 'the urge to destroy is a creative urge'. Influenced by evolutionary theory Bakunin argued that everything should be attacked and challenged. If it survived, according to the Darwinian law of the survival of the fittest, it deserved to do so. If a person or institution or idea collapsed under the assault, something stronger and better suited would take its place. It is very likely that Bakunin and his followers were more influential than Marx in turning Volodya Ulyanov into Vladimir Il'ich Lenin. However, there is not enough evidence for us to be sure. Our information on this issue has also been polluted by generations of Soviet dissemblance. The hagiographic requirement was, as we have seen, to produce Lenin as a full-blown instinctive Marxist from day one of his revolutionary career. To allow the influence of a thinker, albeit a Russian, who was the chief opponent of Marx in the First International and in the left-wing doctrinal arguments of the 1860s and 1870s, would not fit that requirement.

However, it is most likely that the young Lenin was influenced, directly or indirectly, by Bakuninist ideas. In some respects the development of his thought, which involved Russifying Marx, showed certain key Bakuninst elements throughout his life. In particular, Bakunin prioritized political struggle especially against church and state, hence his encouragement of terrorism particularly against state officials. For Marx, the key was class struggle which involved very different dimensions and practices, Marx, like Lenin, being largely sceptical about the revolutionary value of isolated acts of terrorism. Such violence could, the Marxists argued, lead more easily to greater repression than to liberation. However, despite his later impeccable Marxist affiliation, Lenin's thought and, above all, his practice, showed a Bakuninite framework. Lenin was a quintessential political animal and state and church were in the forefront of his targets. In his disputes of the early twentieth century with Mensheviks and the so-called Economists, Lenin took a rather Bakuninist line against the more apparently orthodox Marxism of his opponents. However, that lay in the future.

Much of what has been said in the preceding paragraphs is speculative and at best circumstantial. It does, none the less, seem likely that the first ideological impulse turning Volodya into Lenin arose from the populist tradition. First, as has already been stressed, there was no other widespread tradition to which he could turn in the late 1880s. There are also tantalizing hints in the memoirs of Lenin's future lifelong companion, Nadezhda Krupskaya. She recalls in several places that Lenin, despite polemicizing mercilessly against their younger followers, retained a great respect, almost affection, for senior populists and the pioneers of populism. Obviously we have already encountered the influence of one leading populist inspiration, Chernyshevsky, whom he appeared to read for the first time in these formative years. According to one source, Lenin claimed it was Chernyshevsky who had 'ploughed me over again completely', a striking metaphor and one which exactly describes the process of turning the conventional Volodya into the radical Lenin.[2] Finally, as we shall see, Krupskaya herself hints at early populist influence.

In the end, it must be said, there is not much firm ground on which to base a sound judgement about exactly why Volodya decided to become a revolutionary and what his earliest principles were. The overwhelming effect of his brother's arrest and execution must be in the forefront. In addition, it may help explain Lenin's extraordinary hatred of tsarism and the old Russia which had swallowed up his beloved brother. It would be vapid to reduce Lenin's revolutionary energy to a personal grudge against the system but at the same time it would be evasive to ignore the intensely personal element which appears to form a core source of Lenin's immense revolutionary drive.

One other factor must be taken into account, one which illustrates the autocracy's unfailing ability to dig its own grave, in this case by confirming its potential enemies in their convictions. As the brother of a convicted terrorist Volodya was himself an object of increased government surveillance. The first key problem was his educational career. As a top student Volodya would have been entitled to walk into the best of universities. However, it took a long struggle for his headmaster, Fyodor Kerensky, to get him admitted to the local university in Kazan. Within months, he was expelled. Once again the hagiographic tradition had Volodya as a youthful student protest leader who was thrown out for his radical activities. Once again, we do not know for sure but there is no evidence to back up claims of precocious leadership. The thought that a young, newly arrived student would take the lead in radical protests is most unlikely though he might well have taken part. In any case, once disturbances had broken out, the authorities expelled all students considered to be potential as well as actual risks, such as those with terrorist brothers, as well as actual activists. Whatever the precise details, we do know that Volodya was expelled from Kazan and a regular career was almost closed to him, like thousands of others, throwing them further into radical and revolutionary activities as 'straight' career paths closed off in front of them.

As it turned out, expulsion was not the final nail in the coffin of Volodya's university career. Though he was not allowed to attend classes, he was later permitted to study law by correspondence at the University of St Petersburg.

LENIN BEGINS TO EMERGE: LIFE AND ACTIVITIES

The eight years following his expulsion from Kazan in 1887 were among the most significant of Lenin's life. Like any young person he developed rapidly in that time, between the ages of 17 and 25. It was not only in the intellectual and political sense that he matured but also in the personal and moral sense. The chrysalis of Volodya increasingly fell away and Lenin slowly, but not yet completely, emerged. The period is of particular interest because Lenin was still an ordinary person, albeit a tremendously intellectually gifted one. He lived a more normal, everyday existence than at any time subsequently in his adult life. Though we do not have a mass of material on these years they are the last ones in which we can look at Volodya/Lenin as an ordinary person.

What characteristics can we discern? What kind of life did Lenin lead? Paradoxically, the most accurate way to describe his way of life at this moment would be to say that he led the life of a gentleman, in the sense that he did not have to earn a living but lived on inherited family money and rents, but a gentleman with radical tendencies. His awakening political sense brought him to dabble increasingly in radical circles but, as yet, he was far from being what he later described as a professional revolutionary. In fact, he seems to have engaged on a massive programme of self-education, formal and informal. The formal side led to superb results in his law degree. The informal side built up a massive curiosity about the world, about society and about the state of knowledge of that epoch. He became a voracious reader and we will examine the results in due course. Before that, there are a number of points we can make about Lenin's developing personality.

In 1886–8 the young Volodya had received a number of severe jolts, each of which would certainly be called 'traumatic' today. In January 1886 his father had died unexpectedly of a brain haemorrhage. Following that there was Alexander's arrest in March 1887, followed by his execution two months later. Consider this conjuncture in Volodya's life. On 17 May 1887 he began his final school exams which continued until mid-June. Three days later Alexander was hanged. In the harsh climate of the nineteenth century no concession was made for private grief. Today, all kinds of representations would have been made and postponements organized. This was not open to Volodya Ulyanov. Instead, he had to deal with his emotions and get on with his exams, which he did with great success. The experience did not appear to have fundamentally altered his personality in the direction of bitterness or cynicism, which would have been quite understandable in the circumstances. Lenin did claim later that it was in 1886 that he broke with religion and became a confirmed atheist – no halfway measures even for the young Lenin – but, otherwise, he remained much the same person he had been before in terms of his character. Despite the trauma, at the end of the exam period he was, as we have already seen, awarded a gold medal, the first of several significant intellectual achievements.

Sadly Volodya's triumph over adversity was not the happy ending to his troubles. His acceptance and then expulsion from Kazan University was next in line and there were, as we shall see, further personal blows to be suffered a little further ahead. However, Lenin's development continued to be extraordinarily normal from the point of view of personality, though exceptional in the sense he was drawn more and more onto the path of revolution.

It was not, however, inevitable that Volodya/Lenin should have become a revolutionary. Exclusion from university was followed by police surveillance and a refusal of permission to travel abroad or, indeed, to Moscow or St Petersburg. For the next few years Lenin was trapped in the provinces and, for long periods of time, in the countryside. His uncle's estate at Kokushkino was replaced, in 1889, by a small estate inherited by his mother at Alakaevka, near Samara. For two years the only city in which he spent any time was Kazan. It appears that his mother harboured hopes that she might persuade her son to become a farmer. Volodya certainly spent time working on the Alakaevka estate but his recorded reason for not taking up the rural way of life is interesting. According to Krupskaya, he commented later that 'My mother would have liked me to have taken up farming. I started but soon realized that things were not going right. Relations with the peasants were abnormal.' [Krupskaya 35] What did Lenin mean? Most probably, he was complaining that it was impossible to have free and equal relations – person to person – with the peasants. It was already almost half a century since Turgenev had fallen foul of the authorities over his *Sportsman's Sketches*, which suggested the peasants were human beings too, but, for Lenin, relations between peasants and gentry remained strained. What a difference it would have made to the world had Volodya become a farmer and Lenin would never have been heard of!

It is also a rare, indirect admission by Lenin of the significance of his nominally noble and landowning status. In cold-war historiographies, and in some more recent ones, critics of Lenin have made a great deal of his landowner status and inherited title to infer that he was an aristocrat in the western sense. However, this really shows a profound misunderstanding of the situation. In Russia, titles, like that of Lenin's father, were given for state service, for being promoted as a civil servant. This was a long way from the life of the true aristocratic elite chronicled by, for example, Tolstoy in *Anna Karenina*. Lenin's sisters were not presented at grand balls, nor were they courted by devil-may-care army officers. Their way of life was, as we have seen, privileged but much more modest than that of the aristocracy. Lenin was not above occasionally using his title and status, especially when appealing to the authorities for permission to move out of the provinces, but it never amounted to very much. Lenin's upbringing was more akin to that of the comfortable middle class rather than the aristocracy.

If Volodya was not cut out for farming the same is not true of his other career near-miss, the law. In 1890 and 1891 the pace of his qualification as a lawyer speeded up. He was granted permission to visit St Petersburg to take his exams as an external student. He took his first exams in September 1890, intermediates in April–May 1891 and his finals in autumn 1891. In his finals he obtained first place with excellent marks and was awarded a first-class degree in law in January 1892. This has to be seen as a stupendous achievement for someone who never attended a regular class or course of lectures. Once again, it showed the developing intelligence and capabilities of Lenin's mind.

He was not, however, much interested in putting those mental qualities to use in a law career. He was employed fitfully as an assistant in a legal practice in late 1893–4, but his real interests were elsewhere. Deep in the soul of Volodya Ulyanov, Lenin continued stirring, becoming more and more restless. When he was able to visit cities he made contact with revolutionary circles. When confined to the countryside, he immersed himself in revolutionary literature.

After his initial burst of eclectic reading, including his life-changing encounter with Chernyshevsky in late 1888, the emerging Lenin was taking a more explicitly Marxist path. At about the same time as he 'read and re-read' [Weber 3] Chernyshevsky's *What is to be Done?* he also read Marx's *Das Kapital*, with considerably less dramatic effect. The new direction coincided with his involvement with a small Marxist circle in Kazan led by N.E. Fedoseev. Luckily for Volodya, the family moved shortly afterwards, in May 1889, to Alakaevka and he thus avoided being arrested when police moved in on Fedoseev's group in summer. [CW 33 452] Nonetheless, his Marxist reading continued and he translated *The Communist Manifesto* in late 1889. In summer 1890 he read Engels' *The Condition of the Working Class in England* and is recorded as having practised singing 'The Internationale' in French with his beloved sister, Olga, further evidence of the extraordinary solidarity of the Ulyanov family and of its increasingly radical hue.

One persistent, hostile 'explanation' of why people become revolutionaries is that they are social misfits who find it difficult to relate to real people rather than to abstractions of class, gender, race or whatever.[3] As far as Lenin is concerned nothing could be further from the truth. He had very close, warm, lifelong relationships with his family. It was family tragedy that had sparked his revolutionary interest and it was, most likely, the memory of Alexander that added limitless fuel to his hatred of tsarism and of Russian backwardness, as the radical intelligentsia saw it. According to what Lenin told Krupskaya later, part of his contempt for liberalism may have arisen from the same incident because, as a result of Alexander's 'disgrace' in the eyes of the local community the Ulyanov family was shunned. When Maria Alexandrovna needed a riding companion to enable her to make the first stage of her journey to visit Alexander in jail, no one would accompany the mother of a convicted terrorist. 'Vladimir Il'ich told me that this widespread cowardice made a very profound impression on him at the time. This youthful experience undoubtedly did leave its imprint on Lenin's attitude towards the Liberals. It was early that he learned the value of Liberal chatter.' [Krupskaya 17]

The execution of Alexander was not the last family tragedy of the formative years. While Volodya was in St Petersburg to take his exams in 1891 his sister Olga was also there studying and keeping an eye on him. On 20 April she wrote to reassure her mother that Volodya, who was prone to illness especially at moments of stress, was bearing up well.

> I think, darling Mamochka, that you have no reason to worry that he is over-exerting himself. Firstly, Volodya is reason personified and secondly, the examinations were very easy. He has already completed two subjects and received a 5 in both. He rested on Saturday (the examination was on Friday). He went early in the morning to the river Neva and in the afternoon he visited me and then both of us went walking along the Neva and watched the movement of the ice. [Weber 4]

The idyllic picture of family affection was soon to be shattered. Only a month later, on 20 May, Olga died of typhoid at the age of only nineteen. Maria Alexandrovna came to St Petersburg for the funeral and, on 29 May mother and son travelled back to Samara, spending the rest of the summer quietly in Alakaevka remembering not only Olga, who had just died, but also, perhaps, the first daughter named Olga who had died shortly after her birth in 1868. Lenin's life was marked by family tragedy, family affection and family solidarity throughout his life. One of the hardest consequences of his future exile was that he was out of Russia when his mother died in July 1916. On his return to Russia in the heat of the Revolution and his sensation-causing proposals for Party tactics, one of the first things he did was visit the graves of his mother and Olga.

Olga's poignant letter of 20 April 1891 also reminds us of two other aspects of the developing Lenin's outlook, his love of nature and his tendency to stress-related illnesses. While abroad for the first time in 1895 he showed great appreciation of the grandeur of the Swiss landscape, describing it, in a letter to his mother, as 'splendid. I am enjoying it all the time ... I could not tear myself away from the window of the railway carriage.' [CW 37 73] He spent many hours walking in the mountains, an occupation he returned to whenever he was in Switzerland. He was also ill while he was there. Before his departure from Russia he had suffered a bout of pneumonia. In Switzerland, as he wrote to his mother in July 1895, he 'landed up at a Swiss spa; I have decided to take advantage of the fact and get down seriously to the treatment of the illness (stomach) that I am so fed up with ... I have already been living at this spa for several days and feel not at all bad.' [CW 37 75] Ironically, as we shall see, his fast-approaching exile in Siberia helped him regain his health.

In addition to his immediate family, Lenin also had a circle of devoted friends, which amounted to a kind of extended family, with Nadezhda Krupskaya in the forefront. Her description of their first meeting in February 1894 is well known but remains very evocative. The occasion was a Shrovetide political gathering disguised as a pancake party.

> I remember one moment particularly well ... Someone was saying that what was very important was to work for the Committee for Illiteracy. Vladimir Il'ich laughed, and somehow his laughter sounded quite laconic. I never heard him laugh that way on any subsequent occasion. 'Well,' he said, 'If anyone wants to save the fatherland in the Committee for Illiteracy, we won't hinder them.' [Krupskaya 16]

Lenin's sarcasm did not put her off. They became friends, attending meetings together and walking together through the city of St Petersburg. He also helped her revolutionary preparation. Krupskaya noted that, by the time of her meeting with him in February 1894, Lenin was already an expert in many conspiratorial techniques which he passed on to her. She tells us that in 1895

> police surveillance began to increase. Of all our group Vladimir Il'ich was the best equipped for conspiratorial work. He knew all the through courtyards, and was a skilled hand at giving police spies the slip. He taught us how to write books in invisible ink, or by the dot method; how to mark out secret signs, and thought out all manner of aliases. [Krupskaya 22]

Krupskaya was not always the perfect pupil. After a group of six had taken a train journey out of St Petersburg during which they pretended not to know one another, they discussed how to preserve the group's essential contacts. 'We sat nearly the whole day discussing which contacts should be preserved. Vladimir Il'ich showed us how to use cipher, and we used up nearly half a book. Alas, I was afterwards unable to decode this first collective ciphering!' [Krupskaya 23]

Why was Lenin so adept at conspiracy? Krupskaya drops a very large hint about what was fairly obvious but taboo in Soviet times – the early influence of the populist tradition. 'In general', she wrote, 'one felt the benefit of his good apprenticeship in the ways of the *Narodnaya Volya* party. It was not for nothing that he spoke with such esteem of the old nihilist Mikhailov who had earned the name "Dvornik" ("the watchman") by dint of his prowess at conspiracy.' [Krupskaya 22]

Krupskaya also records that Lenin was admired by Lydia Knippovich, one of the most redoubtable former populists who had transferred her allegiance to the developing Marxist and social-democratic trend. 'Lydia immediately appreciated the revolutionary in Vladimir Il'ich.' [Krupskaya 23] The comment is all the more significant in that Lydia Knippovich organized the printing of many social-democratic works, including early pamphlets by Lenin, by means of the *Narodnaya Volya* printing press. Elsewhere, Krupskaya also records Lenin's frequent defence of populist elders, while in Siberian exile for instance, though he was completely opposed to their younger successors who should, Lenin argued, have realized that the time had come to switch to social democracy.

By the end of 1895, despite her incompetence over ciphers, Krupskaya was the one Lenin trusted most with sensitive materials. At the moment of his arrest she had one of only two sets of proofs of the proposed newspaper *Rabochee Delo*. The other one appears to have been seized during the arrests. Krupskaya took the remaining copy to her old friend Nina Alexandrovna Gerd who held on to it until it was thought to be relatively safe to publish it some months later. So strong had the bond become that Krupskaya unhesitatingly applied for permission for her and her mother, at their own expense, to join Lenin in his Siberian exile, which they did. Very often Lenin seems to have found it easier to maintain friendships with women whereas he was constantly quarrelling with other men (and quite a few women) in the revolutionary movement. There were fewer long-term male associates. Sooner or later he broke with almost all of them, at least for a time.

Krupskaya claims that it was through her influence that Lenin first got closer to actual workers than had hitherto been the case, since the secret circles to which he had belonged were largely intellectual. Krupskaya, on the other hand, had for some years been a dedicated teacher in worker education at the Smolensk District Sunday Evening Adult School. She taught many of the workers who were in Lenin's developing worker study circle in the nearby Nevsky district. Krupskaya's deeper knowledge of working-class life brought her into closer contact with Lenin.

> On Sundays, Vladimir Il'ich usually called to see me, on his way back from working with the circle. We used to start endless conversations. I was wedded to the school then and would have gone without my food rather than miss a chance of talking about the pupils or about Semyannikov's, Thornton's, Maxwell's and other factories around the Neva. Vladimir Il'ich was interested in the minutest detail describing the conditions and life of the workers. Taking the features separately he endeavoured to grasp the life of the worker as a whole – he tried to find out what one could seize upon in order better to approach the worker with revolutionary propaganda. [Krupskaya 21]

According to Krupskaya, Lenin had already developed what became the classic Leninist technique of agitation and propaganda. As she describes the situation, 'Most of the intellectuals of those days badly understood the workers. An intellectual would come to a circle and read the workers a kind of lecture. For a long time a manuscript translation of Engels' booklet, *The Origin of the Family, Private Property and the State*, was passed round the circles.' [Krupskaya 21] One wonders what they could possibly have made of a rather complex, not to say obscure, text of that nature. On the other hand Lenin did not shy away from complicated texts but went through them with the workers.

> Vladimir Il'ich read with the workers from Marx's *Capital* and explained it to them. The second half of the studies was devoted to the workers' questions about their work and labour conditions. He showed them how their life was linked up with the entire structure of society, and told them in what manner the existing order could be transformed, The combination of theory and practice was the particular feature of Vladimir Il'ich's work in the circles. Gradually, other members of our circle also began to use this approach. [Krupskaya 21]

While one might doubt Lenin's technique was that clear-cut in 1894–5, the issue of linking theory and practice was one which was about to burst forcefully into the radical arena following the appearance, in 1894, of Arkadii Kremer's pamphlet *On Agitation*. Essentially, two related issues began to emerge. First, it was deemed to be time for the nascent social-democratic, that is worker-oriented and Marxist-influenced, movement to put less emphasis on analysis and more on revolutionary practice. By that was meant the attempt to build a mass movement not follow the example of isolated acts of terrorism which had traditionally been the hallmark of the populist *Narodnaya Volya*. Second, the issue of the relationship between so-called economic struggle and political struggle began to raise its head. Economic struggle meant, essentially, building organizations such as trade unions which would primarily pursue workers' economic interests. Political struggle implied action against the tsarist state and its repressive institutions. The relationship between these two aspects became increasingly controversial as the social-democratic movement emerged. As we have seen, Lenin already showed something of a 'Bakuninist' streak, that is he put great stress on political struggle and attacking the state though he seems to have always been sceptical about terrorism as a method of conducting such struggle. In fact, one of Lenin's first major personal contributions to social-democratic theory and practice was in this area and we will return to it shortly. For the moment, however, we need to look at the content of Lenin's ideas as they had developed up to early 1895.

LENIN BEGINS TO EMERGE: IDEAS

In the first place there is no doubt that, whatever Volodya's earliest convictions, the emerging Lenin was definitely in the social-democratic camp. In particular, this meant that he accepted the orthodox Marxist line that the workers were the potentially revolutionary class. Alongside them the peasants played a subsidiary role and were, in any case, doomed to disappear as capitalism divided them into a minority of small landowners and a majority of landless labourers, sometimes known as the rural proletariat. Lenin's own ideas on this fundamental Marxist point had important twists and turns ahead but the basic orientation was already set. Lenin was in the camp of the workers and had little time for romantic ideas about revolutionary peasants.

Although many of Lenin's earliest writings have not survived there is ample evidence to show that, at least from 1891, he was criticizing the fundamental propositions of populism. For the first few years of his political career Lenin was an anti-populist polemicist. In 1891, in Samara, he took part in an illegal meeting at the house of a dentist named Kaznelson at which he opposed populist theory on the economic development of Russia. [Weber 4] Presumably this meant that he argued in favour of Russia having to go through the capitalist stage of development before it could attain socialism, it being a basic belief of the populists that perhaps Russia could avoid capitalism and build socialism directly on its already existing semi-socialist institutions.

However, there is an irony about Lenin's vigorous pursuit of the Marxist line. It was not what Marx himself thought was the case. As we have seen, Marx had been approached directly by Russian populist leaders on this very question. After much hesitation he replied that it was indeed possible that Russia might, under certain conditions, avoid capitalism. One could argue that on this issue the populists were more Marxist than Lenin.[4]

Be that as it may, and we will have to return to the issue again, for the time being the emerging Lenin was decidedly anti-populist. In early

1893, in his first surviving work, Lenin argued once more against the populist view that capitalism was not developing in Russia. Further works developed the same theme. The essence of his argument, as it appeared in a letter to a fellow social democrat, P.P. Maslov, was that 'The disintegration of our small producers (the peasants and handicrafts-men) appears to me to be the basic and principal fact explaining our urban and large scale capitalism, dispelling the myth that the peasant economy represents some special structure.' [CW 43 37]

1894 marks Lenin's emergence as a significant figure in the as yet tiny social-democratic circles. In early 1894 a police agent reported that, when the populist Vorontsov got the better of his Marxist opponent Davydov, 'the defence of his [Davydov's] views was taken over by a certain Ulyanov (supposedly the brother of the hanged Ulyanov) who then carried out the defence with a complete command of the subject.'[5] His first major work, 'Who the "Friends of the People" are and how they Fight the Social Democrats', was completed in spring 1894. In autumn he was engaged in dialogue with one of the leading Marxist economists of the time, Peter Struve, who later became a liberal, criticizing certain of Struve's propositions on the Russian economy but joining with him in April 1895 to criticize the populists in a collectively written book of articles entitled *Material on the Nature of our Economic Development*.

A corollary of his polemics against populism and, although it was still rather embryonic, his tendency to defend 'orthodox' Marxism against heretics, was present in other of his lost writings. Krupskaya, in particular, points to Lenin writing a number of pamphlets for circulation in the Semyannikov and LaFerme factories in St Petersburg. However, this turn to worker pamphleteering also reflects the experience of his first trip abroad from May to September 1895.

ENCOUNTER WITH THE GREATS: LENIN'S FIRST TRIP ABROAD

It is fashionable to put thoughts into the head of historical characters, though no historian has the power to verify such speculations. But whatever Lenin was thinking as he left Russia, he could hardly have seen what fate had in store for him. It would be twenty-two tumultuous years before tsarism would finally collapse. In that time Lenin was destined to spend only a few more months in Russia proper. Indeed, over the rest of the twenty-nine years of life ahead of him fewer than seven in total would be spent at liberty in Russia. It is also unlikely to have entered his head that he, rather than the great figures of social democracy at whose feet he planned to learn on this first foreign trip, would become the dominant character of the future revolution and the world's first Marxist ruler.

At the top of Lenin's visiting list was the 'father of Russian Marxism' George Plekhanov, who was living in exile in Switzerland. According to one account, Lenin was overawed in the presence of the great man. [Weber 8] Nonetheless, Plekhanov took to the new arrival. He looked 'not without warm sympathy, at the able practitioner of revolution he found in front of him'. Plekhanov recommended Lenin to Wilhelm Liebknecht, one of the leading figures of German social democracy whom Lenin visited later in his travels when he was in Berlin, as 'one of our best Russian friends'. [Weber 9] Before leaving Switzerland Lenin spent a week with him near Zurich. Paris, and a meeting with Marx's son-in-law Paul Lafargue, followed, then a month and a half in Berlin. He was only able to prolong his trip thanks to the generosity of his mother. He had run out of money by mid-July and was only bailed out by drafts sent in August and September which, ironically, came from Maria's state pension as the widow of a noble.

On 19 September he returned to Russia complete with illegal literature concealed in the false bottom of his suitcase. He also had a new mission, to help set up a paper aimed at workers and a more formal social-democratic group. The paper was prepared under the name *Rabochee delo* (*The Worker's Cause*) and the group was formed, with Lenin as a co-founder, under the cumbersome title of The League of Struggle for the Emancipation of the Working Class. However, both initiatives were abortive. The police were one jump ahead on this occasion and, in the night of 20–21 December 1895, the leadership of the League was arrested. Along with the others Lenin was remanded in custody. A new phase of his life was about to begin, one in which imprisonment and Siberian and foreign exile were to dominate.

VOLODYA/LENIN ON THE EVE OF EXILE

According to Trotsky, a fully fledged Lenin had already emerged as early as autumn 1893. 'It is, thus, between his brother's execution and the move to St Petersburg [i.e. 1 September 1893], in these simultaneously short and long six years of stubborn work that the future Lenin was formed ... all the fundamental features of his person[ality], his outlook on life and his mode of action were already formed in the interval between the seventeenth and twenty third years of his life.' Was Trotsky correct? Before looking at the next phase of his life let us think who Lenin was by late 1895.

One thing which was, almost symbolically, evolving was Lenin's physical appearance. The unfamiliar look of the young Volodya gave way early in life to the well-known iconic figure with a bald head and short beard. The process had already begun in 1889, before he was twenty, when he first grew his beard which, at that time, retained a slightly reddish tinge. He also started losing his hair around then. By the mid-1890s he already appeared old before his time and this, as his associate Krzhizhanovsky pointed out, led to him receiving one of his longest lasting nicknames. Describing the meeting at which he first met Lenin, Krzhizhanovsky wrote 'He drowned us in a torrent of statistics ... His tall forehead and his great erudition earned him the nickname *starik*' ('the old man'). [Weber 6–7] One of the best descriptions comes from the memoirs of Potresov, who accompanied him on his travels in Switzerland. Looking back in 1927 on his first meeting with Lenin at around the same time, Potresov, who had become a political opponent of Lenin in the meantime, points to similar features but in a more hostile manner:

> He had doubtless passed his twenty fifth birthday when I met him for the first time in the Christmas and New Year holidays ... Lenin was only young according to his birth certificate. One could have taken him for at least a 35–40 year old. The face withered, the head almost bald, a thin reddish beard, eyes which observed one from the side, craftily and slightly closed, an unyouthful, coarse voice.

The effect on Potresov was of 'a typical merchant from any north Russian province – there was nothing of the "radical" intellectual about him.' This last comment is very hard to understand unless Potresov meant he lacked urban, gentlemanly finesse. His concluding comment, which backs up this interpretation, is also interesting. 'No trace either of the service or noble family from which Lenin came.' [Weber 7] One suspects Lenin would have taken such comments as a compliment on his ability to overcome his class background.

So, was Trotsky right? Had Volodya disappeared and been replaced by Lenin already? Not entirely. Some Volodya-style features, such as a respectful deference before the elder statesmen of the social-democratic and populist movements, remained. Lenin was not noted for deferential respect to anyone. Also, Lenin had not yet developed broad themes of argument. For the time being a well-grounded but repetitive intellectual critique of populism was his stock in trade, with a certain amount of attention to worker agitation beginning to develop. In no way did he stand out from the crowd as a potential leader, nor had he set out on his devastating course of splitting groups and splitting them again in pursuit of the finest degree of intellectual and doctrinal purity. It was in the next phase of his life, from his arrest through the fateful Second Congress of the Party in 1903 and on to the Revolution of 1905 and its aftermath, that Lenin truly emerged.

2

LAYING THE FOUNDATIONS OF LENINISM (1896–1902)

Trotsky's conclusion that Lenin emerged fully fledged in 1893 belongs to the realm of hagiography and propaganda. The Lenin who went into exile was certainly a rising star of the Social-Democratic movement but he still lacked some of the basic characteristics of the mature Lenin. He remained deferential towards his superiors in the movement and had not developed the steely edge and the frightening self-confidence which was to come later.

Even so, by 1903, he began to play his personal hand. He opened up a split in the Party, though he was reluctant to break fully with Plekhanov and some of the most prominent leaders of the movement just yet. His manipulativeness and dogmatism were in full flow. What was it that put extra steel into Lenin in the years between 1895 and 1902, by which time the foundations of Lenin's own distinctive revolutionary theory and practice – Leninism, in other words – were being laid?

It would be tempting to say that after his arrest in December 1895, along with the other leaders of the League of Struggle, some of the harsh experiences of the next few years of his life, notably imprisonment, interrogation and Siberian exile, had hardened Lenin. Ironically, however, exile appears to have been one of the more relaxed periods of his life. Far from bringing out the vindictive side of his personality Lenin appears to have been more healthy and oddly stress-free.

Clearly, the conditions of tsarist imprisonment and exile, which varied enormously according to the class, status and criminal activity of the detainee, were much more lenient, for gentlemen and lady political prisoners, than the average twentieth-century place of detention. Prisoners were under loose surveillance but, provided they stayed in their allocated villages and only moved elsewhere with permission, they could do much as they pleased. The very nature of the system meant that a number of like-minded people were gathered in the same region so lively discussions about politics were possible from time to time. Lenin himself undertook some translation work to earn a little money and was able to continue some of his own research into the state of Russian agriculture and the economy.

His ability to work creatively was in no small part due to the unhesitating support of Nadezhda Krupskaya. When sentenced to exile herself she applied for permission to join Lenin, describing herself as his fiancée. This polite fiction was not accepted by the authorities who insisted that, if they were to be allowed to live together, they must marry. The wedding duly took place on 22 July 1898. Since she was also responsible for her mother, Nadezhda brought her along, too. Once again, Lenin found himself living in a supportive, female cocoon.

According to Krupskaya, Siberia brought out the best in Lenin. His love of nature and of hunting translated itself into long, invigorating walks in all seasons of the year, accompanied by his hunting gun as often as not, which provided some substantial additions to their diet. Clearly, exile in tsarist times was far less onerous than it was to become in Soviet times. The thought of Soviet prisoners strolling around the Siberian forests with hunting guns is just too bizarre to entertain. For Lenin and Krupskaya the only real restriction was confinement to their assigned village under the eye of an individual appointed as an assessor by the government. They would live freely within the village – receiving and sending letters and getting parcels of books and even occasional luxuries and delicacies from home. It was also possible on occasion to obtain permission to visit other exile centres in the region. The simple way of life restored Lenin's health and brought the colour back to his cheeks and the twinkle to his eye.

Lenin, of course, was not satisfied to treat this period as an enforced and prolonged vacation but continued developing his ideas and following, as closely as the controls on him would allow, the evolution of Russian and world politics. Some of his most important ideas matured

while he was in exile. Clearly, these were important years in the formation of Lenin. Let us take a closer look at them.

LIFE IN PRISON AND SIBERIAN EXILE

After his arrest, Lenin was at first kept in prison in St Petersburg and
subjected to a series of interrogations. Prison, as opposed to exile, was a
particularly miserable experience and, eventually, 'even Vladimir Il'ich
was affected by the prison melancholy'. [Krupskaya 29] Lenin, like
other prisoners, was kept in near solitary confinement. Communication
with the outside world was carefully scrutinized. Prisoners on remand
were, however, allowed a large number of books and Lenin was able to
occupy much of his time preparing his work on the development of
Russian capitalism. He pressed on in the knowledge that, in Siberia,
books would be much harder to acquire. Books also had the advantage
of being used for coded messages. By putting barely visible dots in letters messages could be spelled out. Invisible writing, usually in milk,
could also evade the censor. Messages could be revealed by heating the
paper against a candle flame. According to Krupskaya, Lenin devised
another method. Dipping the paper in hot tea also revealed the message.
[Krupskaya 28] The method was also used to get messages out of
prison. Small 'inkwells', made of bread and filled with milk, could be
concealed from an unexpected visit by guards by the simple expedient
of eating them. In one day Lenin consumed six inkwells. [Krupskaya 29]

Eventually, after four interrogations, Lenin was sentenced in
February 1897 to exile in Siberia. In April, he travelled to Krasnoyarsk
and was exiled to the village of Shushenskoe in Minusinsk district, a
remote area some two hundred miles from Achinsk, the nearest stop-
ping point on the Trans-Siberian railway. In the meantime, Krupskaya
had also been arrested. She was sentenced to three years exile in the less
remote area of Ufa in the Urals/Western Siberia. However, as we have
seen, she applied to join Lenin and she was allowed to do so.

When she arrived, Lenin was, characteristically, out hunting and this
gave his friends the opportunity to play a practical joke on him.
Without mentioning the arrival of Krupskaya they told him a local
drunk had broken into his room and thrown his books around. 'Lenin
quickly bounded up the steps. At that moment I emerged from the *izba*
[hut]. We talked for hours and hours that night.' [Krupskaya 33]

Although exile was exile, there was a certain amount of pleasure and joy in the lives of Lenin and Krupskaya. Even before Krupskaya's arrival Lenin had written in May and June 1897 to his mother that Shushenskoe was 'not a bad village', [CW 37 107–8] that 'life here is not bad' [CW 37 112] and that 'I am very satisfied with my board and lodging.' [CW 37 116] There was a nearby spot on the river Yenisei where Lenin bathed and he had already 'travelled twelve versts [about 12.8 kilometres] to shoot duck and great snipe.' His expectation in June that 'I shall not be bored' [CW 37 116] had, by August, become a complaint that his surroundings were 'very monotonous' and that his work was progressing too slowly. [CW 37 122] Things only began to change for the better the following May when Krupskaya and her mother arrived, easing his boredom and lightening his work load. They found him living in quite comfortable surroundings. 'In the Minusinsk region', Krupskaya reported, 'the peasants are particularly clean in their habits. The floors are covered with brightly-coloured, homespun mats, the walls whitewashed and decorated with fir branches. The room used by Vladimir Il'ich, though not large, was spotlessly clean. My mother and I were given the remaining part of the cottage.' [Krupskaya 32] However, the little household was increasingly inconvenient and they moved to a larger lodging, an entire house with a yard and kitchen-garden in which they grew cucumbers, carrots, beetroots and pumpkins. After a summer of fighting with the Russian stove and knocking over the soup and dumplings with an oven-hook, the two intellectuals were able to engage the services of a local 13-year-old girl, Pasha, as their housekeeper. Their household was completed by a dog Lenin trained for hunting and a kitten.

While conditions were by no means idyllic life could go on despite the long and bitter winters stretching from October to April, with their short days and long nights. Looking back Krupskaya describes the awesome majesty of spring. 'After the winter frosts, nature burst forth tempestuously into the spring. Her power became mighty. Sunset. In the great spring-time pools in the fields wild swans were swimming. Or we stood at the edge of a wood and listened to a rivulet burbling or woodcocks clucking ... One felt how overwhelming was this tumultuous awakening of nature.' [Krupskaya 37] Winter was different but it too had its attractions. Krupskaya describes 'a magic kingdom' of ice and snow:

> Late in the autumn, when the snow had not yet begun to fall, but the rivers were already freezing, we went far up the streams. Every pebble, every little fish, was visible beneath the ice, just like some magic kingdom. And winter-time, when the mercury froze in the thermometers [−39 °C], when the rivers were frozen to the bottom, when the water, flowing over the ice, quickly froze into a thin upper ice-layer – one could skate two versts [two kilometres] or so with the upper layer of ice crunching beneath one's feet. Vladimir Il'ich was tremendously fond of all this. [Krupskaya 38]

Hunting was a major daytime occupation and Lenin became addicted. At first, Krupskaya was taken aback by all the talk about ducks. 'They talked for hours on the subject, but by the following spring I had also become capable of conversing about ducks – who had seen them, and where and when ... Vladimir Il'ich was an ardent hunter, but too apt to become heated over it. In the autumn we went to far-off forest clearings. Vladimir Il'ich said: "If we meet any hares, I won't fire as I didn't bring any straps, and it won't be convenient to carry them." Yet immediately a hare darted out Vladimir Il'ich fired.' [Krupskaya 37] Massacre of hares was common. In winter, they were trapped on islands in the Yenisei. 'Our hunters would sometimes shoot whole boat loads.' Krupskaya also recalls that Lenin still hunted much later in life when they had returned to Russia proper but 'by that time his huntsman's ardour had considerably ebbed. Once we organized a fox-hunt. Vladimir Il'ich was greatly interested in the whole enterprise. "Very skilfully thought out," he said. We placed hunters in such a way that the fox ran straight at Vladimir Il'ich. He grasped his gun and the fox, after standing and looking at him for a moment, turned and made off to the wood. "Why on earth didn't you fire?" came our perplexed inquiry. "Well, he was so beautiful, you know," said Vladimir Il'ich.' [Krupskaya 38]

The long winter nights were an opportunity for reading. According to Krupskaya Lenin read Hegel, Kant and the French naturalist philosophers or, 'when very tired', Pushkin, Lermontov or Nekrasov. He also read and reread Turgenev, Tolstoy and Chernyshevsky's *What is to be Done?* plus what Krupskaya calls 'the classics' apparently including Zola and Herzen. [Krupskaya 38] They also translated the Webbs' book on trade unionism into Russian, though how they did this when their English was, as they later discovered, rather poor is hard to explain. It seems that they were only able to do so by having the German translation by their side. Nonetheless, it did bring in a little money. They also wrote and read drafts of Lenin's first major book, *The Development of Capitalism in Russia*, about which more later.

Their social life was largely circumscribed by the village to which they were confined and its immediate surroundings. The situation brought Lenin an opportunity to observe Siberian rural life at first hand. Not unnaturally, on arrival at Shushenskoe, Lenin tried to establish good relations with the local schoolteacher, the only educated person in the immediate vicinity. However, the teacher spent his time with the local elite, consisting of the priest and a couple of shopkeepers, and he showed no interest in social problems. Lenin did, however, get to know several local peasants quite well, one of whom, a certain Zhuravliev, he described as 'by nature a revolutionary' who opposed the rich and fought against injustice. Another, named Sosipatych, was a typical stubborn *muzhik* [peasant] who accompanied Lenin on hunting trips. Through these acquaintances and his observation of local life Lenin observed what he called the 'ruthless cruelty' of small landowners typical of Siberia whose labourers worked 'as if in servitude, only snatching a little rest at holiday time'. [Krupskaya 34]

Krupskaya also describes a practice of Lenin's which brought broad contact with local problems. On Sundays he set up a juridical consultation to advise peasants of their rights and, as was the way in the Russian countryside, also to deal with personal and informal problems. According to Krupskaya he began to have an impact. 'It was often sufficient for the offended person to threaten to complain to Ulyanov and the offender would desist.' Of course, Lenin was not authorized to conduct such consultations 'but these were liberal times in Minusinsk'. Apparently their assessor was more concerned to sell the middle-class couple some of his veal than to control their activities. [Krupskaya 35]

'Liberal times' also meant that, occasionally, journeys could be made, on some, often devious, pretext or other, which would bring them into contact with other exiles. Once permission was granted for them to make a trip to see the unusual geographical formations of an area which just happened to contain other exiles. Another time they met up with other exiles to pass a resolution on a growing debate in social democracy. They might also go to the funerals of comrades who died in exile. Krupskaya mentions a particularly large New Year (1899) gathering in the town of Minusinsk at which a premature escape by a social-democratic exile provoked a 'scandal' with other, mainly older, *Narodnaya Volya* exiles who had not had time to conceal things before the inevitable police searches which followed such an event. It is less surprising that Lenin and the social-democratic exiles broke with the elderly populists over this 'scandal' than the spirit of sympathy in which it was done. 'These old men have got bad nerves,' Lenin said. 'Just look at what they've been through, the penal sentences they have undergone.' In Krupskaya's words, 'We made the break because a break was necessary. But we did it without malice, indeed with regret.' [Krupskaya 41–2] Once again, Lenin's latent respect for the older generation of revolutionaries was in evidence.

Altogether, Krupskaya's comment that 'Generally speaking, exile did not pass so badly. Those were years of serious study' [Krupskaya 42] was entirely appropriate. In no area was that more true than that of Lenin's health. Throughout his life Lenin had a tendency, which we have already observed, to work himself into a nervous frenzy which would bring on illness at critical moments. Being remote meant Lenin had to face fewer crises and less excitement. As a result his health was better than ever, despite temperatures as low, on occasions, as −40 °C. The initial detention in prison had put a strain on him, pointed out by his mother-in-law in terms familiar to many sons-in-law. 'My mother,' wrote Krupskaya, 'told me he had even got fatter in prison and was a terrible weight.' [Krupskaya 30] However, on meeting him in Shushenskoe, Krupskaya noted that 'Il'ich looked much fitter and fairly vibrated with health.' [Krupskaya 33] Only when the time was approaching for Lenin to leave Shushenskoe and return to the hurly-burly of political conflict did his anxieties return. 'Vladimir Il'ich began to spend sleepless nights. He became terribly thin.' [Krupskaya 43]

In these later years he also had less time for 'distractions'. At one time he had asked for a chess set to be sent out to him because there were a number of players in the area. He even played by correspondence, but, like hunting, once he returned to Russia proper he gave it up because he had no time for it. Similarly, he gave up skating as a boy because 'it tired me so that I always wanted to go to sleep afterwards. This hindered my studies. So I gave up skating.' He even abandoned his interest in Latin because 'it began to hinder other work.' [Krupskaya 39–40] The image of the single-minded Lenin, the determined revolutionary, was already being moulded. Although, as we shall see, he did not entirely cut himself off from relaxing pastimes and hobbies, he was concerned to keep them under great control. The most famous, and most frequently quoted example, comes from Gorky's obituary of Lenin in which he referred to Lenin confessing to a love of Beethoven's *Appassionata* sonata, which he said he could listen to every day because it was 'marvelous superhuman music'. The problem was that

> I cannot listen to music often, it works on my nerves, I want to say sweet stupidities and stroke the heads of people who, living in this dirty hell, can create such beauty. But at the present time one must not stroke people's heads, they will bite your hand, it is necessary to hit them over the head, hit without mercy, even though in our ideal we are against using any violence against people. Hmm, hmm, our duty is devilishly hard.[1]

As in other areas of Lenin's life his virtues – in this case revolutionary determination – were often the flipside of his vices – an obsession with politics and principles too frequently at the expense of actual individuals. A softer, more sympathetic Lenin who worked through his feelings rather than suppressed them might have been a more effective Lenin. However, he was not alone in believing strength of will implied trampling on one's own feelings, let alone those of others. It was a common motif of an increasingly Nietzschean age.

'YEARS OF SERIOUS STUDY'

The carousel of history did not stop just because Lenin had been forced to step off for four years from 1896 to 1900. Indeed, they were particularly eventful times as imperialism continued to carve up the globe and the world slid towards total war. Socialism, too, was in deepening crisis. Significant Marxist movements were emerging across the capitalist world but their appearance brought conflict with earlier radical movements. Not only that, disagreements about interpreting the writings of Marx became more acute. The question of questions facing Marxists was why had no Marxist revolution appeared? In many ways, early twentieth-century Marxism was a series of answers to that crucial conundrum.

From the Russian point of view three great debates were dominating the radical scene. In the minds of many the three debates have become confused with one another so it is as well to define them and separate them as clearly as possible.

We have already mentioned the first. Was the growth of capitalism in Russia inevitable? Although populists had been divided on tactics between those who urged long-term persuasion and propaganda and those who saw terror as catalyst of revolution, they were united over one fundamental principle. Russian society was already deeply saturated with socialism. Peasants, it was argued, were not petty-capitalists but proto-socialists. They held property in common; they redistributed it in accordance with ancient principles of social justice; their lives were largely self-governing through the local commune (*mir* or *obshchina*). The collective mentality was translated into industrial society through co-operative workshops (*artely*). The existence of these institutions and the mentality of equality and fairness which underpinned them could, it was thought, provide a basis for a direct transition into socialism without Russia having to pass through the super-exploitative agonies of a capitalist industrial revolution. Inventive minds embroidered the arguments in many ways. A leading populist economist, N.F. Danielson, put forward an argument which merits attention today given the tribulations of Russia's post-Soviet version of capitalism. He argued that capitalism could never be competitive in Russia because its size and educational/cultural backwardness inhibited its infrastructural growth, and intractable factors such as distance and climate pushed the costs of production above those of more fortunate countries. Whether or not that was the case, populists believed that Russia could, possibly, leap straight from decaying feudalism to socialism.

For social democrats, as they increasingly began to call themselves, these ideas were anathema. Peasants were not the building blocks of the future, they were a transitional hangover from the past. They may not have been capitalist proprietors but, it was argued, their aspirations were precisely to become such. Rather it was workers who were the bedrock of future socialism. Populist optimism also violated one of the basic assumptions of social democrats. Marx, they argued, had laid down a theory of stages. Primitive communism gave way to property-owning societies of which the most recent were feudalism and capitalism. The one developed into the other and capitalism would develop into socialism and, at the end of history, into communism. The stages were clearly defined and, all social democrats believed, central to Marx's theory.

Lenin, as we have seen, cut his social-democratic teeth on defending these assumptions. The seminal work, which Lenin admired deeply, was Plekhanov's *Our Differences* which, as its title suggested, marked out the principles of social democracy as opposed to those of populism. In his earliest writings the young Lenin did little more than develop Plekhanov's insights.

However, it was during his Siberian exile that Lenin focused on the question in greater detail. In an article, evocatively entitled 'The Heritage We Renounce', written in 1898, Lenin summarized his position. First and foremost he had absolutely no time for populist sentimentality about the life of the peasants. In no way was rural society to be idealized. For Lenin, peasants were the victims of unremitting repression by landowners and state. They were poor, ignorant and often lived short, brutish lives curtailed by alcohol and domestic violence. They were not 'noble savages' or homespun philosophers as depicted by Tolstoy. Their way of life was artificially kept in the past by oppressive legislation. Emancipation, he argued, had worsened their condition. The commune was not an emanation of their collectivist spirit, it was an alien and inefficient body imposed on them by the state. In Lenin's words: 'the Narodnik [populist] falls so low that he even welcomes the police rule forbidding the peasant to sell his land. ... Here the Narodnik quite definitely "renounces the heritage", becomes a reactionary. ... For the "peasant" who lives chiefly from the sale of his labour-power, being tied to his allotment and commune is an enormous restriction on his economic activity.' [SW 1 77] The peasants' future lay in casting off the shackles of feudalism and allowing rural society to develop towards capitalism. For Lenin, the inner instincts of the peasantry were directed towards becoming small-scale individual proprietors, not socialists. Those who did not succeed in making the transition would fall into an ever-increasing class of agricultural labourers who would be the basis of a rural proletariat, the natural ally of the urban proletariat. This was the class that would provide a foundation for socialism, not the peasantry as a whole, which was doomed to disappear as capitalism worked its way through rural Russia.

Within this fundamental argument the article contained a number of additional interesting motifs. It followed that Lenin, to a degree, was defending the development of a liberal form of capitalism in Russia. Indeed, he referred without irony to Adam Smith as 'that great ideologist of the progressive bourgeoisie'. [SW 1 65] Even further, he based his article on a forgotten book by a Russian advocate of liberal capitalism, Skaldin (whose real name was Fyodor Yelenev). Although the article was undoubtedly polemical in tone, Lenin retained certain courtesies which later disappeared from his writings. For example, he was prepared to accept Skaldin's good faith, referring to him as 'a bourgeois enlightener' whose views were based on 'the sincere belief that the abolition of serfdom would be followed by universal well-being and a sincere desire to help bring this about'. [SW 1 63 and 64] The writer whom Lenin used as his example of populist romanticism, Alexander Engelhardt, was also treated with some respect, being described as 'much more talented than Skaldin and his letters from the country are incomparably more lively and imaginative' and that his account was 'replete with deft definition and imagery'. [SW 1 66] There was also an overtly 'democratic element' to Lenin's thought at this time. In an article on Engels' death written a few years before, he pointed out that Marx and Engels were democrats before they were socialists. In his 1898 article he also, as he continued to do, posited political freedom as the indispensable prerequisite for any further progress. He also reaffirmed it in an article of 1900 entitled 'The Urgent Tasks of Our Movement' which opens 'Russian Social-Democracy has repeatedly declared the immediate task of a Russian working-class party to be the overthrow of autocracy, the achievement of political liberty.' [SW 1 91] This created ambiguities over his position with respect to the second controversy of the time, that relating to so-called Economism which we will examine shortly.

Before moving on to that we need to remember that, as was mentioned in Chapter One, it has been suggested that, in the polemic over the development of capitalism, Lenin, ironically, was championing ideas of the unavoidability of the capitalist stage abandoned by Marx, whereas the populist argument was closer to that of Marx himself. While this argument is ingenious and in many ways compelling, Lenin himself developed beyond such early assumptions. His most complete work of this period, *The Development of Capitalism in Russia*, written largely in 1896–7 and corrected in 1898, was published in 1899. Here the stress is not so much on whether Russia could avoid the capitalist stage. Lenin's essential argument was that capitalism had already developed to such an extent in Russia that the issue was no longer a live one. Russia was already in the capitalist stage. Examining rural society Lenin identified the growth of capitalist traits. For example, there was greater differentiation of production – that is areas were becoming less self-sufficient and producing what the region was best at and trading it for what other regions were best at. In other words an incipient national market rather than a series of local market economies was developing. Further signs were a growing tendency to produce cash crops, that is crops for sale rather than local consumption; a growth of individual as opposed to communal proprietorship; growing class differentiation between rich (kulak), middle and poor peasants/labourers. All these were signs of the hold which capitalism had already taken on Russian society and economy. The debate was over. Russia was firmly on the capitalist path.

Implicit in this was, of course, Lenin's acceptance of the theory of stages. It is also clear that Lenin followed the Marxist tradition, as mentioned above, of admiring the constructive, modernizing aspects of capitalism when it came to overthrowing feudal relations. Without the development of capitalism, socialism was out of the question.

This did not mean that Lenin took a rose-tinted view of capitalism. Indeed, the second controversy of the period showed exactly the opposite side of his view of capitalism. Other thinkers had taken the view that the nature of capitalism was such that it would almost automatically turn into socialism of its own accord. No revolutionary, especially political, transition would be needed. In European terms, Eduard Bernstein became the foremost advocate of this tendency known as evolutionary socialism. This is not the place for a detailed discussion of Bernstein's views. From our perspective we need to note that Bernstein was facing up to the key question of why Marxist revolution had not yet occurred, indeed, seemed rather remote in the late 1890s, by pointing to what he considered deficiencies in Marx's theory as it was understood at the time. In particular, he argued that capitalism did not lead to the impoverishment of the workers, which would have led them to the situation described by Marx and Engels in *The Communist Manifesto* with the proletarians having nothing to lose but their chains. Instead, through trade unions and labour militancy, they were able to build up an increasingly comfortable and respectable way of life. Instead of polarizing into rich proprietors and impoverished proletarians, capitalist society (like Marx, Bernstein drew his example from the most advanced

capitalist society of the age, Britain) was creating a solid
Property, ownership of land and capital, was diversifying throu_
ety. The middle classes were not disappearing but growing fast.
Bernstein's conclusion was that the struggle by trades unions and
labour-oriented political parties for escalating reforms was the way forward. Revolution was unnecessary. Capitalism was socializing itself.

In Russia such ideas were taken up by a group of social democrats.
Two of them, S. Prokopovich and E. Kuskova, put forward their principles in a pamphlet, dubbed their *Credo* by Lenin's sister Anna, and it is
by that name that it is generally known today. In it, they argued that
political struggle was a distraction and the social-democratic movement
should put its emphasis on economic struggle – that is the day-to-day
battle between employers and employees for better wages and conditions.

For the majority of social democrats, including Lenin, such ideas
were heresy of the worst kind. He was completely opposed to them and
insisted on the absolute necessity of political struggle to be conducted
alongside economic struggle. Indeed, Lenin might be thought to have
actually done the opposite of what the Economists did, namely priori-
tize political struggle over all others. After all, this was the starting
point of the Russian revolutionary movement some forty years earlier
and was associated with one of the greatest Russian revolutionaries,
Bakunin. For Bakunin, it was not economic systems and the associated
classes which tyrannized human society, it was two institutions, the
state and the church, which were in the forefront of oppression. They
had to be destroyed through direct confrontation before any freer society
could be constructed.

Many Russian revolutionary groups and thinkers, including Lenin,
had a somewhat Bakuninist edge to their revolutionary thought and
practice. Lenin's hatred of religion was notorious, for a start. Along with
others he also put the overthrow of tsarist despotism and the inaugura-
tion of a democratic republic as the starting point of social progress. His
later works brought this out and he was not infrequently accused of
being an anarchist. His polemic against the Economists certainly
showed his absolute commitment to political struggle and its primary
importance. In a sense, the consequence is that Lenin might be seen as
being on the wrong side of yet another Marxist tenet here, the priority
of economics over politics and the basic assertion that the emancipation
of the workers would be accomplished by the workers themselves. Lenin

actually quoted exactly this phrase in his article on the death of Engels
[SW 1 40] but, arguably, his career expressed increasing doubt about its
validity.

However, Lenin was not alone in putting political struggle at the top
of the agenda. Along with the Economist controversy, his isolation in
Siberia had made him a spectator at the founding of the Russian Social
Democratic and Labour Party, a grand name for a small gathering in
Minsk which inaugurated it in 1898. Its early leaders were quickly
arrested but its main work, establishing a Party programme, drafted,
ironically, by the soon-to-be-renegade Peter Struve, survived. It, unambiguously, put the overthrow of tsarism as the primary Party task.

The Economist debate is one of the largely overlooked issues of early
Russian Marxism. Indeed, the key themes of both these two debates –
the theory of stages and the primacy of politics – have, by a strange
twist of fate, become inextricably entwined with the third argument of
the period, which is by far the best known, the splitting of the Social
Democratic Party into Bolshevik and Menshevik wings in 1903.
However, before we can approach that we need to pick up the thread of
Lenin's life after his exile and up to the fateful days during and following the Second Party Congress of 1903.

RETURN TO RUSSIA; RETREAT TO WESTERN EUROPE

Eventually, Vladimir Il'ich's sentence of exile was served. Not having
been caught in any major infractions, no additional time was added. On
11 February 1900 the Ulyanovs began their long journey back. The first
stage was a 320-kilometre horseback ride along the Yenissei. According
to Krupskaya, the moonlight allowed them to continue travelling at
night, wrapped up in their elkskin coats to protect them from the sub-
zero temperatures. Even so, Krupskaya's elderly mother felt the cold
intensely. Once they reached the road system, the greater comfort of a
horse and carriage was employed. Finally, at Achinsk, civilization came
within reach in the form of the Trans-Siberian Express. From there it
was only a few days back to Moscow, one more to St Petersburg, except
neither Vladimir Il'ich nor Krupskaya had permission to live in either.
Even worse, although Vladimir Il'ich's sentence was served Krupskaya's
was not and she had to remain in Ufa in the Urals which they reached
on 18 February. As she commented somewhat ruefully in her memoirs,

'it did not even enter Vladimir Ilyich's head to remain in Ufa when there was a possibility of getting nearer to St. Petersburg.' Krupskaya was saddened by the thought that 'it was a great pity to have to part, just at a time when "real" work was commencing.' [Krupskaya 45]

Indeed the major cities beckoned. Vladimir Il'ich, however, was only permitted to reside in the provinces. He opted to take up residence in Pskov, in North-Western Russia. He supported himself with a hum-drum government office job in the Bureau of Statistics, but his real interests were, of course, in getting back in touch with the mainstream of the social-democratic movement. Unsanctioned visits to Moscow and St Petersburg in February and March fulfilled this purpose. A further journey in June brought arrest and ten days' imprisonment. Such inter-ference made his work in Russia impossible since he would remain under frequent surveillance and face constant interrogation. Emigration seemed the better option and he resolved to take it. Before that, how-ever, he had things to do. As soon as he was released from prison he spent six weeks visiting Krupskaya, who had been ill. He travelled via Nizhny Novgorod and Samara where he made contact with local social democrats. After a final visit to his mother and other family members now living in Podolsk, he left Russia for western Europe on 29 July. Barring a few months, he was to be out of Russia proper until the eve of the October Revolution.

But where should he go? The main exile centres were in Germany, Switzerland, France and Britain. The decision as to which to choose depended on many factors. Not least was the cost of living for these, by and large, modestly financed revolutionaries. Contact with other exiles and the best conditions to work and, especially, conduct propaganda, were the other main criteria.

At first, the inviting openness of Switzerland, the home still of Plekhanov and Axel'rod, was the first choice. Within weeks, however, he had upset several apple carts. Bavaria was his next destination. He was drawn there by contact with people who advised him on the main project of the moment, the production of a newspaper, *Iskra (The Spark)*. Nuremberg gave way to Munich where Lenin settled down for the time being. He was even able to enjoy the cultural life, writing to his mother about theatre and opera visits which brought him 'the greatest pleasure' [CW 37 317]. He also told her in February, during Fäsching, 'that peo-ple here know how to make merry publicly in the streets.' [CW 37 319]

A visit to Vienna brought the comment that it was 'a huge, lively and beautiful city'. [CW 37 323]

Life was not, however, a holiday. Even though he was out of Russia, Lenin was by no means beyond the reach of the police. He was forced to live a clandestine life including, in order to protect himself, making extensive use of false names to confuse the police. He used no less than 150 pseudonyms in his writings including Meyer, Richter and others. In January 1901, for the first time, he used the name Lenin in place of Tulin and Ilyin which he had used most frequently hitherto. However, this was still not the name under which he is best known today because he usually combined it with the first name Nikolai. Forwarding addresses, false passports and false national identities – including German and Bulgarian – were also part of the covert game. The police were not the only ones who were confused. In April 1901 Krupskaya finished her term of exile in Ufa and she lost no time in joining Lenin whom she believed to be living under the name Modraczek at an address in Prague. The scene Krupskaya describes is worthy of a comedy movie:

> I sent a telegram and arrived in Prague. But no one came to meet me … Greatly disconcerted I hailed a top-hatted cabby, piled him up with my baskets and started off … We … stopped at a large tenement building. I climbed to the fourth floor. A little, white-haired Czech woman opened the door. 'Modraczek,' I repeated, 'Herr Modraczek.' A worker came out and said: 'I am Modraczek.' Flabbergasted, I stammered: 'No my husband is!'

It was soon realized what the mistake was and Krupskaya was then told that Lenin was in fact in Munich, living under the name Rittmeyer. Unfortunately Rittmeyer, like Modraczek, was actually the name of an associate used for forwarding mail. The scene was set for a partial repetition:

> Arrived in Münich … having learned by experience, I left my baggage in the station and set out by tram to find Rittmeyer. I found the house and Apartment No. 1 turned out to be a beershop. I went to the counter, behind which was a plump German, and timidly asked for Herr Rittmeyer, having a presentiment that again something was wrong. 'That's me,' he said. 'No, it's my husband,' I faltered,

completely baffled. And we stood staring at one another like a couple of idiots.

Help, however, was at hand. Rittmeyer's wife saw what had happened and said 'You must be the wife of Herr Meyer. He is expecting his wife from Siberia. I'll take you to him.' She took the thoroughly bemused Krupskaya to a nearby apartment. The door opened, and there, at a table, sat Vladimir Il'ich and his sister Anna Il'inichna, and Martov. 'Forgetting to thank the landlady I cried: "Why the devil didn't you write and tell me where I could find you?"' The misunderstanding had come about because 'a friend, to whom had been sent a book containing the Münich address, kept the book to read!' Krupskaya concludes the comic episode: 'Many of us Russians went on a wild goose chase in a similar fashion. Shliapnikov at first went to Genoa instead of Geneva; Babushkin, instead of going to London, had been about to start off for America.' [Krupskaya 49–50]

The Ulyanovs overcame this family tiff and took an apartment in Schwabing where, as Krupskaya laconically puts it, we 'lived after our own fashion'. They engaged in their usual mixture of sampling the local atmosphere and immersing themselves in Russian politics. 'Local life did not attract our attention particularly. We observed it in an incidental manner.' [Krupskaya 62] The lack of intensity of German social democracy struck them. They attended May Day celebrations. They observed fairly big columns of social democrats. 'In dead silence they marched through the town – to drink beer at a country beer-garden. This Mayday celebration did not at all resemble a demonstration of working-class triumph throughout the world.' [Krupskaya 62] Visitors were frequent and here there was no lack of intensity. The ferocity of discussion undermined Lenin's delicate health. In particular, Martov would often turn up full of news, gossip, energy and indignation which fuelled daily conversations of five or six hours. They made Lenin 'exceedingly tired' and eventually Lenin 'made himself quite ill with them, and incapable of working'. [Krupskaya 59] Indeed, Lenin's health had already taken a turn for the worse since his return from Siberia. Catarrh had plagued his early months of European exile and worse was to come. In 1903, at the time of the split in the Party, 'everything lay on Vladimir Il'ich. The correspondence with Russia had a bad effect on his nerves ... Il'ich would spend sleepless nights after receiving letters [with bad news] ... Those sleepless nights remain engraved on my memory.' [Krupskaya 78] By that time the couple were living in London and the health of others was also affected. 'Potresov was ill; his lungs could not stand the London fogs.' [Krupskaya 77] Ultimately, at the time the Ulyanovs left London for Geneva in May 1903, Lenin went down with a painful nervous illness, probably shingles, described by Krupskaya as 'holy fire' which caused what she identified as 'shearer's rash'. 'On the way to Geneva, Vladimir Il'ich was very restless; on arriving there he broke down completely, and had to lie in bed for two weeks.'

Lenin had not wanted to leave London but had been outvoted by the rest of the editorial board which decided to move the *Iskra* office to Geneva. The Ulyanovs had initially come to London on 14 April 1902, having left Munich on 12 April because the local printers would no longer take the risk of publishing *Iskra*. They journeyed through Germany and Belgium, combining sightseeing – Cologne Cathedral, for example – with visiting left-wing activists. At first, London evoked ambiguity. In a letter to Axel'rod Lenin wrote 'The first impression of London: vile. And everything is quite expensive.' [CW 43 81] Krupskaya gives a more nuanced view. According to her she and Vladimir Il'ich were 'astounded at the tremendous size of London. Although it was exceedingly dismal weather on the day of our arrival, Vladimir Il'ich's face brightened up and he began casting curious glances at this stronghold of Capitalism, forgetting for the while, Plekhanov and the editorial conflicts.' [Krupskaya 64] Could any impact be greater than that!

The London of 1903 was the capital of the world, the focus of globalization, the richest city in the world with a formidable gap between rich and poor. It was the centre of finance capital and cultural capital. Its riches included the Reading Room of the British Museum where Lenin, like Marx before him, was able to study uninterruptedly. London was also a political capital, not only of the world's most powerful country but also of a global empire of unprecedented size. London, as it had been in Marx's day, was the chief citadel of world capitalism and the focus of a mighty, military and colonial empire. Where better for Lenin to observe the massive contrasts of rampant imperialism? 'Ilich studied living London.' [Krupskaya 65]

He and Krupskaya lost no time in exploring their new environment from corner to corner. Leaving their home on Holford Square in St

Pancras they would take rides on the upper decks of omnibuses which acquainted them with the many faces of one of the world's most intriguing cities. From the quiet squares and detached houses of Bloomsbury and the West End to 'the mean little streets inhabited by the working people, where lines of washing hung across the streets', [Krupskaya 65] which they explored on foot because the buses could not penetrate them, nothing escaped their analytical gaze. 'Observing these howling contrasts in richness and poverty, Il'ich would mutter through clenched teeth, and in English: "Two nations!"' [Krupskaya 65] Street brawls, drunkenness, a bobby arresting an urchin-thief. The Ulyanovs were eager observers. They attended socialist meetings and listened to rank-and-file workers expressing themselves. Though contemptuous of the 'labour aristocracy', which included most of the labour leaders who had, according to this view, been 'corrupted by the bourgeoisie and become themselves petty-bourgeois', Lenin 'always placed his hope on the rank-and-file British workman who, in spite of everything, preserved his class instinct.' 'Socialism', he said, 'is simply oozing from them. The speaker talks rot, and a worker gets up and immediately, taking the bull by the horns, himself lays bare the essence of Capitalist Society.' [Krupskaya 66]

According to Krupskaya, who herself was highly instrumental in implanting them in post-revolutionary Russia, it was in London that Lenin first observed reading rooms which anyone could enter to read files of current newspapers. 'At a later period, Il'ich remarked that he would like to see such reading rooms established all over Soviet Russia.' [Krupskaya 66] The Ulyanovs also, like generations of culture-vulture intellectuals before and since, took advantage of London's fabulous cultural riches. Tchaikovsky's latest symphony (the *Pathéthique*), theatre visits and even walks in the countryside occupied them. 'Most often we went to Primrose Hill, as the whole trip only cost us sixpence. Nearly the whole of London could be seen from the hill – a vast, smoke-wreathed city receding into the distance. From here we got close to nature, penetrating deep into the parks and along green paths.' [Krupskaya 68]

From the conspiratorial point of view liberal Britain had great advantages. 'No identification documents whatever were needed in London then, and one could register under any name. We assumed the name Richter.' [Krupskaya 69] It was easy to travel and in June/July 1902 Lenin spent a month in Loguivy, near Pointe de l'Arcouest on the beautiful north coast of Brittany, with his mother and sister Anna. 'He loved the sea with its continuous movement and expanse. He could really rest there.' [Krupskaya 69] He also made trips to Switzerland and Paris to meet and discuss politics. This also made it easy for others to visit him. It was in London that 'there was a violent knocking at the front door ... It was Trotsky' [Krupskaya 75] who had, at least, managed to find the right door without trouble. Lenin became his patron and recommended him to Axel'rod as 'a young and very energetic and capable comrade from here (pseudonym: "Pero") to help you.' [CW 43 95–6] Lenin's recommendation was not enough for Plekhanov whose suspicions were raised that Trotsky was simply a young protégé of Lenin's. The impression was heightened when Lenin, unsuccessfully, tried to have Trotsky co-opted onto the board of *Iskra* in March 1903.

Not everything in London suited them, however. 'We had found that the Russian stomach is not easily adaptable to the "ox-tails", skate fried in fat, cake, and other mysteries of English fare.' [Krupskaya 68] With its positives and negatives London was the most overt, living, breathing example of capitalism that Lenin had encountered and it made a deep impression on him. It even, of course, housed the grave of Karl Marx. No wonder he did not, despite its drawbacks, want to abandon it for the backwater of Geneva.

'REAL WORK' COMMENCES

Krupskaya's presentiment that 'real' work was about to begin on their return from Siberia was spot on. Lenin's anxieties about the critical situation of social democracy were already giving him sleepless nights. According to his wife, 'Vladimir Il'ich longed passionately for the formation of a solid, united Party into which would be merged all the individual groupings whose attitude to the Party was at present based on personal sympathies or antipathies. He wanted a party in which there would be no artificial barriers, particularly those of a national character.' [Krupskaya 78] The task facing Russian Social Democracy was enormous. Essentially, the movement was composed only of loosely related groups scattered throughout Russia and western Europe. There was no organizational framework, and nor was there more than the flimsiest foundations of an agreed theory. It was fighting for its identity against other political movements. It seems curious that, at this time and throughout Lenin's career – and one is tempted to say, the entire history of the socialist left – the closer the opponent the more vigorous the polemic. Opposition to conservative and, to a lesser extent, liberal parties was practically self-evident. Differences with other radical movements, notably the populists who were themselves organizing into the Socialist Revolutionary Party, created great arguments. But the worst quarrels came with others who claimed to be social democrats. Lenin's sleeplessness was seldom caused by worrying about what capitalists would do next, rather it was about what his friends and apparent allies would do next. His energies were not devoted to refuting the principles of liberalism, rather they were expended on arguing about differences of interpretation of Marxism. At one level, to the outsider, this characteristic makes the debates appear scholastic, the equivalent of discussing how many angels could dance on a pin head. To insiders, however, and especially to Lenin, it was the heretics who adopted a large proportion of the true doctrine who were the most dangerous. In Lenin's mental universe, there was no danger of workers falling directly for the lure of liberalism or conservatism. However, they could be led surreptitiously into the bourgeois camp by misguided leaders who thought they were Marxists and/or socialists. Time and time again Lenin turned on fellow leftists with much greater venom and far greater frequency than on the imperialists themselves.

To follow the debates, shifting alliances and splits of these years in detail would take us beyond the scope of our current enquiry. We do, however, need to look at the main contours of what was happening. We have already examined two of the three big debates wracking the movement – with the populists over Russian capitalism and the revolutionary role of the peasantry on the one hand and with the revisionists/ Economists on the other. The third, best known, argument revolved around the construction of a unified social democratic party, an endeavour which brought about the famous split of 1903 into Menshevik and Bolshevik branches of the Party. Let us plunge into this complex whirlpool of polemic.

Building a unified party was an obvious task. The problem for social democrats in exile was that they had an excess of architects and no bricklayers. Everyone knew how he or she wanted the Party to look. As a result, there were very many different views. Theoretically, the Party already existed. Its small conference at Minsk in 1898 had at least brought a Party programme into existence, one which, though amended, retained some influence until 1917. The growing problem was also underlined by the fact that one of its main drafters, Peter Struve, was rapidly withdrawing from Marxism towards liberalism and eventually conservative imperialism. For Lenin, the most striking phrase of the programme was the one in which Struve wrote that 'The further east in Europe one proceeds, the weaker, more cowardly, and baser in the political sense becomes the bourgeoisie and the greater are the cultural and political tasks that devolve on the proletariat. The Russian working class must and will carry on its powerful shoulders the cause of political liberation.'[2] This insight remained basic to Lenin's, and others', adaptation of Marxism to Russian conditions. Clearly, it also tied in with the polemic over capitalism. Capitalism and the bourgeoisie might be weak in Russia but the point was not to sit back until they were strong but to overthrow them while they were still weak. The responsibility of the proletariat would then include making up ground lost by capitalism through its weakness before moving on to socialism. Already, in embryo, in those few phrases, we have Lenin's strategy of 1917–24.

However, such implications lay far in the future. For the time being the intractable problems of Party construction around agreed principles continued. One can categorize the participants in different ways. One could see the conflict as being one between an older and younger generation or, what is almost the same thing, between long-term exiles and those who had only recently left Russia. There is some truth in this but it does not explain why the close friends and allies of the early debates – Martov and Lenin – should become the spearheads of the later rival factions. However, the disputes of 1900 to early 1903 were affected by such features. For the new arrivals the old guard, whom they had revered from afar and continued to respect as long as they could, had become infected with a spirit of exile which, according to Lenin and others, had cut them off from real developments in Russia. The exiles were much more dogmatic, less ready to expect a successful socialist revolution in the near future.

The major focus of dispute was control of the Party newspaper. This follows from the fact that the real central intent and purpose of a party, given that all overt political activity was illegal in pre-1905 Russia, was to produce a Party newspaper and arrange for its clandestine distribution. For this to happen a lot of work was necessary. First, funds had to be raised. If that could be done then printing facilities capable of dealing with the Russian alphabet which were also beyond the direct and indirect reach of the tsarist police had to be found. As we have already seen, one German printer was unwilling to continue printing Russian material because of the risk and Lenin had had to move to London to find a new one. He was welcomed by British socialists who had a printing press at Clerkenwell Green. As Lenin described it, 'British Social Democrats, led by Quelch, readily made their printing plant available. As a consequence, Quelch himself had to "squeeze up". A corner was boarded off at the printing works by a thin partition to serve him as an editorial room.' [CW 19 369–71]

Having printed the paper, distribution was the next, and perhaps greatest, difficulty. A variety of ingenious routes to get material into Russia were developed. False-bottomed suitcases were often enough to evade half-hearted border searches but only small quantities could be moved that way. More ambitious methods involved links with Russian sailors in western ports. One route took packages of newspapers and other material from French Mediterranean and Italian ports to the Black Sea where watertight packages would be tossed overboard for collection by locals in smaller boats. Couriers, concealment on trains and many other methods were tried. Such manoeuvres of course entailed crude clandestine communications to inform recipients of what was arriving and when and how. There was also a reverse traffic of Party news and of newspaper contributions. Simple code names for people, places and operations were embedded in apparently innocuous letters. Odessa was 'Osip', Tver 'Terenty', Pskov 'Pasha'. Lenin's sister Maria was 'the little bear', Trotsky 'the Pen'. Consignments of newspapers from the printing works were 'beer' from 'the brewery'. [Krupskaya 69–71] If all these obstacles were overcome, and some estimate that only one in a hundred copies got through, once in Russia the materials then had to be distributed as widely as possible around the vast country. Consequently, provincial Party cells were mainly occupied in newspaper distribution. The Party and the newspaper would thus become one and the same thing.

However, the problem causing the splits was bigger than all these practical issues. It was the question of questions. Who would control what went into the papers? On the one side, the old hands, especially Plekhanov and Axel'rod, believed they had a natural right to predominance since they were the founders of the movement. On the other, younger and more energetic spirits, like Lenin and Martov, wanted their say. They believed the spirit of exile had softened the revolutionary edge of the elders. Both factions, however, needed each other. A major split in such a small and weak group, comprising only a few thousand activists at most, would have been suicidal, or so it seemed then. Consequently, compromises ruled the day. Two newspapers came out. *Iskra* (*The Spark*) was dominated by Lenin and Martov. The symbolism of the title was obvious, indicating not only the editors' belief that Russia was ready to catch fire but also their own apparent weakness as a mere spark, though one with the potential to start an uncontrollable fire. The elders produced a less frequently appearing journal *Zarya* (*The Dawn*). Without reading too much into it, the title itself suggests a slower, less violent and more evolutionary process of change. The compromise did not run smoothly. Party unity and harmony seemed far away. Frequent quarrels and disputes broke out. In May 1902 Lenin complained to Plekhanov that he had dealt with one of Lenin's articles in a summary manner. 'If you have set yourself the aim of making our common work impossible, you can very quickly attain this aim by the path you have chosen. As far as personal and not business relations are concerned, you have already definitely spoilt them or, rather, you have succeeded in putting an end to them completely.' [CW 34 103] Lenin was taking a chance alienating Plekhanov and was all too obviously relieved when a reconciliation was brokered in June. 'A great weight fell from my shoulders when I received your letter, which put an end to thoughts of "internecine war" ... That I had no intention of offending you, you are of course aware.' [CW 34 104–5] Lenin implied that his nervous illness had been to blame. A break with Plekhanov at that point might have been fatal to Lenin's career.

In the middle of all this Lenin wrote and produced one of his best known works entitled, like Chernyshevsky's influential novel, *What is to be Done?* It appeared in March 1902. In it Lenin tried to formulate his views on what the Russian Social Democratic Party should be. Also like Chernyshevsky, Lenin apologized in the Preface for the 'serious literary shortcomings' of the pamphlet since he had to work in great haste. [SW 1 100] Indeed the subtitle of the 150-page pamphlet is 'Burning Questions of our Movement', defined as 'the character and main content of our political agitation; our organizational tasks; and the plan for building, simultaneously and from various sides, a militant, All-Russian organization.' [SW 1 99] The Preface also makes clear what Lenin's prime intention was – to challenge Economism. Lenin's response to the burning questions revolved around discussion of the relationship of the Social Democrats to the spontaneous mass movement; the difference between so-called trades-union politics and Social Democratic politics; and finally, promotion of the plan for an All-Russian Social Democratic newspaper. [SW 1 100] The work is one of Lenin's most controversial writings, not least because it is supposed to contain the blueprint for Bolshevism. Does it? In order to find out we need to look at its main arguments.

The nearest thing to an underlying response running through the entire work is the idea that the Economists and their 'Freedom of Criticism' allies, by which is meant mainly Peter Struve, idealized the current state of affairs in the labour movement while Lenin believed it needed to be raised to a higher plane. In the first section Lenin lambasted his opponents for raising lack of theory to a virtue. The Economists quoted Marx's words that one step is worth a dozen programmes. For Lenin, to say this 'in the present state of theoretical disorder is like wishing mourners at a funeral many happy returns of the day.' [SW 1 116] Marx insisted on theoretical rectitude first. In Lenin's words, 'Without revolutionary theory there can be no revolutionary movement.' [SW 1 117] Lenin was already insisting that his opponents' views amounted to nothing more than opportunism. The theme came out even more clearly in the second section of the pamphlet when Lenin attacked the Economists' dependence on spontaneity. By contrast, Lenin formulated one of his most important and characteristic ideas, the need for and nature of consciousness in the revolutionary movement. In one of the most-quoted parts of *What is to be Done?* Lenin wrote:

We have said that *there could not have been* Social Democratic consciousness among the workers. It would have to be brought to them from without. The history of all countries shows that the working class, exclusively by its own efforts, is able to develop only trade union consciousness, i.e. the conviction that it is necessary to combine in unions, fight the employers, and strive to compel the government to pass necessary labour legislation etc.

He then goes on to say quite plainly and unambiguously where this consciousness comes from:

> The theory of socialism, however, grew out of the philosophic, histori-cal and economic theories elaborated by educated representatives of the propertied classes. By their social status the founders of modern scientific socialism, Marx and Engels, belonged to the bourgeois intel-ligentsia. In the very same way, in Russia, the theoretical doctrine of Social Democracy arose altogether independently of the spontaneous growth of the working-class movement; it arose as a natural and inevitable outcome of the development of thought among the revolu-tionary socialist intelligentsia. [SW 1 122]

Clearly, the two elements had to be brought together. 'Spontaneous', 'trade-union' consciousness was inadequate. It had to be infused with correct socialist theory to raise it to a higher level.

Much of the rest of the work is taken up with discussing the rela-tionship between spontaneity and consciousness. The point, for Lenin, was that spontaneity alone would not be sufficient, it needed the con-scious guidance of those who had formulated and guarded the theory. A major problem with the Economists, as far as he was concerned, was that they idealized spontaneity and did not see the need to go beyond it. For Lenin, the two elements had to come together. It was even the case, according to Lenin, that spontaneity 'in essence, represents nothing more or less than consciousness in an embryonic form'. [SW 1 121] Workers could climb up to greater consciousness through strikes, as, Lenin claims, they had done in Russia where, compared to the primitive and reactive machine-smashing revolts of the sixties and seventies, 'the strikes of the nineties might even be described as "conscious" … Even the primitive revolts expressed the awakening of consciousness to a cer-tain extent.' [SW 1 121] The point was it had a limit – trade-union consciousness. To leave the workers' movement to its own devices was to allow it to fall prey to bourgeois ideology, a fate to which, he believed, the Economists were contributing. By not building up a protective shield of socialist theory they were allowing bourgeois influences to dominate. 'Why … does the spontaneous movement … lead to the domination of bourgeois ideology? For the simple reason that bourgeois ideology is far older in origin than socialist ideology, that it is more fully developed, and that it has at its disposal *immeasurably* more means of dissemination.' [SW 1 131] What Lenin meant was that reformism would take hold rather than revolutionary consciousness and he pointed to various German and British examples to prove his point. Spontaneous working-class activity was good, but not, in itself, sufficient, even where it attained advanced forms. At the end of the day, 'the greater the spontaneity of the masses and the more widespread the movement, the more rapid, incomparably more so, the demand for greater consciousness in the theoretical, political, and organizational work of Social Democracy.' [SW 1 141] The Economists, instead of going beyond spontaneity, were 'bowing' to it. They were dragging at the tail of the movement and this was even worse than opportunism. [SW 1 140]

Although Lenin's distinctions were clear-cut, the difference in the actual formulations and propositions of the two sides seem rather similar. Even those propositions quoted by and condemned by Lenin seem somewhat similar to his own. For example, two Economist propositions were: 'The political struggle of the working class is merely the most developed, wide and effective form of economic struggle' and 'The economic struggle is the most widely applicable means of drawing the masses into active political struggle.' [SW 1 145] Both sides saw the need for both aspects of struggle and, with goodwill, one can see that they might have reached compromise. But the argument was not fully reflected in the written propositions. What Lenin feared was Bernsteinian revisionism and the Economists appeared to be the most likely point of entry of reformist and revisionist ideas despite their protestations. The subtext of their position was more important than their actual formulations. It was also the case that the two factions had identified each other as opponents from the moment of the founding of *Iskra* and much of the energy of *Iskra* and the Economist paper *Rabochee delo* had been expended in sniping at one another. It was the implications which Lenin thought he perceived and attacked which were so important. He pointed specifically to the Webbs, whose writings on trades unions he and Krupskaya had, of course, translated while in Shushenskoe, and the experience of British trade unions to show that, although they claimed to 'lend the economic struggle a political character', they remained at the reformist, trade-unionist level. In Lenin's words, 'the pompous phrase about "lending the economic struggle *itself* a political character", which sounds so "terrifically" profound and revolutionary, serves as a screen to conceal what is, in fact the traditional striving to *degrade* Social Democratic politics to the level of trade union politics.' [SW 1 148]

In the fourth section of the pamphlet Lenin developed a similar argument based on the current level of disorganization of Party and movement which was the starting point of the whole debate. Lenin's fear was that the Economists were idealizing the current state of affairs which, for Lenin, was nothing more than 'amateurism' or 'primitiveness'. The point was to escape from current conditions of poorly prepared cadres and ill-thought-out and uncoordinated methods of struggle. Instead it was necessary to build a strong, theoretically well-armed, well-organized, disciplined movement. According to Lenin, Economist principles provided too narrow a base for such developments. While Lenin admitted both Economists and Social Democrats were beset by the problems of 'primitiveness', what he called 'growing pains that affect the whole movement', [SW 1 182] there was a crucial difference. The Economists 'bow to the prevailing amateurism' while for Social Democrats 'our primary and imperative practical task [is] to establish *an organization of revolutionaries* capable of lending energy, stability and continuity to the political struggle.' [SW 1 183]

It is in expounding this last point that Lenin's ideas take what his critics see as a sinister turn. What was the fuss about?

At the core of Lenin's argument lies the assumption that in autocratic conditions the problems of political struggle were more complex and extensive than those of political struggle in more democratic countries. 'Here and further on,' he says, 'I, of course, refer only to absolutist Russia.' [SW 1 189] The revolutionary organization had to be secret and, following from that, small and select. While, of their nature, trades unions should be organized on as broad a basis as possible and as publicly as prevailing conditions would allow, 'on the other hand, the organization of the revolutionaries must consist first and foremost of people who make revolutionary activity their profession ... Such an organization must perforce not be very extensive and must be as secret as possible.' [SW 1 189–90] As Lenin strikingly put it, the problem of a broad organization would be that, while it 'is supposedly most "accessible" to the masses ... [it] is actually most accessible to the gendarmes and makes revolutionaries most accessible to the police.' [SW 1 196] Lenin defended his conception against certain obvious criticisms by arguing that, 'to concentrate all secret functions in the hands of as small a number of professional revolutionaries as possible does not mean that the latter will "do the thinking for all" and that the rank and file will not take an active part in the *movement*. On the contrary, the membership will promote increasing numbers of the professional revolutionaries from its ranks.' [SW 1 200] Lenin further elaborated that while the Party organization was centralized the movement should be broad. The illegal press was, for example, to be read as widely as possible, demonstrations should be broad as should every function of the movement. [SW 1 201] Summarizing his outlook, Lenin argued that the 'task is not to champion the degrading of the revolutionary to the level of an amateur, but to *raise* the amateurs to the level of revolutionaries.' [SW 1 201] Similarly, the point was to *raise* 'the workers to the level of revolutionaries; it is not at all our task *to descend* to the level of the "working masses" as the Economists wish to do.' [SW 1 205]

The talk of raising and descending points to one of the two key implications of Lenin's theory around which argument has raged. First it implies elitism – only the advanced, conscious revolutionaries can guide the political struggle and they will be the wider movement's natural leaders. Second, under such conditions the normal elements of democracy – equality of all; open, mass voting and so on – were inappropriate. Lenin makes no bones about this. '"Broad democracy" in Party organization, amidst the gloom of the autocracy and the domination of the gendarmerie, is nothing more than a *useless and harmful toy*', harmful because it 'will simply facilitate the work of the police'. No party could practise broad democracy under such conditions 'however much it may have desired to do so'. [SW 1 212] Once again Lenin is absolutely explicit that what he was saying was based on the conditions of tsarist Russia. His final conclusion on the issue of organization was that 'the only serious organizational principle for the active workers of our movement should be the strictest secrecy, the strictest selection of members, and the training of professional revolutionaries. Given these qualities, something even more than "democratism" would be guaranteed to us, namely complete, comradely, mutual confidence among revolutionaries. This is absolutely essential for us, because there can be no question of replacing it by general, democratic control in Russia.' [SW 1 213–14]

By comparison, the final section of the pamphlet, on organizing a newspaper, is relatively uncontroversial in that it is occupied chiefly with a direct polemic with *Rabochee delo* of limited broader significance.

Does *What is to be Done?* constitute a blueprint for Bolshevism? Does it contain a peculiarly Leninist outlook which foreshadows the 'totalitarianism' of the later Soviet Union? Lenin's discourse on the conspiratorial organization of selected professional revolutionaries has led many to argue exactly this.[3] Should we agree with them? Not necessarily. On the one hand, Lenin quotes many mainstream Social Democrats in support of his position, including Karl Kautsky who is quoted at great length on the key issue of where class consciousness comes from. In Kautsky's view the idea that 'socialist consciousness appears to be a necessary and direct result of the proletarian class struggle' is said to be 'absolutely untrue'. Scientific, academic knowledge is required for modern socialist consciousness to arise, Kautsky argues, and 'the vehicle of science is not the proletariat, but the *bourgeois intelligentsia* ... Thus, socialist consciousness is something introduced into the proletarian class struggle from without.' [Quoted by Lenin in SW 1 129] Similarly, Lenin points to existing examples of educated, conscious, permanent, stable leadership in the form of Liebknecht and Bebel and the leaders of the German Social Democratic Party. [SW 1 197] Surely these points indicate that Lenin was being less radical than appeared later to be the case? One could also add to it that, among Social Democrats, the pamphlet was broadly welcomed at first.[4] It was only as the split began to occur that Plekhanov and others began to have second thoughts. For the moment, however, Lenin's pamphlet was welcomed as a defence of orthodox Social-Democratic thinking, not as a clarion call to heresy.

A close reading might have given cause for concern in that Lenin's other great model for the Party leadership comes from the early period of Russia's own populist revolutionary movement. 'A circle of leaders, of the type of Alexeyev and Myshkin, of Khalturin and Zhelyabov, is capable of coping with political tasks in the genuine and practical sense of the term.' Once again, his own youthful populism and his constant admiration of the early populists were in evidence. 'Do you think our movement cannot produce leaders like those of the seventies?' he asked the Economists. [SW 1 185] Again he refers to 'the magnificent organization that the revolutionaries had in the seventies, and that should serve us as a model.' [SW 1 208] But even here Lenin was at pains to defend himself against accusations of following the example of the terrorist *Narodnaya volya* too closely. He points out that its parent party, *Zemlya i volya*, which stressed peaceful propaganda, was organized on the same lines. Its leaders were the ones who created the 'magnificent organization'. [SW 1 208]

For all these reasons we would have to conclude that Lenin was not yet stepping over the boundaries already set by Social Democracy. His thoughts on how to operate under tsarist conditions were no more than common sense. The problems began to arise when the culture of centralization and secrecy inculcated by autocratic conditions became a habit which could not be shaken off even when the conditions no longer prevailed.

Before leaving this most important of Lenin's formative writings there are two other points we need to take note of. Although the issue of consciousness was raised, the full implications were yet to work themselves out. In particular, there was very little on exactly what 'Marxist', 'proletarian' or 'revolutionary' consciousness consisted of. What was permitted, what was not? What were the precise features of 'advanced' consciousness among Party members? These, at various times, became contentious issues and we will have to return to them. Consciousness is one of the most potent of Leninist concepts and has often been underestimated as a foundation of much of his thinking. Throughout his life propaganda and persuasion were the instruments which would 'raise' the consciousness of sceptics and bring them into agreement with Lenin. In the end, the revolution would stand or fall according to the degree to which this could be successfully achieved. He had no mechanism to deal with the possibility that the result of raising workers' consciousness could have any other outcome.

Finally, we have noted that the differences over which the polemic was conducted were infinitely small compared to the common ground between both sides and that the actual written formulations were only part of the battle. Like any politician, Lenin had become entangled in a party discourse. The Economists were identified as opponents; the sniping had been going on for years; whatever they said had to be combated not always because of what it meant but because of perceived implications or subtext. Such arguments crop up with increasing frequency in the next phase of Lenin's life but none is more crucial than the upcoming debates which led to the fateful split into Bolsheviks and Mensheviks. Here too, paper formulations do not seem enough to warrant the polemical energies they apparently unleashed. Once again, subtexts, discourse, supposed implications and even personal antagonisms are more important than written texts. With this in mind let us turn to the next step in the emergence of Lenin and Leninism.

THE SPLIT IN THE PARTY

The formal story of the split at the Party Congress is simple enough and has often been told. The Party was in a general state of flux, uncertain of its theory, its immediate political programme, its organization and its membership. The founding conference in Minsk in 1898 had been an ephemeral affair bequeathing a programme and a name, the Russian Social Democratic Labour Party, but little else. It was decided that the time had come to organize the Party more comprehensively. Its rivals, the populists, had formed the Socialist Revolutionary Party in 1901 and the liberals were moving towards what eventually became the Constitutional Democratic (Kadet) Party. Things were on the move in Russian politics and it was time for the social democrats to join in. The Second Party Congress, called to assemble in Brussels, was, in effect, intended to be the founding congress of a properly constituted Social Democratic Party. The Congress convened secretly in a former warehouse in Brussels on 30 July 1903. It was discovered by the police on 6 August and it was decided to decamp en masse to London. After crossing the Channel from Ostend, still arguing, the delegates re-formed in a Congregationalist church in Southgate Road, north London, which was run by a committed socialist. It continued until 23 August.

All the factions we have been discussing – *Iskra*, *Zarya* and the Economists – were present. One other significant group was the Jewish Workers' Party, the Bund, which was strong in western Russia for the obvious reason that that was the area in which most Jews lived. There were 43 voting delegates with 51 votes altogether and 14 consultative delegates allowed to speak but not vote. *Iskra/Zarya* had 27 delegates with 33 votes, obviously a comfortable majority. There were seven Economists, five Bund delegates and four undecided. After preliminary discussion about a Party programme the Congress, now in London, moved on to the Party constitution. It was over the very first paragraph, defining a Party member, that the first major clash occurred on 15 August. After initially agreeing, the *Iskra* group then split. Martov wanted a broad definition of Party membership, namely that someone 'who regularly supports one of its organizations' should be deemed a member. Lenin wanted a narrower formula. A member should engage 'in personal work in one of the party organizations'. Martov was prepared to accept supporters, Lenin wanted only activists. Lenin's formulation lost by 28 votes to 23. Martov's majority included the votes of the Bund and the Economists. The *Iskra* group split. 19 voted for Lenin, 14 for Martov. When, on 18 August, two Economists and the Bund left the congress the power balance shifted. As well as his majority of *Iskra* delegates Lenin had a majority of congress delegates, 24 to 20 supporting Martovites. It was from this 'majority' (*bol'shinstvo* in Russian) that the terms Bolshevik and Menshevik (*menshinstvo* – minority) were eventually to derive, though for the time being the simple terms majority and minority were used. In final elections to the Central Committee, the leading body of the Party between congresses, and to the editorial board of *Iskra*, Lenin's candidates predominated, not least because Plekhanov still supported him. Martov was elected to the *Iskra* board but refused to serve as token oppositionist to a Lenin/Plekhanov majority. Having completed its work, the congress broke up. On 24 August many of the delegates visited Karl Marx's grave in Highgate Cemetery and then dispersed.

The formal story, however, conceals more than it reveals. From our point of view, the crucial and controversial question is not so much what happened at the congress, rather it is how did Lenin achieve his objectives? On the one hand, his opponents accused him of a ruthless, almost Machiavellian, pursuit of success. To his defenders it was a great moment, the emergence of a single-minded, determined Lenin armed with correct tactics he would not see compromised establishing the basis of a movement that was eventually to sweep him into power and control half the planet.

It cannot be doubted that Lenin's behaviour was at times boorish in the extreme. His intensity led him into almost frenzied interventions. Indeed, he later admitted as much in a letter to Potresov of 13 September. He wrote that he had 'often behaved and acted in a state of frightful irritation, frenziedly' and was even prepared to admit to 'this *fault of mine*'. [CW 34 164] He was not, however, prepared to accept that any of the congress decisions he had forced through were wrong. The congress had seen a new side of Lenin, the ruthless, stop-at-nothing side. He had not hesitated to split the movement though he does not appear to have foreseen the development coming. It also showed the side of his personality that was prepared to sacrifice anything if political necessity demanded it, in this case the relationship with his close friend Martov.

Lenin appeared to be riding high as the congress broke up. He had established himself as second in the Party pecking order to the venerable Plekhanov and, in practice, as the most active and, apparently de facto, leader. Plekhanov was almost a symbolic chairman, Lenin a hands-on chief executive. In fact, however, appearances were deceptive. Plekhanov was no extinct volcano and he was at pains to try to reverse the split that had taken place. After all the Party did not have resources to squander. In Plekhanov's eyes the Martovites were first-rate Marxists and revolutionaries who must be brought back into the fold. Lenin, however, was determined that the decisions made should be upheld. His stubbornness appeared to have brought his own downfall. His refusal to compromise risked making him an outcast.

Almost all the main protagonists seemed to feel that the acrimonious falling-out at the congress was really just an incident which could be patched up. For a year or so afterwards an elaborate chess game of political relationships was conducted. In September and October 1903 Lenin and Plekhanov tried to reach agreement with Martov. However, in late October and November, when progress was being made, it was Lenin who dug his heels in. He complained to Plekhanov, resigned from the Party Council and urged Plekhanov: 'do not give everything away to the Martovites.' [CW 34 185] In his resignation letter he stated 'I by no means refuse to support the new central Party institutions by my work to the best of my ability.' [CW 7 91] On 4 November he complained to a friend that Plekhanov had 'cruelly and shamefully let me down' and that 'the situation is desperate'. On 6 November it was Lenin who resigned from the editorial board of *Iskra*, a painful wrench after he had done so much for the newspaper. From that point on Plekhanov sided with the Mensheviks. Lenin for the time being led the Central Committee but the Mensheviks controlled the newspaper, the key to the Party. A bitter struggle between the factions continued. Without money, resources or influence he was forced to remake his career and, eventually, build, in Bolshevism, a personally loyal instrument which, he hoped, would never let him down.

3

CONSTRUCTING LENINISM

The previous chapters have shown how, by 1904, Lenin had almost constructed himself from the raw material of his younger self, Volodya. The next step was to forge a party in his own, self-made likeness.

FAMILY LIFE 1903–4: FROM LONDON TO GENEVA

The struggles of 1903–4 had, as we would expect, taken their toll on Lenin's often delicate health. However, he had come through. Despite the energy-sapping background of the constant bickering in the Party the Ulyanovs continued to lead a full and, often, happy life in exile. Early in 1903, just a few weeks before they left London, Nadezhda Krupskaya continued to write about their diversions to Lenin's mother: 'You will probably think that we have no amusements here at all but we go somewhere almost every evening; we have been to the German theatre a number of times and to concerts, and we study the people and the local way of life. It is easier to observe here than anywhere else. Volodya is very keen on these observations and gets as enthusiastic about them as about everything he does.' [CW 37 606]

At the time Krupskaya wrote this letter Lenin was away lecturing in Paris. He spent more and more of his time travelling in western Europe giving lectures to intellectual audiences and occasionally addressing workers' meetings. His main activity, however, remained editorial work, at that time on *Iskra*. He and Martov wrote much of the contents, often under a variety of pseudonyms. Lenin also had major responsibilities for seeing successive issues through the press. The pattern of spending most of his time on journalism continued right up until the outbreak of the war in 1914. Indeed, at times, Lenin accurately described himself on official documents as a journalist. A succession of papers and journals, especially *Iskra*, *Vpered*, *Proletarii* and eventually *Pravda*, occupied the core of Lenin's life in the exile years. He wrote an astonishing number of articles for his journals. The first issue of *Vpered* appeared in January 1905, the last, the eighteenth, in May. In all Lenin contributed forty articles to it. It was replaced by *Proletarii* (*Proletarians*). From May to his return to Russia in November, he spent three days a week working on it. He contributed ninety articles to its twenty-six issues. In the short time between his return to Russia and the closure of Gorky's paper, *Novaia zhizn'* (*New Life*), in December he had contributed twenty articles. His style, however, was less extraordinary. Typically there would be an acutely observed, often polemical, central point to his articles but there was no subtlety of argument or style. The point would be rammed home through invective, sarcasm, repetition and padding apparently aimed at filling the pages of the journals rather than adding to the argument. His journalism was more akin to the bludgeon than the rapier. It is hard to say what effect it had on his readers. His articles are often hard to read and were clearly aimed at an intellectual rather than mass audience. He had little gift for directly propagandizing his ideas to the masses. Nonetheless, journalism remained the focus of his life. For Lenin, being a professional revolutionary was more or less synonymous with being, like his mentor Karl Marx, a professional political analyst and commentator.

There were, none the less, still possibilities for extensive recreation. Returning to Geneva unwillingly in May 1903, Vladimir and Nadezhda took frequent trips to the mountains which they loved. In January 1904 they had 'a wonderful outing to Salève. ... Down below, in Geneva, it was all mist and gloom, but up on the mountain ... there was glorious sunshine, snow, tobogganing – altogether a good Russian winter's day.' [CW 37 359] In summer they spent four weeks backpacking including a week in Lausanne and mountain walks near Montreux. Lenin signed a postcard to his mother 'from the tramps'. [CW 37 363] Krupskaya wrote 'The new impressions, the natural tiredness and the healthy sleep had a healthy effect on Vladimir Il'ich. His thoughts, his joie de vivre, his good humour returned.' Politics still intruded, however. Krupskaya's account of the idyll concludes: 'We spent August near Lac de Brêt where Vladimir Il'ich and Bogdanov drafted the plan for the continuation of the struggle against the Mensheviks.' [Weber 38] The Ulyanovs also continued their cultural pursuits while living in Geneva, Krupskaya noting that in late 1904 they attended a performance of *La Dame aux Camelias* the cast of which included Sarah Bernhardt. [Weber 40]

Lenin's life continued to be balanced between writing, intriguing and relaxing. Among the forces which sustained him, especially in demanding times like those of 1903–5, was the support of his natural family and of his supporters and friends who made a kind of second family. The latter differed from the former in that those who made it up were constantly changing according to the alliances of the day. At one point, Lenin had been particularly close to Martov, the only comrade with whom he communicated at this time using the familiar form '*ty*' rather than the formal '*vy*' but he did not hesitate to break with him in 1903 when it appeared to be necessary. Similarly, Bogdanov, his companion in mountain walks and discussions, was eventually expelled from the little community. Lenin never allowed sentiment to stand in the way of his political principles. He might have been a better, more empathic leader had he done so, but firmness of will was the fashion of that, and many other, times.

However, the one unshifting support mechanism was that of his family, including Krupskaya who occupied a curious role of lover, wife, secretary and, at times, almost an extra sister. It was often Krupskaya who kept Lenin's mother and brother and sisters informed of their doings. Indeed, the collective radical commitment of all the Ulyanov siblings is remarkable. Far from being an isolated renegade, as he is sometimes portrayed, Lenin remained the darling of his mother, whose affection Lenin constantly and fulsomely returned, and the favourite of his sisters and brother who all, to a greater or lesser degree, shared his political commitment. The Ulyanovs were an extraordinary revolutionary family. It was not simply that Alexander's execution marked them out. Many other families of convicted political prisoners distanced themselves from or even disowned their radical family member but Lenin's brother and sisters actively embraced the struggle against tsarism in varying ways. The depth of their commitment, and of Lenin's bond with them, was made manifest in late 1903 and early 1904 when Lenin and Krupskaya learned that his brother Dmitrii and sisters Anna and Maria had all been arrested in Kiev. Krupskaya wrote to her mother-in-law that the news 'came as a great shock to us – and it is so sad'. In any case, she wrote, 'We are not living too well in Geneva; Mother is often poorly. We feel unsettled somehow and the work goes badly.' [CW 37 607] Only Lenin's mother remained outside political activity but she still remained the much-loved head of the family whom Anna, in particular, took care of and who was well looked after by all her children. They brought her on holiday to France and elsewhere and she kept in touch with all of them. Without doubt, the Ulyanovs were a close-knit and extraordinary family.

THE INTENSIFICATION OF THE PARTY STRUGGLE

Without such support the years of bitter struggle would have been even harder for Lenin. The Second Congress did not forestall further discussion. Far from it. The dispute became generalized. Alliances came and went. Issues rose and disappeared. Tempers were pushed to the limit and beyond. To the outsider, real differences still seemed minimal compared to the immense acres of common ground between the contending parties. Principles continued to be bound up in personality clashes and no overall, universally respected, mediating force emerged. Instead, the debate went on and on.

How can we best understand the arguments in the years from 1903 to 1905 and beyond? Simply following the ins and outs would be confusing not to mention tedious. From our point of view, the main contours are the most important. The fundamental point underlying the debate was that Lenin, and his supporters, were more determined than ever to defend a truly revolutionary policy and were mainly afraid that any loosening of revolutionary commitment would eventually lead to the abandonment of revolutionary principles and the adoption of a never-ending reformism. To prevent this Lenin opposed what he saw as the slightest compromise over basic principles. Indeed, his position hardened between 1902 and 1904 so that what had been consensual in 1902 – his attack on the Economists – had become more specifically 'Bolshevik' in that the notion of the vanguard, elite party was becoming increasingly divisive. As time went by Lenin was carving out a more and more radical and solitary path.

Why? It is far from easy to answer this question. Indeed, in many ways, it is the central question about Lenin. How did he come to believe so strongly in himself? Why did he take such a strong, revolutionary line? Why was his position hardening at this point?

Lenin, more than most of his opponents, believed in the imminent collapse of capitalism, providing the revolutionaries played their part. To his opponents, this was utopian. Capitalism around 1900 seemed secure. Globalization, in the form of the New Imperialism, was rampant. Africa had been swallowed up by competing colonizers. In 1900 London controlled the main financial and political tentacles which reached around the globe. Economies were expanding. Thanks to resistance movements – trades unions above all and political pressure groups – living standards and civil and political rights were expanding. Far from polarizing society into rich and poor a broad, prosperous lower middle class was forming. Workers were carving out decent lives for themselves, especially if they had skills. Of course there remained many social problems including a vast underclass of, often, migrant unskilled labour and extreme exploitation in the colonies, but there could be no doubt that capitalism, far from being in crisis, appeared to be expanding without any sign of limits. It was an expansion in which broad sectors of the European population were participating. It was exactly such phenomena which had led Bernstein to his revisionist position in the first place. In practice, Bernsteinian conceptions were seeping into the social-democratic movement. Lenin was determined to resist them. Over the next phase of his intellectual development he had to give his answer to the question of why, in his view, capitalism, none the less, appeared to be unstable. However, this was not in the forefront of his mind at this time.

Many observers have attributed Lenin's revolutionary intransigence to the execution of his brother which, they claim, had made him implacable and vengeful. However, as we have seen, Lenin had not been the isolated fanatic that such authors suggest. Before 1903 he had, by and large, maintained friendly and warm relations with the rest of the movement and been a psychologically balanced individual with no obvious traumas. While the execution of his brother certainly had considerable significance, to help understand the growing rift other points need to be weighed up. First, as Lenin matured his convictions also became more sharply defined. He had, as it were, gone from a learning stage, in which they developed, to a teaching stage in which they should be spread and implemented, not to mention defended, with full force. It is also apparent that opposition to his proposals brought out the worst in Lenin. It made him ill. It made him, as he recognized himself, overly insistent and even, in his own word, 'frenzied' as we have seen. [CW 34 164] He became excessively abusive and caused ruptures in his personal relationships with opponents. Such was the depth of his commitment to his ideas and his frustration with opposition that he became less and less courteous towards his opponents. Sometimes, if his interests demanded that there should be no break, for instance with Gorky whose financial support was essential, he could sometimes bite his tongue and tone down the vitriol. However, these were exceptions to the rule. He had become a determined conviction politician.

On the face of it, Lenin's opponents appeared to be correct. Capitalism was an ever-expanding and increasingly stable juggernaut that seemed unlikely to be brought down in the near future. However, events were, to some extent, favouring him in that, in Russia, revolution was just around the corner and Lenin was to throw himself into it with increasing enthusiasm and optimism. The events of 1905 were to lead him to urge the workers of Moscow into a hopeless conflict with the authorities. Ironically, the inevitable failure of the uprising was to cause Lenin himself to tone down his revolutionary expectations. With these considerations in mind, let us look more closely at Lenin's work in the exciting period of revolution and the longer, more energy- and morale-sapping years of post-revolutionary defeat and endless Party squabbling.

ONE STEP FORWARD OR TWO STEPS BACK?

The hardening of Lenin's position after the Second Congress first became apparent, as far as his published writings are concerned, in his *Letter to a Comrade on Our Organizational Tasks*, written in mid-September 1903. Lenin's key phrase was that a 'disciplined party of struggle' was needed. His pamphlet circulated widely in Russia in a sort of *samizdat* (self-published) form and was then published as a pamphlet in both Russia and Geneva in January 1904. However, his main declaration of new principles came in the more extensive *One Step Forward: Two Steps Back – The Crisis in Our Party* which appeared in March 1904. It is actually longer than the much better known *What is to be Done?* and could be said to contain many of the propositions which are harder to find in the earlier pamphlet.

One Step Forward: Two Steps Back is an unusual piece of work. It is a detailed commentary, from Lenin's perspective, on the minutes of the Second Congress. It goes, issue by issue, through the debates and resolutions of the Congress. It maintains a high level of vitriolic energy towards Lenin's increasing band of opponents. The excruciating detail, the childishly sustained heavy sarcasm and the difficulty of reviving the context in which it was produced make it a very difficult and unprepossessing item to read today. Lenin's words that it will only be the occasional reader who will have 'the patience to read' the whole or some of his opponents' writings could apply to readers of Lenin's pamphlet also. [SW 1 298] Its importance lies in the fact that it appears to tighten up the looser concepts of *What is to be Done?*

Lenin complained that 'Shells rained on my head' [SW 1 409] and he sought to return fire. Three words, above all, characterized Lenin's views on Party organization: authority, centralism and discipline. The key concepts he was attacking were autonomy, reformism, anarchism and, even, democracy, a term Lenin used in a particular sense in this pamphlet to mean something like decentralization, a situation in which the members could readily overrule the leaders rather than the other way about. Altogether, they made up the ever-expanding category of 'opportunism'. In his view the demands from certain quarters for 'autonomy', that is decentralization, were inappropriate. For Lenin, the moment was one of transition. 'Previously, our Party was not a formally organized whole, but merely a sum of separate groups', a point he reiterated several times. The looser relations this imposed were no longer applicable: '*Now* we have become an organized Party, and this implies the establishment of authority ... the subordination of lower Party bodies to higher ones.' [SW 1 398–9. See also 420] Lenin supported 'top downward' [SW 1 424] organization and, in a phrase that resounds today, defended bureaucracy over democracy in that 'Bureaucracy *versus* democracy is in fact centralism *versus* autonomism; it is the organizational principle of revolutionary Social-Democracy as opposed to the organizational principle of opportunist Social-Democracy.' [SW 1 424] The crucial point here is: what did Lenin mean by bureaucracy? Earlier Lenin had argued that bureaucracy, in the sense of careerism, place-seeking and wrangling over co-option rather than ideas, was unquestionably 'undesirable and detrimental to the Party'. [SW 1 396] Looking further into the debate it seems that what Lenin meant by bureaucracy in the positive sense was a permanent central Party apparatus which issued instructions to the lower ranks. 'Democracy' weakened the principle if it meant the lower ranks had the right to decide whether to accept or reject instructions from above. So do we have, in *One Step Forward*, the blueprint for Bolshevism that is somewhat elusive in *What is to be Done?*

At one level, as the extracts above indicate, Lenin was being more forthright about the need for a strongly led party where the organizational principle was, in his expression, from the 'top downward'. In addition the rhetoric indicated an increasingly unbridgeable gulf between the participants. Actual manoeuvrings and deep squabbles had become endemic. Lenin's determination and lone battle had, indeed, brought shells raining down on him from all directions. Plekhanov had written an article pointedly entitled 'What Should Not Be Done' and Martov had complained of *A State of Siege* in the Party in a pamphlet of that name. Discussions to bring unity led to deeper disaster. In October Lenin wrote that 'You can't imagine even a tenth of the outrages to which the Martovites have sunk. ... War has been declared.' [CW 36 128] Party bodies voted in favour of one side and then the other as the search for compromise continued. Plekhanov said he could not bear to 'fire on his comrades' and that 'rather than have a split it is better to put a bullet in one's brain.' [quoted in SW 1 400] Lenin himself was so preoccupied with his thoughts that he walked into the back of a tram and, according to Krupskaya, 'very nearly had his eye knocked out.' [Krupskaya 94] He resigned from central Party bodies, including the *Iskra* editorial board, in November, and wrote harshly about Plekhanov who, he said, had 'cruelly and shamefully' let him down by reopening discussion with the Martovites. [CW 34 186] By late November he was co-opted onto the Party Central Committee. The bewildering array of attacks and counter-attacks continued. However, in the light of the actual struggle, can one conclude that, as Lenin wrote later, 'Bolshevism exists as a political movement and as a political party since 1903'? [Weber 34]

Some of the ambiguities present in *What is to be Done?* continue into *One Step Forward: Two Steps Back*. Kautsky is presented as an example of a centralizer. A contemporary dispute in the German Social Democratic Party about the right of the centre to intervene in the affairs of constituencies is held up as an analogy to what Lenin is writing about. He also claimed that he stood for 'Social-Democratic European' practices against his opponents who were 'Social-Democratic Asiatics'. [SW 1 424] There are occasional tones of conciliation. The day after writing that 'war has been declared' Lenin joined Plekhanov in offering to co-opt Martov on to the *Iskra* editorial board! On several occasions he stated that he recognized his opponents were honourable, though sometimes in such a patronizing way that one might doubt the sincerity involved. For example, Lenin said 'it would be unwise to attribute to sordid motives even the most sordid manifestations of the squabbling that is so habitual in the atmosphere of émigré and exile colonies. It is a sort of epidemic disease engendered by abnormal conditions of life, disordered nerves, and so on.' [SW 1 392] He used the same concept much more crudely towards the end of the pamphlet where he talked about a 'sordid story brought about by [Martov's] morbid imagination' plus reference to 'a number of *incorrect statements* (evidently due to his wrought-up condition)'. [SW 1 447–8] However, there is no doubt that the only way Lenin would join with the transgressors would be if they capitulated to his principles.

One Step Forward: Two Steps Back also merits consideration beyond its detailed contents. Overall, Lenin was seeking a new level of Party organization which corresponded to the situation. His demand for a unified and disciplined party with a strong central executive, and this is clearly what he meant by 'the bureaucratic principle' of organization, was not unreasonable in itself. Other parties were evolving in much the same way, notably the liberals, who emerged as the Constitutional Democratic (Kadet) Party, and the Socialist Revolutionary (SR) Party. The degree to which his conception of Party organization was fundamentally different from theirs is open to dispute. Many will also sympathize with his complaint that one of the roots of the problem lay in 'intellectual individualism' [SW 1 398] which accepted only 'purely Platonic and verbal' acceptance of organizational relations. [SW 1 399] At heart, Lenin could be seen to be trying to instil necessary discipline into a chronically individualist body of people. He said as much. 'Sneering at discipline – autonomism – anarchism – there you have the ladder which our opportunism in matters of organization now climbs and now descends, skipping from rung to rung and skilfully dodging any definite statement of its principles.' [SW 1 431]

By contrast, Lenin's extraordinary insistence on following rules and minutes showed a mind desperate for a fixed point in an ever-shifting universe. He was looking for a solid foundation from which to build a disciplined party devoted to the undiluted goal of revolution and eluding the siren grasp of opportunism. In concrete terms this meant that, though he admired the heroic deeds and potential of the workers he believed they had to be guided, kept under control and that their movement must show discipline not the dreaded spontaneity beloved of the Economists and other of Lenin's opponents.

However, few saw it in exactly that light, nor did they believe the issue was a matter of life or death. A decisive turning point was reached in summer 1904. Since February a group of Lenin's supporters had urged conciliation. By July and August they completely dominated the Central Committee. Lenin had lost control of his last institutional redoubt. He was being edged out into the wilderness. Heavy blows from the international socialist community followed. In September he was attacked in print by the widely respected Rosa Luxemburg who accused him of 'ultra-centralism' and being 'full of the spirit of the overseer'. His principles threatened to 'bind' the movement rather than develop it. His concern, she argued, was 'not so much to make the activity of the party more fruitful as to control the party'.[1] Kautsky, in turn, refused to print Lenin's reply. No major figures in the European or Russian movements came to Lenin's defence. He was desperate. Loss of influence also left him without funds and without an outlet for his writings. The leading figures of Russian and German Social Democracy – Plekhanov, Axel'rod, Zasulich, Martov, Kautsky and Luxemburg – were all opposed to him. His own supporters – Lengnik, Essen and Zemlyachka – were comparative nonentities. Stalwarts like Nosov, Krasin and Krzhizhanovsky had gone over to the 'conciliators'. Even at this point Lenin refused to compromise. For him, the split was essential and had to be maintained despite the odds against him. He was alone with his own mini-group. As we shall see, his stance eventually attracted a rising generation, including Bogdanov and Lunacharsky, not to mention the crucial support of Gorky, but for the time being Lenin had alienated all the major figures of European Marxism.

Why had he become so implacable and how was he to dig himself out? The answer to the first question seems to be that Lenin, now thirty-four years old, had reached a decisive and maturing point in his development. The ideas of *What is to be Done?* and *One Step Forward: Two Steps Back* had become sacred to him. His interpretation of what they meant was his guiding light. He was no longer prepared simply to learn from and defer to the older generation. In addition, he wanted to assert his own ideas. As we have seen, at their heart was the deep conviction that the Party should be small, advanced and secret. To see his beloved Party adopting what he considered suicidal principles of broad membership was too much for him to accept. He would fight the process all the way. We might surmise here that Lenin's background of prison and exile had convinced him of the need for conspiracy while many of his opponents had spent long years in western Europe and had been more deeply imbued with the spirit of liberal democracy and wanted to adapt it. Lenin had a different vision, which the struggle was hardening rather than softening. He was becoming a fundamentalist, unwilling to compromise what he considered to be the essence of his faith. He had always been self-confident and it was a virtue that stood him in good stead. At this conjuncture, however, one could say that it was, like other of his virtues at various times, threatening to turn into a vice. It was becoming a basis for dogmatism, narrowness and intolerance. Lenin knew what he wanted and had stopped listening even to his close friends if they tried to tell him any different. To his supporters it was admirable determination and clear-sightedness. His opponents could only shake their heads in sorrow and disbelief.

The confidence and determination were, however, what pulled him through. While one might argue about the exact meaning of Lenin's written text, his actions seemed less ambiguous – he was building a centralized, revolutionary party around himself over which he would exert decisive influence. For the moment, however, it was only a small acorn.

The language of *One Step Forward: Two Steps Back* is also interesting from the point of view of nomenclature. The term Bolshevik does not appear at all, although the regular Russian word *bol'shinstvo* (majority) from which it is derived is used constantly by Lenin to describe the group to which he claimed to belong. The word Menshevik appears once, in inverted commas [SW 1 398], as does the term Leninism in the phrase 'revolt against Leninism' which Lenin said was coined by Martov. [SW 1 433] Clearly, the terminology still had not been defined any more than the Party differences themselves.

Perhaps the final, and most ironic, comment on the pamphlet, the dispute and the whole two-year obsession with organization, was that it diverted the émigré leadership from keeping a proper watch on Russian politics so that when the revolution of 1905 exploded out of the rumblings of the previous four years or so, the leaders of Russian Social Democracy were caught by surprise. Lenin's schedule in December 1904 and early January 1905 was still taken up with lectures on the Party situation and on making final preparations for the emergence of his new publishing project *Vpered (Forward)*. The revolution was a surprise.

Krupskaya describes how they first heard of the events of Bloody Sunday, 9 January (OS), in St Petersburg the day after they happened.

> We went where all the Bolsheviks who had heard the Petersburg news were instinctively drawn – to the Lepeshinsky's emigrant restaurant. We wanted to be together. The people gathered there hardly spoke a word to one another, they were so excited ... Everyone was so overwhelmed with the thought that the Revolution had already commenced, that the bonds of faith in the Tsar were broken, that now the time was quite near when 'tyranny will fall and the people will rise up – great, mighty and free.' [Krupskaya 108]

1905

Although revolution in the abstract was in the forefront of the minds of the émigrés, its actual outbreak in January 1905 was not. After four or five years of social disorder there was no immediate sign of escalation. In the mid-1890s St Petersburg had seen its first major strikes, beginning with women workers in a cigarette factory and later among metalworkers. In 1899 there was a student strike which led to university closure in St Petersburg. From then on rural and urban crises came and went. There were general strikes in Rostov, Odessa and elsewhere. Troops were called in with increasing frequency to deal with disturbances in town and country. One compilation suggests the army dealt with 19 disturbances in 1893; 33 in 1900; 271 in 1901 and 522 in 1902.[2] The newly formed SR Party, the deadly populist rival to the Social Democrats, instigated a terror campaign which brought about the death of many government officials from local policemen and police chiefs to several government ministers.

Yet, the main blows against the government did not come from radical bombers but were self-inflicted. In the face of growing internal disorder the autocracy embarked on an ill-fated war with Japan. Arrogant assumptions of easy victory turned into nightmare defeats on land and sea. Tsarist inefficiency was exposed in a bitter war of massive firepower and trench defences. The final straw came in January 1905 when one of Russia's major strongholds in the Far East, Port Arthur, fell. The news arrived in St Petersburg at the same time as the Bloody Sunday demonstrations were being prepared and had a considerable impact, especially among the educated middle class.

A second self-inflicted blow came in the form of police socialism. This evolved from an idea of a Moscow police official named Zubatov. Rather than allow workers to be organized illegally by left-wing sympathizers, why not have loyalist leaders who would encourage them to support the autocracy? Wherever they were set up Zubatov unions became a cover for radicals and blew up in the face of their sponsors. The Bloody Sunday demonstration was organized by such a union, the Assembly of Russian Factory Workers, and led by a priest, Father Gapon. It was not the massive demonstration which provoked revolution. There was a third, fatal, self-inflicted blow. Local security officials gave a lunatic order to fire on the demonstrators and, even more ludicrously, to fire on disorganized bystanders later in the day. It was tsarist credibility which was shot to ribbons, though not all parts of Russian society were equally alienated. A revolutionary process had been started.

As 1905 progressed workers, peasants, professors, industrialists, financiers, some landowners and nationalists joined in for a variety of reasons. Even military units like the famous battleship *Potemkin* mutinied. Autocracy was under assault from all quarters and it only escaped by the skin of its teeth. The most acute phase of the crisis came in October. It was precipitated by a general strike which spread to many cities and a railway strike which shut down large parts of the country. For once, the path of concession was chosen to resolve the crisis but only because everyone involved except Nicholas believed a repressive response would only lead to another Bloody Sunday debacle and perhaps a troop mutiny which might bring down the tsar and even the dynasty.

Against his instincts and principles Tsar Nicholas was forced by his court camarilla to sign a manifesto apparently promising democratic reforms. In early 1906 a parliament, known as the Duma, was set up. It supported radicals and was disbanded. The same happened to the Second Duma though after its disbandment in June 1907 the laws were changed by the Prime Minister, Peter Stolypin, to limit the vote essentially to the propertied classes. Bit by bit the apparent concessions of the October Manifesto were shown to be misleading. The autocracy retracted as many of its concessions as it could. However, the Manifesto had done its work. It split the opposition. Large parts of the propertied elite went back to support the tsar's initiative since it appeared to give them what they wanted – namely a say in how the country was governed. The eruption of revolution had caused them to lose confidence in the tsar and they believed they would be better able to control their own fate themselves. In the meantime, however, the autocracy was climbing back into the saddle.

An important sign of the success of the manoeuvre was the fact that in the next major crisis, the Moscow uprising of December, the government was able to use guards troops to shell the rebel districts and restore order. Throughout 1906 and into 1907 troops fought strikers in cities and peasant rebels in villages. Thousands died on both sides but there was no doubt by then that the government would prevail and by early 1907 the revolution had failed. Tsarism was unable to retract all its concessions but it did retain the upper hand in government.[3]

Stuck in Geneva and other centres of emigration, Lenin and the rest of the Russian radicals abroad agonized over events which were only dimly and belatedly reported. They had not foreseen the dramatic turn the revolution took in January because their own sources of information were intermittent and partial and the major west European press was largely imperceptive and not very interested up to that point. From January onward, however, the Russian revolution was the great cause of democrats, liberals and socialists throughout the continent. Autocracy, the cossack, the knout (a Russian whip) and the 'Stolypin necktie' (the hangman's noose) were universally hated symbols of the anachronism that was Russian government. This opened up many platforms in the west to Russian speakers and helped raise funds for political and humanitarian causes. None the less, many of the radicals, particularly the younger ones, wanted to be closer to the action. Trotsky returned in

February. After the October Manifesto broader circles deemed it safe to make a cautious return. Plekhanov and the older generation, by and large, did not join them, in Plekhanov's case because of health reasons.

For Lenin, in particular, 1905 was a complicated year. Faction fighting did not diminish. If anything, the raised stakes made it yet more bitter. Then there was frustration, something that, as we know, Lenin supported rather badly. There was the frustration of not knowing exactly what was going on and the even greater frustration of not being able to exert influence on events. At the same time, of course, there was also hope and, from time to time, elation. The long-awaited revolution was on the move. At last, theory could be put into practice and practice could confirm old theories or stimulate new ones.

THE REVOLUTION SEEN FROM GENEVA – 1905

For Lenin, the new situation did not so much stimulate new initiatives, though there were some, as reinforce the importance of the themes he was already dealing with. His major concerns – breaking with the circle mentality and developing a proper Social Democratic party and analysing what form a revolution could take in Russia's peculiar conditions – became increasingly important and dominate his writings and actions in the first phase of the revolution. Unlike 1917, when the abdication occurred at the beginning of the revolution and conditions of relative freedom emerged rapidly, in 1905 it was only after the October Manifesto that Lenin felt the situation had changed sufficiently for him to venture back to Russia. For the first ten months of 1905 Lenin remained in western Europe. Despite a growing number of articles analysing events in Russia the old themes of the Party dispute continued to be uppermost in Lenin's thoughts.

Lenin and the Party in 1905

A central focus of the dispute, and the centrepiece of Lenin's strategy for ending it, was the idea of convening a new Party Congress to thrash the issues out. Although his detractors would claim he was being insincere, Lenin appealed time and time again for a Third Congress to represent the whole Party. However, the minority had adopted boycott tactics towards Party bodies on and off since 1903 and continued to do so with respect to the proposed congress. In the last issue of *Vpered* to appear before Lenin's departure from Geneva for the congress in London he published his 'Open Letter' to Plekhanov [CW 8 335–43] imploring him one more time to submit 'the entire conflict to the judgment of the Party itself'. [CW 8 343] Even though this appeal was rhetorical and the earlier ones may have been bluff, they were a bluff that should have been called. Through them, Lenin was able to command at least a substantial proportion of the moral high ground in the eyes of Party members. They, too, were largely baffled by the vehemence and obstinacy of the leadership factions particularly in the eye of an increasing revolutionary storm.

It was thus not entirely Lenin's fault that when the Third Congress convened in London on 25 April 1905 all the delegates were Leninists. Lenin used the congress, which lasted until 12 May, to establish a Leninist grip on key Party institutions. Existing papers – *Iskra* and *Vpered* – were declared disbanded and a new paper, *Proletarii*, set up as the official Party newspaper under Lenin's editorship. An all-Leninist Central Committee was elected composed of Lenin, Bogdanov, Krasin, Postalovsky and Rykov. Lenin even wrote to the International Socialist Bureau in Brussels in June demanding it recognize *Proletarii* as the only official newspaper and de-recognize *Iskra*. Calls for unity became muted in the face of the new tactic. It was at this point that the split looked at its deepest and most irreconcilable. However, appearances were still deceptive. The International Socialist Bureau was not prepared to grant Lenin his victory and his tone became more conciliatory. Once again detractors might say the apparent willingness to compromise was tactical and insincere but that is speculative and is not necessarily true. Lenin's stunning letter to Plekhanov of late October underlined the complexity. In it he said the 'need for social democratic unity can no longer be put off'. In a sentence which could only be heartily endorsed by any baffled observer trying to thread a way through this labyrinth, Lenin continued 'We are in agreement with you on over nine-tenths of the questions of theory and tactics, and to quarrel over one-tenth is not worthwhile.' [CW 34 364]

None the less, the new sense of urgency over reconciliation was clear as was its prime motivation. The October Manifesto had changed the situation making revolutionary unity more imperative than ever, not least because there was agreement that there should be a united front to get real democratic concessions out of the autocracy.

Lenin's views on revolutionary tactics and strategy in 1905

One thing the Party factions did agree on was that the upcoming revolution in Russia would be bourgeois. Sadly, however, that did not mean they agreed on what was meant in practice by a bourgeois revolution. Lenin's own version evolved as the revolutionary year unfolded. Lenin was particularly inspired by the already quoted ringing phrases in the original 1898 Party manifesto, drafted by Struve, that 'The further east in Europe one proceeds, the weaker, more cowardly, and baser in the political sense becomes the bourgeoisie and the greater are the cultural and political tasks that devolve on the proletariat. The Russian working class must and will carry on its powerful shoulders the cause of political liberation.'[4] In March 1905, in an article in *Vpered*, Lenin launched his concept of a 'democratic dictatorship of the proletariat and peasantry'. A further article in April elaborated his views and was published as a separate pamphlet. The formulation had already changed and was now, as the title proclaimed, *The Revolutionary-Democratic Dictatorship of the Proletariat and Peasantry*. It achieved its most developed exposition in Lenin's main pamphlet of 1905, *Two Tactics of Social Democracy in the Democratic Revolution*, which Lenin worked on in June and July and was published in August. Here it interacted with the theme of the Party's attitude to a provisional revolutionary government and to the theme of armed uprising.

Though sometimes apparently contradictory, Lenin's views expressed in this pamphlet help clarify a great deal about his tactics and strategy in 1905 and in 1917. For those who doubted that he believed in the importance of the bourgeois revolution he stated clearly and unequivocally that 'A bourgeois revolution is *absolutely* necessary in the interests of the proletariat.' [CW 9 50] However, the complications began from there. An issue which arose immediately from that assumption was, what role would the Social Democrats play in such a revolution? Lenin's formula was perhaps evasive but not unreasonable. Echoing the decision of the Third Party Congress on the issue he said participation in a provisional revolutionary government was possible but was 'subject to the alignment of forces and other factors which cannot be exactly predetermined'.

[CW 9 24] It was, he said, 'impossible at present to speak of concrete conditions' under which the decision to join or not join should be made. [CW 9 32] For example, should the wavering bourgeoisie ultimately turn to tsarism for protection, the result would be disastrous for the left. 'Social Democracy will find its hands actually tied in the struggle against the inconsistent bourgeoisie. Social Democracy will find itself "dissolved" in bourgeois democracy in the sense that the proletariat will not succeed in placing its clear imprint on the revolution.' [CW 9 58]

Lenin's fear that the distinctive proletarian imprint would 'dissolve' in the thick porridge of bourgeois democracy was, of course, related to his view of the fate of revolutionary socialism in the bourgeois democratic countries of the west. Lenin was determined to keep the distinctive proletarian imprint and remembering this helps us to see a consistency between his ideas in 1905 and 1917.

The parallels with 1917 do not end there. The issue of armed uprising had also raised its head and the deeper into the revolutionary year he went, the more anxious Lenin became that this question should be clearly addressed. Once again arguing more sensibly than some of his opponents on this uncomfortable issue, Lenin started out from the assumption that 'Major questions in the life of nations are solved only by force. The reactionary class themselves are usually the first to resort to violence ... as the Russian autocracy has systematically and unswervingly been doing everywhere ever since 9 January.' [CW 9 132] However, far from being carried away with the prospect of violence Lenin's views, though based on realism, seemed rather simplistic. In late October in a much-quoted passage he made one of his most sustained analyses of force which appears more naive than penetrating. Giving instructions on setting up revolutionary army contingents he said:

> The contingents may be of any strength, beginning with two or three people. They must arm themselves as best they can (rifles, revolvers, knives, knuckledusters, sticks, rags coated in kerosene for starting fires, ropes or ropeladders, shovels for building barricades, pyroxilin cartridges, barbed wire, nails (against cavalry), etc. etc.). Under no circumstances should they wait for help from other sources, from above, from the outside; they must procure everything themselves.
> [CW 9 420]

The idea that such rag-taggle bands could fight their way into power was truly ludicrous.

What did these various formulations add up to? In brief, Lenin was saying that Russia's revolution would be bourgeois, but it would have its own special characteristics. Clearly Lenin did not believe the socialist revolution was just around the corner. As in 1917 he pointed to the backwardness of the workers and the need to raise their consciousness as a process that would take some time. Exactly how much time Lenin was not prepared to say and, in 1905 as in 1917, the question remained ambiguous.

Be that as it may, the October Manifesto had changed the situation sufficiently to allow Lenin and other, but not all, the leading revolutionary émigrés, to consider returning to Russia. Lenin made up his mind and arrived in St Petersburg on 21 November.

LENIN IN RUSSIA AND FINLAND (NOVEMBER 1905–DECEMBER 1907)

Lenin spent the next two years based in Russia and Finland. In the early weeks he had to report to the police and lived apart from Krupskaya who had arrived separately ten days after him. Because of irksome restrictions and police surveillance Lenin went underground on 17 December. Using a false passport he took a trip to Finland returning on 30 December. From the middle of March he was mainly based in Finland, at Kuokkala and later Styrs Udde. He travelled frequently to St Petersburg and Moscow as well as to overseas Party and associated meetings in Stockholm, Copenhagen, London, Stuttgart and elsewhere. He finally left in December 1907, making a perilous journey over thin ice that almost gave way beneath him. For two full years. Lenin was closer to the heart of events than he had ever been or was to be again until 1917 itself. What do his writings and actions of this period tell us about him?

One of the first articles he produced after his return contained some unexpected twists and turns. Writing in Gorky's newspaper *Novaia zhizn'* in November 1905 Lenin discussed 'The Reorganisation of the Party' in which he called for its democratization. [CW 10 29–43] It was, of course, consistent with his views before and after, that underground and conspiratorial tactics were not ideal, they were simply the necessary response to oppressive conditions. Once those conditions changed such tactics were no longer obligatory. More conventional open and democratic Party relations could be embarked upon, in this case in the form of what was becoming known as 'democratic centralism'. Lenin had already outlined this in *One Step* and *Two Tactics*. He was determined the centre would remain the decisive element of the Party but local bodies would have the right to approach it and fight for changes in its outlook without having the right to go their own way on any significant policy issues.

Also at this time, as part of an initial drive to clarify the role and tasks of the Party, Lenin wrote two more articles destined to have an important impact later on. In 'Party Organisation and Party Literature' (13 November 1905) he expressed the view that all Party publications should be approved from the centre. Without going into the complexities here it is clear that Lenin was making the eminently sensible point that anything published in the Party's name should be officially approved by it. It is also clear that what Lenin meant by Party literature was political pamphlets. This article came to haunt Soviet literature in the Stalin era when its strictures were applied not only to political pamphlets but to all kinds of written material including artistic literature. It also came to apply not only to official Party publications but to everything published, since in Stalin's day there was little scope for publishing anything independently of the Party. It remained a guiding light of Soviet publishing and censorship policy almost until the end.

A second article which came to have baleful consequences was devoted to 'Socialism and Religion'. It was published in mid-December 1905 in the last issue of *Novaia zhizn'* before its closure by the police. Lenin condemned all forms of religion and expressed the view that they should not be tolerated in the Party. He quoted Marx's dictum that religion was 'the opium of the people' without reference to Marx's further elaboration that it was 'the sigh of the oppressed creature; the heart of a heartless world; just as it is the spirit of a spiritless situation: it is the opium of the people.'[5] For Marx religion was more subtly understood as a comfort in the alienating world of capitalism while Lenin saw it solely as an agent of stupefaction and corruption. It marked a significant turn away from Marx in the direction of Bakunin who also put hostility to religion in the front rank of the revolutionary's outlook. Together with an article of 1909 entitled 'The Attitude of the Workers' Party Towards

Religion' – in which Lenin disagreed with wider European practice that religious belief was a private matter for each Party member and instead insisted that the Party should be actively opposed to religion at all levels – it laid down guidelines for Party policy on religion for much of the Soviet era.

The fact that Lenin occupied his first weeks back in revolutionary Russia writing organizational articles is, in itself, rather extraordinary, even though the pattern was to be repeated in 1917. Lenin had arrived in the middle of the most tumultuous upheaval Russia had, so far, endured. And yet he played little practical role in it. He was not an active member of the St Petersburg Soviet and visited it on only a few occasions. He advocated armed uprising and fully supported the Moscow workers when they embarked on one, but his contribution to it was minimal. Ironically, for a movement which later came to pride itself on its revolutionary praxis, that is the active combination of theory and practice, Lenin eschewed direct activism. Theory was his practice. Where one might expect to find an active revolutionary out on the street encouraging and organizing protest and rebellion, Lenin preferred the committee room, the study and the printshop. He did make the occasional public appearance. Krupskaya describes one in May 1906 when he spoke in front of three thousand people, using the name Karpov to put the police off the scent. 'Il'ich was very excited. ... One immediately felt how the excitement of the speaker was being communicated to the audience. ... At the end of Il'ich's speech, all those present were swept with extraordinary enthusiasm.' [Krupskaya 135–6] He focused his activities in 1906 and 1907 on attending important Party policy-making meetings including a variety of conferences and congresses.

In fact, Lenin had missed the main revolutionary action. By the time of his return the authorities, by means of massive repression, were regaining control. Lenin remained committed to the idea of armed uprising but its moment had, for the time being, passed. For him, 1906 and 1907 were dominated by ambiguous joint activity between the two Party factions. Each side needed the other though each wanted to gain the upper hand in a 'united' Party. Both realized that without unity social democracy would be totally irrelevant, leaving the stage to the better organized SRs and even the liberals of the Kadet Party. Thus a kind of shared yoke bound the two sides together. There were violent arguments followed by hollow reconciliations. At one point Lenin even declared his faction was closed down and talked of 'the former Bolshevik fraction'. However, as the revolutionary wave receded through 1906 the need for unity gave way to a renewed struggle between Bolsheviks and Mensheviks, the terminology being in general use by this time.[6]

In any case, the issues dividing the factions were also in a state of evolution. In 1906 and 1907 no one was arguing about Party membership and professional revolutionaries. Democratic centralism, Lenin claimed with some justification, was 'now universally recognised'. [CW 10 147–63] The central issue was armed uprising and, in Lenin's case which is our concern here, convoluted tactics opposing constitutional illusions and electoral pacts but also boycotting and then opposing the boycott of the various Dumas.

Despite its failure, the Moscow armed uprising remained Lenin's ideal pretty well throughout 1906. He continued to write about the growing prospects for a successful repetition, criticized Plekhanov for his opposition to it in February 1906 and was heartened by the Kronstadt and Sveaborg insurrections which were sparked off in July 1906 by the dissolution of the First Duma. Even in September he drew the 'Lessons of the Moscow Uprising' which he continued to see as a peak of revolutionary effort and a model for the future since he wrote 'A great mass struggle is approaching. It will be an armed uprising.' [CW 11 61–8]

In reality, however, the revolutionary wave was subsiding and the issue of the Party's attitude to the Duma was more pressing. Lenin, having at first called for a boycott of the First Duma, which sat from late April to July 1906, changed his position vis-à-vis the Second, which sat from March to early June 1907. In Lenin's view, made clear in his denunciation in February 1907 of a group of thirty-one Mensheviks urging electoral agreement with the Kadets, the Party should stand alone without making any deals with anyone. As we have seen, he had already warned against mistaking support for, or at least an expectation of, the bourgeois revolution with a policy of getting too involved in it. In March 1907 he continued to argue that the revolution was bourgeois but could only be brought to fruition through the joint action of the proletariat and the peasants. [CW 43 175] As ever, the distinctions were very fine but none the less real to Lenin. The class principle had to be remembered and any blurring of it by over-enthusiastic relationships with class enemies was to be avoided. The main barbs were directed at

Plekhanov, whose plans to return to Russia had been thwarted by illness. He had not only opposed the Moscow armed uprising but had also promoted a policy of the Social Democrats making electoral pacts with other parties, notably the Kadets in the Second Duma elections.[7] In July, Lenin continued to argue that, despite the changes in the electoral system, the correct position for the Party was to participate in the elections to the Third Duma, as a separate, distinct group. The ebbing of the revolutionary tide meant that, instead of promoting armed uprising about which he was now silent, Lenin was prepared to settle for using the Duma delegation as a publicity mouthpiece for the movement.

He spent less and less of his time and energy on Russia and, in the summer of 1907, spent more and more time liaising with the International Socialist Bureau, not least in his never-ending quest for Party funds. In August he attended the International Socialist Conference in Stuttgart. The excitement of Russia was beginning to pall, the revolutionary opportunity clearly over for the time being, though Lenin did not overtly acknowledge this fact. Back in Finland Lenin wrote one of his best-known descriptions of émigré life in a letter to Grigorii Aleksinsky: 'Over there, you are frightfully out of touch with Russia, and idleness and the state of mind which goes with it, a nervous, hysterical, hissing and spitting mentality, predominate ... there is no *live* work or an environment of live work to speak of.' [CW 43 176]

Perhaps Lenin had a premonition because he was almost disengaging from Russian politics as the summer turned to autumn. Reaction was back in control. In early December 1907 the first volume of a selection of his major works, including *One Step* and *Two Tactics*, was seized by the police. Lenin needed no further hint. He went into deeper concealment, moving from Kuokkala to Helsinki. Krupskaya recounts Lenin's tale of how he then left the Russian Empire altogether. Despite having a false identity as Professor Müller, a German geologist, police surveillance caused him to take the almost fatal decision to avoid joining the steamer to Sweden at Abo, since there had been arrests of revolutionaries escaping via this route. Instead, he decided to walk across the treacherous ice to a neighbouring island and pick the boat up there. It was too dangerous for any sensible guide to lead him. He had to entrust himself to the care of 'two rather tipsy Finnish peasants. ... [I]n crossing the ice at night they and Il'ich very nearly perished. In one place the ice began to move

beneath their feet. They only just managed to extricate themselves. ...
Il'ich told me that when the ice began to slide from beneath his feet, he
thought, "Oh! What a silly way to have to die."' [Krupskaya 146]

Lenin had left Russia behind and only returned via the Finland
Station in April 1917. From intense polemic and the intoxication of the
nearness of revolution Lenin returned to the nerve-jangling world of
exile. Its pangs were softened by an immersion in philosophy, sojourns
in Italy and the establishment of rival Party schools in Capri and Paris.

CONSOLIDATING BOLSHEVISM: PHILOSOPHICAL WARS

Defeat was a bitter pill for the left to swallow. From our perspective of
knowing that tsarism had only a decade to live it is easy to minimize
how depressed the left was. From the contemporary perspective the situation looked bleaker than ever. The Russian revolution, that had been
expected by radicals, centrists and conservatives for half a century,
appeared to have come and gone. Indeed, had tsarism displayed minimal
political sense the chance might have gone forever. Above all, the left
feared the emergence of a Russian Bismarck, that is, an authoritarian
monarchist who would bring the new industrial and financial propertied elite into the government-supporting alliance, harshly repress left-
wing parties and buy off workers with minimal measures of, for
instance, social insurance.

In Peter Stolypin, governor of the troublesome province of Saratov, the
autocracy had just the man who might have done it. He was appointed
Prime Minister in 1906 in succession to Witte. However, Nicholas II was
so far detached from reality that he remained obsessed with maintaining
an undiluted autocracy despite the existence of the Duma. As a result,
he not only had to face opposition from the left, but the tsar also dis-
mayed liberals. Their leader Miliukov believed 'nothing had changed' as
a result of the October Manifesto.[8] He also lost the confidence of the far
right. The fright they had experienced in 1905 led them to attack him
for the minimal concessions he had made. The period showed, especially
through the Duma, that Nicholas had little support and even the carefully gerrymandered right-wing dominated Third Duma showed up the
continuing fissures in the body politic. Certainly there was no sign of
the emergence of a new alliance of old and new property, that is the

landowners and the new capitalist bourgeoisie, around the autocracy. Both sides of this potential alliance doubted the autocracy's ability to guarantee their security. The problem beyond that was that, on the one hand, liberals believed greater concessions to democracy were needed to preserve Russia's current class structure and prevent a redistributive upsurge from below. On the other, the ultra-right believed there should be a turn to what amounted to military dictatorship under the autocrat based on nationalism, anti-semitism, opposition to democracy and anti-intellectualism, an almost proto-fascist programme. Nicholas himself was firmly in this camp. Stolypin saw the need for more flexibility and had lost the confidence of the tsar before his assassination in 1911.

There has been a tendency, revived in post-Soviet Russia, to idealize the last years of tsarism as a time of Russian economic expansion and transition to democracy. The first half of the proposition is indubitably true, the second half demonstrably false. In fact, one could more readily argue that the disparity between the two – a booming economy fuelled by government armaments orders and a restless middle class and a dilapidated, anachronistic and inefficient government which hated modernization and deeply distrusted the middle class as a westernizing force that would sap the distinctiveness of Holy Russia – was making a revolution more rather than less likely. Such a revolution would have been bourgeois rather than socialist in its early phases but would have ended the autocracy, though maybe not the monarchy. Arguably, this is what actually happened: the elite began the Revolution in 1917, not the masses. However, that was for the future and by then the massive influence of the First World War had also intervened.

For the moment, however, the situation looked bleak for the Russian left in 1907. Bolshevik membership, insofar as one can judge from scanty evidence, appears to have peaked at 150,000 in the revolutionary years and dropped to 10,000 or so by 1909/10. The atmosphere was one of defeatism and a search for new beginnings.

A prominent group of former Marxists, with Struve in the forefront, continued their transition from Marxism to philosophical idealism and individualism. Indeed, given the difficulty of political activity, theoretical and philosophical issues began to loom large among the radical intelligentsia. Lenin himself picked up his philosophical studies, which had been rather desultory since the end of his Siberian exile, but only, in an increasingly typical fashion, to batter the head not only of his opponents but also of his only prominent allies. How did this come about?

As we have seen, Lenin had manoeuvred himself into a position of near isolation among prominent Marxists by the end of 1903 and 1904. However, his intransigent stand began to attract a new generation of supporters who breathed new life into Bolshevism. The main figures in this group were the brothers-in-law Anatoly Lunacharsky and Alexander Bogdanov. Their importance to Lenin was massively enhanced by the fact that they had links to Russia's second (after Tolstoy) most popular living writer of the period, Maxim Gorky, who himself had links with wealthy art patrons among Russia's rising industrial class whom he could tap for money for radical causes. Gorky became a major link in the crucial chain of Bolshevik finance.

Bogdanov and Lenin first met in Geneva in 1904. They established an immediate rapport. Bogdanov had been drawn to Lenin's intransigent stand against opportunism and Lenin was enthralled by Bogdanov's knowledge of and contacts with the worker movement back in Russia where Bogdanov was based. The result, rather unusually, seems to have been that Lenin bent some of his ideas in Bogdanov's direction. In particular, Bogdanov was resolutely workerist. Taking as his fundamentalist text Marx's injunction that the task of liberating the workers would be undertaken by the workers themselves, Bogdanov attempted to eliminate all non-proletarian influences from the worker movement. Though he was acutely aware of the obvious contradiction here, namely that he himself was an educated intellectual, not a worker, he attempted to carry through his principles. It is not too fanciful to suggest that Bogdanov's influence can be detected in Lenin's writing of this time.[9] *One Step Forward: Two Steps Back* differs mostly from its more famous predecessor in that it criticizes the anarchist, individualist tendencies of a radical intelligentsia which refused to accept discipline. *What is to be Done?* had given a much more positive role to the intelligentsia as the bringers of socialist consciousness from without to the proletariat.

Although there were many points of difference which soon exploded into a bitter argument, for the time being the two men were happy to collaborate with each other. The need to work with Bogdanov had overridden Lenin's disagreements with him on fundamental principles, not least because he was dependent on Bogdanov for access to Gorky's funds but also because he had so few supporters at the time. However, once Lenin was forced back into exile and partly because he now had a direct line to Gorky and didn't need Bogdanov's mediation so much, the differences began to emerge. The wave of savage repression in Russia from late 1905 to 1907 and even beyond pushed literary and philosophical activity back to the top of the agenda since direct activism was no longer possible. In these years Lenin turned back to philosophy to confront Bogdanov.

Bogdanov was much more of a philosopher than Lenin. He had been deeply influenced by the fashionable German philosophers Ernst Mach and Richard Avenarius. He had, if anything, taken their principles even further than they had done themselves to produce what he called 'monism'. Put crudely, monism was a denial of idealism and dualism. Idealists argued, following Plato, that there was an element of every object akin to its spirit, soul or essence. Thus, a tree, apart from being a tree, embodied 'treeness', a table, in addition to its specific characteristics such as construction material, size, shape and purpose, would exemplify a generic 'tableness' and so on. Dualists argued that there were two levels of existence – material and spiritual. The spiritual could resemble the essence of the idealists. Bogdanov's monism dismissed all such concepts. For him there was only one level of existence, the material. On this basis he constructed a complex philosophy based on the axiom that everything in the universe was material, including human consciousness.

In addition to his direct philosophical concepts he also discussed the implication of his ideas for socialism.[10] In particular, he focused on the question of consciousness. Like everything else, for Bogdanov consciousness was a material entity. But it was also a crucial component of revolution. Bourgeois revolution had been preceded by a long period of developing bourgeois culture going back to the Renaissance. Could there be a proletarian revolution without a corresponding cultural revolution challenging the domination – or hegemony – of bourgeois ideas? For Bogdanov, the answer was a resounding no! To his discomfort, some of his friends and admirers, notably Gorky and Lunacharsky, attempted to popularize this form of socialism as the last great religion – the religion of humanity replacing the religions of God. As a result, the group became know as God-builders because they saw humanity as the creators of God (in the form of the perfect socialist society) rather than the other way round.

Lenin could not abide any of this and he fought it ferociously. One might surmise that, at least in part, Lenin's animosity arose from political differences and the breakdown was postponed while Bogdanov was sitting on the Bolshevik money pot, but when the break came Lenin's attack was tempestuous. He attacked Bogdanov more directly since it was still in his interest to maintain good relations with Gorky who could still be useful to him. Lenin even decided to devote himself to catching up on his philosophical studies, largely in the British Museum Reading Room, in order to refute the heretics. The result was another of Lenin's major works, *Materialism and Empiriocriticism*, published in 1909. It was later enshrined as a philosophical masterpiece in the Soviet Union.

As a philosophical treatise *Materialism and Empiriocriticism* stands almost alone in terms of the depth and ferocity of its insulting language. It is certainly true that Marx and Engels could combine philosophical argument with ridicule in works such as *The German Ideology* and *Anti-Dühring*, but Lenin's language was even more crude. Only 'an inmate of a lunatic asylum' or 'a charlatan or utter blockhead' could disagree with him. For Lenin, the German developers of monist ideas, Avenarius, Mach and their followers, wrote 'gibberish' and 'sheer nonsense'. Bogdanov was 'a jester'. Remarkably, Lenin's sister Anna, who had helped prepare the volume for publication in Moscow, had urged him to tone down the language and he had, apparently, complied though he insisted in a letter of 9 March that there was no reason for toning down the polemics against the 'clerical reaction' (*popovshchina*) of Lunacharsky and Bogdanov [CW 37 414] and again on 21 March that the attacks on the two are 'not under any circumstances to be toned down'. [CW 37 417]

In the end, the volume is more memorable for its polemic than its philosophy. Its content has not unduly troubled the world philosophical community. At its heart is the simple proposition that there is an objective world that exists outside the consciousness of the individual. In a breathtaking sweep of reductionism, Lenin argued that all idealists, not to mention their opposites, Bogdanov and the monists, denied this and ended up taking the solipsistic position: that is, that we cannot prove anything outside the existence of consciousness itself. Lenin offered little but repetitive assertion of dogmas derived largely from Engels as his contribution to the debate.

While anyone with any philosophical sensitivity would be appalled by the crudity of Lenin's thought, the volume helped bring the conflict with the Bogdanovites to a crisis. The dispute came to a head at a meeting of the extended editorial board of *Proletarii* which met in Paris from 21 to 30 June 1909. After a tense struggle Lenin won and Bogdanov and his followers were classed as opponents along with the Mensheviks. 'Bolshevism,' Lenin said, 'must now be strictly Marxist.' Lenin in private correspondence and conversation several times referred to Bogdanov and his group as 'scoundrels'. He refused to participate in Bogdanov's Party school held in Gorky's villa on Capri.

Once again Lenin was determinedly purging his party of heretics. Once again he had broken with the only intellectually serious equals in his movement. Once again he was isolated, though he still tried to maintain good relations with senior figures of international socialism like Rosa Luxemburg, to whom he sent a copy of *Materialism and Empiriocriticism*. However, her attitude to Lenin remained lukewarm. Nothing summed up Lenin's situation better than a letter to Zinoviev, now one of his closest comrades, a man distinguished by his enthusiastic support for Lenin rather than any originality or creativity on the intellectual or political fronts. Menshevik polemics were described as 'very vile'; Bogdanov and his supporters were 'scoundrels'. As for Trotsky, who was making overtures to team up with Lenin, he behaved like 'a despicable careerist and factionalist' surrounded by 'a rascally crew'. He was also a 'scoundrel' and 'swindler' who 'pays lip service to the Party and behaves worse than any other of the factionalists'. [CW 34 399–400]

The letter was written from the countryside outside Paris to which Lenin and Krupskaya had withdrawn to recover from the customary nervous exhaustion he suffered after a hard fight. They walked in the forest and added the new activity of cycling to their repertoire. The fresh air and summer sun quickly restored Lenin's equilibrium and, after six weeks' holiday, he returned fully to the fray in Paris. Lenin had won the disputes and had tightened the definition of Bolshevism even further. While he still retained a sense of belonging to a wider movement of international socialists to which many of his opponents also belonged, he believed intensely that unity would only come about by the whole movement following his principles rather than through any compromise. Unity on any other terms was completely out of the question.

CONSOLIDATING BOLSHEVISM: ORGANIZATIONAL WARS

The break with Bogdanov and his associates, including Gorky with whom Lenin's relations became very tense for some years, left Lenin bereft once again of major intellectual peers within Bolshevism. By 1909 the fortunes of all the political parties of the left had foundered in the wake of the failure of 1905, swamped by waves of depression and disillusion. These developments did not, however, stop Lenin from continuing his favourite pastime, splitting an ever-smaller party. In particular, he had to resist efforts by the Bogdanovite left to establish themselves, rather than the Leninists, as the true heirs to the Party and, crucially, its funds which were still being held in trust by German socialists in the International Socialist Bureau until such time as the Russian squabbles were resolved. There seemed little prospect of this happening. Lenin was now fighting on two fronts within the Party itself. To the right, the dispute with the Mensheviks had, to some extent, stabilized though Lenin continued to hold out hopes of winning Plekhanov and his immediate supporters over to Bolshevism. But it was the left which offered the greater threat.

Lenin's writings of the next few years were focused on the struggle against what he termed liquidators and recallists (*otzovists* from the Russian) or ultimatumists. They did not exactly correspond to the two separate factions and were, at times, used almost interchangeably or in tandem. The term liquidator was not new. It had been used to describe the Mensheviks. It continued to refer to those whose policies of decentralization, in Lenin's view, would lead to the liquidation of the Party in the continuing conspiratorial conditions of post-1905 repression. Recallists were so termed because they wanted to recall the Bolshevik delegates from the Third and Fourth Dumas. They believed Bolshevik participation in what all agreed was a reactionary institution only served to legitimize that institution. As we have seen, Lenin had shared their scepticism in 1906 and supported boycott but in 1907 was converted to the virtues of having elected deputies. His main reason was that the Duma could serve as a tribune from which Bolshevik policies could be proclaimed openly and be reported in the wider press. The deputies' immunity from arrest (at least until the outbreak of war) also gave them a privileged position. For Lenin, the handful of Bolshevik Duma delegates, numbering six at the most, became a crucial component of the Party from 1913, when the group was formed, until 1914 when they were arrested. The faction leader, Roman Malinovsky, elected to the Duma in 1912, worked closely with Lenin and was one of his most trusted and widely known supporters.

For the last half decade, before the war that changed everything broke out, Lenin was, in a sense, at his most Leninlike. He was a prominent figure known to other European socialist activists but no more so than Martov, Bogdanov and many others. Plekhanov remained the most widely known among the Russians and was one of the few sharing the prestige and broader recognition of the main leaders of German and French socialism such as Kautsky, Bebel, Jaurès, Lafargue and others. By comparison Lenin was still obscure. His actions seemed likely only to make him even more so. The years were filled with intense squabbles with three opponents – Trotsky, Bogdanov and the Mensheviks. Time after time Lenin announced a complete break with one or other of the groups, only, bewilderingly, to hold out hopes of unity shortly afterwards.

Writing to his sister Anna in March 1909 about *Materialism and Empiriocriticism* Lenin stated 'We have *completely broken off* relations with them' [CW 37 414], that is with the Bogdanovites. Even so, only a couple of weeks earlier he had invited them to put their case in *Proletarii*. Lenin continued to attack in uncompromising terms. Recallism was 'the worst political travesty of Bolshevism'. [CW 15 357] and 'a caricature of Bolshevism'. [CW 15 393] In late June Lenin and Bogdanov both attended a meeting of the editorial board of *Proletarii*. Lenin persuaded the meeting to exclude Bogdanov from the *Proletarii* group though not from the Party.

That was not the end of disputes by a long way. For the time being, only Plekhanov was exempt from his wrath because he still held out hopes of winning him over. In November 1909 he believed 'Things [were] moving towards an alignment with the Plekhanovite Mensheviks' [CW 34 408] but, despite blowing hot and cold for several years, nothing came of it. In the meantime he refused to participate in the Capri Party school set up by Lunacharsky and Bogdanov with the assistance of Gorky whose island home was its base of operations. Lenin also wanted to split Gorky off from Bogdanov and he made several attempts to do so, at times chiding Gorky, at others apologizing for his own rashness. [CW 34 403–4 and 405–6]

Throughout 1910 and 1911 the arguments went on. Passions began to run so high that, in a Paris café in January 1910, Aleksinsky, a former Bolshevik, and others now close to Bogdanov gatecrashed a Bolshevik meeting. The confrontation degenerated into fisticuffs. Even so, at certain moments resolution appeared to be near. In November 1909 Lenin proposed a draft resolution on unity to the editorial board of *Sotsial Demokrat*. Its rejection caused him to resign, though he withdrew his resignation two days later. More significantly, the Party Central Committee, meeting in Paris from 15 January to 5 February 1910, seemed to have reached a compromise, forced in part by Bolshevik 'conciliators' who urged Lenin to reach an agreement. Lenin wrote to his sister Anna on 1 February that he had agreed to close down 'the factional newspaper *Proletarii*' and was 'trying harder to promote *unity*'. [CW 37 451] His article 'Towards Unity' was published in *Sotsial Demokrat* (26 February) [CW 16 147–55] but by mid-March Lenin was back in attack mode criticizing the position of the Bogdanovite journal *Vpered* and Gorky. In April he told Kamenev in a letter that a 'Party core' was needed but could not be built 'on the cheap *phrases* of Trotsky and Co but on *genuine* ideological rapprochement between the Plekhanovites and the Bolsheviks.' [CW 43 243–4; Weber 70] In autumn his tone was the same. In a letter of 9 October he talked of 'Martov's and Trotsky's most incredible absurdities and distortions' [CW 36 174] and in another, on 14 October, that 'We can and should build the Party only with the Plekhanovites', possibly because he agreed with Plekhanov that 'nothing can be done with Trotsky.' [CW 34 430] Remarkably, Lenin had earlier correctly prophesied, in September 1909, that Trotsky 'will win over some people from the Mensheviks, a few from us, but in the end he will inevitably lead the workers to Bolshevism'. [CW 43 222] None the less, bitter polemic continued until the white heat of the Revolution itself.

In an article, unpublished at the time, written in July 1911 Lenin claimed that at the January 1910 plenum 'the Bolsheviks dissolved their group *on condition* all other factions would be dissolved. This condition has not been carried out as everyone knows.' [CW 36 182] Lenin, naturally, blamed everyone else but he was as guilty as any. He did not accept it, even, on one occasion, chiding Gorky for attacking the whole Party for its squabbling without distinguishing right from wrong. [1 August 1912, CW 35 50–1] But it was not only principle that was at stake. Quite large sums of money, notably a bequest from a wealthy supporter called Shmidt, meant that whoever could claim to be the legitimate party had the right to the cash. For the time being, however, it was only doled out by the trustees in dribs and drabs to Lenin and the other factions when they were in extremis financially.

Although it did not stop the infighting, in January 1912 Lenin took the most decisive steps so far towards forming his own separate party at a conference in Prague attended by eighteen Bolsheviks and two Mensheviks. Lenin dominated the conference and was elected to the Party Central Committee and as its representative on the International Socialist Bureau. None the less, the squabbles continued more or less unabated. The disputed funds remained undistributed and struggles with Bogdanov and others continued. The most famous newspaper in Party history, *Pravda*, was established in May 1912 as a legal Bolshevik publication. It appeared until June 1913 and then, under a variety of names, until July 1914. Lenin contributed a massive 280 articles to its 636 issues. [Weber 82] But even so it was the object of Lenin's wrath for not pursuing the fight against the liquidators with sufficient energy and even 'stubbornly and systematically cut[ting] out any mention of the liquidators both in my articles and in the articles of other colleagues.' [CW 35 47] Just as bad, if not worse, Bogdanov collaborated with *Pravda* and Lenin, from exile, could do no more than complain. Only in February 1914 was Bogdanov forced out and even then thirteen 'Left Bolsheviks' wrote a letter of complaint about it.

A few months later the mirage of unity made its last pre-war appearance. In June 1914 Lenin wrote an article entitled 'On Unity' which more or less said unity could only be achieved on his terms. The issue had come up because the International Socialist Bureau in Brussels had called a meeting to try to unify the Russian groups. Lenin used all his charm and influence to persuade Inessa Armand to represent him because, he said, her French was so much better and, not least, she was more tactful than Lenin who admitted afterwards that she had handled the affair better than he would have done. 'Language apart I would probably have *gone up in the air*. I would not have been able to stand the hypocrisy and would have called them all scoundrels.' [CW 43 423] Even relations with Plekhanov had taken a turn for the worse. In May 1913 Lenin had defended him to colleagues in *Pravda* saying they should write 'kindly and mildly' to him because he was valuable as he was fighting the enemies of the working class. [CW 35 99] However, in June Lenin referred to him in a letter to Kamenev as a 'sly boots, Ignatius Loyola, the master shuffler'. [CW 43 357] It was only the outbreak of war which ended the round of infighting and began a major realignment which, as we shall see, found Lenin and Plekhanov on completely opposite sides while Martov, and to some extent Trotsky, came closer together.

While the Prague Conference did not end the squabbling it did have one important effect. From that time on Lenin had gathered around him many of the figures who made up the team with which he was to conduct the Revolution. The Kamenevs and Zinovievs followed him in his wanderings. Bukharin, living in Vienna, Rykov and Radek all took Lenin's side. At no point would anyone have predicted that these people would eventually become victims of another group that was already forming within the wider team. Stalin, with whom Lenin began to get better acquainted, not least because Stalin was one of the few Bolsheviks who was interested in questions of nationality from a socialist point of view, became editor of *Pravda*. The secretary of the paper was a young, well-connected, rising star of the Party Vyacheslav Molotov (whose real name, Scriabin, revealed his kinship to the composer) who had the most extraordinary career of all. He returned to Petrograd in 1917 before Lenin and was still in the Soviet leadership in 1957, four years after Stalin's death. He served as Stalin's right-hand man. Stalin's industrial chief, Ordzhonikidze, a fellow Georgian, was elected to the Central Committee at the Prague Conference. At another level Demian Bednyi, churner-out of Stalinist doggerel in the 1930s, also emerged and was defended against criticism by Lenin himself. [CW 35 99–100, May 1913] All remained fiercely loyal to Lenin. With a few exceptions, notably Trotsky, the core of Bolshevism had formed even though it was to split disastrously after Lenin's death.

However, there was one member of Lenin's entourage who was not what he seemed, the leader of the Duma delegation, Roman Malinovsky, Party spokesman in the Duma and member of the Central Committee since 1912, who was eventually exposed as a double agent. Lenin had already been alerted to suspicions about Malinovsky by Elena Rozmirovich and Bukharin among the Bolsheviks, but Lenin had rejected them as an SR or Menshevik plot to slander a redoubtable Bolshevik. In the end, in an irony typical of the complex situation of late tsarism, it was the government itself which exposed its agent after tipping him the wink to get out of Russia first, which he did in May 1914. Why such a bizarre turn of events? At the time Malinovsky was exposed, Bolshevik support was rising and it was an excellent opportunity for the tsarist authorities to undermine this by exposing one of the best-known figures in the Party as a government agent. The scandal did, indeed, rock the Party and damage its standing. In a Dostoevskian coda to his story, after the war and revolution Malinovsky returned to Russia to make amends for his treachery and turned himself over to an astonished Cheka who, at first, had no idea who he was. After checking the records they summarily tried and executed him.

OBSERVATIONS ON THE WIDER WORLD

While intense squabbles and recovery from the nervous strain they caused occupied most of Lenin's time and, with the dubious exception of *Materialism and Empiriocriticism*, he produced no major works of theory until the war itself approached, there were a number of interesting observations on current developments which help us round out our picture of Lenin's ideas at this time and refute one or two myths.

The early twentieth century was a time of rapid economic and social change based not least on the arms race and the scramble for colonial territory. Lenin was aware of the pace at which capitalism was developing. While its growing strength discouraged many on the left Lenin was not at all downcast. Writing to Gorky in January 1911 he argued that wherever capitalism went it devoured the workers and it was the task of socialists to point it out. 'We say: capital devours you, will devour the Persians, will devour everyone and go on devouring until you overthrow it. That is the truth. And we do not forget to add: except through the growth of capitalism there is no guarantee of victory over it.' Even more interestingly he went on to say that:

> *Resistance* to colonial policy and international plundering *by means* of organizing the proletariat, *by means* of defending freedom for the proletarian struggle, *does not retard* the development of capitalism but *accelerates* it, forcing it to resort to more civilized, technically higher methods of capitalism. There is capitalism and capitalism ... The more we *expose* capitalism before the workers for its 'greed and

cruelty', the more difficult it is for capitalism of the first order to persist, the more surely is it bound to pass into capitalism of the second order. And this just suits us, this just suits the proletariat. [CW 34 438–9]

Lenin went on to say that crude capitalism had been almost completely replaced in Europe by 'democratic capitalism' forcing crude capitalism out into the wider world, a process which 'enlarges the base of capitalism and brings its death nearer'. [CW 34 439]

He echoed the theme in public in May 1912 in an article about the approaching elections to the Fourth Duma entitled 'Political Parties in Russia'. [CW 18 44–55] In it he defended participation in the parliamentary process. 'In the absence of representative institutions there is *much more* deception, political lying and fraudulent trickery of all kinds, and the people have much fewer means of exposing the deception and finding out the truth.' He continued: 'The greater the degree of political liberty in a country and the more stable and democratic its representative institutions, the easier it is for the mass of the people to find its bearings in the fight between the parties and to *learn politics*, i.e. to expose the deception and find out the truth.' [CW 18 45]

In a short but key article on 'The Awakening of Asia', published in *Pravda* on 7 May 1913, he exulted in how quickly Asian countries were being drawn into the struggle against capitalism. 'Was it so long ago that China was considered typical of the lands that had been standing still for centuries? Today, China is a land of seething political activity, the scene of a virile social movement and of a democratic upsurge. Following the 1905 movement in Russia the democratic revolution spread to the whole of Asia – to Turkey, Persia, China. Ferment is growing in British India.' [CW 19 85] The Asian 'liberation movement' would link up with 'the advanced proletariat of Europe' in order to 'take the place of the decadent and moribund bourgeoisie'. [CW 19 86] He also praised migration for its 'progressive significance' in drawing 'the masses of the working people of the *whole* world, breaking down the musty, fusty habits of local life, breaking down national barriers and prejudices, uniting workers from all countries in huge factories and mines in America, Germany and so forth.' [CW 19 454] Here Lenin was, in a sense, predicting globalization. He believed it would benefit the revolution in the long run. It would bring workers from all over the world 'face to face with the powerful, united, international class of factory owners' [CW 19 454] and, optimistically, create internationalism among them. 'Class conscious workers, realizing that the breakdown of all national barriers by capitalism is inevitable and progressive, are trying to help to enlighten and organize their fellow-workers from the backward countries.' [CW 19 457] The multitude of ways in which capitalism has prevented the realization of this vision has exercised many Marxists and other radicals. Far from uniting the working class of the world, ethnicity and nationality have become weapons to divide the masses, to such an extent that Lenin's perspective looks hopelessly naive.

In September 1913 he was even more explicit about the value of reforms but not of reformism. He explained his position thus: 'Unlike the anarchists, the Marxists recognize struggle for reforms, i.e. for measures that improve the conditions of the working people without destroying the power of the ruling class. At the same time, however, the Marxists wage a resolute struggle against the reformists, who directly or indirectly, restrict the aims and activities of the working class to the winning of reforms.' [CW 19 372] The crucial point was that reforms were fine as a means but not as an end.

It is clear from the above quotations that Lenin was not, as many suggest, a person who believed in 'the worse, the better', that is that the worse the situation of the workers the more likely they were to support revolution. Rightly or wrongly, Lenin believed the opposite. Only politically conscious, relatively sophisticated workers could form the backbone of a revolutionary movement and it was only advanced, democratic, relatively civilized capitalism that could produce them. Lenin's frequently expressed scepticism about Russian workers stemmed from his belief that they had not, under oppressive tsarist conditions, had the opportunity to rise to the required levels.

Lenin touched on many other points in these years. Marxism was not to be understood as a dogma. 'Our doctrine – said Engels referring to himself and his famous friend [Marx] – is not a dogma but a guide to action.' [CW 17 39] Nor was it utopian – 'Marxists are hostile to *all and every* utopia.' None the less, they can extract what is valuable from utopian ideologies, notably populism (*narodnichestvo*). 'The Marxist must extract the sound and valuable kernel of the sincere, resolute, militant democracy of the peasant masses from the husk of Narodnik utopias.' [CW 18 359] Although not yet entering the argument about imperialism in a major way, he criticized Rosa Luxemburg for having 'got into a shocking muddle' in her book on *The Accumulation of Capital*. [CW 35 94]

He also showed awareness of the latest developments of capitalist industry. On one hand, he had no illusions that the Taylor system of so-called scientific management which had developed production-line assembly was anything other than 'the latest method of exploiting the workers' and showed that 'In capitalist society, progress in science and technology means progress in the art of sweating' (that is of super exploitation of labour). This, he argued, is what the European bour-geoisie would borrow from America, not its 'democratic institutions ... nor political liberty, nor yet the republican political system, but the lat-est methods of exploiting the workers.' [CW 18 594] On the other hand, he remained an enthusiast for big industry. The automobile industry, he argued in 1913, had enormous potential. He noted that in Germany, for example, the increase in production 'of motor vehicles of all kinds, including motor cycles, was 27,000 in 1907 and 70,000 in 1912'. Nonetheless, under capitalism this potential could not be real-ized because motor cars 'are available only to a relatively narrow circle of rich people' whereas 'industry could produce hundreds of thousands of motor vehicles' to serve the people by, for example, replacing 'a large number of draught animals in farming and carting'. This would mean vast tracts of land would be liberated from producing fodder for horses and could be converted to improving food supplies for humans. [CW 19 283–4] Clearly, although Lenin's mind was primarily on Party struggle, he was still observing what was going on in the wider world.

THE ULYANOVS ON THE EVE OF THE FIRST WORLD WAR – FROM FINLAND TO GENEVA – PARIS – KRAKOW

The years of bitter infighting took their toll on Lenin's health. The cycle of increasingly intense activity producing illness and the need to with-draw and recuperate soon reasserted itself. In June 1907, after the con-tentious Fifth Party Congress, he and Krupskaya moved to a house near the lighthouse at Styrs Udde (Stjernsund) in Finland. Lenin told his mother, 'I came back terribly tired. I have now completely recovered.' According to Krupskaya, 'We have all put on so much weight it's not decent to show ourselves in public ... Here there is pine forest, sea, magnificent weather, in short, everything is excellent.' [CW 37 366]

Writing to Maria at about the same time, Lenin claims: 'I am having a rest such as I have not had for several years.' Krupskaya wrote that 'We are bathing in the sea, cycling ... Volodya plays chess, fetches water.' [CW 37 368 and 369]

The convenience of Finland was not to last. It had only been made possible by the granting of autonomy to the Finnish province by the tsar in 1905 and the increasingly reactionary atmosphere of 1907 meant that it was no longer safe for revolutionaries to use Finland as a half-way house between Russia and exile. In December, in the guise of 'Professor Müller', he crossed to Sweden, almost, as we have seen, at the cost of his life.

The Ulyanovs returned to Geneva in January 1908. A little Bolshevik community formed. Krupskaya's mother joined them, as ever, plus Lenin's sister Anna, the Zinovievs and Kamenevs. The consolation of Geneva was the proximity of the mountains. Lenin continued to enjoy walks and excursions, and even tried to tempt his brother Dmitrii to come from Russia so that 'we could go for some splendid walks together'. [CW 37 390] But even so its attractions palled. Lenin described the city in letters to Lunacharsky and his sister Maria as 'accursed' [CW 43 179] and 'damned'. 'It is an awful hole but there is nothing we can do.' [CW 37 372] Even the usually positive Krupskaya wrote that 'Geneva looked cheerless.' [Krupskaya 147] When they had settled down there once more, however, they were persuaded to move to Paris in December 1908 but it had also lost its charm. It, too, was 'a rotten hole' as Lenin described it in another letter to Anna of February 1910. [CW 37 451] Lenin's second period of exile in western Europe was much harder for him to bear than the first. Places which had been tolerable were no longer attractive.

The reason for the disillusion is obvious. The prospects of 1905 had raised expectations to undreamed of heights. Then they had been totally dashed. Emigration was a more bitter pill to swallow in the atmosphere of defeat compared to the hopes before 1905. According to Krupskaya, 'in Paris we spent the most trying years of exile.' [Krupskaya 166] Writing to Gorky in April 1910 Lenin said: 'Life in exile is now a hundred times harder than it was before the revolution.' [CW 34 421] The new exile was no less prone to the old disease. Describing the January 1910 Central Committee Plenum to Gorky, he said it was 'three weeks of agony, all nerves were on edge, the devil to pay'. [CW 34 420]

However, on this occasion, the squabbling was purgative: 'Life in exile and squabbling are inseparable. But the squabbling will pass away; nine-tenths of it remains abroad; it is an accessory feature ... The purging of the Social-Democratic from *its* dangerous "deviations", from liquidationism and otzovism (recallism) *goes forward* steadfastly.' [CW 34 421]

Once again, holidays helped Lenin maintain his equilibrium, starting with ten days in Nice – 'the place is wonderful – sunny, warm, dry and a southern sea' [CW 37 412] – with his brother-in-law in March 1909 and, after the showdown with Bogdanov in July, six weeks in Bombon near Clamart where the walking and cycling began again.

However, not all Lenin's encounters with the bicycle were happy ones. In January, on the way to watch an air display at Juvisy-sur-Orge near Paris, an expensive motor car driven by a viscount ran him down and smashed his bike. Lenin was barely able to jump clear. However, the episode did enable him to reactivate some of his legal training. He brought a suit against the driver. By the end of the month, thanks to the help of witnesses, he was able to report to his sister Maria that 'My bicycle case ended in my favour.' [CW 37 450] It did not put Lenin off. Cycling remained one of his favourite recreations. He and Krupskaya frequently took rides at the weekend, pedalling out of Paris into its wooded and rural suburbs they loved so much.

Illnesses and constant travel from meeting to meeting – San Remo, London, Liège, Brussels, Copenhagen, Stockholm – continued to punctuate Lenin's life. His philosophical research in 1909 had been badly disrupted by illness, which even endangered the whole project. On 13 July 1909 he wrote to Maria: 'My illness has held up my work on philosophy very badly. I am now almost well again and will most certainly write the book.' [CW 37 386] In July 1910, despite his earlier hostility to the Party School there, he visited Capri for a fortnight, meeting not only Gorky but Bogdanov, Lunacharsky and Bazarov as well. The visit was recorded in a series of photos. The summer of 1910 also saw Lenin and Krupskaya departing on 22 July for a month's holiday in Pornic, near Nantes, in South Brittany. Lenin told his mother he was having a wonderful holiday. However, immediately it ended he was on the way to Copenhagen for the Congress of the Socialist International. He took advantage of being in the Baltic region to arrange for his mother, now 75, and his sister Maria to take the steamer from St Petersburg to Stockholm where he met them and they spent almost a fortnight together. His mother even attended one of his public meetings which, according to Maria, 'made her very excited'. After 'she listened quite attentively', she commented that he spoke 'so impressively and skilfully but why does he exert himself so much, why does he speak so loudly, that is so harmful' adding, like innumerable mothers, 'He is not looking after himself.' [Weber 72] It was Lenin's last direct contact with her. She lived on until 1916 but Lenin's exile did not end, of course, until 1917. He was clearly aware that he might not see her again and, according to Krupskaya, when the time came for Maria and their mother to return, 'it was with sad and wistful eyes that he followed the departing steamer.' [Krupskaya 182]

1910 was also the year in which Lenin developed a friendship with Inessa Armand, who arrived in Brussels from Moscow with two of her five children in 1909. She was a steadfast Bolshevik and a beautiful and energetic woman of half-French, half-English descent. She was a lively presence and, in Krupskaya's words, 'soon gathered our Paris group around her'. Without doubt Lenin developed a great affection for Inessa and, most probably, fell in love with and embarked on an affair with her. Krupskaya, not surprisingly, is very low key about Inessa in her memoirs but the three of them maintained good relations with each other and Inessa often accompanied Lenin and Krupskaya on trips. Once again Lenin appeared to be copying Chernyshevsky, though unlike the husband who stood aside to allow his wife to have her lover in Chernyshevsky's novel, Krupskaya did not withdraw to the United States but continued to work just as devotedly for the cause and for her husband. It was, however, a feature of Chernyshevsky's 'New People' that they could overcome petty jealousy and show deeper love for one another than bourgeois convention allowed. The Lenin love triangle, though never a *ménage à trois*, did follow Chernyshevskyean principles not least in Lenin's eventual stoic rejection of Inessa in favour of Krupskaya, putting the interests of the revolution first, but none the less maintaining friendship and collaboration between the three of them.

Neither the presence of Inessa nor the resumption of cycle rides in spring 1912 was sufficient to drive away the emigration blues. The delights of Paris continued to pall. Writing to Lenin's sister Anna, Krupskaya said: 'Life goes on so monotonously here that I don't know what to write about … We went to the theatre, the play was idiotic … Today we are going to see Sophocles' *Elektra*.' [CW 37 612]

The growing irritation was fuelled by a return to labour militancy in Russia which began to revive hopes for a renewed challenge to the autocracy. War clouds were also forming. Though Lenin rightly predicted during the 1912 Balkan crisis that there would not be a general war [CW 37 482], it was clear that something deeper was brewing. Lenin's attention was increasingly drawn by two issues – what strategy to pursue in Russia and the international entanglements caused by the conflicts of imperialism. They dominated his writing for the years to come. The apparently rising revolutionary tide strengthened the urge to be near events. But a return to Russia was out of the question. Lenin's solution was to get as close as possible, this time Poland rather than the still inaccessible Finland. From 1912 to 1914 Lenin and Krupskaya lived in Krakow accompanied by the Zinovievs and others. The relief of returning to a near-Russian environment was unmistakable. Krupskaya wrote that 'Ilich liked Krakow very much; it reminded him of Russia.' [Krupskaya 206] Lenin himself showed his relief in a letter to his mother: 'This summer we have moved a long way from Paris – to Krakow. Almost in Russia! Even the Jews are like Russians and the Russian frontier is only 8 versts [about 8 kilometres] away.' [CW 37 479] According to Krupskaya: 'Exile in Krakow was only semi-exile. In Krakow we were almost entirely absorbed in the work in Russia. Close connections with Russia were quickly established.' [Krupskaya 204] Enthusiasm mounted. In a letter to Gorky Lenin commented that 'in Russia the *revolutionary* revival is not any kind of a revival, but a revolutionary revival.' [Krupskaya 204] Lenin's spirits clearly rose. 'The change of environment, the absence of émigré squabbles, soothed our nerves somewhat.' [Krupskaya 206] In another letter to his mother Lenin wrote from Krakow:

> The weather here is wonderful and I frequently go cycling. No matter how provincial and barbarous this town of ours may be, by and large I am better off here than I was in Paris. The hurly-burly of life in the émigré colony there was incredible; one's nerves got worn down badly and for no reason at all ... Of all the places I have been in my wanderings I would select London or Geneva, if those two places were not so far away. [CW 37 519]

There were also walks in the woods and bathing in the River Vistula. In summer 1913 there was the irresistible lure of the Tatra mountains and the Polish resort of Zakopane. They rented a large bungalow in the cheaper spot of Poronin, seven kilometres from Zakopane. 'The bungalow was situated 700 metres above sea level at the foot of the Tatra Mountains. The air was wonderful and, although there were frequent mists and drizzle, the view of the mountains during the clear intervals was extremely beautiful. We would climb up the plateau which was quite close to our bungalow and watch the snow-capped peaks of the Tatra mountains.' [Krupskaya 228] However, Krupskaya's health meant a trip to the specialist and an operation in Berne. The operation, conducted without anaesthetic, appears to have brought some relief. Ever making the best of the situation, they travelled to Vienna and returned via old haunts in Munich. They returned to Krakow for the winter but returned to Poronin the following May.

Unfortunately, as enemy aliens, they were not able to stay in Austrian-controlled Poland once the war began on 4 August. They soon began to attract the attention of the local police and the population who were suspicious of the presence of strange Russians so close to the frontier. What could they be but spies? On 7 August their holiday home in Poronin, near Zakopane, was raided by the Austrian police. Lenin recounted the comic opera scenario to a colleague and neighbour: 'The head of the local police was in charge ... the blockhead left all the Party correspondence but took my manuscript on the agrarian situation. He thought the statistical tables in it were a secret code.' [Weber 103] The following day, Lenin was arrested. Through the good offices of the Austrian Social-Democratic leader Victor Adler, he was released and Lenin and Krupskaya were able to leave, via Vienna, for neutral Switzerland where they arrived on 5 September. Though they did not, of course, know it, it was the last staging post of their exile before the tornado of war tore into their world and turned it upside down in the most astonishing circumstances.

4

IMPERIALISM, WAR AND REVOLUTION

For a revolutionary, bad news can be good news. From 1912 onwards the fragile post-1905 balance of the autocracy began to be lost as the strike movement got under way. Once again, the main agent of revolution was the autocracy itself rather than the radical parties. In April 1912, some 200 people, striking miners and members of their families, were shot by police in a single massacre in the Lena goldfields in Siberia. Once again, single-handedly and without provocation, the autocracy had found a way to plunge itself into unnecessary crisis. In a single day its agents had undone more than six years of precarious recovery. Without its revolutionary or liberal opponents lifting a finger they had been presented with a dramatic confirmation of their diagnosis of the terminal ineptitude of the autocracy. At a stroke, the real situation in Russia was laid bare. Labour was still ruthlessly exploited and was prepared to stand up for itself. Sensitive middle-class souls were embarrassed by the anachronistic barbarism that was their government. Revolutionaries were energized by a new wave of labour unrest as Russia's armaments-led mini-boom of 1908–12 collapsed into a rising cycle of unemployment and renewed worker militancy. It was a new Bloody Sunday, putting the political clock back almost a decade, exposing the farce of quasi-constitutionalist Russia. Not that the opposition were above using the opportunities presented by the limited parliamentary system. The massacre became a *cause célèbre* taken up by opponents of the autocracy in the Duma as well as on the street. Their case was put by a rising young leftist civil-rights lawyer named Alexander Kerensky, the son of Lenin's headmaster and another product of Simbirsk. On the wider horizon the complex series of Balkan wars and crises which led to the general war of 1914 had already begun. Here, too, tsarist incomprehension and ineptitude reaped a heavy harvest. In its domestic and foreign policy choices the autocracy would have been hard put to find a more effective way of committing suicide.

SOCIALISTS AND THE APPROACH OF WAR

Lenin, correctly as it turned out, saw such developments as the birth of renewed revolutionary opportunity. As the various clouds gathered Lenin's hopes began to rise again. It should not, however, be inferred that Lenin in any way lauded violence and misery. Quite the opposite. His whole life had been devoted to abolishing misery and war. Marxism was the mechanism by which it could be done. The iron laws of history were not of Lenin's making but he believed he could interpret them. If capitalism was heading towards open conflict it meant, Lenin believed, it was on its deathbed and was bringing forward the moment of liberation from its yoke. That alone should be celebrated. The terrible cost should not. If there was any way to avoid it, so much the better. But there wasn't and that was the fault of capitalism, not its opponents. The consolation was that it was the last convulsion after which there would be no more.

From his home in Krakow he observed carefully what was going on in Russia. The turn in the international situation also brought him to focus on international relations – diplomatic and economic – and the phenomenon of imperialism which, he believed, linked them together. Just as the war, when it came in August 1914, was the culmination of a series of imperial, diplomatic, military and internal crises for the participants which blew apart the old systems and the old assumptions, so it was for the socialist movement. At the level of analytic discourse and national and international organization, the approaching war brought a series of crises to the socialist movement and, as the war broke out, the crises culminated in the destruction of the remnants of socialist solidarity at the national and international levels. Although prone to factionalism before the war there was still a sense that all socialists belonged to the same family despite its quarrels. After it the socialist movement was totally divided with no prospect of meaningful reunification for the rest of the century.

The growing international crisis, which reached new levels of acuteness by 1912, focused attention on what was at the heart of the events and on what should be done. Socialists were in the forefront of this analysis. Though Lenin had been largely preoccupied with internal questions of class and revolutionary struggle in Russia, he had begun to show an increasing interest in international issues from the turn of the century. Ingeniously, in a dimension often lost on his later adulators, Lenin's interpretation of the growing international conflict, as we shall see, also impinged heavily on and arose directly out of the fundamental dilemmas of Russian Marxism. Three major themes dominated the thinking of Lenin and all other socialists. The first was the catastrophic split in the movement induced by the war; second, why the war was as it was; third, what were the prospects for revolution in the new circumstances?

Despite the gathering storm clouds many observers believed there would not be a war. Some of them even believed a major war was impossible. From the liberal perspective there were a number of people who followed the reasoning of the utopian thinker St Simon. He had argued that modern technology and communications (writing in the mid-nineteenth century he was deeply impressed by the emergence of railway networks, the Internet of that age) created greater and greater interdependence and mobility of peoples from country to country. This would, he thought, blur sharp national identities and antagonisms and, in the economic sphere, make the prosperity of one country dependent on the prosperity of its neighbours, reversing ancient enmities and zero-sum games in which success could only be bought at the expense of another's failure. Instead, war would be mutually ruinous, destroying the international system and all the participant economies. There could be no victors, so rational leaders would shy away from war. While, in some respects, the European Union has created a kind of St Simonian oasis out of one of the areas which generated the world's worst conflicts of the nineteenth and twentieth centuries, there was insufficient recognition of the consequences of war in 1914 to make such ideas convincing. There was concern, however. On the eve of war powerful industrialists from Britain, France and Germany tried to stave it off. The City of London was nervous and days before the war began, the British Foreign

Secretary, Grey, warned the French ambassador that 'the commercial and financial situation was extremely serious, there was danger of a complete collapse that would involve us and everyone in ruin.' Individuals like Albert Ballin, a personal friend of the Kaiser, and Sir Ernest Cassel lobbied actively against the war.[1] Tragically, common sense was overwhelmed by the uncontrollable tide of jingoism on all sides, the contrary interests of heavy munitions companies and the ongoing culture of diplomacy linked to defence of national 'credibility' as it is thought of today. The existence of anti-war capitalists showed the existence of contradictions within the elite but Lenin, for one, was little impressed. As the war went on, he increasingly developed a theory of capitalism based on its rampant, aggressive, imperialist tendencies.

However, before he turned his attention in that direction, the other force which, it was thought, might successfully throw itself in front of the juggernaut of war, was the internationalist socialist and labour movement. The Second International had been set up in Paris in 1889 to continue the work of the First International which had broken down through a split between Marxists and Bakuninite anarchists among other things. The Second International had brought together a wide variety of left-wing groups from moderate labourists to revolutionary socialists like Lenin. In 1914 they were united about one thing. The war was not in the interests of workers. It was an imperialist dispute between conflicting capitalist elites. The workers would be enrolled only as cannon fodder. In a famous statement of 1911 – which, incidentally, shows that, like Lenin, he also believed revolution might arise out of the war – the moderate Belgian socialist leader Emile Vandervelde pointed to the two major forces working against war: 'There are in Europe at present too many pacifist forces, starting with the Jewish capitalists who give financial support to many governments through to the socialists who are firmly resolved to prevent mobilization of the nations and in the event of defeat to spring at the throats of their rulers.'[2]

Tragically, the socialist movement proved to be much less 'firmly resolved' than Vandervelde had predicted. Although the majority of socialist leaders probably shared his outlook they did very little to implement a practical anti-war strategy. They held a series of meetings, passing resolutions against the war right up until late July, and even believed at that point that, although they would have to move their scheduled international congress from Vienna since Austria-Hungary had already declared war on Serbia, it might still be held in August in Paris. Like the rest of Europe they were soon to be overwhelmed by the chain of events.

There were obviously weaknesses in the socialists' expectations. Above all, workers were not immune to national enmities. In Vienna, for instance, the working class was deeply anti-Serb and supported their government. The key weakness, however, lay in Germany and had been pointed out at a Party conference in 1891, long before the war crisis took hold, by none other than the veteran German socialist August Bebel. 'If Russia, the champion of terror and barbarism, were to attack Germany to break and destroy it ... we are as much concerned as those who stand at the head of Germany.'[3] It was through this opening that the worm of national self-defence entered into and started to eat away the body of the labour movement and its much-vaunted international solidarity. While international resistance was a fine thing, when it came to the crunch, the majority of German socialists decided, after an agonizing debate, that they must support their government once Russia had mobilized. That swayed the debate elsewhere. If Germany was threatening invasion then the left would have to join in the defence of France. If Belgium were to be invaded British workers could not stand idly by and watch the Kaiser reach the Channel and so on. The brittle chain snapped. Majorities succumbed to patriotism. Only a rump of opponents stood firm against the war. It was a disaster for the socialist movement.

At first sight, it might appear that the minorities would find it easy to come together, which is what they tried to do in an anti-war coalition. However, their national governments put severe restrictions on them even in 'democratic' Britain, France and Germany, hampering international travel and contacts, suppressing newspapers and organizations and turning opinion firmly against the 'white feather' brigade, accusing them of cowardice. That, however, was not their greatest problem. Despite sharing opposition to the war they remained a widely disparate group comprising pacifists, 'moderate' labourists like Ramsay MacDonald and radical Marxists like Lenin motivated by class solidarity and dreams of class struggle and even civil war. Attempts to bring the anti-war movement together foundered on its broad disparities. Attempts were made to hold anti-war conferences in Switzerland at Zimmerwald in September 1915 and Kienthal in April 1916 but they had no practical consequences as far as the war was concerned, serving only to emphasize the differences. The only one that promised to achieve something was called in Stockholm in 1917, largely at the behest of Russia's Provisional Government which needed to appear to have a peace policy for internal political reasons. However, Britain and France ensured that it did not succeed.

From the outset of the war Lenin's position was clear. The war was an imperialist struggle in which the workers of the combatant countries had no stake. They would, sooner or later, recognize this basic fact and act accordingly by throwing off the imperialist yoke imposed by their bourgeoisie, hence Lenin's call as early as September 1914 to turn the imperialist war into a European-wide civil war. The prospect of civil war remained fundamental to Lenin's strategy in the war years although, for obvious tactical reasons, he chose not to emphasize or even admit to it on occasions. He outlined his ideas in a pamphlet entitled *The War and Russian Social Democracy* written in October and published in November 1914. The opening paragraph is an excellent encapsulation of many of the main themes of Lenin's analysis of the war:

> The European War, which the governments and the bourgeois parties of all countries have been preparing for decades, has broken out. The growth of armaments, the extreme intensification of the struggle for markets in the latest – the imperialist – stage of capitalist develop-ment in the advanced countries, and the dynastic interests of the more backward East-European monarchies were inevitably bound to bring about this war, and have done so. Seizure of territory and subju-gation of other nations, the ruining of competing nations and the plunder of their wealth, distracting the attention of the working masses from the internal political crises in Russia, Germany, Britain and other countries, disuniting and nationalist stultification of the workers, and the extermination of their vanguard so as to weaken the revolutionary movement of the proletariat – these comprise the sole actual content, importance and significance of the present war.

The solution, Lenin continued, was in the hands of the revolutionary left:

> It is primarily on Social-Democracy that the duty rests of revealing the true meaning of the war, and of ruthlessly exposing the falsehood,

> sophistry and 'patriotic' phrase-mongering spread by the ruling
> classes, the landowners and the bourgeoisie, in defence of the war.
> [SW 1 657]

The rest of the short, sharp article largely expanded these thoughts. The
bourgeois leaders of both warring camps had 'hoodwinked' their respec-
tive peoples by disguising a war of plunder as a 'war of defence'.
'Neither group of belligerents is inferior to the other in spoliation,
atrocities and the boundless brutality of war' but each distracts the
masses from the true struggle – 'a civil war against the bourgeoisie both
of its "own" and "foreign" countries ... with the help of false phrases
about patriotism'. [SW 1 658] Lenin's views could not be clearer. Only
class struggle, not national struggle, could truly liberate the toiling
masses. So convinced was Lenin of the primacy of class struggle that he
introduced a remarkable theme into his argument which recurred
throughout the war. Despite squaring up to each other, and in the case
of the Anglo-French bloc 'spending thousands of millions to hire the
troops of Russian tsarism, the most reactionary and barbarous monarchy
in Europe, and prepare them for an attack on Germany', [SW 1 658]
the two blocs would, nonetheless, in the event of a revolution in Russia,
work together to defend their class interests. 'In fact, whatever the outcome of the war, [the German] bourgeoisie will, together with the
Junkers, exert every effort to support the tsarist monarchy against a revolution in Russia.' [SW 1 657]

Having outlined his views on the war the remaining two-thirds of
the article is devoted to denouncing opportunist, right-wing Social
Democrats. Their role in 'hoodwinking' the workers was, if anything,
gaining prominence in Lenin's analysis. If revolution had not come
about as it should have done, who could be more to blame than these
class traitors? The bourgeoisie acted in its own interests, which in
Marxist theory meant digging their own graves, but the role of the
'petty-bourgeois opportunists' was to make the workers believe their
interests were close to those of the bourgeoisie and could be achieved by
reform. Instead of opposing their governments' 'criminal conduct' they
'called upon the working class to *identify* its position with that of the
imperialist governments'. [SW 1 659] In a diatribe which brought
together many elements of the case against the Social-Democratic right
wing Lenin said:

The opportunists have long been preparing the ground for this collapse [of the Second International] by denying the socialist revolution and substituting bourgeois reformism in its stead; by rejecting the class struggle with its inevitable conversion at certain moments into civil war, and by preaching class collaboration; by preaching bourgeois chauvinism under the guise of patriotism and the defence of the fatherland, and ignoring or rejecting the fundamental truth of socialism, long ago set forth in the *Communist Manifesto*, that the workingmen have no country; by confining themselves, in the struggle against militarism, to a sentimental, philistine point of view, instead of recognizing the need for a revolutionary war by the proletarians of all countries, against the bourgeoisie of all countries; by making a fetish of the necessary utilization of bourgeois parliamentarianism and bourgeois legality, and forgetting that illegal forms of organization and propaganda are imperative at times of crisis. [SW 1 661]

Socialists everywhere should follow the example of the Russian Social Democrats (nowhere does he use the terms Bolshevik and Menshevik) who suffered for their opposition to the war through loss of their legal press, the forced closure of most of their associations and arrest and imprisonment of members but who still voted against war credits and denounced the war as imperialist. [SW 1 660]

Idealistically, Lenin concluded with a number of assertions about the next steps. First, socialists should adopt the slogan of 'the formation of a republican United States of Europe', that is for the revolutionary overthrow of the German, Austrian and Russian monarchies. However, Russia itself was not, Lenin argued, ready for socialism. 'Since Russia is most backward and has not completed its bourgeois revolution, it still remains the task of Russian Social Democracy to achieve the three fundamental conditions for consistent democratic reform, viz., a democratic republic (with complete equality and self-determination for all nations), confiscation of the landed estates, and an eight-hour working day.' This contrasted with 'all the advanced countries' in which 'the war has placed on the order of the day the slogan of socialist revolution' and where the proletariat will have to bear a heavy burden 'in the re-creation of Europe after the horrors of the present "patriotic" barbarism'. [SW 1 662] Workers must unite with one another, so that 'The conversion of the present imperialist war into a civil war is the only correct proletarian slogan.' [SW 1 663]

In these few short pages Lenin laid down many of the principles that were to guide him into and beyond the seizure of power. His opposition to the barbarism of war was clear, but he was no pacifist – the 'sentimental, philistine' opponents of militarism being the Ramsay MacDonalds of the left. Instead, there would have to be a class war, a civil war, a revolutionary war to achieve the overthrow of the bourgeoisie. The socialist right wing also made the mistake of 'making a fetish of the necessary utilization of bourgeois parliamentarianism and bourgeois legality, and forgetting that illegal forms of organization and propaganda are imperative at times of crisis', in other words they mistook the useful tools of parliament and bourgeois rights as ends in themselves rather than means that had to give way to more direct methods of struggle at crucial moments.

Around this time, Lenin also clarified other important aspects of internationalism. First, the internationalist could not be blind to the existence of nations and the diversity of cultures associated with them. True, they were destined to disappear, but, in the meantime, like social classes, they had to be dealt with. Early in 1914 he had written a treatise on national self-determination emphasizing the freedom and equality of all nations and national cultures. However, implementation of these principles was complicated. While socialists should struggle for the equality of nations it was imperative that the socialist struggle itself should not be broken down into a series of national struggles. Instead, it should be conducted above the level of individual nations. In Russia, this meant that socialists would assert the rights of all nationalities but not break the movement down into Ukrainian, Georgian, Polish or Armenian parties. No, the struggle must be conducted over the whole empire at once. In asserting this he was opposing, in particular, Rosa Luxemburg for whom Polish independence was a goal in itself. Lenin mistrusted such 'separatism'. Instead, he argued:

> The proletariat of Russia is faced with a twofold or, rather, two-sided task: to combat nationalism of every kind, above all, Great Russian nationalism; to recognize, not only fully equal rights for all nations in general, but also equality of rights as regards polity, i.e., the right of nations to self-determination, to secession. And at the same time, it

> is their task, in the interests of a successful struggle against all and
> every kind of nationalism among all nations, to preserve the unity of
> the proletarian struggle and the proletarian organizations, amalga-
> mating these organizations into a close-knit international association
> despite the strivings for national exclusiveness.

Lenin summarized the apparently paradoxical principle thus: 'Complete
equality of rights for all nations; the right of nations to self-determination; the unity of the workers of all nations – such is the national programme that Marxism, the experience of the whole world, and the
experience of Russia, teach the workers.' [SW 1 652]

Some months later, after the war had begun and Lenin was thoroughly denouncing bourgeois chauvinism, he had to make allowances
for the inroads nationalism had made on the identity of workers. In
another article, entitled 'On the National Pride of the Great Russians',
Lenin made the distinction between justified and unjustified feelings of
national pride. 'Is a sense of national pride alien to us, Great-Russian
class conscious proletarians? Certainly not! We love our language and
our country.' [SW 1 665] He continued, 'We are full of a sense of
national pride, and for that very reason we *particularly* hate our slavish
past ... and our slavish present.' [SW 1 665]

Little attention was paid to these writings when they first came out
as they were swamped by the tidal wave of war fever gripping Europe,
but they were to have greater and greater resonance, Lenin's ideas on
self-determination even supposedly affecting US President Woodrow
Wilson's Fourteen Points for ending the war. The statements about
Russian national pride could have been penned by Stalin and were used
to justify socialism in one country and socialist patriotism in the Second
World War. The kernel of Lenin's much better known pamphlet
Imperialism can be found in these brief articles and much of Lenin's strategy
for 1917 can be traced back to them. The capitalist elites of the warring
blocs would relentlessly prolong the bloody and barbarous struggle for
domination over their rivals. In the process, the war would increasingly
polarize the combatant countries. The masses would increasingly look to
opponents of the war for leadership. In central and western Europe
socialism was a possibility while in Russia a bourgeois democratic revolution would open the road to further progress. Interestingly, Lenin
makes no reference to the United States. Within a few weeks of the war

beginning, at a time when societies were still intoxicated with the elixir of nationalist fervour, the left was in disarray and the internationalists apparently a tiny, isolated minority, Lenin was calmly looking forward to a moment of triumph hardly anyone else could foresee.

However, there was still a long way to go from autumn 1914 to February 1917 and, though the goal of revolution was achieved, it did not necessarily come about for the reasons Lenin expected. None the less, for the next two-and-a-half years, Lenin retained this framework of analysis. He developed aspects of it, notably being more specific about the approach of revolution in Russia and in producing a more elaborate theory of imperialism which shaped twentieth-century thinking beyond the confines of the revolutionary left.

THEORIZING IMPERIALISM AND WAR

The ever-deepening crises of early twentieth-century Europe drew the best analysts of the radical left into attempts to uncover the fundamental dynamic driving international relations. They did not have to look far to find their villain, imperialism, but delving into what it actually was and how it worked caused great controversy.

Before going any further we need to pause for a moment to consider what phenomena the theory of imperialism was supposed to explain. The features which dominated economic and political life in the late nineteenth century were certainly dramatic. In 1870, the year of Lenin's own birth, Germany had fought a war against France and emerged as a budding superpower right in the heart of Europe. This alone destabilized the pre-existing balance of power. Europe's other predominantly German-speaking Great Power, Austria-Hungary, was fading as was its neighbour Turkey. The contraction of these two declining empires opened up all sorts of areas of conflict. Germany increasingly took on the role of Austria-Hungary's patron in the Balkans and Near East. This, in turn, antagonized Britain and France, who feared German expansion into the Middle East and Egypt where the Suez Canal had altered the strategic significance of the Eastern Mediterranean. Russia, too, was alarmed to see German influence arriving at the Straits, in addition to its existing enemies Britain, France and Turkey. It meant that Germany effectively blocked Russia's two main sea routes to the west, the exits from the Baltic Sea and the Black Sea.

Increasing international antagonism coincided with a second industrial revolution. The first industrial revolution had been characterized by steam, coal, iron and the emergence of railways. The second was based on steel, electricity, chemicals, and later oil. The new features came together in rapid technological developments, notably a worldwide telegraph system, steam ships, dynamite, machine-guns and massive steel artillery and shells. A military revolution ensued, as did an ever-escalating arms race.

However, perhaps the most striking phenomenon of the late nineteenth century was the division of the globe. From 1880 to 1905 almost all the world fell under the direct political or indirect economic hegemony of one or other of the Great Powers. India, China, Africa and South America all came under foreign domination. In 1900 London was the focus of the first global economy. Within hours, companies and the government could communicate with Hong Kong, Sydney, Alexandria, Buenos Aires, San Francisco or Cape Town. Economic shifts in the City of London translated into boom or bust for Bolivian miners and Chinese traders as much as they did for British farmers and industrialists. As we have seen, it was this intoxicating atmosphere which had brought Lenin and Krupskaya into direct contact with the contradictions of capitalism on their visits to London.[4] But from the Marxist point of view the astonishing two decades needed some explanation. What was the driving force or forces? Had capitalism itself changed since Marx's heyday? Was the evidence used by Marx, taken largely from British data for the 1840s and 1850s, still relevant? What impact did the new phenomena have on the prospects for revolution? Did the new situation help explain the critical fact that no Marxist revolution had taken place or even appeared likely, in 1900? These were the questions pondered by the analysts of the left.

Lenin had become interested in such phenomena at least from August 1904 when he and Krupskaya translated one of the great liberal analyses of imperialism by the British economist J.A. Hobson. [Weber 38] In Hobson's view, imperialism was underpinned by increasingly competitive economic forces. In place of the free trade and *laissez-faire* ethos of the mid-century a more militaristic and aggressive form of capitalist expansion had evolved, as easy opportunities for profit in industrial capitalism's early years gave way to a harsher environment as the number of competing investors increased exponentially.

Two fundamental features of Hobson's analysis were adopted by many Marxist theorists. First, they picked up the idea that imperialism had an economic basis derived from increasing competition to invest capital profitably. Second, they shared the liberal critique of the aggressive and inhuman nature of the phenomenon which uprooted native communities, obliterated resistance with overwhelming military force and cared nothing for the humanitarian and environmental consequences of its ever-deepening exploitation of the resources of the globe. Not surprisingly, this led to a very hostile interpretation of imperialism on the part of radical Marxists.

The most sophisticated analyses in the Marxist tradition came from the Austrian Marxist Rudolf Hilferding and from Rosa Luxemburg. In a seminal book, entitled *Finance Capital*, Hilferding set out to link the origins of increasing international tensions, the arms race and the economic and political division of the globe to basic social changes observable in Europe. His starting point was the changing nature of capital since Marx's day. Early capitalism had been characterized by direct contact between investor and his investment. In other words, the investor would usually know the entrepreneur or industrialist to whom he or she was entrusting his or her money. Decisions to invest were taken directly by those whose money it was. Since that time, however, banks had come to take an ever-increasing role in controlling the flow of capital. Individual investors were rapidly giving way to institutions which held vast capital resources and, consequently, had more and more power over the economy. In place of hundreds of thousands of competing small investors, national economies were seeing the emergence of a few dozen banks.

The relative simplification of the investment process meant that, although they still competed against one another, the possibility of controlling the market began to arise. Where, under early capitalism, the market was the unpredictable ocean in which investors and producers alike were tossed uncontrollably, the construction of the new capitalist super-institutions meant they could be less subject to market anarchy. Indeed, far from showing capitalism's supposed commitment to competition, the institutions emerging at this time showed its even greater appetite for subduing and fixing the market. In addition to banks, producers were also coming together in larger and larger institutions. Mega-companies were emerging, the predecessors of twentieth-century global corporations. Bosch, Krupp, Siemens, Schneider, Vickers and more became vast enterprises employing tens of thousands. Many of them were arms producers, an area where the free market never dominated for obvious reasons. Hilferding, though he was not the first to do so, called these large economic players monopolies, a term that was not literally true since a monopoly meant domination by one entity. However, it emphasized what Hilferding saw as the tendency of capitalism to produce a smaller and smaller number of dominant companies.

This tendency was reinforced by the grouping of these monopolies into cartels. The purpose of the cartel, for Hilferding and the left, was to control prices so that the fluctuations of the market could be reduced and, if possible, prices kept high. By doing this, all members of the cartel would benefit though they might still compete in other ways, for instance to win more contracts than their competitors. However, the emergence of what became known on the left as monopoly capitalism meant that a small number of more-or-less unbankruptable major companies came to dominate some 70 per cent or so of key sectors – steel, chemicals, coal, oil, capital (i.e. banks) – while a mass of smaller players were left exposed even more to the chill winds of competition. If a sector contracted, when demand for, say, coal started to fall, the smaller players would go to the wall first and the big companies pick up the pieces. It was also the case that smaller companies were often the most innovative while large companies were risk-averse since they had so much to lose. However, a successful innovation, pioneered by a small producer, could, once it had been tried and tested so the risk was minimized, be taken over by the large company once the risk element had been taken out and its success proved.

Hilferding also pointed to one more crucial aspect of monopoly capitalism. As large companies became more powerful, so their links with the state became stronger as they lobbied for legislation and policies appropriate to their activities. These varied from country to country. Where industrial capitalism was weak, in Russia, Italy and to a lesser extent in France and Germany, protectionism was high on the industrialists' agenda. In dominant countries, where they did not fear the competition of others, free trade dominated. As is still the case down to the present, one of the key differences between the ideology of free trade and that of protectionism, apart from their essence, is that protectionism can be implemented by each country for itself but free trade often requires an active policy to impose it on unwilling countries. This might take the form of economic retaliation against protectionist nations to nullify the impact of their tariff barriers but could also lead to direct political and military intervention to assert the 'right' of free trade. Countries might also arm to defend themselves against such threats.

In a myriad of ways, Hilferding and the radical left argued, the tentacles of contemporary capitalism were closing around the emerging nation states. The outcome was that states were increasingly representing the interests of their great companies in colonial and international economic policies. Competition between capitalists was now bloc versus bloc rather than individual versus individual. The outcome was the growth of international tensions and the economic division of the globe. The tensions also sparked off the arms race. Governments and arms companies became merged in what President Eisenhower memorably described half a century later as the military-industrial complex. In this way, Hilferding had produced a brilliant account which brought together the key phenomena of the age.

However, his analysis did not stop there. For Hilferding finance capital was a major step towards organized capitalism. In this fact, there were some crumbs of comfort for the left. Despite having described contemporary finance capitalism as a major juggernaut crushing all in its way, he also believed that the system raised some hopes for socialists. He saw it as a system in which, within its limits, capitalism was trying to organize itself. Marxist socialism was, first and foremost, supposed to be about rational organization of resources to satisfy human needs. This would require replacing the anarchy of the market by some form of rational planning and control. For Hilferding, capitalism itself was beginning to produce the means and mechanisms of planning and control. In its own hesitant and ambiguous fashion, through monopolies, cartels and ever-tightening links with the state, capitalism itself was throwing up the means by which a future socialist revolution could control the aggressive juggernaut. Lenin seized on this aspect, in particular, of Hilferding's ideas and, as we shall see below, drew consequences crucial to his strategy and tactics in Russia in 1917.

Hilferding's ideas were first comprehensively compiled in 1910 when the original German edition of his book came out. The impact was instantaneous. It was the book the revolutionary left had been waiting for. In a sense it was the answer to Bernstein. Like Bernstein, Hilferding was dealing with that most tantalizing of questions for Marxists at that time – why had there not been a revolution? In reply, Bernstein had painted a picture of a less and less aggressive capitalism settling into a reformist path to social justice. Hilferding, however, ripped away the mask of complacency and hypocrisy which surrounded liberal capitalism and revealed a beast within. Hilferding had started out from the classic Marxist premise of concentration of capital leading to monopoly. Far from being benevolent, the monopolies were wild beasts stalking the entire globe for profit. Anything and anyone in their path was doomed. Hilferding pointed to the fate of native Americans, of north and south, who had been massacred and their cultures destroyed by the onslaught. Now Black Africans faced the same processes.

Capitalists themselves were transformed in the process. Many free-trade liberals had been humanitarians, believing a benign capitalism would bring the world together and the interconnected economies make war impossible. Not so the expansionist monopolists of the early twentieth century. In Hilferding's words:

> The desire for an expansionist policy revolutionizes the entire view of life held by the bourgeoisie. They are no longer peace-loving and humanitarian. The old free-traders did not look on free trade simply as being the best economic policy but as a starting point for an era of peace. Finance capital lost this belief a long time ago. It does not believe in the harmony of capitalist interests, but recognizes that competition develops more and more into a political struggle for power. The ideal of peace fades away, and the ideal of greatness and power of the state replaces the humanitarian ideal.

It should be remembered that Bernstein had been basing his views on developments in Britain and Hilferding on what was happening in Germany where exaltation of the state and bellicose nationalism were indeed sweeping all before them. He continued:

> The ideal of the nation ... is now transferred into belief in the exaltation of one nation over all other nations. Capital is now the conqueror of the world, and every new country it conquers represents a boundary which it has to cross. This struggle is going to be an economic

necessity, for to lag behind lowers the profits of finance capital, reduces its ability to compete and, in the end, could make the smaller economic unit a tributary of the larger.

He also goes on to describe the associated decline in morality. The new capitalist argues 'realistically': 'Eternal justice is a beautiful dream, but one cannot even build railways at home with moral principles. How can we conquer the world if we wait for our rivals to be converted to our principles.' Racism is the inevitable outcome of the new capitalism: 'Subjugation of foreign nations by force ... leads the ruling nation to attribute this domination to its special natural characteristics – i.e. to the character of its race. Thus, in the ideology of race there develops, disguised as natural science, the reality of finance capital's striving for power.'[5]

Hilferding had brilliantly analysed a world tumbling into war in a spirit of aggressive nationalism. He linked the burgeoning ideology of 'social Darwinism' – notably that competition was necessary because it conformed to the 'natural' law of 'survival of the fittest' – to the nature of finance capital itself. He also argued that the profits made in imperialist adventures made it possible for working-class living standards in the home countries to rise and thereby fend off revolution. Hilferding had linked the dominant social characteristics of the era and produced a revolutionary analysis which has deeply affected the revolutionary left down to the present. His depiction of monopoly and corporate capitalism as a hungry tiger prowling the entire globe in search of prey is still influential and was the essence of many later Soviet polemics and propaganda campaigns against capitalism. No matter how benevolent it looked, the wild beast still lived underneath the more humanitarian mask.

Ironically, Hilferding himself moderated his political position and associated himself with Kautsky after the split in the International. Later he became a junior figure in the Weimar government of the 1920s and eventually died in Gestapo custody in 1941. However, his drift to the 'opportunist' camp made the reception of his ideas on the revolutionary left rather ambiguous. Indeed, it helps to explain his obscurity since his ideas are better known to us through those who built on them rather than through Hilferding himself. Of all those who are indebted to Hilferding none is better known than Lenin, two of whose main writings – *Imperialism* and the closely connected *State and Revolution* – would not have been possible without Hilferding.

However, Lenin being Lenin and Hilferding being who he was, the relationship between the ideas of the two of them is not simple. While he adopted large swathes of Hilferding's analysis Lenin strongly defined differences between the two of them. Reading Lenin's pamphlet one would hardly notice its debt to Hilferding as much as the polemic. Indeed, Lenin more readily acknowledges the influence of Hobson than that of Hilferding on the grounds that Hobson is an unambiguous bourgeois liberal while, as a supporter of Kautsky, Hilferding is a petty-bourgeois disguised as a socialist and therefore more dangerous.

None the less, the similarities between Lenin's and Hilferding's analyses are striking. Concentration of capital, monopolies and cartels are equally at the heart of both analyses. The insatiable appetite for profits and the worldwide striving to realize them are fundamental to both. The ensuing hypocrisy of 'democratic' and 'humanitarian' values alongside racism, exultant nationalism and a colossal arms race and, by the time Lenin was writing, the most horrible war of all time, are roundly denounced by both. Lenin also seizes on, and indeed quotes favourably, Hilferding's point about the superprofits of imperialism funding the rising living standards of the 'aristocracy of labour'. For Lenin, the existence of these beneficiaries of imperialism explains the emergence of reformist social democracy – it is the ideology of precisely these elements who rise above the true proletariat.

However, Lenin also attempted to emphasize a number of what he considered crucial differences from Hilferding. Openly following Hobson, Lenin argued that the system described was not dynamic but parasitic and moribund. This is an interesting argument in that, for its originator Hobson, the existence of a large, idle, class of speculators who lived on the profits made by others was disgusting, immoral and unsustainable. It seems likely that Hobson's humanitarian disgust at the existence of such rich idlers carried away his judgement in that there is no convincing argument to say that they are a sign of the system's decadence. Immoral though it was, there is no reason why the system should be undermined by it. It is perhaps even more extraordinary that Lenin should seize on this point to distinguish himself from Hilferding. He follows Hobson in his contempt for idle 'coupon-clippers' living on unearned income but, no more than Hobson, does he show that the system is unsustainable. Just because it was repulsive did not make it unworkable.

Writing in 1915 and 1916 Lenin's perspective was somewhat different from that of Hilferding, whose book had come out four years before the war. Lenin focused more on why the war was happening. Without understanding these ideas it is impossible to understand what Lenin meant by his central mantra that the war was an 'imperialist war'. In his view, as we have seen in his writings of the very early days, the war was essentially brought about by the conflict between the Anglo-French and German capitalist blocs competing with each other for markets and for the ruination and despoliation of the other bloc. Russia was involved as the hireling of the Anglo-French bloc. In a preface to the postwar French and German editions of *Imperialism* Lenin pointed to the Treaties of Brest-Litovsk and Versailles to make his point. In both cases the victors had attempted to ensure the economic ruination of the vanquished and the takeover of assets by the victors. Brest-Litovsk was the most draconian peace treaty of modern times with Germany taking vast tracts of land, population, infrastructure and mineral resources plus imposing an indemnity payable in gold. Left to France and some of the British delegates Versailles would have been equally draconian. However, America, motivated by a desire to restructure Europe for 'business as usual' and an increasing fear of the spread of revolution leading to the setting up of a *'cordon sanitaire'* (the predecessor of the iron curtain), modified the terms of the treaty. However, this was not enough for John Maynard Keynes who pointed out that the economic destruction of one power would weaken the trade and finance system as a whole. None the less, Lenin was satisfied that his basic point was supported by events. The war was fought for markets, colonies and the destruction of competition. His pamphlet has become a classic statement of the radical Marxist view of war in the capitalist era and is much better known than the analysis of Hilferding on which much, though not all, of it depends.

One further point. Hilferding's analysis, as modified and added to by Lenin, depicted an aggressive, bloodthirsty, racist, immoral capitalist class drawing closer to the nation state and to militarism in its desire to annex the world and subdue its major competitors. In this way they were, inadvertently, opening the way for the Marxist interpretation of fascism as the ultimate, decadent phase of capitalism preceding its fall. Arguably, this interpretation had fatal consequences in blinding the dogmatic left to the ever-present contradictions between capitalists. As we have seen, Lenin had a tendency to believe that, despite imperialism, if threatened from the left, the warring capitalist blocs would put their mutual interest in suppressing revolution above their conflicting imperial interests. In fact, animosity between Germany and Britain and France continued for at least half of the century, revolution or no revolution. As such, the essence of this theory contributed to the fatal decision of the German Communist Party (instructed from Moscow in 1928) to treat all non-communist parties – Social Democrats, Liberals, Centre Party Catholics, Nationalists and Nazis – as equally fascist. Only when it was too late for Germany did they turn to alliances with all anti-fascist parties. However, such consequences could not be foreseen in 1916 when Lenin first formulated his ideas in detail.

There was, however, one more important dimension of Lenin's pamphlet which distinguished it from its inspirers. Like all Lenin's writings, *Imperialism* had a Russian dimension to it in that it addressed peculiarly Russian preoccupations. In fact, it addressed the oldest of Russian Marxist issues, the one with which Lenin had first made his name in the 1890s, namely, what is the fate of capitalism and hence of Marxist revolution in Russia? One of the main themes of the leftist interpretation of imperialism, shared by other theorists such as Rosa Luxemburg and Nikolai Bukharin, was the globalization of capitalism through imperialism. Indeed, Bukharin's book was entitled *Imperialism and the World Economy*.[6] Lenin, among others, seized on this aspect of the debate. If capitalism were now a global system, the issue of which countries were ripe for Marxist revolution was less important in that the system could be challenged anywhere. Bukharin, adapting a phrase from Alexander Bogdanov, even went so far as to say that the chain of capitalism would break at its weakest link. For Lenin, this was not entirely the case. While it would not be the weakest link that would break the chain it could, at least initially, be one of the weaker links. The weakest links, in Lenin's view, were in the periphery and he did not believe capitalism would break down there. A classic weaker link, however, was Russia which was much more strategically important to international capitalism. In Lenin's view, the dilemma of whether one could have a Marxist revolution in a country which he, among others, considered 'backward' from the Marxist point of view, now had another resolution. A Marxist, class struggle against capitalism could be begun in Russia, but it could not be ended there. It would have to be supported by revolutions in the 'advanced' capitalist countries, notably Germany. However, for Lenin, there was no doubt about the applicability of Marx's theories even to 'backward' Russia. Two fundamental points distinguished his view from that of the populists and the right-wing Social Democrats. First, as he had argued from the late 1890s, the question of Russia's capitalist future was beyond dispute, since it was already irreversibly on the capitalist path. Second, because of the globalization of capitalism, the Russian revolution, though unsustainable in Marxist terms if it remained isolated, could spark off the final collapse of capitalism in its heartlands of Britain, France and Germany in particular. It is worth repeating that this did not mean that Lenin differed from his Marxist rivals by ignoring the orthodox Marxist 'theory of stages' whereby capitalism had to exhaust its creative potential before it gave way to socialism. Rather, his view was that Russia was already in the capitalist stage and therefore, given the new conditions of globalization, the socialist stage could be on the agenda even in 'backward' Russia. As we shall see, the assumption that Russia was 'passing from the first stage of the revolution', i.e. the bourgeois capitalist stage, to the 'second stage', i.e. the socialist stage, was a basic orientation for Lenin's analysis and strategy in 1917.

THE ULYANOVS IN WARTIME

Imperialism became one of Lenin's best-known works. Ironically, one of the reasons he had written it in the first place, was that he was, as usual, desperately short of money. By the time it was finally published in full, in 1917, Lenin's material and political situation had changed beyond all expectation. Looking at his life during the war there is no sign of such a transforming prospect on the horizon.

In the bright summer sun of August 1914 Europeans joyously went through the first stages of their own self-destruction. Troop trains set off for the fronts. In the main cities of the warring blocs, Berlin, Vienna, Paris, St Petersburg, London and the rest, the scenes were similar. Bands, patriotic songs, flags, banners and cheering crowds sent the first victims of a doomed generation to their fate. Peace protestors were outnumbered and often bullied into silence. Those who foresaw the horrors to come were, in most cases, overwhelmed by a paroxysm of jingoism.

The sombre expectations of the right-wing Social Democrats who reluctantly voted for war credits were not noticed by the mainstream. The prophetic words of 3 August 1914 of Britain's Foreign Secretary, Sir Edward Grey, that 'The lamps are going out all over Europe; we shall not see them lit again in our lifetime', were ignored. It was to take several years of pointless sacrifice before the sceptics began to muster a significant audience, but even then they were a minority in most countries.

Unnoticed in the continent-wide mobilization the Ulyanov couple made their way from Krakow, in 'enemy' Austria-Hungary, to neutral Switzerland. As had often been the case in the past, Lenin needed favours from his political opponents. In this case, Austrian Social-Democratic leaders, notably Victor Adler, intervened on his behalf despite the fact that Lenin denounced them regularly as opportunists. Unlike most socialists Lenin did not abide by the principle of having no enemies on the left. None the less, he was prepared to take advantage of the sentimentality of others if he felt he had to. Here as elsewhere in his life, Lenin's morality was dominated by the need to do whatever seemed necessary to promote the true revolution.

Throughout the turmoil of the Marne, the Masurian Lakes, Passchendaele, the Somme, Verdun and the other disasters of war Lenin continued to live the life of a scholar and litterateur. His life revolved around libraries and publications. Communications were obviously hampered in wartime as was travel and he was unable to leave Switzerland. The continuous contact with Russia which he had enjoyed was no longer possible. There was no question of producing a newspaper on the scale and with the frequency of previous ventures. Even so, Lenin threw himself into doing what he could and in November revived *Sotsial Demokrat* (*The Social Democrat*) which appeared fairly regularly. Over twenty issues and two volumes of articles had appeared before Lenin departed Switzerland in March 1917. It is inconceivable to think of Lenin being without some sort of mouthpiece at this critical period.

At first the Ulyanovs lived in Berne, which he described as 'a dull little town, but ... better than Galicia' and occupied himself 'poking around in libraries – I have missed them.' [CW 43 432] Oddly, given the unfolding drama, Lenin returned to the great philosophers, including Hegel and Aristotle, about whom he compiled his *Philosophical Notebooks*. His studies were notable for his 'discovery' of dialectics. The dialectic became a major philosophical cudgel for Lenin because, to his own satisfaction at least, he was able to claim that all other Marxist philosophers, from Plekhanov onwards, had overlooked its significance. Even in his last writings as his death approached nearly ten years later, he said of Bukharin, the acknowledged philosopher of the Communist Party, that he had never understood dialectics. In other words, no one but Lenin had really understood Marx. This lack of understanding was no side issue because, for Lenin, it was absolutely crucial to understanding the philosophical underpinnings of Marx's theory. In Lenin's opinion the dialectic was the Marxist theory of knowledge. [CW 38 355–63] Why was it so important? Dialectics proved that thought operated through the conflict of ideas. An idea, a thesis, would engender its opposite, its antithesis. In the conflict between the two a new concept, the synthesis, would emerge. This would form a new idea/thesis and the process would continue. Essentially, for Lenin, the dialectical process undermined all static, and therefore conservative, ways of thinking. Dialectics posited the constant interaction and struggle between concepts, resulting in new concepts rather than the pure triumph of one of the original combatants. Transferred into the natural world it suggested that stasis, i.e. things being unchanging, was not their natural state. Rather, they were in a constant state of change. For a revolutionary like Lenin, this meant that revolution, a form of change, was more natural than its illusory opposite, the notion longed for by conservatives, that ideas, history, tradition and so on were, or could be, unchanging. In fact, dialectical thinking was by no means a monopoly of revolutionaries. Liberals, social Darwinists and even some of the more subtle conservatives, believed that interaction of opposites and ensuing change were inevitable. However, for the more extreme conservatives and reactionaries, who abounded in Russia, such ideas were anathema and fitted in badly with, for example, traditional religious assumptions about the revelation of absolute truth. If truth was known through revelation how could it evolve? Lenin keenly adopted dialectics as the philosophical underpinning of a world moving inexorably towards revolution, using dialectics as a tool to ridicule those fighting a constant rearguard action against innovation in the name of revelation.

However, Lenin's philosophical musings were not published at this time. Instead, he went full steam ahead with the polemic with the majority of the Second International which had supported the war and wrote his predictions about the war hastening the revolution which we have already examined. The new situation caused him some, usually temporary, re-evaluations. According to a newspaper report of a speech against the war which he gave in Lausanne on 14 October Lenin praised his former friend Martov for 'doing precisely what a social democrat should do. He is criticizing his government.' [CW 36 300–1]

The routine in Lenin's life in Switzerland was based, as usual, on libraries, writing and lecturing, largely in Russian émigré circles which included Plekhanov, Axel'rod, Martov, Trotsky and Angelica Balabanoff, as well as the core Leninist group itself. In this respect the Shklovskys and the Zinovievs were Lenin's closest companions and comrades in arms along with Bukharin, G.L. Pyatakov, E.F. Rozmirovich and Evgeniia Bosh. Key correspondents included Alexander Shlyapnikov and Alexandra Kollontai who spent the war years in the other main neutral zone, Scandinavia. Of course, some Leninists were in prison and exile including Kamenev and Stalin. The latter had yet to fully make his mark on Lenin who, despite having called him 'his splendid Georgian', had actually had to be reminded of his name during the war. [CW 43 469] Later, when released from prison after the February Revolution, Stalin was to become one of Lenin's closest and most reliable assistants. Also in prison were the five Bolshevik deputies to the State Duma who were arrested for their opposition to the war in late 1914. It was still a tiny group.

Cultural and recreational distractions appear to have been less frequent in wartime but, as before, Lenin and Krupskaya took many, sometimes lengthy, visits to the mountains. The routine was disrupted by family bereavements, the arrival of Inessa Armand as a near-neighbour and companion and the convening of several important left-wing conferences in Switzerland which meant that, if Lenin could not travel to meet other socialists in other countries, at least a trickle of them were able to come to Switzerland. As ever, the Ulyanovs' existence involved a constant battle for funds to keep the wolf from the door.

Once they had settled in Berne Lenin was quick to invite Inessa Armand, who was also living in Switzerland, to join them. She did so and by October was living 'across the road' [Krupskaya 252] from Lenin and Krupskaya. Krupskaya describes the relationship. The autumn of 1914 was, she recalled, 'glorious' and they took frequent walks in the nearby forest.

> We would wander for hours along the forest roads, bestrewn with fallen yellow leaves. On most occasions the three of us went together on these walks, Vladimir Il'ich, Inessa and myself. Vladimir Il'ich would develop his plans of the international struggle. Inessa took it all very much to heart. In this unfolding struggle she began to take a most direct part, conducting correspondence, translating our documents into French and English, gathering materials, talking with people etc. Sometimes we would sit for hours on the sunlit, wooded mountainside while Il'ich jotted down outlines of his speeches and articles and polished his formulations; I studied Italian with the aid of a Toussain textbook; Inessa sewed a skirt and basked with delight in the autumnal sun – she had not yet fully recovered from the effects of her imprisonment. [Krupskaya 252]

If there ever had been an affair between Lenin and Inessa it was certainly over by this time. They remained close friends and comrades in the struggle but there is no evidence of the transient heat which characterized their relationship in 1910. While they were apart from 1912 to 1914, their letters were frequent and cordial but less intimate than Inessa's letter in which she said she was in love with Lenin. Throughout, Nadezhda and Inessa maintained an unaffectedly friendly relationship.

The spring of 1915 brought a deep personal blow for Krupskaya. Her mother died on 20 March and was cremated and her ashes buried on 23 March. Her death brought an unexpected problem. It exposed the Ulyanovs' irreligious outlook to their pious landlady who, in a singularly unchristian and uncharitable way, requested her tenants to look for a room elsewhere so she could rent hers out to Christians. Mourning was brief as the two of them threw themselves into an International Socialist Women's Conference held in Berne from 26 to 28 March. As it happened the war years also brought the death of Lenin's mother on 25 July 1916. Lenin maintained a revolutionary stiff upper lip but his love and affection for his mother remained undimmed and, within a few hours of his eventual return to Petrograd in April 1917, he visited the grave where she lay next to Lenin's sister Olga.

LENIN'S WARTIME POLITICS

Conferences and meetings were the restricted arenas in which Lenin was able to play out wartime politics in Switzerland. The first confrontation came in Lausanne on 11 October 1914. Plekhanov was scheduled to make a speech to rally Mensheviks to the defence of Russia (defensism). Like other socialist groups they were splitting over the war and a left wing, including Martov, was inclining towards internationalism. Lenin decided to go although he was uncertain as to whether the organizers would let him in. We do not have the text of his speech but we do have accounts of the event. Lenin was allowed in and listened intently to Plekhanov's speech. The first part, which enunciated some general Marxist principles, brought applause from Lenin. However, the second half was an argument in favour of defensism. Plekhanov's remarks were met with warm support. Indeed, the audience were Plekhanov's people. Even Lenin still respected him and hoped he would be converted to internationalism. At the end of his speech, there was a call for comments from the audience. Only one person responded. Lenin walked nervously forward, glass of beer in hand. It was rather like a bull entering the arena after the matador's parade and early flourishes. In the teeth of the enemy Lenin courageously stood up and put forward the point of view we have already seen him articulating in his articles of September, the need for working-class solidarity and the transformation of the war into a civil war. He spoke for about ten minutes. Plekhanov took the floor to despatch the brave bull which he did to great adulation from the audience, which was, in any case, predisposed to his side. None the less, Lenin had made his point even though he appeared to have lost that particular fight. Needless to say, the intensity of the occasion affected his nerves and he was in a state of great excitement after it. However, his nerves and his confidence were somewhat restored on 14 October when he spoke at a meeting of his own. He stressed working-class solidarity in the face of imperialist war and it was on this occasion that he even partially praised Martov for doing the right thing. He also lectured on the war and socialism in Geneva on 15 October. His positions were very well received by his audience.

Switzerland was one of the only places left in Europe where vestigial international conferences of the left could be held. One of the earliest was the International Conference of Socialist Women held in March 1915, a few days after the death of Krupskaya's mother. Lenin himself could not be a delegate but he directed the Bolshevik delegation, which consisted of Nadezhda, Inessa and Lilina Zinoviev. In true Bolshevik fashion they split the conference and refused to budge. After some tense wrangling a compromise was reached whereby the majority resolution stood but the minority Bolshevik resolution was minuted. The Bolshevik culture of hard-line confrontation was not being softened by the war. They remained a supposedly democratic group which refused to accept majority decisions, other than their own. It was a similar story a week later when an International Socialist Youth Conference also met in Berne from 5 to 7 April. Again excluded from direct participation Lenin held court in a nearby café, and sympathetic delegates came and went in a steady stream looking for guidance on what steps to take next in the conference.

The two most important such conferences, however, were the anti-war conferences held at Zimmerwald (5–8 September 1915) and Kienthal (24–30 April 1916). The timing of the Zimmerwald Conference meant it interrupted the Ulyanovs' usual summer mountain holiday. In fact, for once it was Krupskaya's health, her persistent problems with Graves' disease – a thyroid condition which caused her goitre, bulging eyes, heart palpitations and infrequent periods – which flared up once more after her mother's death, that caused them to leave Berne for a base near the mountains. They chose Soerenberg at the foot of the Rothorn. As usual, they enjoyed almost idyllic surroundings. 'We were quite comfortable at Soerenberg; all around there were woods, high mountains and there was even snow on the peak of the Rothorn.' The punctuality of the Swiss post and the efficiency of Swiss organization meant that Lenin could request any book from the Berne or Zurich libraries and it would arrive two days later – 'a complete contrast to bureaucratic France ... This arrangement enabled Il'ich to work in this out-of-the-way place. Il'ich had nothing but praise for Swiss culture.' Their way of life contrasted with the turmoil of war going on around them and against which Lenin was directing his intellectual energies:

It was very comfortable to work at Soerenberg. Some time later Inessa came to stay with us. We would rise early and before dinner, which was served at 12 o'clock everywhere in Switzerland, each of us would work in different nooks of the garden. During those hours Inessa often played the piano, and it was particularly good to work to the sounds of the music that reached us. After dinner we sometimes went to the mountains for the rest of the day. Il'ich loved the mountains – he liked to get to the crags of the Rothorn towards evening,

> when the view above was marvellous and below the fog was turning
> rosy ... We went to bed with roosters, gathered alpine roses, berries;
> all of us were mushroom-pickers ... and we argued with so much
> heat about their classification that one might have thought it was a
> question or resolution involving important principles. [Krupskaya
> 264–5]

Despite wrenching himself away from this magical world, Lenin threw
himself heart and soul into the conference. Even though this was a conference largely of the left and of anti-war socialists many of whom
shared Lenin's approach, he was unable to command a majority. His left-
wing platform was outvoted nineteen to twelve. It seemed that, for
Lenin, opposition, rather than being in the majority, continued to be his
natural stance. Not that Lenin enjoyed defeat. Once again he had to
recuperate. He rejoined Krupskaya back in the mountains. Il'ich, she
recalled,

> came back from the Zimmerwald Conference in a state of irritation.
> The day after Il'ich's return from Zimmerwald we climbed the
> Rothorn. We climbed with a 'glorious appetite', but when we reached
> the summit, Il'ich suddenly lay down on the ground in an uncomfort-
> able position almost on the snow, and fell asleep. Clouds gathered
> then broke; the view of the Alps from the Rothorn was splendid and
> Lenin slept like the dead. He never stirred and slept over an hour.
> Apparently Zimmerwald had frayed his nerves a good deal and had
> taken much strength out of him. It required several days of roaming
> over the mountains and the atmosphere of Soerenberg before Il'ich
> was himself again. [Krupskaya 267]

While the beauties of the scenery and the delights of country and
mountain walks and cycle rides were essential to Lenin they were only
the backdrop and support to his real passion of revolutionary politics.
Defeat at Zimmerwald found him ready for the fray once more as the
follow-up conference at Kienthal approached. True to his conception of
the way the war would go he detected a steady, but still minority, growth
of anti-war sentiment in Europe and a strengthening of the 'Zimmerwald
left' in particular. However, Kienthal itself was no more Leninist than
its predecessor. There were twelve delegates out of forty-three

supporting the left, including the Bolshevik delegation of Lenin, Zinoviev and Inessa Armand. Once again there were fierce disputes but, try as he might, the majority remained firmly opposed to Lenin's position, essentially still that of turning the imperialist war into a European-wide class and revolutionary civil war. Even so, Lenin was optimistic, summing the results up in a letter to Shliapnikov. 'After all, a manifesto was adopted … that is a step forward.' 'On the whole,' he continued, 'despite the mass of defects' it was 'a step towards a break with the social patriots'. [CW 36 390–1]

Kienthal does not seem to have taken it out of Lenin the way Zimmerwald had done. The Ulyanovs had been living 'quietly', as Lenin put it, in Zurich since early 1916 when they had gone there for a fortnight for Lenin to use the libraries in connection with his pamphlet on imperialism which was the centre of his attention. They kept postponing their return until they eventually settled down there, finding it more lively than Berne. It also brought them into contact with members of the sparse Swiss working class. They rented an unsuitable room from a shoemaker rather than a better one they might have had because they 'greatly valued their hosts'. The house had a mixture of German, Italian and Austrian, as well as Russian, inhabitants. There was no atmosphere of chauvinism. One day, when the women of the various nationalities were talking around the gas stove the shoemaker's wife, 'Frau Kammerer, exclaimed indignantly: "The soldiers ought to turn their weapons against their governments!" After that Il'ich would not listen to any suggestions about changing quarters.' [Krupskaya 272]

Krupskaya also gives another anecdote from later in the year when they had moved out of the city into the mountains for summer, once again for her health as much as Lenin's. They chose an inexpensive 'rest resort' in Chudivise 'amidst wild mountains, very high up and not far from the snow peaks'. It had three drawbacks. The first was a milk diet 'which we positively howled against' and supplemented 'by eating raspberries and blackberries which grew in the vicinity in great quantities'. Second, the rest home was an eight-kilometre donkey ride from the station. Apart from delaying the post this also meant guests returning home had to leave early. As a result, almost every morning at six some guests would leave and a song of farewell, with a refrain about 'goodbye cuckoo', would be sung. 'Vladimir Il'ich, who liked to sleep in the morning, would grumble and bury his head under the quilt'. Finally, the place was non-political, 'they did not even talk about the war'. 'Among the visitors was a soldier' sent at state expense to help a lung condition. 'He was quite a nice fellow. Vladimir Il'ich hovered about him like a cat after lard, tried several times to engage him in conversation about the predatory character of the war; the fellow would not contradict him, but he was clearly not interested. It seemed that he was very little interested in political questions in general, certainly less than in his stay at Chudivise.' [Krupskaya 278–9]

The Ulyanovs stayed at Chudivise from mid-July to the end of August. Although Lenin thought about politics a great deal and talked to Krupskaya about his ideas, there were no Russians there, it was too remote for visitors and there were no libraries so Lenin was completely unable to work in his usual way. Eventually, it was their turn to leave and have 'goodbye cuckoo' sung to them.

> As we were descending through a wood, Vladimir Il'ich suddenly noticed white mushrooms, and in spite of the fact that it was raining he began eagerly picking them, as though they were so many Zimmerwald Lefts [i.e. his opponents from the Zimmerwald Conference]. We were drenched to the bone, but picked a sackful of mushrooms. Of course we missed the train and had to wait two hours at the station for the next one. [Krupskaya 279]

It is hard to realize that this delightful moment – of two committed intellectual companions, harmlessly picking mushrooms, failing to engage locals in political conversation and generally spending a delightful six weeks cut off from the world – was only six months before Lenin's return to Russia and only a year before he was to find himself running the world's largest country. It was the last time the Ulyanovs were able to be quite so carefree. Once they returned to the Kammerer's in Zurich the approaching revolution slowly rose in their perspective.

Though, of course, they did not know it, the Ulyanovs' return to Zurich, still wet but triumphantly carrying their sack of mushrooms, opened up the final phase of their long exile. The autumn and winter were largely spent in the usual round of lectures, libraries and articles. Lenin continued to live more like the professor he often passed himself off as than a revolutionary activist. 'In the autumn of 1916 and the beginning of 1917 Il'ich steeped himself in theoretical work. He tried to utilize all the time the library was open. He got there at exactly 9 o'clock, stayed until 12, came home exactly at ten minutes past 12 (the library was closed from 12 to one), after lunch he returned to the library and stayed until six.' [Krupskaya 284] Working at home was difficult not least because of the distraction of unwanted visitors trying to get Lenin involved in the overheated intrigues of the Russian émigré colony in Zurich. To make matters worse there was a sausage factory across the street which gave out 'an intolerable stench' [Krupskaya 284] which prevented the window from being opened during the day.

Throughout the war finances had been a problem, particularly after Maria senior's death since the pension handed on from her husband had, for many years, provided a secure but small base income to which Vladimir Il'ich could turn. The saga of who controlled Social Democratic Party funds had rumbled on from 1906 to 1914 without clear resolution. Much of the funding had been frozen in this period. Despite constantly bumping along the borderline of impecuniousness, Lenin, as we have seen, managed to live the life he desired and to accomplish his main aims of publishing. However, in autumn 1916 the financial situation looked particularly dire. 'Il'ich searched everywhere for something to earn – he wrote to Granat [a publishing house], to Gorky, to relatives and once even developed a fantastic plan to publish a "pedagogical encyclopaedia".' [Krupskaya 284] It was so bad that, for the first time, Krupskaya even contemplated getting a job! For what she describes as a 'semi-mythical' income, she became secretary of the Bureau for Political Emigrant Relief. Even so there was still time for the beloved walks in the mountains:

> On Thursdays, after lunch when the library was closed, we went to the Zürichberg mountain. On his way from the library Il'ich usually brought two bars of nut chocolate, in blue wrappers, at 15 centimes a piece, and after lunch we took the chocolate and some books and went to the mountains. We had a favourite spot there in the very thick of the woods, where there was no crowd. Il'ich would lie there on the grass and read diligently. [Krupskaya 284]

What was Lenin reading? What was the theoretical work in which he steeped himself in these last few months of his intelligentsia way of life? Largely it was the issues of imperialism, opportunism, war and the coming revolution which continued to be at the centre of his attention. Imperialism had raised questions of the role of the state in advanced capitalist society and, conversely, of its role in the socialist transition. No doubt, much of his thinking laid the foundation for *State and Revolution* which he wrote later in 1917.

Reading was also Lenin's lifeline to the outside world. During the war, Switzerland was the peaceful eye of a hurricane raging all around. It was from this protected bubble that Lenin peered into the maelstrom. Though it did not happen all at once the world was changing. The melting pot of war was altering social relations of class and gender. The massive incorporation of the male population into the military via conscription led to rising expectations. Above all, a determination that such things should never happen again got stronger and stronger. Having been expected to pay the butcher's bill, working-class men began to insist on some return and, as a minimum, greater rights in making national decisions. Working-class women also came out of the home in larger numbers than ever though many were happy to return to it after the war, if they still had partners, in order to get back to the deferred task of having families. Middle-class women began to agitate anew for the vote. National rivalries and alliances were deepening. After the war, large multi-ethnic empires collapsed and a whole raft of new states came into existence. Harder to pinpoint but perhaps more profound in the long run, a cultural revolution was under way. In the face of a mass slaughter that more and more people saw as unnecessary the remnants of scientific optimism about progress were blown away. The end products of human scientific and technological ingenuity seemed only to be more and more effective engines of death. Intellectual and social escapism took hold in certain circles. Left-wing parties burgeoned and, particularly in defeated countries, revolution approached.

While much of this remained concealed or only half-formed in 1916, Lenin would have been able to perceive some of it. In particular, he was following, as closely as he could, the developing crisis in Russia. 1915 had been a disastrous year, with massive military defeats leading to retreat and loss of territory. Masses of refugees were cast adrift and flowed through the Russian home front as a major destabilizing factor. Many of them were Jews and their flight completely broke down the attempt to confine them to the 'Pale of Settlement' in the west. Panicky generals talked of falling back even further. Some of them found a handy scapegoat for their own ineptitude in 'Jewish spies' who supposedly gave away vital secrets to the enemy. Vicious pogroms broke out in the remnants of Russian Poland as the army retreated. The appalled government called for them to stop, not only on humanitarian grounds, but also because they alienated the British, French and American bankers on whom Russia relied to finance the war.

The crisis came to a head in August 1915. Nicholas, foolishly, decided to promote himself to the rank of Commander-in-Chief of the armed forces. His ministers objected on two grounds, one overt, the other, more serious but covert. The former argument was that by taking such a step, Nicholas was associating himself too closely with the fate of the army, which looked bleak at that moment. More seriously, they were concerned that the decision imposed a virtual military dictatorship in that Nicholas would spend more time at military headquarters in western Russia and less with them in Petrograd. His absence did cause a vacuum and most of the objecting ministers were rapidly replaced. Their replacements were also soon replaced with an apparent reduction in competence at each change. A sinister game of 'ministerial leapfrog' was being played and everyone's candidates for gamemaster were Rasputin and Alexandra, Nicholas's wife. The rumour spread that they headed a pro-German faction determined to bring Russia down. Such legends, for there was no truth in them, were extremely powerful in undermining loyalty at all levels. Even more unsettling were three other areas of developing crisis. A broad swathe of conservative and 'moderate' members of the Fourth Duma began to agitate for more power. Their position was simple. The autocracy was increasingly incompetent and only they, the Duma members, could bring it back to its senses before disaster struck. They set up a Progressive Bloc in August 1915 which became the foundation for Duma action in the February Revolution of 1917. Its leading members formed the Provisional Government. Their middle- and upper-class anxieties were being fuelled by a gradual but unmistakable return of working-class militancy from late 1915 on and also by a developing food crisis. This was partially caused by oversupply to the military but also by a reduction in the peasants' incentive to market grain as the price of scarce industrial goods soared out of their reach. Gloomy news for the Duma politicians was balm to the eyes of Lenin as he read of the growing turmoil in his homeland.

In the long term, as we have seen, there is no doubt that Lenin expected the war to turn into a European revolution. However, some observers have argued that Lenin did not foresee the collapse of tsarism. Indeed, like the vast majority of people, including those from all sides on the spot and Nicholas II himself, the actual downfall of the autocracy was to be a shock. While many thought its days were numbered hardly anyone was prepared for the actual collapse. In faraway Switzerland, dependent on inaccurate newspaper reports, Lenin could not be expected to be more clairvoyant than anyone else. However, it is frequently claimed that he wrote, at about this time, that he would not live to see the coming revolution. Nothing could be further from the truth.

The misunderstanding comes from a misreading of the conclusion of one of the last two important public speeches Lenin made before his return. In a 'Lecture on the 1905 Revolution' given to young Swiss workers in German on 22 January 1917, the twelfth anniversary of 'Bloody Sunday', Lenin outlined the main features of the first Russian Revolution. He stressed several points which were key to his own strategy in 1917, namely, the rapidity with which a revolutionary situation can arise; the leading role of striking proletarians; the rapid spread of revolution to the peasant countryside which looked to the workers of the towns for leadership; and the fracturing of the army, since 'militarism can never and under no circumstances be defeated and destroyed, except by a victorious struggle of one section of the national army against the other section', that is by civil war. The purpose of the speech was, of course, to arouse the revolutionary enthusiasm of the young audience to which he was speaking. At the end, Lenin exhorted them not to be 'deceived by the present grave-like stillness in Europe. Europe is pregnant with revolution. The monstrous horrors of the imperialist war, the suffering caused by the high cost of living everywhere engender a revolutionary mood.' [CW 1 802] A few moments later he made the statement which is so misunderstood. 'We of the older generation may not live to see the decisive battles of the coming revolution.' [CW 1 802] Clearly this did not mean Lenin was not expecting revolution. It meant exactly the opposite. The revolution was 'coming' but it might not reach its conclusion in Lenin's lifetime, quite another matter. It could, Lenin implied, take decades for the total overthrow of capitalism to be ensured.

It has, indeed, also been suggested that, as a result of consultations with physicians in Switzerland, Lenin may have been aware that his lifetime was likely to be short, that he was suffering from the same complaint that had cut his father down at the age of fifty-four (and he was already forty-six). Lenin did in fact die at the age of fifty-three after being seriously ill for nearly two years.[7]

Be that as it may, Lenin was certainly expecting revolution, as he had been since the beginning of the war, but exactly what revolution and where it would break out first was impossible for anyone to foresee with precision. In the event, the news of the fall of the tsar in March 1917 hit the Russian community in Zurich like a thunderbolt. 'After dinner, when Il'ich was getting ready to leave for the library, and I had finished with the dishes, Bronsky ran in with the announcement, "Haven't you heard the news? There is a revolution in Russia."' The Russians flocked to the lake where the latest editions of the newspapers were displayed. There was no doubt. Revolution had broken out, the tsar had gone. In a moment, the Ulyanovs' lives had been turned upside down. The routine of the library gave way to a feverish desire on the part of Lenin and most of the other exiles to get back to Russia. Where there had been diffidence in 1905, largely because the tsarist authorities remained intact throughout, there was now eagerness to return. But how? The British and French would not want to allow Russians opposed to the war to return for obvious reasons. Taking a passage through Germany was risky as it might open them to the charge of collusion with the enemy. Indeed, in July 1917 exactly that charge was laid at Lenin's door. Clandestine return by aircraft was too fantastic. A Swedish passport might be possible but no one knew any Swedish. Krupskaya teased Lenin that if they did disguise themselves as Swedes then he would give them away because in his dreams he would see Mensheviks and start swearing out loud at them in Russian as he slept. [Krupskaya 288]

In the end, Lenin's Swiss friend, socialist politician and fellow internationalist, Fritz Platten, negotiated conditions with the German ambassador for émigrés to return through Germany to Sweden and then to Finland and Petrograd. It was on this basis that 32 returnees, including Lenin, Krupskaya, Inessa Armand, the Zinovievs and Radek plus Fritz Platten, boarded their special railway carriage and set out across Germany on 9 April. They left and crossed to Sweden on 12 April where they were greeted by local socialists including the mayor of Stockholm on the 13th. Lenin left Stockholm that evening and eventually arrived in Petrograd's Finland Station at 11pm on 16 April. He, and the rest of the group, were welcomed by a noisy crowd at the station. The most significant phase in the life of Lenin and of the Revolution had begun.

5

FROM THE FINLAND STATION
TO THE WINTER PALACE

From the moment the news of the February Revolution broke, Lenin and most of the Russian émigré community in Switzerland were in a fever. Every scrap of information and rumour was scrutinized; plans were made for future tactics; a desperate desire to get back to the centre of events in Petrograd consumed most of them. According to Krupskaya, Lenin wrote to Alexandra Kollontai in Sweden, 'Never *again* along the lines of the Second International! Never *again* with Kautsky! By all means a *more revolutionary* programme and more revolutionary tactics ... revolutionary propaganda, as heretofore, agitation and struggle for an *international* proletarian revolution and for the seizure of power by the "Soviets of Workers' Deputies" (but not by Kadet fakers).' [Krupskaya 287] Though he probably didn't realize it he had already unlocked the gateway to power. By establishing his party as the opponents of the emerging Provisional Government led by Kadets (i.e. liberals like Miliukov of the Constitutional Democratic Party), Lenin was eventually to gather in all the growing opposition to that government on the left. However, in the early stages of the Revolution his position was very much that of a small minority. We will, of course, trace the stages by which the majority came to support Lenin.

Lenin had no sense that standing against the Provisional Government would be crucial. In March and April, it was only one aspect of a series of principles and strategies he proposed to his Party to guide them in the crisis. In particular, he wrote a series of *Letters From Afar* while he was still in Switzerland and in his first intervention on his return, *The Tasks of the Proletariat in the Present Revolution* laid down his ten commandments which have come to be known as *The April Theses*. For the moment, however, Lenin led nothing. Only the first of his five *Letters From Afar* was published at the time and *The April Theses* were met with incredulity by many Party leaders. What was Lenin saying in these crucial weeks up to his return?

There was little that was new in these works. Rather, they were the encapsulation of the themes which had already emerged. Fundamental to everything was Lenin's identification of the war as a continuing imperialist war – not a war of national defence, still less a revolutionary war – and Russia's new Provisional Government as the handmaiden of Anglo-French capital. The Revolution, he argued, had been instigated to strengthen Russia's part in the imperialist dogfight. The first *Letter from Afar* made these points crystal clear. 'That it is an imperialist war on *both* sides is now … indisputable.' [SW 2 3] One of the main forces behind the February Revolution, and the one which had assumed its leadership, was

the conspiracy of the Anglo-French imperialists who impelled Milyukov, Guchkov and Co. to seize power *for the purpose of continuing the imperialist war*, for the purpose of conducting the war still more ferociously and obstinately, for the purpose of *slaughtering fresh millions* of Russian workers and peasants in order that the Guchkovs might obtain Constantinople, the French capitalists Syria, the British capitalists Mesopotamia, and so on. [SW 2 5]

From the point of view of Marxist revolution Lenin repeated his view that February represented the beginning of the transition from the first stage of the Revolution to its second stage. In the third, unpublished, *Letter from Afar* Lenin referred to 'the *factual* conclusion I drew in my first letter, namely: that the February–March Revolution was merely the *first stage* of the revolution. Russia is passing through a peculiar historical moment of *transition* to the next stage … to a "second revolution".' [CW 23 323]

The first *Letter from Afar* also went into greater detail about the main contending forces at work in Russia. For Lenin these were threefold: the autocracy, the bourgeoisie and the workers. The antagonism between the first two was, he said, not deep. He even believed the Provisional Government would work for a tsarist restoration and that 'the *whole* of the new government is monarchist, for Kerensky's *verbal* republicanism cannot be taken seriously, is not worthy of a statesman and is, *objectively*, political chicanery.' [SW 2 8] In fact Kerensky remained a republican and formally introduced the Russian Republic in September. Lenin was, however, partly correct in that the instinct of Miliukov and others was to preserve the monarchy but they were prevented from pursuing their hopes by popular opposition and the absence of a credible candidate. He was also right about the first two forces coming together and was particularly scathing about leftists who ignored this process and claimed they were supporting the bourgeoisie as a lesser evil than tsarism. 'He who says the workers must *support* the new government in the interests of the struggle against tsarist reaction (and apparently this is being said …) is a traitor to the workers.' [SW 2 8] For Lenin, it was still the same imperialist monster and must be opposed: 'this new government is *already* bound hand and foot by imperialist capital, by the imperialist policy of *war* and plunder.' [SW 2 8] The government was 'as regards the *present* war but the agent of the billion-dollar "firm" "England and France"'. [SW 2 7]

One aspect of Lenin's thought in 1917 which differed substantially from his ideas of 1905 was a greater appreciation of the role of soviets. Initially set up in the earlier revolution as committees to co-ordinate strikes they quickly took on the role of organs of mass self-expression but Lenin barely noticed them and rarely visited them. In 1917 they emerged rapidly in towns across the length and breadth of the Empire. Like the most important of them, the Petrograd Soviet, they brought together masses of workers, plus a crucial component of soldiers and/or sailors, together with radical intellectuals who took the lead. There were even some soviets in rural areas though in most of the countryside the political space occupied by soviets in the urban areas was more likely to be filled by village and *volost'* (parish) committees. Having learned from 1905, Lenin immediately identified the Soviets of Workers' Deputies as the focus of mass proletarian action describing them as 'an organization of the workers, the embryo of a workers' government, the representative of the entire mass of the *poor* section of the population, i.e. of nine-tenths of the population, which is striving for *peace, bread* and *freedom*' [SW 2 7], a broad front which may reflect a populist substrate still present in Lenin's outlook. In more Marxist fashion he identified the 'broad mass of rural semi-proletarians and partly also the small-peasant population' as its allies along with the proletariat of other countries. 'With these two allies,' he concluded, 'the proletariat, *utilizing the peculiarities* of the present situation, can and will proceed first to the achievement of a democratic republic and complete victory of the peasantry over the landlords, instead of the Guchkov–Miliukov semi-monarchy, and then to *socialism*, which alone can give the war-weary people *peace*, *bread* and *freedom*.' [SW 2 10]

He did not leave his analysis there. In these last émigré writings he made a number of other important points, many of which stayed with him in 1917 and are crucial to understanding his strategy and tactics. He believed 1905 had been a practice run and in February 'this eight-day revolution was "performed", if we may use a metaphorical expression, as though after a dozen major and minor rehearsals; the "actors" knew each other, their parts, their places and their setting in every detail' [SW 2 2], but it had 'required a great, mighty and all-powerful "stage-manager", capable … of vastly accelerating the course of world history' in order for the revolution to evolve from its 1905 to 1917 stage. 'This all-powerful "stage-manager", this mighty accelerator, was the imperialist war.' [SW 2 2] In accordance with his predictions of September 1914 he concluded that the imperialist 'war was bound, to turn into a civil war between the hostile classes'. [SW 2 3] But one should not forget that the fact that the February Revolution succeeded so rapidly was 'only due to the fact that, as a result of an extremely unique historical situation, *absolutely dissimilar currents*, *absolutely heterogeneous* class interests, *absolutely contrary* political and social strivings have merged, and in a strikingly "harmonious" manner.' [SW 2 5] These will soon break up into the capitalist-imperialist interest on one hand and the 'as yet underdeveloped and comparatively weak *workers' government*' [SW 2 7] focused on the soviet.

Other crucial Leninist themes emerged. The third, also unpublished, *Letter from Afar*, pointed to themes of the necessity to organize; to prepare for civil war; to contemplate a new form of state organization with, at its heart, a citizen-militia. He already formulated the key text of his later pamphlet *State and Revolution* when he wrote that bourgeois revolutions only perfected and transferred the state machine from the hands of one party to another when the point was to smash it. [CW 23 325–6]

Here, and in the important *Farewell Letter to the Swiss Workers* of 8 April, he argued that even a massive, soviet-based worker–peasant revolution would still not be socialism but only a step towards it. He also returned to his ambiguities about the revolutionary potential of the Russian working class:

> To the Russian proletariat has fallen the great honour of *beginning* the series of revolutions which the imperialist war has made an objective inevitability. But the idea that the Russian proletariat is the chosen revolutionary proletariat among the workers of the world is absolutely alien to us. We know perfectly well that the proletariat of Russia is less organized, less prepared and less class-conscious than the proletariat of other countries. It is not its special qualities, but rather the special conjuncture of historical circumstances that *for a certain, perhaps very short, time* has made the proletariat of Russia the vanguard of the revolutionary proletariat of the whole world.
>
> Russia is a peasant country, one of the most backward of European countries. Socialism *cannot* triumph there *directly* and *immediately*. But the peasant character of the country ... *may* make our revolution the *prologue* to the world socialist revolution, a *step* toward it. [CW 23 371]

However, the future really hinged on another proletariat: 'The German proletariat is the most trustworthy, the most reliable ally of the Russian and the world proletarian revolution.' [CW 23 372]

In these words, before he had even left Switzerland, Lenin had interpreted the February Revolution in the light of his earlier predictions and, to at least his own satisfaction, had confirmed his expectations. His prediction of the war turning into a civil war was, he said, ridiculed by the opportunists but now 'only the blind can fail to see' that 'transformation of the imperialist war into civil war is *becoming* a fact.' [CW 23 372] The future·promised a massive battle of workers against capitalists and peasants against landowners by means of armed force. But even this would only lead to the establishment of the 'democratic republic of workers and peasants'. It would only be a step towards socialism, not socialism itself.

On arrival in Petrograd Lenin, who had been working hard on the journey, produced his brilliant theses. They had the impact of a hand

grenade and shocked many, even among his closest allies. [SW 2 13–16]
Partly this was caused by context, partly by content. The Petrograd to
which Lenin returned was still celebrating its liberation from autocracy
and, while the initial euphoria of February had worn thin, there was still
a lingering sense of national honeymoon, bringing the whole country
together in a spirit of hope and renewal around the new situation.
When Lenin and the rest of the group of revolutionaries returned to the
city via the Finland Station it was an excuse for a radical party. It has
often been suggested that his return was seen as being especially porten-
tous but that is largely an anachronistic accretion from the later cult of
his personality. Lenin was welcomed as a prominent radical but not in
fundamentally different terms from many others. However, he was soon
to show his distinctiveness. Even his closest loyalists could hardly
believe what they were hearing. His injunctions caused widespread
bewilderment. Like a schoolmaster in front of a dim class Lenin, as he
said himself, read out his theses twice, very slowly. That was not
enough. It took some three weeks of intense struggle in the Party to
persuade the majority that he was correct.

The point that caused most immediate controversy was his injunction that there should be 'no support for the Provisional Government'.
Lenin was not the first of his group to arrive back in Petrograd. He had
been preceded by returned exiles, notably Kamenev and Stalin. They
had made policy as they thought appropriate in Lenin's absence and had
gone along with the mainstream in the Soviet who accepted the
Provisional Government and worked with it in order to consolidate the
overthrow of tsarism. The accepted wisdom among the Soviet leaders
was that, if they alienated or opposed the Provisional Government, they
might drive it, and the middle class it represented, back into the arms
of the autocracy. Added to that, many Mensheviks also argued that
Russia was not ready for a full-scale Marxist revolution. As we have
seen, even Lenin shared their scepticism about the Russian working
class, but he was prepared to pursue radical revolution in Russia with
the overwhelming aim of spreading it to the rest of Europe.

There were other key points in *The April Theses*. The theoretical
underpinning of his views remained that the war 'unquestionably
remains on Russia's part a predatory imperialist war' and as a result 'not
the slightest concession to "revolutionary defencism" is permissible'. He
meant by this that those who said it was now right to fight for Russia

because it was a democracy overlooked the fact of 'the capitalist nature of [the] government'. Only a worker and poor peasant government which renounced conquest and made 'a complete break' with 'all capitalist interests' could conduct a war of revolutionary defence. Closely related to this was his assertion that Russia was '*passing* from the first stage of the revolution to its *second* stage which must put power into the hands of the proletariat and the poorest sections of the peasantry'. His reason for the revolution being only at the first, bourgeois, rather than second, proletarian, stage is interesting. Lenin attributed it to 'the insufficient class-consciousness and organization of the proletariat'. Once again he made a point of working-class backwardness.

A whole host of Leninist themes poured out in the theses. Soviets should take the lead. In an easy phrase to write but a concept that was much more difficult to realize, Lenin called for 'Abolition of the police, army and bureaucracy', that is the smashing of the existing state machine. It was the greatest of ironies, and one of the most profound historical processes for us to analyse, that the system Lenin created was characterized precisely by its police, army and bureaucracy.

On the land question he called for 'Confiscation of all landed estates' and followed this with a proposal for 'Nationalisation of *all* lands in the country, the land to be disposed of by the local Soviets of Agricultural Labourers' and Peasants' Deputies.' Large estates should not be broken up but maintained by the local soviets as model farms. We will return to the deeper implications of this crucial point, but for the moment we can see several immediate ones. The peasants' desire to take over estates should be resisted. Their land, too, should be taken over – in order to equalize 'rich' 'kulak' and poor peasant holdings. The model farms should show the advantages of large-scale over small-scale farming as beacons guiding the peasants to their more productive future. Lenin certainly did not envisage peasant farming as anything other than a brake on Russia's progress. There were also concerns, spread across the whole political spectrum, that the large estates produced most of the surplus that fed the army and towns. To allow the peasants to take it over would endanger the food supply to the non-rural population since peasants would use much of the extra capacity to raise their own living standards rather than market the surplus. One should also note Lenin's care not to put local soviets in the hands of the peasants as a whole but to put 'the weight of emphasis in the agrarian programme' on agricultural labourers and poor peasants who should be organized separately from each other and from wealthier peasants, the point being to further class struggle between different peasant groups. His discourse about class differentiation among peasants, going back to the 1890s, was still prominent in his approach to the peasant question, though he changed the nuances of it many times in the next five years.

Surprising to his audience, but not to us since we have seen him use the concept already, was his assertion that 'It is not our *immediate* task to "introduce" socialism'. Instead, they should initially be satisfied with bringing 'social production and the distribution of products at once under the *control* [that is, supervision] of the Soviets of Workers' Deputies.' Combining that with his previous point, about calling for the amalgamation of all banks into a single, national bank and control of that also to be exercised by the soviets, comprised the skimpy elements of Lenin's economic policy or, more precisely, policy of economic transition which we will need to look at in much greater detail later. Suffice it to say, despite being a Marxist who understood the economy to be the foundation of the culture and politics of an era, Lenin's theses were almost entirely political. His, in a sense, Bakuninist streak, of putting emphasis on political struggle and the destruction of the state, was more prominent than his economically 'determinist' Marxism.

Although these were the points which were most stressed by Lenin we must not overlook others which were made briefly and almost in passing. It was only point nine out of ten that referred to 'Party tasks' listed briefly as 'convocation of a party congress', 'alteration of the party programme' – especially when it came to the issues of imperialist war, the 'commune state', as he called it, and amendment of the minimum programme – and 'change of the party's name'. All these shared the implication that they would define the Leninist group, the Bolsheviks, more clearly not only against the Mensheviks but also, as the next point showed, against the whole array of defensist social democrats of the collapsed Second International. The final point, 'a new international' carried the same concern to the international arena, in other words made a clear division between a new 'revolutionary international' and the '*social-chauvinists*' and the 'Centre' in which Lenin placed 'Kautsky and co'. Incidentally, insertion of the word 'fraternization' in the first point, about the war, was also tied in with Lenin's internationalist vision in that he saw contact across the front-lines as a way of building the international class solidarity he believed was being generated by the war. If Russian and German troops got together they would see they had no quarrel with each other and turn instead on their rulers. In practice, such expectations turned out to be naive.

Such were the main points of Lenin's vision of revolutionary policy. They caused great hostility, not only among the usual suspects such as the Menshevik and SR right, but even within his own party which was not ready for such an apparently gung-ho approach. Many historians have also claimed Lenin was calling for a new revolution. However, there are certain signs, even within the text of the theses, that, for the moment at least, that was not so. Calling for 'no support' for the Provisional Government should be distinguished from calling for its overthrow. Elsewhere Lenin seemed to envisage a process which might take some time. Putting the ideas across would require 'patient, systematic and persistent *explanation*' of the errors of the masses. Similarly, 'In view of the undoubted honesty of those broad sections of the mass believers in revolutionary defencism ... it is necessary with particular thoroughness, persistence and patience to explain their error to them.' Finally, of course, he said it was not their '*immediate* task to "introduce" socialism', only soviet supervision of production and distribution and of the banks. Arguably, this last point foresaw a radical political revolution preceding a transformation of the economy. It could be understood to imply left-wing political supervision of a, for the time being, continuing capitalist, market economy. In fact, it is hard to understand it any other way. In all these respects we need to think carefully about Lenin's vision for the revolution, but we can assert that none of the principles of *The April Theses* was new. All of them arose organically from Lenin's longer-term assumptions about the war and continued to envisage the transformation of the imperialist war into a Europe-wide revolutionary civil war. Had they had access to or read Lenin's writings of 1905 and 1914–17 more carefully, his comrades should not have been so surprised. This leads us to the suspicion that even his closest comrades did not read Lenin's latest writings as holy writ and went their own way within what they saw as the larger parameters of their political position. Lenin was right to focus on the need to overhaul the Party. When he arrived back he did not, in any real sense, have a party. It was vital to consolidate one.

FROM RETURN TO THE BRINK OF DISASTER – APRIL TO JULY

Whatever the interpretive nuances surrounding *The April Theses* one thing was beyond doubt. Lenin was back. A new value had entered into the revolutionary equation. The atmosphere of revolution was intoxicating after the leafy suburbia of Berne and Zurich. Krupskaya's own description brilliantly captures the atmosphere of revolutionary festival in Petrograd.

> Those who have not lived through the revolution cannot imagine its grand, solemn beauty. Red banners, a guard of honour of Kronstadt sailors, searchlights from the Fortress of Peter and Paul illuminating the road from the Finland Station to the Kshesinskaya mansion, armoured cars, a chain of working men and women guarding the road. [Krupskaya 297]

Dignitaries, including Soviet leaders Skobelev and Chkheidze, came out to meet Lenin in the tsar's lounge at the station. Lenin, who had wondered if they would all be arrested when they returned, was 'a little taken aback' when approached by an army captain but it was only that he should take part in inspecting a guard of honour! Even at the station Lenin was already outlining his theses. At the Bolshevik headquarters, the commandeered mansion of the tsar's one-time mistress, the ballet dancer Ksheshinskaya, he spoke to 'a huge crowd of workers and soldiers' which 'surrounded the house'. [Krupskaya 297]

It was also a time of personal joy. That first evening Lenin and Krupskaya were squeezed into a room at Lenin's sister Anna's house in Shirokaya ulitsa (literally Broad Street) in the Petrogradskaya Storona region of the city. Another sister, Maria, was also living there. The members of this always-close family were once again being reunited and supporting one another. Krupskaya recalls that the children of the house hung a welcome banner, saying 'Workers of the World Unite' over her and Lenin's bed. 'I hardly spoke to Il'ich that night – there really were no words to express the experience, everything was understood without words.' [Krupskaya 296] The happiness was, of course, tinged with sadness that Lenin's mother, Maria, had failed to live through to this happy day by only eight months. As we have already mentioned, Lenin's first duty on his first day back was to visit her and beloved Olga's graves.

After that, it was straight into the fray. Lenin went to one of the revolutionary powerhouses, the Tauride Palace, former home of the Duma and current home of the Petrograd Soviet, first to report his journey officially to the Executive Committee of the Soviet and then, in one of the committee rooms, to meet Bolshevik delegates and, in effect, give them their instructions. He presented his ten theses to an increasingly bemused audience. 'For the first few minutes our people were taken aback.' [Krupskaya 297] That was putting it mildly. Lenin had dropped something of a bombshell.

Critics within and without the Party were not slow to join in. Lenin was particularly indignant that a former Bolshevik now defensist had accused him of 'planting the banner of civil war in the midst of revolutionary democracy', [SW 2 16] which was more or less exactly what Lenin had wanted to do. There was also severe opposition within the Party. It was only three days later that his *Theses* appeared in *Pravda* followed the next day by an article by Kamenev criticizing him for upsetting the delicate balance and pointing out that the propositions were 'the expression of Lenin's private opinion', not the official policy of any part of the Bolshevik Party. Kamenev was wasting his energy. The moment was fast approaching when Lenin's private opinions were to weigh much more heavily than any Party resolution, but for the moment he had to make a great effort to get *The April Theses* accepted. In a letter, Lenin complained that the *Pravda* editorial board, which he himself joined on 19 April, had 'wobbled towards "Kautskyism"', a deviation he 'hoped to correct'. [CW 36 444–5] Lenin bombarded the Party press and meetings with articles reiterating the themes of the wartime writings and *The April Theses*. In *Letters on Tactics* he criticized 'Old Bolsheviks' (incidentally launching a fateful phrase for many of his comrades) for repeating stale dogmas rather than reacting to new realities. Though he only mentioned Kamenev by name, most of the Party leadership in Petrograd – including Stalin and Kalinin – were implicated. As we have already had occasion to comment, the narrower the issue the more intense the debate and that certainly appears to be the case here. Even a close examination of the polemics seems to show a relatively small gap between the contending groups. Lenin's opponents were mainly upset by his apparent desire to rush into a new, socialist phase of the revolution when they believed it was still necessary to consolidate the bourgeois phase. Lenin defended himself by saying that he had spelled out clearly that an immediate transition to socialism was not on the cards. Lenin summarized his key point as follows:

> The revolutionary-democratic dictatorship of the proletariat and the peasantry has already become a reality (in a certain form and to a certain extent) ... 'The Soviet of Workers' and Soldiers Deputies' – there you have the 'revolutionary-democratic dictatorship of the proletariat and the peasantry' already accomplished in reality. This formula is already antiquated ... A new and different task now faces us: to effect a split *within* this dictatorship between the proletarian elements (the anti-defencist, internationalist, 'Communist' elements, who stand for a transition to the commune) and the *small-proprietor* or *petty-bourgeois* elements (Chkheidze, Tsereteli, Steklov, the Socialist-Revolutionaries and the other revolutionary defencists, who are opposed to moving towards the commune and are in favour of 'supporting' the bourgeoisie and the bourgeois government). [CW 24 44–5]

Some of Lenin's supporting arguments were less than clear. What did it mean to say that 'Bolshevik slogans and ideas *on the whole* have been confirmed by history; but *concretely* things have worked out *differently*'? [CW 24 44] Such comments smack more of someone who has the greatest difficulty in admitting he was wrong in the slightest degree, certainly a characteristic of Lenin. However, the argument was notable for two modifications Lenin was already making to his original formulations in April. First, he began to talk about the existence of what he called 'Dual Power'.

> The highly remarkable feature of our revolution is that it has brought about *dual power*. This fact must be grasped first and foremost: unless it is understood we cannot advance ... What is this dual power? Alongside the Provisional Government, the government of the *bourgeoisie, another government* has arisen, so far weak and incipient, but undoubtedly a government that actually exists and is growing – the Soviets of Workers' and Soldiers' Deputies. [CW 24 38]

The second modification was precisely the prominence Lenin was now giving to soldiers' soviets. Before his return he had not thought about them. As soon as he got back the role of soldiers was obvious. Immediately Lenin had grasped the importance of incorporating soldiers into the revolutionary equation and, in fact, they were to prove in many ways the decisive force in 1917.

So exactly what was Lenin saying that so upset his critics? At the end of the pamphlet on *The Dual Power* he made three points. First, the Provisional Government should be overthrown because it was a bourgeois government unable to fulfil the people's demands for peace, bread and freedom. Second, it could not be overthrown 'just now'. Third, it could not be overthrown 'in the ordinary way' because it rested on the support of the second government, the soviets. Significantly he concluded: 'to become a power the class-conscious workers must win the majority to their side. *As long as* no violence is used against the people there is no other road to power. We are not Blanquists, we do not stand for the seizure of power by a minority.' [CW 24 40] In his *Theses* and the articles backing them up Lenin was really trying, first and foremost, to get the Party to move on. It had been focused on the first stage of revolution, the overthrow of the tsar, since its origin. That had now happened and the second of his three forces of revolution, the imperialist bourgeoisie, was now in power. Since that was an established fact, it was now necessary to work towards its overthrow. However, there was no indication of whether this would take an historical epoch or would happen in weeks. Somewhere between the two seemed most likely, Lenin's own definition being the time it would take for the workers' cause to win over the majority. In the event, Lenin played fast and loose with even this proviso.

This debate was the first occasion on which Lenin was able to resume battle for control of his party. After a short, sharp conflict his views prevailed at the Seventh All-Russian Conference of the Bolshevik Party held from 27 April to 5 May (OS). Lenin opened the conference, gave its main report and was elected to the Central Committee with the highest number of votes. Unsurprisingly, he was the undisputed leader of the movement he had founded and nurtured. It was unthinkable that there should be any rival. After all, Lenin had made loyalty to himself and to his ideas the key condition of membership. One could hardly set up what amounted to a kind of political club of one's fans and then not get to lead it.

Of course, the Party was not an end in itself. Its purpose was to exert influence on the course of events. Lenin might 'control' his party but could his party exert any power? In the conditions of spring and early summer 1917 the answer must be a resounding no. For the time being it was too weak. The torrent of revolution was sweeping through Russia with little reference to the ideologies and preferences of Lenin and his supporters. In rural areas peasants set up committees; reduced rents they paid; forced their wages up if they were labourers; sowed seed on land abandoned by landowners who had no labour to work it; and even drew up inventories of estates to stop landowners stripping the assets. Soldiers and sailors established a vigorous but varied network of committees to protect their interests. By and large, they asserted that soldiers and sailors would defend the country against attack but would not freely go on the offensive. Workers set up militias to defend their factories and its stocks and also their homes; massive numbers joined trades unions; factory committees kept a close eye on management and even slowly encroached on managerial functions.[1]

No one did any of this because the Bolsheviks told them to. Most would never have heard of Bolshevism let alone have the first idea of what it stood for. In fact, the learning process was the other way round. Lenin began to absorb the revolutionary processes he saw around him and began to theorize a new kind of revolutionary state based on Marx's writings on the Paris Commune. In fact, Marx had gone through a process like that through which Lenin was going. A radical revolution which did not look to him for guidance showed him ways of organizing about which he wrote. Lenin saw similar spontaneous revolutionary creativity which resembled that of Paris in 1871 and built on it. Smashing the state machine and replacing it with directly elected, recallable officials and a nationwide militia all based on a system of soviets became Lenin's recipe for a post-revolutionary state. *The April Theses* mentioned that 'the salaries of all officials, all of whom are elective and replaceable at any time, not to exceed the average wage of a competent worker.' [SW 2 15] In *Letters on Tactics* he talked about the 'commune state' which, based on Soviets, was 'a *state* of a special type' [CW 24 52] which would 'make the independent activity of the *masses* a reality more quickly than a parliamentary republic'. [CW 24 53] It would be 'a state *without* a standing army, *without* a police opposed to the people, *without* an officialdom placed above the people'. [CW 24 48]

Clearly Lenin was tremendously excited by the situation. During the months of April to June the revolutionary ferment continued to bubble.

The government was defeated and a minority of socialist ministers joined it in May to form the first coalition. Soviets called for quicker action by the Provisional Government on implementing its promises of land reform, peace negotiation and a constituent assembly to prepare the transition to democracy. In a major piece of wrestling with the Soviet leadership and Provisional Government, the Bolsheviks were forced to call off a demonstration on 10 June (OS) in favour of one called officially by the Soviet a week later. What looked like a sign of weakness on the part of the Bolsheviks actually turned into a triumph when Bolshevik slogans predominated. It was one of the first major signs of the process Lenin had predicted. The masses were already becoming disillusioned with the Provisional Government and the 'opportunists' of the Soviet right wing.

However, it would be wrong to translate this into an assumption that Lenin was becoming triumphalist. In fact, his speeches and writings of these crucial weeks counsel caution. His main concern was that the left might overstretch itself and provoke a right-wing counter-revolution. His concern was based on the fact that what might seem possible in the heady political atmosphere of Petrograd would precipitate forces in that city into taking steps for which the rest of the country and, indeed, the continent was not yet ready. He spelled this out unambiguously in his speech calling on the Petrograd Committee of the Party to call off the June demonstration. The crisis, he said, showed that the leaders of the Petrograd Soviet, in which the Bolsheviks were still a minority, 'are calling an offensive against us' based on the fear that the Bolsheviks were conspiring to seize power by means of the demonstration. Lenin took the threat to the Bolsheviks very seriously and said: 'The proletariat must reply by showing the maximum calmness, caution, restraint and organization ... We must give them no pretext for attack.' [CW 25 80]

Of course, the Soviet majority, in their turn, might be forgiven for thinking the Bolsheviks were planning something. Only a week before this speech, Lenin had told the First All-Russian Soviet Congress (3–24 June (OS)), in response to the Menshevik leader Tsereteli's comment that there was no party in Russia prepared to take power, that there was one, the Bolsheviks, who were 'ready to take over full power at any moment'. [SW 2 143] In reality, Lenin's point had only been rhetorical, intended to show up the resolve of the Bolsheviks compared to the

Mensheviks' tendency to compromise, or, in their own view, to be realistic. But Lenin, too, was realistic. Out of more than a thousand delegates at the Congress from all over Russia only 105 declared themselves to be Bolsheviks. It was not surprising that Lenin maintained his note of caution.

The Congress, into which Lenin characteristically threw all his nervous energy and strength, was followed by the furore over the proposed Bolshevik demonstration of 10 June (OS), plus the stress of the Soviet-approved but Bolshevik-dominated demonstration which actually took place on 18 June (OS). They all combined to create an intense period of activity. As usual, tension played havoc with Lenin's nerves and his health. He was completely exhausted and had pushed himself beyond his limits. After the Congress concluded, on 24 June (OS), it seemed that the moment of tension had passed and Krupskaya prevailed on him to take a break. Krupskaya had, herself, become deeply involved in the burgeoning committee and representational structure of the revolution, being voted on to the Vyborg raion soviet, an equivalent of a London borough council. She was also busy with educational and youth work. In her own, characteristically vivid words: 'I greedily absorbed the life around me.' [Krupskaya 299] The result was that she was unable to accompany Vladimir on his break. Instead, his sister, Maria, went with him. On 28 June (OS) he left Petrograd for the Finnish village of Neivola to stay with his old friend Vladimir Bonch-Bruevich. Once again, he surrendered to the calming powers of nature, walks in the woods, fresh air and recuperation. He did not stop thinking or writing but he was ready to enjoy a period of meeting-free tranquillity as the pace of revolution appeared to be slowing, temporarily. However, nothing could have been further from the truth. On 4 July (OS) he hurried back to Petrograd because, in his absence, the Revolution had reached its most critical point since February itself.

THE JULY DAYS

As the Revolution radicalized, so its opponents in the propertied middle and upper classes became increasingly fearful for their privileges. Krupskaya herself records seeing signs on the streets of Petrograd of the growing resistance to the left and the breakdown of the February honeymoon. In her work with young people she noted: 'Young workers presented a striking contrast to the older groups of the middle school ... The latter often approached the Kshesinskaya mansion in a crowd, hurling abuse at the Bolsheviks. It was apparent that they were put up to it by someone.' [Krupskaya 300] During the crisis of April, when the Provisional Government came under pressure because of the publication of the Miliukov Note promising the Allies that Russian imperialist war aims had not changed as a result of February, Krupskaya noted a large workers' demonstration coming from the Nevsky Gate. 'Another crowd, wearing hats and bowlers moved towards the workers' demonstration ... The workers predominated near the Nevsky Gate but nearer to Morskaya Street and Poitsevsky Bridge the bowlers and hats were more numerous.' Krupskaya quickly became aware of one of the most effective devices being used in such circles to undermine the Bolsheviks and other parts of the internationalist left. 'The story was passing from mouth to mouth among the crowd of how Lenin had bribed the workers with German gold and now all were following him. "We must beat Lenin!" shouted a stylishly dressed young woman. "Kill all these scoundrels," someone in a bowler roared.' Krupskaya's conclusion was that the events revealed the growing realities of the moment: 'Class against Class! The working class stood for Lenin.' [Krupskaya 301]

The patriotic card was being played increasingly by the government which had few other weapons in its locker for rousing public support. For a variety of reasons, from early May, the government was trying to reinvigorate the war by means of an offensive. This put it on a collision course, especially with the soldiers whose committees were frequently coalescing around the policy of supporting defensive operations only. They would resist attack but not take part in attacking the enemy. The government, which had promised not to remove troops from Petrograd in its foundation agreement with the Soviet in March, saw the renewed offensive as an opportunity to renege on this commitment and to move the most troublesome, that is the most radical-minded, military units out of Petrograd. There was a problem of where they might go because front-line officers did not want what they saw as a mutinous rabble dumped on their doorsteps. Be that as it may, the crisis boiled up. The failure of the offensive in early July added to the heat, each side blaming the other. The left said it should never have been undertaken in the first place, the right blamed the soldiers' committees and soviets for undermining its efforts. In Petrograd the conjuncture had also brought a political crisis and the first coalition government had broken up on 2 July (OS) and no second coalition had been formed to replace it. At this crucial moment Russia had only a caretaker government.

The situation in the city came to a head when left-wing regiments, notably the First Machine Gun Regiment, were ordered out of the city. On 3 July (OS) they held a stormy meeting and resolved to overthrow the government. The radical stronghold of Kronstadt, a chief port of the largely inactive Baltic Fleet, had been, in effect, an oasis of soviet power for some months. The decision was made to send a large contingent – some say 10,000, others 25,000, armed sailors – to join anti-government demonstrations in the city in support of the Machine Gunners. They arrived on 4 July (OS). Workers, too, joined in. They were exasperated by falling output, unemployment, lockouts and other employer tactics intended to cut their wages and break their vastly burgeoning representative institutions. The two days of demonstration represented the greatest crisis the government had so far faced. There is no doubt it could have been overthrown, indeed the forces on the street were greater than in the October Revolution itself. However, no one, apart from the rather small anarchist left, was prepared to lead them. The sailors went to, among other places, the Bolshevik headquarters, the Kshesinskaya Mansion, to beg for leadership. Lenin, who had rushed back from his recuperative rest in Finland, spoke a few words of praise for their fortitude but did not call on them to seize power. Instead, he pushed the Party orator, Anatoly Lunacharsky, who had newly arrived in the Bolshevik ranks along with Trotsky and the rest of the 'Interdistrictite' faction, out onto the balcony to deal with them, effectively to praise them but also tell them to remain peaceful and to go home. N.N. Sukhanov, the great chronicler of the Revolution, describes the scene on 4 July (OS):

> When the Kronstadters surrounded Kshesinskaya's house, expecting to receive instructions, Lenin made an extremely ambiguous speech. He didn't demand any concrete action from the impressive force standing in front of him; he didn't even call on his audience to continue the street demonstrations … During the ovation given him by the Kronstadters, Lenin called [Lunacharsky] over and suggested that he speak to the crowd. Lunacharsky, always ablaze with eloquence, didn't wait to be urged.[2]

The demonstrators' efforts to find leadership were no more successful at the Tauride Palace where the Petrograd Soviet was based. In their frustration they threatened leaders of the Soviet and briefly held the SR leader Chernov captive. It was only through the timely intervention of Trotsky and others that Chernov was released unharmed.

Exactly what Lenin intended in July has remained controversial but a fairly reliable view has emerged.[3] The revolutionary pressure was coming largely from below and in radical centres like Kronstadt the popular mood was to the left of the Bolsheviks. This caused their local representatives much embarrassment and they often led groups in July which were determined to seize power. Others complained that the Central Committee was calling on them to be 'firemen', that is they had to damp down the revolutionary enthusiasm of their constituency. Thus, different levels of the Party in the Petrograd region had different views on what policy should be. The grassroots Party cells, especially in Kronstadt, were being pushed by their constituents to support radical action while bodies higher up remained cautious. The confusion has led to arguments that the Bolsheviks planned to use the July Days to seize power. However, a ten-day rest in Finland is hardly the likely preparation Lenin would make for such a venture. None the less, they were tempted to lead the movement as it gathered momentum. The Central Committee agonized all night on 3/4 July (OS). However, Lenin was far from certain that the moment was right. From his perspective there were a number of shortcomings to the movement at that time. First, although it would have been possible, indeed simple, to arrest the government, the turmoil was largely confined to Petrograd and there was a danger that sufficient force could be raised in the rest of Russia, possibly with allied help, to crush the rising in the city and set up a military dictatorship. Second, the movement was a spontaneous one, it was not under Bolshevik control despite many lower-ranking Bolsheviks leading component parts of the demonstrations. Both these reasons appear to have weighed heavily with Lenin and the decision was taken to persuade the demonstrators to disperse peacefully.

The fact that the Bolsheviks did not lead the demonstrations did not prevent many, probably most, of their enemies from believing that they had been responsible. A new government, led for the first time by Alexander Kerensky, who had earlier been Minister of Justice and later Minister for War responsible for the disastrous offensive, quickly seized its opportunity to attack the left. The dispersal of the demonstrators put the left into disarray, since many had supported them, and made it defenceless for the moment. Kerensky took advantage of the moment to begin an assault on the Bolsheviks. The patriotic card was played prominently. The failure of the offensive was blamed on the left but worse was to come. Papers were produced by a former Bolshevik, Grigorii Alexinsky, purporting to prove that the Bolshevik leaders, and Lenin in particular, were German agents. Taken together with exaggerated claims about the 'sealed train' in which Lenin had travelled across Germany on his journey home from Switzerland, many were led to believe the stories. The issue of 'German money' has played a persistent but misleading role in the mythology of the Revolution, similar in some ways to the myth of Rasputin in that, while there may have been some basis in truth for aspects of the stories, the real significance of them is grossly exaggerated. German money may have found its way into Bolshevik coffers but no way was Lenin a German agent, taking orders from Berlin.[4] Germany and the Bolsheviks had some common interests, the weakening of the Russian war effort most obviously, but for quite different reasons. Lenin wanted to use Russia as a springboard to overthrow the German Empire, too. Hardly an objective of the Kaiser's policy! None the less, the story was persistent and we will meet it again.

Though it was in essence false, the accusation was effective. Rightwing 'patriots' attacked the Bolsheviks' premises, including the *Pravda* office, and personnel. Government troops occupied the Kshesinskaya mansion. Various homes of Bolsheviks were trashed by mobs or searched by the authorities. Lenin himself narrowly avoided being caught by a group of renegade officers who, on 9 July (OS), ransacked the flat of Lenin's sister, Anna, and brother-in-law, Mark Elizarov, on Shirokaya ulitsa, where Lenin and Krupskaya had been living. They arrested Krupskaya and the Elizarovs and took them to the General Staff Headquarters but later let them go. 'These are not the people we want,' their colonel is reported to have said. According to Krupskaya 'If Il'ich had been there they would have torn him to pieces.' [Krupskaya 312] The Bolshevik Party was officially proscribed and warrants were issued for the arrest of its leaders, including Trotsky who had just thrown in his lot with Lenin. The Party circumvented proscription by using a different name but the threat of arrest brought problems for individuals. At first, Lenin wanted to give himself up but, after some discussion, in which Stalin was one of the leading protagonists urging Lenin not to hand himself over to the authorities, the Central Committee decided that it would be unwise and that he should go into hiding instead. He, and others including Zinoviev, were so valuable to the Party that they must remain free, so they went into hiding in Finland. Trotsky, on the other hand, walked into a police station and demanded to be arrested, arguing the government was not strong enough to hold him for long. The police obliged and arrested him on the spot.

Using the historian's most powerful asset, hindsight, we might be inclined to minimize the importance of these events since their impact was, in the end, short-lived. From Lenin's point of view, however, the conjuncture seemed to be a disaster of the first order. He proposed radical changes of policy and tactics to meet the crisis. The basic theoretical assumption behind his policies was, as he wrote in the opening section of *The Political Situation: Four Theses*, that 'the counter-revolution has become organized and consolidated, and has actually taken state power into its hands.' [CW 25 176, 10 July (OS)] Once again, he was viewing events through the prism of his earlier analyses, he was seeing events as a confirmation of his predictions. This was emerging as one of the key aspects of Lenin's politics and could be said to have hampered clear analysis of actual events. The July Days were a case in point. The earlier prediction was that the tsarists and the Provisional Government would close ranks against the left and that, in effect, is what happened in the aftermath of the July Days. In fact, the new coalition government that emerged included more ministers from the defensist left and, as later events like the Moscow State Conference and the Kornilov mutiny were to show, the nationalist right hated Kerensky and the Provisional Government and wanted to see it removed and replaced by something more under their control, notably a military dictatorship. So, in that sense, Lenin was wrong. The counter-revolution had not seized power but Lenin had interpreted events that way because that is what he had been predicting.

With a weak premise it is no surprise that Lenin's conclusions also look dubious. First, the balance between peaceful development through the soviets and the alternative policy of armed uprising now tipped in favour of the latter. Once again it fulfilled a prediction that the left would use peaceful means unless force was used against it. Lenin understood the reaction to the July Days to be just such a change on the part of the authorities. Of course, he was partially correct here although the force seemed to have emanated from the far left first and the government was reacting to threats to itself. However, Lenin was in no doubt about the new course. Strategy was now to be based on preparing an armed uprising. 'All hopes for a peaceful development of the Russian revolution have vanished for good. This is the objective situation: either complete victory for the military dictatorship, or victory for the workers' armed uprising.' [CW 25 177] Even the slogan 'All Power to the Soviets!' was deemed to be outdated. It had been 'a slogan for the peaceful development of the revolution which was possible … up to 5–9 July (OS) … This slogan is no longer correct, for it does not take into account that power has changed hands and that the revolution has in fact been completely betrayed by the SRs and Mensheviks.' [CW 25 177–8] Finally, Lenin also was so impressed by the turnabout that he concluded extremely pessimistically that, in certain respects, the situation had thrown Bolshevism back to the pre-war situation and that it was now necessary to combine legal with illegal activity: 'The party of the working class, without abandoning legal activity, but never for a moment overrating it, must *combine* legal with illegal work, as it did in 1912–14. Don't let slip a single hour of illegal work. But don't cherish any constitutional or "peaceful" illusions. Form illegal organizations or cells everywhere and at once for the publication of leaflets, etc. Reorganize immediately, consistently, resolutely, all along the line.' [CW 25 178]. In other words, it was now necessary for key assets of the Bolshevik Party, its leadership, its press, to go back underground. As chief asset this is exactly what Lenin himself plus Kamenev and Zinoviev, the numbers two and three in the Party, actually did. In fact, for the next seven or eight weeks the legal segment of the Party continued to function through the simple expedient of circumventing the proscription by tactics from the tsarist period like changing names. The Party called itself Social Democratic Internationalists when its candidates stood for election. The newspapers changed their names and continued to circulate. For example, the banned *Pravda* appeared as *Rabochii Put'* from September to 26 October (OS). The Party even held an illegal congress (its sixth) from 26 July to 3 August (OS).

Far from being hamstrung by it, proscription was, in fact, a major boost for the Party in the medium term, turning them into martyrs and giving them the mantle of being the opponents most feared by the authorities. Conversely, this meant that as the number of critics and opponents of the authorities grew, so many of them saw the Bolsheviks as the natural leaders of the opposition. Lenin's tactic of no support for the Provisional Government was reaping rich dividends.

Before looking at Lenin's life in renewed exile, one more aspect of the events, one which is often overlooked as a relatively minor, or perhaps inevitable, development, needs our attention – the reconciliation between Lenin and Trotsky. It happened relatively smoothly and by stages, being completed at the underground Party Congress in the absence of both Trotsky, who was in jail, and Lenin, who was in hiding. It does show that Lenin's political will could overcome his personal likes and dislikes in both directions. We have seen him most frequently expelling his friends and allies, like Martov, Plekhanov, Bogdanov and others including Trotsky, from his faction if he believed political expediency required it. In this case, because their political differences had fallen away, Lenin was prepared, more so than most of the other Party leaders around him, to welcome one of his most devastatingly outspoken critics back into the Party. In the long years of polemic between them, from 1906 to 1917, Trotsky had made many savage attacks on Lenin. His most noteworthy was his attack on Lenin's concept of the Party and associated 'democratic centralism'. In 1904 Trotsky had described Lenin as a 'despot and terrorist' and compared him to Robespierre. In *Our Political Tasks* (1904) he had made one of the most acute and devastating attacks on Lenin's conception of the Party. 'Lenin's method leads to this: the party organization at first substitutes itself for the party as a whole; then the Central Committee substitutes itself for the organization; and finally a single "dictator" substitutes himself for the Central Committee.' From the moment of reconciliation onwards, however, they worked smoothly together as though nothing had ever happened. Political expediency could work in both directions.

EXILE ONCE MORE

When the officers and cadets raided Anna Ulyanova and Mark Elizarov's apartment on Shirokaya ulitsa it was not surprising they did not find Lenin. Krupskaya herself commented that 'After our arrival in Petrograd I saw little of Il'ich.' [Krupskaya 299] This appears to have remained the case for the whole period between April and October.

They worked in different places on different projects. Krupskaya was occupied in matters cultural and educational, Lenin in the Central Committee and *Pravda*. Lenin also had a wide range of formal and informal meetings which took him all over the city and would sometimes find him sleeping over at people's apartments wherever he happened to be. The Ulyanovs' devotion to the revolutionary cause and the revolutionary way of life remained total throughout these months. At the ages of forty-seven (Lenin) and forty-eight (Krupskaya) they did not have so much as a flat to call their own and had no possessions to speak of beyond the clothes they had frequently packed in their suitcases on their travels around Europe. They did not own a stick of furniture or anything of value or bulk. Their peripatetic life had created ingrained habits and there was no certainty that they would not have to move quickly once again. However, they were also completely uninterested in the acquisition of wealth and goods. Their focus remained on liberating the oppressed of Russia and the world and in this light what was needed were the means to conduct the struggle, resources for a newspaper, for organizing the Party and a simple subsistence for Lenin and Krupskaya. Personal possessions were not even on the agenda. It may also help explain why they had no children, although the possible inability of either one or the other of them to have children because of the effects of certain of their illnesses has also been proposed. However, we do not know the reason with any certainty. We do know children would scarcely have fitted into their life together.

In July Lenin remained untrammelled by material constraints and was able to cut ties immediately the decision was made and disappear from the view of the authorities. What followed was the last peaceful oasis in his active life. Armed with various false documents and living in a variety of places, Lenin had several months of separation from the front line of political struggle. Initially, he and Zinoviev lived in a grass-covered hut in a field near Razliv, some 35 kilometres from Petrograd. About the end of August, with documents describing him as a worker named Ivanov, Lenin, with the help of an engine-driver, disguised himself as a fireman and crossed the border into Finland, living in Lahti and then Helsinki. Even in Helsinki caution continued to reign supreme. He even reverted to old habits. He wrote to Krupskaya, using invisible ink, to invite her to visit him in Helsinki, drawing a rough map to help her. Clearly Krupskaya, who, as we have seen, had had problems mastering conspiratorial techniques back in the mid-1890s, was out of practice. She scorched the edge of the letter when she heated it over the lamp to make the invisible writing appear. This had unfortunate consequences: 'Everything went off well, except for a delay caused by the lack of directions contained on that part of the map which I had burned. I wandered through the streets for a long time before I found the street I wanted.' [Krupskaya 315] Did memories of other chases after Lenin in hiding, in Prague and Munich for example, spring to her mind? Her second visit, two weeks later, also had its difficulties when she lost herself briefly in a forest as night fell. When she arrived she found Lenin's 'mind was not on what he was saying, it was fixed on rebellion and how best to prepare for it.' She continues: 'His mind was constantly engaged on the problem of how to reorganize the whole state apparatus, how the masses were to be re-organized, how the whole social fabric was to be rewoven – as he expressed it.' [Krupskaya 316]

Despite the welcome visits by Krupskaya, the frustration caused by Lenin's exile mounted, even though he was kept in touch by reading newspapers and receiving a series of messengers. His immense writings and correspondence of September, urging a more proactive policy on his party, showed the force of his pent-up anxiety. Before that, however, he reverted to the analytical mode which was second nature to him. Once more, Lenin the intellectual and professor came out ahead of Lenin the activist.

As we have seen, earlier in the year in the *Third Letter from Afar*, not to mention *The April Theses*, Lenin had been reflecting on the problem of the post-revolutionary state. Clearly, events had pushed this issue right to the top of the agenda. The revolution was evolving and, despite the apparent setback of July, Lenin believed it would continue to do so. The more it did, the more imperative it was to envisage what would happen once the existing authorities were overthrown and the masses took over. Exile at least gave him an opportunity to develop his thoughts on this crucial issue, which he did in the last of his major works, *State and Revolution*. Before analysing its content, one fundamental point, present in the very title, should not be forgotten. Lenin, in looking at the problems of transition from existing reality to socialism, chose to think first about politics. One might have expected of a Marxist, particularly at a time when economic determinism was thought to be the basis of the doctrine, that the issue of the economy might present itself. It is remarkable that, in the course of revolution, indeed throughout his life, Lenin paid far less attention to economics than he did to politics. Where economics was a focus it was, as with the work on *Imperialism*, very much tied to politics. Economic questions – what, on the day after the revolution, would be the policy towards prices and money? what would the market economy do? where would investment come from? and so on – were issues that Lenin barely considered. Where he did, he had largely offered political and institutional solutions such as amalgamating and nationalizing banks. The very title and key phrase of the new work, namely that the state machine should not be taken over but smashed, echoed Bakunin as much as Marx (even though the concept originated with Marx) and even critics in his party were not slow to point out this aspect of Lenin's thought and he included a rather unconvincing section in *State and Revolution* in which he attempted to distinguish his ideas from anarchism.

Let us take a look at this work, mainly in order to trace Lenin's thinking at this time. The pamphlet itself was not influential in 1917 for the simple reason that it was not published until 1918 and a small extra section, Chapter II, part iii, was added for the second edition which was published in 1919. Lenin, who had been working on the theme in 1915 and 1916, considered the item to be of some importance, so much so that he asked Lev Kamenev, in the event of his, Lenin's, death, which was a real possibility in the pogrom atmosphere of July, to publish his notebook 'Marxism and the State', which had been held up in Stockholm. He was, however, able to retrieve it and work on it further and it emerged as *State and Revolution*. What was in it that Lenin considered to be so vital?

The core of the work consists of Lenin's interpretation of Marx's writings on the Paris Commune. The Commune (1871) took over Paris in the vacuum caused by the German siege of the city and the government's withdrawal and collapse. It was the first example, of many the left hoped, of the people rising up and governing themselves. Incidentally, the majority of Communards (members of the Commune) were influenced by French radicals such as Blanqui rather than by Marx, hence the aura of anarchism detected by many in Lenin's work.

The core insight, smashing the existing state rather than transforming it, opened the way up to all sorts of questions. How would one replace the legislative, administrative, judicial, police and defence functions it performed for society? Why did existing forms have to be smashed?

To answer the second question first, in Marx's conception the state was the instrument by which the ruling class ruled. They took over the state and imbued it with the values and priorities of the ruling class. It therefore followed, in Marx's view, that it was too tainted by its connections with the rulers to be transformed and, as the Communards had instinctively seen, its remnants had to be completely broken before a new organization, part and parcel of the mass of the population, could take its place. In addition, in the Marxist perspective, the classless society would be a stateless society so the transitional forms should also be constructed with this aim in view.

Most of *State and Revolution* is taken up with an examination of the principles behind the new organization. The point was to fuse the institutions as closely as possible with the people so they could not be used to oppress the majority – the people would not, it was assumed, repress themselves. This meant having structures fully composed of the people and fully answerable to them at all times. How would this be accomplished following the implementation of Lenin's injunction from *The April Theses* – 'Abolition of the police, army and bureaucracy'? The police and armed forces would cease to be 'special bodies of armed men' (Engels) since this was the characteristic that enabled them to be used for repressive purposes. As special, separate bodies, cut off from society, they identified with their own ethos and orders, not with their brothers and sisters in the society around them. To overcome this it was necessary that as many citizens as possible should be involved in staffing and operating them. There would be a compulsory term of service for all male citizens. The whole country would be trained in arms in order to be able to defend themselves and deprive the state of its monopoly of police and military knowledge and techniques. The people would be armed and therefore they could not be forced into submission by armed external agencies. Bureaucratic and judicial functions would also be democratized by enforcing a regular rotation of administrative tasks in which the whole population would participate. In Lenin's words 'Everyone would govern in turn and soon become used to no one governing.' [SW 2 357] All officials, including delegates to representative institutions, would be subject to annual election and could be recallable at any time should a certain percentage of their constituents demand it. Salaries, too, would be pegged to the wages of an average worker. The point here was to undermine the careerist appeal of comfortable administrative jobs. While, at first, some of these principles were implemented briefly, the emerging Soviet Union was eventually characterized by their precise opposite – a tyrannous, permanent, unresponsive bureaucratic elite of Party and state officials, many of whom were paid high salaries. While we will see some of the forces bringing this about, our main concern is with the development of Lenin's own ideas on such issues.

State and Revolution was also remarkable for some of its other assumptions and sources. In addition to the Marx/Paris Commune core there is also a large measure of Hilferding's ideas present. Hilferding, as we have seen, argued that capitalism was becoming organized and its essential nutrient, capital, was turning into bank capital (finance capital in Hilferding's phrase) controlled not by entrepreneurs and owners of capital but by bank employees, its managers. Take over the banks and one would thereby take over the essence of capitalism. Lenin proposed exactly this in *The April Theses*. He developed the principle even further in *State and Revolution* arguing that all 'political' functions could, similarly, be reduced to accounting and control within the grasp of the average, literate intelligence.

> Capitalist culture has *created* large-scale production, factories, railways, the postal service, telephones, etc., and *on this basis* the great majority of the functions of the old 'state power' have become so simplified and can be reduced to such exceedingly simple operations of registration, filing and checking that they can be easily performed by every literate person, can quite easily be performed for ordinary 'workmen's wages', and that these functions can (and must) be stripped of every shadow of privilege, of every semblance of 'official grandeur'. [SW 2 299]

In a memorable phrase, he claimed running the state would become a routine like the everyday operation of the post office.

> A witty German Social-Democrat of the seventies of the last century called the *postal service* an example of the socialist economic system. This is very true ... To organize the *whole* economy on the lines of the postal service so that the technicians, foremen and accountants, as

well as *all* officials, shall receive salaries no higher than 'a workman's wage', all under the control and leadership of the armed proletariat – that is our immediate aim. This is the state and this is the economic foundation we need. [SW 2 304]

Marx rarely used the phrase 'dictatorship of the proletariat' but Lenin turned it into a key phrase and a key concept. Lenin quoted one of Marx's references to it.

Between capitalist and communist society lies the period of the revolutionary transformation of the one into the other. Corresponding to this is also a political transition period in which the state can be nothing but *the revolutionary dictatorship of the proletariat.* [quoted in SW 2 332]

According to Lenin 'Democracy for an insignificant minority, democracy for the rich – that is the democracy of capitalist society.' [SW 2 333] He added: 'Marx grasped the *essence* of capitalist democracy splendidly when … he said that the oppressed are allowed once every few years to decide which particular representatives of the oppressing class shall represent and repress them in parliament.' [SW 2 334] By comparison, 'during the *transition* from capitalism to communism suppression is *still* necessary, but it is now the suppression of the exploiting minority by the exploited majority.' [SW 2 336] A state is still necessary but it is a transitional one which will, says Lenin, be much less complex since the suppression of a minority of exploiters by the majority of exploited 'is comparatively so easy, simple and natural a task that it will entail far less bloodshed than the suppression of the risings of slaves, serfs or wage-labourers and it will cost mankind far less.' [SW 2 336] Such a mechanism is, Lenin continues, 'compatible with the extension of democracy to such an overwhelming majority of the population that the need for a *special machine* of suppression will begin to disappear.' [SW 2 336] In a rare reference to the soviets he concludes that while the exploiters can only suppress the people by means of a very complex machine, '*the people* can suppress the exploiters even with a very simple "machine" … by the simple *organization of the armed people* (such as the Soviets of Workers' and Soldiers' Deputies …).' [SW 2 336] Remember that, at the point of writing the final piece in August 1917, Lenin was at a point of disillusionment with the soviets as they were then constituted and had explicitly turned back to a policy of workers' armed uprising.

In *State and Revolution* Lenin produced many classic formulae of the left. But few of them found their way into Bolshevik or Communist practice. Where attempted, many of them failed. In the early Soviet state and later in Mao's China, rotation of administrative posts was tried but tended to bring chaos as each wave of newcomers took time to understand the job and, more or less as soon as it did, was replaced by the next set of draftees. Administrative and other tasks were, sadly, more complex than the routine of the post office. Militias, too, were soon abandoned as being undertrained to take on the tasks of modern war. However, critics of the authoritarian streak which emerged in communist societies would point less to the inadequacies of the institutions themselves and more to the communist obsession with control to explain the failure of the ultra-democratic provisions of *State and Revolution*. From our perspective of examining Lenin's life, perhaps the most extraordinary and ironic feature is that, while he retained such ultra-democratic ideas in his head, Lenin later presided in practice over the emergence of one of the most intrusive bureaucratic state structures the world had ever seen. While we will return to this question again it is worth noting that one of the key reasons for the tension was already apparent. In *State and Revolution* Lenin assumes that a free proletarian will share his, Lenin's, principles. It thereby follows, in Lenin's logic, that any proletarian who disagreed was not yet free of the shackles of bourgeois thought. Lenin's solution, before and after *State and Revolution*, was to remove the oppressive ideas, to raise the consciousness of those who disagreed until they reached advanced consciousness, that is, they saw the light and came into agreement. In this respect Lenin's mental world resembles, may indeed have been imbibed subconsciously from, the Orthodox church which envisaged humanity unifying around the absolute truth which it possessed. Be that as it may, the chief weakness of Lenin's intellectual system was that it provided no room for honest disagreement between individuals who were enlightened and advanced. Such enlightenment, it was assumed, would lead to harmony, not dissonance. Reality was to prove otherwise.

The manuscript of *State and Revolution* breaks off after two sentences of Chapter VII entitled 'The Experience of the Russian Revolutions of

1905 and 1917'. It is tantalizing that such a chapter was never written though we may infer from the rest of his writings what Lenin might have said, for instance that the 1905 Revolution lacked organized proletarian leadership and hegemony which was increasingly provided in 1917 by the Soviet, internationalist left. However, we will never know. The postscript to the first edition, written in late November 1917, explains laconically why the section was never completed:

> I was 'interrupted' by a political crisis – the eve of the October revolution of 1917. Such an 'interruption' can only be welcomed; but the writing of the second part of the pamphlet ... will probably have to be put off for a long time. It is more pleasant and useful to go through the 'experience of the revolution' than to write about it. [SW 2 361]

One may doubt that it was truly preferable to experience revolution rather than write about it. It is rather extraordinary to think that, although it was certainly enforced to a large degree, Lenin occupied so much of his time in the maelstrom of events in mid-1917 writing an erudite commentary on Marx and Engels together with scholarly refutation of critics then and now. Most of the pamphlet is brilliant exposition, critique and polemic, practical applications relatively few. From this point on, however, Lenin's life was about to change irreversibly. He was not afforded the time to complete *State and Revolution*, nor did he return in any detail to theory. For the remainder of his life, practice called.

INTO POWER

After the failure of the July Days the propertied classes had attempted to make the most of the weakness and division of the left. Step by step they tried to regain the initiative. Troops were used more frequently to restore 'order'. Landowners and factory owners became more aggressive. In late August the political conjuncture changed dramatically and quickly. Lenin, despite being in exile, was one of the first to spot what was happening, though, as usual, there was an element of interpreting events as fulfilment of his prophecies. Somewhat like the politics of the military offensive in June, the consequence of the right's social offensive was that it overreached itself, collapsed and left the way open to a renewed assault by its opponents.

In mid-August, Prime Minister Kerensky convened a State Conference in Moscow to prepare the way for a genuine Constituent Assembly. The conference members were largely selected but some were elected. Its main significance was twofold. It confirmed the polarization of Russian politics with left and right succeeding each in denouncing the other. Second, it demonstrated that only Kerensky was capable of gaining significant support from both sides.

No left-wing champion emerged from this largely bourgeois body, unless one includes the Bolsheviks of Moscow whose general strike made the everyday life of the conference difficult by paralysing city transport among other things. However, a champion of the right, the Commander-in-Chief of the army, General Kornilov, was emerging, to the extent that he was officially muzzled by Kerensky and his true policies, of suppressing army committees, reintroducing the death penalty in the army and subjecting many factories and transport facilities to military discipline, were presented in a speech by an ally, the Cossack Ataman (Chief) Kaledin. Outside the conference a growing cluster of army officers, landowners, factory owners, bankers and a cluster of politicians from the far right to a number of Kadets, turned to Kornilov in the hope that he would 'restore order'. In late August Kornilov tried to oblige. The flattery and insistence of his camarilla in Moscow pushed him into a foolish adventure which had the exact opposite effect to the one anticipated. He moved troops towards Petrograd which were immediately deemed to be a threat to the soviets in particular and the whole popular revolution in general. The Petrograd Soviet took the lead in disrupting his advance by closing the railways to him and sending propaganda deputations which melted the resolve of his troops, including the Chechens and Ingush of the so-called 'Wild Division'.

However, the key controversy over the incident surrounds the role of Kerensky. This is not the place for a detailed discussion of whether he had earlier supported Kornilov; the point is that, halfway through the mutiny, Kerensky stood Kornilov down and had him arrested (31 August (OS)). Kornilov was astounded. Kerensky armed the Petrograd Soviet and its supporters and, in a concession to the Soviet, released its arrested members from jail including a delighted Trotsky. Incidentally, Lenin was not tempted to end his exile at this point. Instead, he moved to Helsinki from Razliv.

The Kornilov affair produced two victims and one group of major beneficiaries. The victims were, obviously, Kornilov but also, less obviously, Kerensky. By turning against Kornilov he became instantly hated by the army command and the right in general. However, his turn to the left was not received with joy on the left where he was blamed for having appointed Kornilov in the first place and having apparently supported him in the early stages of the coup. The overwhelming consequence of this was a more rapid than ever decline in the standing of Kerensky and the Provisional Government. In effect there was a political vacuum. It was into this vacuum that the main beneficiaries of the affair, the Bolsheviks, stepped. Lenin's predictions had been proved right and his policy of no support for the Provisional Government was now beginning to reap massive dividends. For the first time Bolsheviks began to win majorities in key soviets and to take over the leadership of them. Where was the new wave of support coming from?

Ironically, the Kornilov affair ended up helping Kornilov's enemies by acting as a massive wake-up call to the masses. Soldiers had seen the spectre of the restoration of traditional discipline rise up before their eyes. Workers had been threatened with the introduction of martial law in key factories. Manipulated lockouts and factory closures and the threat of unemployment galvanized workers into further and further steps towards taking over management themselves. Peasants sensed that, if they wanted land, they would have to take it, and soon. Peasant land seizures rose markedly in September. The masses could no longer look for leadership from the Mensheviks and the Socialist Revolutionaries who had formerly attracted most of their votes but were now, because of their closeness to the government, losing credibility. They were the apparent allies of counter-revolution. On the other hand, because they had stayed outside the political game, the Bolsheviks were not tainted by association with the rapidly collapsing Provisional Government. However, winning the masses' votes was not, as we shall see, the same as winning over their hearts and minds. Mass support came to the Bolsheviks as the only significant agents of what the masses wanted – peace, bread, land and all power to the soviets. It was emphatically not a conversion to Bolshevik values and to the dreams embodied in *The April Theses* and *State and Revolution*. In reality, some of the masses' priorities, notably the peasants' desire for land, were directly contrary to Bolshevik policy which, in this case, for example, supported nationalization of land not private or commune-based ownership. It was on practical issues like abolition of the death penalty that they began to win majorities in soviets, not on long-term projects to restructure humanity. These severe contradictions were to make themselves felt almost from the first moment of Bolshevik power. For the time being, however, they were not noticed. What was increasingly evident was that there was a very significant turn to the left in the popular mood.

Despite his physical separation from events Lenin was among the first to seize on the significance of the new conjuncture. True, he claimed much of it was consistent with his predictions of growing disaffection with the Provisional Government, though even he must have been taken aback by the speed at which events moved in the direction of the left. In September he began to radically change the direction of his policies, though for a while he did not turn towards a consistent alternative course. He did, however, embark on an absolutely extraordinary outpouring of letters, articles and pamphlets.

His first communication to the Central Committee illustrated the new characteristics to perfection. It began:

> It is possible that these lines will come too late for events are developing with a rapidity that sometimes makes one's head spin. I am writing this on Wednesday, August 30 (OS) and the recipients will read it no sooner than Friday, September 2 (OS). Still, on chance, I consider it my duty to write the following.
>
> The Kornilov revolt is a most unexpected (unexpected at such a moment and in such a form) and downright unbelievably sharp turn in events.
>
> Like every sharp turn it calls for a revision and change of tactics. And as with every revision, we must be extra-cautious not to become unprincipled. [SW 2 196]

The first point made was that, though the Party was fighting against Kornilov and therefore alongside Kerensky's forces, they still did not support him, they were still not defensists. 'It is', he admitted, 'a rather subtle difference, but it is highly essential and must not be forgotten.' [SW 2 196] He also urged forcing a more aggressive policy on Kerensky including arresting Kornilov's 'allies' such as Miliukov and shutting down right-wing institutions like the Duma which still had a vestigial existence. Peasants should be urged to demand land and '*immediate and unconditional peace must be offered* on *precise* terms' though how one offers unconditional peace on terms is not explained. Implicit in this was a call to the entire left to support this policy since the new conjuncture had so changed the situation that defensism proper could no longer be justified. Implicit in what he said was that the SRs and Mensheviks might join in this enterprise helping either to end the war or turn it into a revolutionary war. This surprising theme of possible reconciliation was repeated two days later in an article often seen as insincere, entitled, in unLeninist fashion, 'On Compromises'. The central point is that the Kornilov conjuncture is so special, 'so abrupt and original a turn' [SW 2 202] that one might envisage offering 'a voluntary compromise' not to their main bourgeois class enemies but 'to our nearest adversaries, the "ruling" petty-bourgeois-democratic parties, the Socialist-Revolutionaries and Mensheviks'. [SW 2 202] Once again the subconscious 'populist' element of an all-embracing 'people's revolution' surfaced through the impeccably crafted Marxist veneer of Lenin's ideas. Under the compromise the Bolsheviks 'would refrain from demanding the immediate transfer of power to the proletariat and poor peasants and from employing revolutionary methods of fighting for this demand' while the SRs and Mensheviks would abandon the Provisional Government and form a new government responsible to the soviets and proclaim the rapid convening of the Constituent Assembly. [SW 2 202–3] Lenin believed that this would create democratic conditions which could only benefit the Bolsheviks. They would use their freedom to continue to win over, by peaceful methods, the majority of the population. Lenin underlined that such a possibility was a fragile one and things changed so fast it might be outdated before his article was read but, even so, it was a chance that should not be allowed to pass by untried. In fact, Lenin added a postscript saying that the article was delayed by two days before publication and that the moment had in fact gone by, 'the days when by chance the path of peaceful development became possible have *already* passed.' [SW 2 206] In fact, he made the same point about the peaceful development of the revolution in an article entitled 'The Tasks of the Revolution' written slightly later and published in late September (OS). By then, however, he had another element to his discourse. He wrote:

A possibility very seldom to be met with in the history of revolutions now faces the democracy of Russia, the Soviets and the Socialist Revolutionary and Menshevik Parties – the possibility of convening the Constituent Assembly at the appointed date without further delays, of making the country secure against a military and economic catastrophe and of ensuring the peaceful development of the revolution. [CW 26 67]

Once again the possibility of a broad democratic alliance was presented, less as a piece of disinformation, more as a serious possibility. If it were pure camouflage why would the suggestion have disappeared rapidly, as it did, once Lenin moved towards a more robust course? At such a time the propagandist element of proclaiming peaceful development would have been more useful. But he dropped the suggestion. However, there was a new note which had only come into Lenin's discourse in the last few days, the insistence on the need for revolution in order to avoid catastrophe. The theme is pursued to its greatest extent in the pamphlet *The Impending Catastrophe and How to Combat It* written at the same time, 10–14 September (OS), but not published until after the seizure of power. It opens: 'Unavoidable catastrophe is threatening Russia' and goes on 'Everybody admits this … Yet nothing is being done.' [SW 2 217] Touching for once on economic questions Lenin catalogues the problems of government paralysis: the need to nationalize and regulate the banks; nationalize cartels; introduce rationing; introduce a heavily graded income tax and thereby struggle against the looming problems of famine and catastrophe. 'Perish or forge full steam ahead' are Lenin's stark choices. [SW 2 253] While these thoughts were not published they do explain a phrase that was. In *One of the Fundamental Questions of the Revolution* he wrote '*Power to the Soviets – this is the only way to make further progress gradual, peaceful and smooth.*' He continued:

Power to the Soviets means the complete transfer of the country's administration and economic control into the hands of the workers and peasants, to whom *nobody* would dare offer resistance and who, through practice, through their own experience, *would soon learn* how to distribute the land, products and grain properly. [CW 25 73]

Apart from the astonishingly naive assumptions that revolution could improve Russia's social and economic order rather than add a potentially fatal further dimension of collapse, that nobody would resist a soviet takeover and that the new, unlettered, peasant and worker authorities 'would soon learn' the complex arts of economic distribution, the quotation is notable for linking the two themes of fending off catastrophe by seizing power and peaceful development which go hand in hand for the last time. Lenin, in his next missives, shocked his colleagues with a dramatic new line.

Lenin's bombshell came in the form of a letter to the Central Committee and the Moscow and Petrograd Committees of the Party written, like the above, between 12 and 14 September (OS). The uncompromising first sentence said it all: 'The Bolsheviks, having obtained a majority in the Soviets of Workers' and Soldiers' Deputies of both capitals, can and *must* take state power into their own hands.' [SW 2 362] This was the first of an ever-increasingly strident series of missives sent by Lenin to a variety of Party bodies but they all revolved around the message contained in that first sentence. No more pretence about peaceful development or power-sharing: the emergence of Bolshevik majorities in the soviets meant the time for decisive, unilateral, revolutionary action had come. The language Lenin uses in his series of letters and articles betrays a desperate sense of urgency. Power must be taken 'at this very moment' [SW 2 363]. 'History will not forgive us if we do not assume power now.' [SW 2 363] Opposition to the idea is 'the most vicious and probably most widespread distortion of Marxism' resorted to by opportunists. 'Vacillations may *ruin* the cause.' [CW 26 58] 'The crucial point of the revolution in Russia has undoubtedly arrived.' [SW 2 372] 'To miss such a moment and to "wait" for the Congress of Soviets would be *utter idiocy*, or *sheer treachery*.' [SW 2 378] 'To refrain from taking power now … is *to doom the revolution to failure*.' [SW 2 380] 'Procrastination is becoming positively criminal.' [SW 2 424] 'Delay would be fatal.' [SW 2 432 repeated SW 2 433] 'Everything now hangs by a thread.' [SW 2 449]

Apart from the obvious fact that, at the end of the day, it was successful, Lenin's campaign has a number of interesting features. In the first place, Lenin's mounting frenzy was occasioned by the fact that, amazingly, he was not being listened to. When the first letter arrived it was proposed that it should be burned as a dangerous piece of evidence that might endanger the whole party. Following further pressure he was so frustrated by 29 September (OS) that he offered to resign from the

Central Committee, a possibility the Central Committee itself did not take seriously. Nor, however, were they prepared to give in to what they saw as a far-fetched demand of Lenin that power should be seized. His colleagues believed his isolation from Petrograd encouraged the breeding of what they saw as unrealistic demands, as fantasies.

Lenin, however, did not. He took the idea deadly seriously and resorted to further stratagems to get round their resistance. In writing, in the first place, to both Petrograd and Moscow he was partly fishing for support. Either would do. 'By taking power in Moscow and Petrograd *at once* (it doesn't matter which comes first, Moscow may possibly begin), we shall win *absolutely and unquestionably.*' [SW 2 364] By 1 October (OS) he was also sending his crucial letter not only to the three committees but also to the Bolshevik members of the Petrograd and Moscow Soviets. Again he invited Moscow to begin if it thought it could. By 7 October (OS) in a letter to the Petrograd City Conference of the Bolshevik Party he was looking to the Baltic Fleet to perhaps kick off the revolution. The following day he wrote to the Bolshevik delegation to the Congress of Soviets of the Northern Region meeting in Helsinki urging that 'the fleet, Kronstadt, Vyborg, and Revel [Tallin] can and must advance on Petrograd.'[5] [SW 2 433] By this time, having met only delay on the part of everyone else, Lenin took the ultimate step of returning to Petrograd, though, still as cautious as ever, he remained in hiding, staying in the apartment of a Party worker named Marguerita Vasilevna Fofanova. A meeting of the Central Committee was set up for 10 October (OS) in the apartment of the Menshevik-Internationalist N.N. Sukhanov and his wife Galina Flakserman who was a Bolshevik. Despite talking all night and resolving to put armed uprising on the agenda, Lenin had still not got his way. At a further meeting called for 16 October (OS) his frustration was still patently obvious. According to the minutes he commented that 'if all resolutions were defeated in this manner, one could not wish for anything better.'[6] Even worse was to come two days later when, in an open letter published in Gorky's paper *Novaia zhizn'*, Kamenev and Zinoviev, the two leading figures in the Party after Lenin, made public their opposition to a Bolshevik seizure of power, thereby revealing what was, in any case, pretty much an open secret that the Bolsheviks were conspiring against the government. Lenin was merciless in his denunciation of them. They were strike-breakers, traitors and blacklegs. Terms such as 'evasive', 'slanderous' and 'despicable' peppered Lenin's letter. At a meeting of 20 October (OS) the Central Committee took a less serious attitude to the article than Lenin, merely calling for the two to submit to Party discipline rather than, as Lenin wanted, expelling them from the Party.

Clearly, while Lenin was undoubtedly the dominant figure in the Party leadership, even he could not snap his fingers and get his way. It is also significant that, within days, despite the extreme invective, Lenin was working closely and harmoniously with Kamenev and Zinoviev. Once again, the political Lenin was in evidence. First he did not spare his close friend and fellow exile, Zinoviev, from coruscating criticism, like that which had rained down on the heads of Martov, Plekhanov, Bogdanov and many others in the past. But also, the moment passed once the political issue was resolved and they were prepared to return to the Bolshevik camp and accept Party discipline. Lenin dropped the invective as quickly as it had arisen. Like the much longer-lasting polemic against Trotsky, once it was over it was almost as though it had never happened. In interpreting Lenin's more outspoken and extreme statements we must remember that Lenin's political instinct worked in both directions to overrule personal feelings. He could sacrifice friendship in order to break a political relationship. He could also ignore former animosities to build a new alliance. In this light, one should take more seriously Lenin's thoughts at various times about reuniting even with SRs and Mensheviks. If the political terms changed and came right, Lenin might well have been prepared in practice to ally with them as he claimed he would in his writings. However, the preliminary condition would have to be fulfilled. The politics would, indeed, have to be right!

The final aspect of Lenin's campaign for an insurrection lies in the arguments he used to promote his policy. The urgency of his campaign was driven above all by the fact that the Bolsheviks had obtained majorities in the county's two leading soviets. However, this did not mean that those soviets were controlled by the Bolsheviks or that the majority of members actually understood Bolshevik objectives. What it meant above all was that they were prepared to support a party which opposed the Provisional Government and stood firmly in favour of soviet power. That the Bolsheviks also proposed a magical incantation against the war – peace without annexations or reparations – also helped even though it was in practice undeliverable and had, lurking behind it,

Plate 1 The Ulyanov family in Simbirsk, 1879, Vladimin is bottom right
© Hulton-Deutsch Collection/CORBIS

Plate 2 Lenin as a university student, 1891
© Bettmann/CORBIS

Plate 3 Lenin and the Petersburg League of Struggle, 1895. Lenin is in the centre seated behind the table.
© Bettmann/CORBIS

Forged passport with picture of himself in disguise enabled Lenin to escape to Finland in the fall of 1917. Warrant for his arrest had been issued in July of that same year.

Plate 4 Forged passport, 1917
© Hulton-Deutsch Collection/CORBIS

Plate 5 Lenin sitting at his desk, c. 1921
© Bettmann/CORBIS

Plate 6 Lenin, Krupskaya and children on a bench, 1922
© Hulton-Deutsch Collection/CORBIS

Plate 7 Lenin in a wheelchair, 1923
© Bettmann/CORBIS

Plate 8 Crowd at Lenin's funeral, 1924. The cult begins

© Hulton–Deutsch Collection/CORBIS

Plate 9 Lenin's work goes on – *Pravda* editors at work (Bukharin and Maria Ulyanova, Lenin's sister), 1925

© Hulton-Deutsch Collection/CORBIS

the assumption of civil war. Indeed, he even went so far as to remind Party colleagues that, in the event of a soviet takeover and a refusal of peace by the enemy (something that was as certain as anything could be in politics), then the Bolsheviks would become real defensists, they would 'be the *war party par excellence*'. [SW 2 368]

This was actually consistent with all Lenin had said on the issue, including *The April Theses*. However, it was not part of the general perception of the party of peace on the part of the masses. Even some of the leaders were still surprised by it. Only perceptive observers really understood longer-term Bolshevik aims. According to the diarist Sukhanov 'We [the Menshevik-Internationalists] were divided [from the Bolsheviks] not so much by slogans as by a profoundly different conception of their inner meaning. The Bolsheviks reserved that meaning for the use of the leadership and did not carry it to the masses.'[7]

However, Lenin asserted several times that the majority of the country now supported the Bolsheviks. His critics, including Kamenev and Zinoviev, were more sober in suggesting the Bolsheviks might attain a quarter to a third of Constituent Assembly votes rather than a majority. Second, Lenin argued that a full-scale insurrection was going on in the country. Here he was on surer ground. As we have seen, the Kornilov revolt had galvanized the left into more active defence of its 'gains of February' as they became known. The Kornilov affair had raised the spectre of counter-revolution; so, for the masses, it was now or never. Peasants speeded up the acquisition of landowners' land. Workers fought to control their factories and keep them running. Soldiers and sailors reasserted the authority of their committees and were more determined than ever not to be pawns in an imperialist struggle. Linked to this, Lenin also argued that the enemies of the revolution were wavering. Kornilov had split the propertied classes and provoked the backlash just mentioned. The arrest of Kornilov, and the ensuing despair of the army officers, was sowing confusion among the former elites. Lenin believed the international conjuncture was also right and Bolshevik action was imperative to realize the international potential of the revolution. On 29 September (OS) he argued the world revolution was reaching its 'third stage' which 'may be called the eve of revolution'. [SW 2 371] Lenin insisted on it many times in the campaign of September–October. For instance, he referred to the German mutinies in the Central Committee resolution of 10 October (OS). All the above arose out of his earlier writings. However, as we have seen, one major additional argument began to take a more and more prominent part in Lenin's armoury, the rather fanciful but powerfully argued notion that only a soviet seizure of power would *prevent* social and economic catastrophe.

Incidentally, the last of Lenin's communications to his comrades in the Central Committee written on 24 October (OS), which was never sent because he broke cover himself and went to join them, stated that power should be taken by the 'armed people' and 'the masses'. Strangely, nowhere in it does he specifically mention workers. For the last time before the actual revolution, Lenin's populist matrix emerged from under the orthodox Marxist surface.

Lenin took no direct part in the seizure of power itself before the night of 24–25 October (OS). The overthrow of the remnants of the Provisional Government was not conducted by the Party as much as by the Petrograd Soviet and its Military Revolutionary Committee with Bolsheviks such as Trotsky but also others including Left SRs, anarchists and Left Mensheviks taking a leading role. However, some have suggested that Lenin's dramatic emergence from hiding was decisive in tipping the balance from a defensive operation to protect the Congress of Soviets which was about to meet and also, perhaps, the city of Petrograd itself which, it was widely though probably incorrectly believed, was on the point of being surrendered to the Germans. We do not know for sure what Lenin did in the vital hours following his arrival at the Smolny Institute, the soviet nerve centre. We do know that he left hiding almost on an impulse and, still in disguise, made his way through the city, narrowly avoiding a Provisional Government patrol. On arrival at the Smolny Institute he handed his disguise to his friend Bonch-Bruevich who had accompanied him. Knowing his retreat might yet be as rapid as his advance, Bonch-Bruevich, only half-jokingly, said he would keep hold of it as it might yet come in handy.

Whether the influence came from Lenin or not, a bolder set of actions emanated from the Smolny in the middle of the night of 24–25 October (OS). The following morning at 10 a.m. the overthrow of the Provisional Government and the establishment of a Soviet Government was proclaimed. Even so, it was only the following evening that, without any significant part being played by Lenin, the Winter Palace was raided and the remaining Provisional Government ministers arrested.

Kerensky himself had already left the city to seek assistance. Later in the day, that is 26 October (OS), Lenin went to the Second Congress of Soviets and was acclaimed as the leader of the Revolution. He was nominated as Chairman of the Council of People's Commissars, that is as head of the new government, though for the moment the full personnel of the government were not named as negotiations were continuing. Lenin introduced Decrees on Peace and Land which were approved. The Menshevik and SR leaders, the chief rivals of the Bolsheviks, suicidally walked out of the Congress into what Trotsky described as 'the dustbin of history'. Lenin, in the midst of these events, commented to Trotsky that 'The transition from illegality and being hounded from pillar to post to power is too abrupt. It makes one dizzy.' [Weber 141] It was a dizziness Lenin would have to get used to.

6

FROM CLASSROOM TO LABORATORY – EARLY EXPERIMENTS

Almost from the very first day of the October Revolution Lenin's hopes and expectations for it began to collapse. His opponents had predicted as much. Lenin's assertion that the transition to soviet power would be 'gradual, peaceful and smooth' was so far off the mark that observers have wondered if he seriously meant it or if it was simply a propaganda device. In October, the Bolsheviks had appeared to offer, as far as the population was concerned, four things above all. They were: soviet power; peace; bread (i.e. economic and material security); and land. The delivery of these promises was faltering at best. At the same time the Bolsheviks were gradually improving the toehold on power they had achieved in October. October was no more than a beginning from which more secure consolidation had to be achieved. Opposition also gained momentum but was divided between the anti-Bolshevik soviet left and the more broadly counter-revolutionary propertied classes of the centre and right. Social and economic disruption deepened at an alarming rate. The war against Germany did not disappear overnight. The essential condition for success – world revolution – showed little sign of appearing quickly.

Such was the unpromising situation into which Lenin stepped on 25 October (OS). Up to that time he had been mainly a professor and teacher of revolution, a frequenter of Europe's great libraries, who constantly produced articles of analysis and denunciation. Even in the crucial weeks and months before the October Revolution Lenin had been in hiding and his weapons continued to be words not deeds. Events over which he had no control, like the Kornilov affair, had propelled him into power. In no sense had Lenin, up to this point, exerted leadership over the revolution. As we have seen, he had found it hard enough to exert his authority over the tiny band of ardent supporters in the various higher committees of his own party. With what success would he make the transition to practical politician, to activist? He was stepping out of his professorial classroom and study into a laboratory where actions were judged by their results. But it was no ordinary laboratory. It was chaotic, near-bankrupt and threatened with external attack. Experiments conducted in these conditions would be risky in the extreme and the odds would be strongly stacked against them working successfully. It is hardly surprising that it took Lenin several attempts to get the formula right – at least to his own satisfaction. Maybe even the final formula he bequeathed to his party and people – the New Economic Policy – was flawed in ways that only came to light after his death. The remainder of our study of his life will centre on how Lenin coped with the immense challenges he, and the Revolution, faced.

INITIAL CONSOLIDATION AND THE FIRST CIVIL WAR

Whose power?

In Lenin's own words in *The Dual Power* of 9 April 1917, 'the basic question of any revolution is state power.' [SW 2 18] The first task was to secure power. But there was an associated problem. Whose power was it that would be consolidated? The slogans of October were unambiguous. They all proclaimed 'All Power to the Soviets'. Lenin, however, had secretly been urging Bolshevik power. Only one of these positions could be implemented.

On the surface, soviet power appeared to reign supreme. It was to the Second All-Russian Congress of Soviets that the Petrograd Soviet and its Military Revolutionary Committee, which had actually spearheaded the takeover, turned to formalize the new system. The government called itself the Soviet Government and retained the title until 1991. It was through soviets and especially their military revolutionary committees that power began to spread throughout the country in its so-called triumphal march. If the local soviet supported the takeover all well and good. However, where Mensheviks and SRs were in the majority, many soviets did not support the new authorities and this included some major army soviets at the front and in the Ukraine. Here tactics were cruder. Local Bolsheviks, plus a minority of non-Bolsheviks from other parties, set themselves up as a military revolutionary committee and used their authority to call on revolutionary regiments to coerce the soviet majority into acquiescence. In other places the soviet forces as a whole were not strong enough to prevail immediately. In Moscow, the left–right balance was much more even and it took six days of fighting before the authority of the soviet prevailed. The fighting was also notable because, hearing reports of damage to the Kremlin, Anatoly Lunacharsky briefly resigned as Minister of Education. Arresting the remnants of the General Staff at *Stavka* (HQ) in Mogilev was a delicate enterprise. The acting Chief of Staff, Admiral Dukhonin, negotiated an uneasy handover but the troops sent by the Bolsheviks could not resist the temptation of revenge and lynched him before they could be reined in.

The military squads used in such operations gradually became the core of the Bolshevik enforcement system on which it relied from its first days. Spontaneous organizations of the people – ironically those closest to the militia pattern supposedly supported by Lenin, such as Red Guards – were disbanded in favour of more tightly controlled groups. The most famous was the Latvian Rifle Regiment, members of which became Lenin's and the Soviet government's bodyguards. They also formed the active arm of the king of all enforcement agencies, the Cheka, when it was set up in December 1917. It is worth pausing here for a moment to reflect, since this was one of the earliest examples of an extraordinary process that affected the whole revolution very quickly. In his writings of only a few weeks earlier, Lenin had insisted on the value of actively democratic ways of conducting state business, or more correctly, what was formerly state business since the state was, in Lenin's words taken from Marx, to be smashed. Far from being smashed and replaced by militias and socially conscious workers in place of civil servants, the new institutions increasingly took on a traditional look. Some issues, like the restoration of ranks and insignia, not to mention the death penalty, in the Red Army, eventually caused Party scandals. Others, particularly in the early days, were passed over without even being noticed. By the time Lenin came to reflect on what was happening he was, as we shall see, already complaining about drowning in a sea of red tape. Lenin was finding out that while one might have ideas about how a completed revolution would look, the exercise of transition — what steps one took the day after the revolution, the day after that and so on — was much trickier than anticipated. No natural instinct to build the revolution emerged from the masses. The new leaders were too pre-occupied with facing a massive wave of events to do more than respond instinctively. By the time they came to take stock they were already well off course and it was not clear that, with the prevailing winds and tides, they would ever be able to regain their expected destination.

Despite the operation against *Stavka*, the main figures in the General Staff, including Kornilov who slipped out of jail, along with other parts of the officer corps and a crystallizing resistance to soviet power, had retreated to the protection of Ataman Kaledin, chief of the Don Cossacks. South Russia and parts of eastern Ukraine became no-go areas for soviet power and General Alexeev formed the anti-soviet Volunteer Army. The remainder of Ukraine was drifting towards independence. Siberia had areas of support for each of the two sides and was of uncertain affiliation for some time to come. However, the Soviet government, with its increasingly effective Red Army also growing from politically active Bolshevik regiments and their allies, appeared, by the beginning of the new year, to be dealing a series of powerful blows to the havens of counter-revolution. In January radical Don Cossacks repudiated the authority of Kaledin. In early February Kiev fell to soviet forces. By the end of February, Rostov and NovoCherkassk were under soviet control and the Volunteer Army was forced to retreat to the Kuban. However, the Germans took Kiev on 2 March and threw out the left and restored the nationalist Rada (Assembly). The following day the peace treaty was signed at Brest-Litovsk handing Ukraine and other territories to Germany and Austria-Hungary, and driving soviet authority out. However, on 14 March Red troops took the last stronghold of the Volunteers, the Kuban capital Ekaterinodar. When, a month later (13 April), Kornilov himself was killed during an unsuccessful attempt to retake Ekaterinodar, it appeared that the Civil War was all but over. Many Bolsheviks were of this opinion. Considering also that peace had been made with Germany, it appeared that fighting might soon cease. Nothing could have been further from the truth. But before we turn to the renewal of the Civil War in May, we need to look at many other aspects of the early months.

As a result of the processes traced above, soviet power appeared to be relatively secure by March 1918. However, such an assertion begs a vital question. Was it soviet power that occupied this position or was it Bolshevik power that had triumphed?

While Lenin had wavered over the issue of soviet power in 1917 he never wavered over Bolshevik power. From his first, rhetorical, assertion that the Bolsheviks were prepared to take power uttered at the First Congress of Soviets he proclaimed his resolve. Even when things turned against them in July Lenin still believed in a Bolshevik-led armed uprising in the context of a nationwide revolution – roughly what happened in October. His drive for power in September and October was ambiguous in the early stages with the uncharacteristic musing about compromise and peaceful transfer of power between soviet-based parties. However, the very titles under which his later letters and articles have come down to us – 'The Bolsheviks Must Assume Power' and 'Can the Bolsheviks Retain State Power?' – tell their own story. At the Central Committee meetings of 10 and 16 October (OS) it was Bolshevik power that Lenin urged.

Lenin's imagination had also, in professorial mode again, been fired by the example of the Jacobins in the French Revolution. This association of ideas is a key to unlocking the seemingly utopian and disparate parts of Lenin's discourse on the revolution in the weeks leading up to October. The Jacobins had inherited a crumbling revolution, threatened by impending foreign invasion, from the temporizing Girondins. Through resolute revolutionary action, including terror and sending out plenipotentiaries (*représentatives en mission*) from the centre, they had turned the situation round. Lenin believed he and the Bolsheviks could do the same, the hapless Menshevik and SR right playing the role of Girondins. As far back as July Lenin had defended the Jacobin heritage. The theme grew as the October Revolution approached. It was their example which inspired some of the more improbable statements which we have seen that he made at the time, notably that only further revolution could defend the left and create a transition that would be 'gradual, peaceful and smooth' [SW 2 261]; that the 'resources, both spiritual and material, for a truly revolutionary war are still immense' [SW 2 368]; that 'the workers and peasants would soon learn' [SW 2 261] and 'will deal better than the officials ... with the difficult practical problems' of production and distribution of grain [CW 24 52–3 (April)]; and that the Bolsheviks, like the Jacobins, would become 'the war party *par excellence*'. [SW 2 368] Lenin increasingly appealed to 'the history of all revolutions', meaning primarily the French. [SW 2 450] He even quoted Marx who was himself quoting one of the Jacobin leaders, Danton: 'Marx summed up the lessons of all revolutions in respect to armed uprising in the words of "Danton the greatest master of French revolutionary policy yet known: *de l'audace, de l'audace, encore de l'audace*"' (boldness, boldness and yet more boldness). [SW 2 427]

Lenin's letter of the night of 24 October (OS) claimed power would be handed over to 'the true representatives of the people' and 'not in opposition to the Soviets but on their behalf' as 'proved by the history of all revolutions'. [SW 2 449–50] The official declaration of 25 October (OS), issued by the Petrograd Military Revolutionary Committee (MRC), claimed power passed to itself, the MRC, and thereby 'the establishment of Soviet power .... has been secured.'[1] [SW 2 451]

The coup was presented to the Second Congress of Soviets in the wrapping of soviet power but the realities were changing. The most formidable of opponents, from the soviet right to Martov on the internationalist left, walked out and formed the never-effective Committee for the Salvation of Russia. That left the entire Congress with virtually no alternative leadership to the Bolsheviks. Many delegates were Bolsheviks and a majority appear to have been mandated to support soviet power before they left their home areas, that is *before* the Bolshevik operation. 612 out of a total of 670 delegates were mandated to end the alliance with the bourgeoisie and only 55 to continue it. Holding to their mandate the majority supported the Bolsheviks and many, but by no means all, declared themselves to be 'Bolshevik', around 390 being the accepted figure.[2] However, there is some difficulty in identifying just what being a Bolshevik meant. Many identified with the Bolsheviks mainly, probably only, because the Bolsheviks supported soviet power. Therefore, more or less by definition, most of those who supported soviet power described themselves as Bolsheviks. It is extremely unlikely that many of them had a developed sense of what the Bolsheviks stood for beyond their immediate slogans.

Many Party leaders, including Kamenev and Zinoviev, had been sceptical about the Bolsheviks taking power alone, hence their 'strikebreaking' outburst. But even after 25 October (OS) some Party leaders believed the emerging path of unsupported Bolshevik power was not only impossible, it was undesirable and could lead to unhealthy dictatorship. An alliance of soviet parties would, they believed, be more democratic. On 4 November (OS) they expressed themselves unambiguously: 'It is our view that a socialist government should be formed from all parties in the soviet ... We believe that, apart from this, there is only one other path: the retention of a purely Bolshevik government by means of political terror.' To follow this path would result in cutting the leadership off from the masses and 'the establishment of an unaccountable regime and the destruction of the revolution and the country'.[3] Amazingly Kamenev and Zinoviev, who had not been expelled as Lenin had demanded, were prepared to criticize again.

Coincidentally, further signs of the well-founded nature of their fears became apparent. On the same day, Trotsky called for a curtailment of press freedom, arguing that earlier demands for complete freedom of the press had represented the Party's 'minimum programme' while control of the counter-revolutionary press, which soon came to mean virtually any non-Bolshevik paper, was its 'maximum programme'. Fears were growing as to what other surprises the 'maximum programme' might reveal. The response of the Central Committee majority, determined largely by Lenin, was as uncompromising as it was possible to be. The dissidents were accused of 'totally disregarding all the fundamental tenets of Bolshevism'. That implied a clear enough definition of what 'Bolshevism' was at that point – one-party dictatorship. As if that were not enough they were also accused of 'criminal vacillation', 'sabotage' and being 'enemies of the people'.[4]

However, two qualifications to the extremism of the response should be noted. First, despite the language, the minority was not expelled but presented with an ultimatum to accept Central Committee authority immediately. Most did so, though some resigned. Those who accepted continued working as normal in the leadership, again showing that Lenin's political personality permitted reconciliation, if the political conditions were right, as readily as enforcing a split where they were not. Second, though slightly hollow, the majority protested that it was not their fault that the one-party government was emerging. The majority declared that:

> The Central Committee affirms that, not having excluded anyone from the Second All-Russian Congress of Soviets, it is fully prepared even

now to re-instate those who walked out and to agree to a coalition within the Soviets with those who left; therefore the claim that the Bolsheviks do not want to share power with anyone is absolutely false.[5]

Sceptics might argue that the other parties were certainly not going to return to the fold and therefore the promise was hollow. They might also add that the previous paragraph but one in the resolution rather contradicted the later one:

The Central Committee confirms that there can be no repudiation of the purely Bolshevik government without betraying the slogan of Soviet power, since a majority of the Second All-Russian Congress of Soviets, barring no one from the Congress, entrusted power to this government.[6]

The majority also claimed several times that the collapse of negotiations for the Left SRs to join the government was not their fault. In fact, largely because of pressure from the Railwaymen's Union (*Vikzhel*), the Left SRs did join in a coalition that lasted four months. However, the weight of the above arguments tends to indicate that Lenin was not only ready but very willing to march on alone. In any case, the only acceptable terms for a coalition would have been complete acceptance of the Bolshevik programme. Those were virtually the terms on which the Left SRs joined the government and it was at the first major obstacle, the peace treaty of Brest-Litovsk, that it broke down.

However, the alliance did last long enough for it to get Lenin past another potentially fatal obstacle, the Constituent Assembly. Here was another issue over which the contradictions of Lenin's personality came to a head. On 26 October (OS) he presented the Second Congress of Soviets with a manifesto it approved which stated clearly that the new Soviet government 'will ensure the convocation of the Constituent Assembly'. [SW 2 457] The new government was 'to govern the country until the Constituent Assembly is convened'. [SW 2 471] On another occasion he claimed the new government would submit proposals for peace 'for consideration to the Constituent Assembly'. [SW 2 462] In discussing land he said the new decree 'is proclaimed a provisional law, pending the convocation of the Constituent Assembly'. [SW 2 470]

He even went so far as to speculate that 'even if the peasants continue to follow the Socialist-Revolutionaries, even if they give this party a majority in the Constituent Assembly, we shall still say – what of it? Experience is the best teacher and it will show who is right.' [SW 2 470]

How could one doubt Lenin's commitment to the Constituent Assembly? Indeed, the elections went ahead more or less on schedule with little controversy in early November. However, once the results became known and it was clear the Bolsheviks did not have a majority Lenin's tone was less accepting. In a *Pravda* article of 13 December (OS), entitled 'Theses on the Constituent Assembly', he attacked the legitimacy of the elections. They did not reflect post-October realities, he said, for two reasons above all. First, the party lists were drawn up before October and did not reflect the split of the SR Party into left and right segments so the electors could not take that major fact into account. Second, the elections took place before the electorate had had time to digest the meaning of October, which, he claimed, they now supported more deeply. The result was, in Lenin's view, a 'divergence between the elections to the Constituent Assembly, on the one hand, and the will of the people and the interests of the working and exploited people, on the other'. The solution was for the elected Assembly to accept the broad lines of soviet government policies up to that point and to support new elections to bring the Assembly into line with the electorate's supposed new allegiances. [SW 2 502]

The Assembly, perhaps naively on Lenin's part, was allowed to convene on 5 January (OS) in the hope that it would accept Lenin's 'painless solution' [SW 2 502] to the dilemma. When it did not, it was forcibly dissolved in the early hours of 6 January (OS). While there were some significant demonstrations in its support in Petrograd, in the course of which there were many deaths and the brutal murder of two former Provisional Government ministers in their hospital beds, the dissolution of the Assembly did not spark off much resistance on the part of the masses. The elections did, however, give some indication of the political allegiances of the nation. The entire right wing, represented almost exclusively by the Kadet Party, received support from no more than a rump of, if generously calculated, around 10 per cent of the voters. The Bolsheviks took about 25 per cent and the, undivided, SR list and allies took about 50 per cent. The Mensheviks got next to no votes. At the actual meeting the best indication of the affiliation of delegates was in the election of a chair. Maria Spiridonova, the Left SR candidate supported by the Bolsheviks, received 153 votes while Victor Chernov, the SR candidate, received 244 votes and was duly elected.

However, that was not the end of the story. Immediately after the Constituent Assembly was dissolved the Third Congress of Soviets was convened as a kind of counterweight. Lenin addressed it on 11 January (OS). Indeed, had it agreed to do so, the Constituent Assembly, or at least that part of it amenable to Bolshevik blandishments, was intended to be merged with the Congress to form – the French Revolution providing the model – a revolutionary Convention. However, it was not to be. The Third Congress showed the Bolsheviks tightening their grip on power with 441 out of the 707 delegates at the first session. The Fourth Congress, which met in emergency session in mid-March to discuss the Treaty of Brest-Litovsk, was even more heavily Bolshevik with 795 Bolsheviks out of 1,232 delegates. In effect, this was the last public meeting at which a significant proportion of non-Bolsheviks was able to take part and it also ratified, as it were, the split between the Bolsheviks and the Left SRs. We will have cause to return to it in discussing the peace question. As far as the question of power is concerned, by the end of March soviet power had been definitively replaced by Bolshevik power. No one other than Bolsheviks ever sat in the Soviet government. Other parties were reduced to token status in central and local soviets. In this respect, Lenin's will had been done.

Land

Compared to the complexities of the central issue of power, the story of the struggle over land in the first few months of the Revolution was a simple one. The complications were to come later. At the Second Congress Lenin quite simply stole the land policy of the SRs, adding a few embellishments. Nominally, land was handed over to the local land committees and soviets with a frequently unheeded proviso that large estates, that is the landowners' land, should be maintained as large model estates under local soviet/committee control. The point was to try to prevent the break up of the large estates because they produced the bulk of the surplus needed for the towns and the army. If they were to be broken up and added to the peasant near-subsistence economy, production might fall and markets collapse. Some estates were transformed into state farms but usually with a hugely reduced land area. Problems were being stoked up for the future.

It was in his speech on land that Lenin made his magnanimous comment that if the peasants continued to follow the SRs, so what? They would soon learn. However, it was unlikely that they would desert the new authorities since the Bolsheviks had implemented the central item of peasant and SR policy. Lenin's tone switched between the laconic and the magnanimous when confronted by hecklers in the Congress who pointed out the proposed decree was essentially SR policy:

> Voices are being raised here that the decree itself and the Mandate were drawn up by the Socialist-Revolutionaries. What of it? Does it matter who drew them up? As a democratic government, we cannot ignore the decision of the masses of the people, even though we may disagree with it. In the fire of experience, applying the decree in practice, and carrying it out locally, the peasants will themselves realize where the truth lies. [SW 2 470]

He then went on to talk about the possibility of an SR majority in the Constituent Assembly. Critics might also detect a large vein of disingenuousness as well!

In Lenin's favour it can be said that he took the obvious pragmatic decision any sensible government would have taken. Since September, largely as a reaction to fears arising from the Kornilov affair, the peasants were no longer ready to wait for the Constituent Assembly to hand out the land. The Kornilov affair demonstrated the danger that the opportunity would be taken away from them. Very sensibly they took action while they could. As a result, from September to February/March 1918, almost all landowner estates were taken under peasant control and most of the land re-distributed.[7] There was no way to stop this tidal wave. Lenin recognized that and held on to power. The Provisional Government – despite the ever more desperate appeals of the former Minister of Agriculture, Chernov, who had been replaced in August – did not feel able to implement it. They had kept it in the background, like other key issues, to avoid breaking up the alliance with the bourgeoisie and thereby risking civil war while the external enemy was still at the gates. This sensible and honourable policy had ceased to be viable after Kornilov. Had Kerensky himself implemented the radical programme things might have been very different, but he did not. He was still hanging on to the extinct hope that the country might be kept together. Kornilov had made this impossible. Even so, in Kerensky's eyes the alternative was an abyss of destruction from within and without. He was not prepared to condemn Russia to such a fate. Lenin, of course, was spared such thoughts by his discourse of revolution as the only path to save Russia from the abyss. Events were soon to prove Lenin wrong, but for the time being bold initiatives won the day.

Potential food shortages and social collapse were not the only delayed problems. No one knows exactly which voices Lenin heard raised when he announced his policy, because they might have come from outraged Bolsheviks as much as from outraged SRs. While the SRs might fume to see their policies stolen, Bolsheviks might also get steamed up at seeing their policies betrayed. The provisions announced by Lenin were very different from the Bolsheviks' real long-term beliefs about land. Above all, the traditional Bolshevik line was to encourage the disappearance of the peasantry, whom they saw as a transitional class. In modern society they would dissolve away. Some would remain as labourers on much larger collectively owned farms which could benefit from economies of scale and compete with American farms in the production and productivity stakes. The remainder would leave the countryside and become urban workers. Thus, whichever path they took, they would be proletarianized and thereby join the chosen people. To achieve this, basic Bolshevik policy was to nationalize land. In fact, they had done the opposite. They had opened the way for a last golden age of the peasant commune and the small peasant economy. It flourished in the 1920s but suffered immensely when Stalin judged that the time had come to tidy up the contradiction through the collectivization campaign. However, there were twists and turns to come in Lenin's own attitude to the peasants, but it was only when the dire consequences of the land decree began to assert themselves that he refocused on rural issues in spring 1918. From October 1917 to March 1918 the peasants were left to themselves. They conducted a complete revolution in landholding.

Peace

Elevation into a position of power meant Lenin had to make real decisions with real consequences over the question of war. Before October, 'peace' polices had been crucial in attracting or repelling popular support. Various approaches existed. 'War to a victorious conclusion' was the slogan of the right; 'revolutionary defensism' and peace negotiations was the policy of the centre; 'peace without annexations or indemnities' (that is, reparations) was the policy of the internationalist left. Lenin, as he stated at several points, was prepared to become a revolutionary defensist once Russia had a real, that is, people's revolution to defend. The far left also lauded the prospect of revolutionary war, meaning exporting revolution on the bayonets of Russian proletarian soldiers. Despite this plethora of policies and their symbolic importance in attracting support, in real terms there was less to choose between them than met the eye. Victorious war and defensive war meant much the same thing to those caught up in it — carry on fighting. In fact, peace without annexations and indemnities meant exactly the same. The implication, that the borders of 1914 could be magically restored, was not on. As Russia fell to rack and ruin, as it was seen in Berlin, so the prospect of the German Army packing up and going home was more remote than ever. That's what no annexations meant. Since that was impossible, fighting would have to be carried on.

Or would it? The one policy no one was contemplating in public, though in many ways it corresponded to a kind of subliminal, unspoken attitude in the minds of many, was unconditional surrender. For four months Lenin tried to evade implementing this logical consequence of his other policies.

Since 1914 Lenin had interpreted the war as a revolutionary opportunity. Its potential in this respect would be tapped by a popular uprising sparked off by opposition to the imperialist struggle. In the *April Theses* Lenin had toyed with notions of revolutionary defensism and later of revolutionary war. However, there was a gap. How would the imperialist war be transformed? How would the required popular uprising be realized? In the *April Theses* there was only one word about this — fraternization. In October the Decree on Peace presented to the Second Congress along with the other key documents did not go much further. The Decree called on 'all the belligerent peoples and their governments to start immediate negotiations for a just, democratic peace'. Such a peace was defined as 'an immediate peace without annexations ... and without indemnities'. [SW 2 459] The Decree went on to expound Lenin's views on international relations and the coming revolution in the usual terms and added a number of provisions. The most important were the promise to publish all secret treaties and abandon secret diplomacy and to offer an immediate three-month armistice. Any terms offered in response would be considered 'but that does not necessarily mean that we shall accept them'. [SW 2 462] Lenin even contemplated the fact that 'War cannot be ended by refusal, it cannot be ended by one side.' [SW 2 462] He did not, however, offer a solution to the dilemma of no one responding to the Decree.

Despite saying 'we are not living in the depths of Africa but in Europe, where news can spread quickly' [SW 2 463] the Decree did not spread. It was barely known outside Russia but, like the other decrees of the Second Congress, had considerable propagandist weight in Russia. That was all very well but it didn't budge the German Army. They would not be moved back by a piece of paper.

Even worse, Lenin had to contemplate what to do about the Russian Army which was, essentially, the remnants of the Russian Imperial Army increasingly denuded of General Staff and senior officers who drifted away to join the counter-revolution. Troops, too, began to drift away. One of the great myths of 1917 was that the October Revolution was led, to a significant degree, by insurgent deserters from a collapsed army. In reality, the army was holding together and the problem of desertion, though worrying throughout 1917, was still under control. In fact, it was the October Revolution which unleashed the tide of desertion, not the other way round. Lenin was caught in a major quandary here. He knew very well, from Engels above all, that no revolution could succeed unless it overcame the police and military resources of the state. But the Bolsheviks still needed an army between them and the Germans. There were two contradictory imperatives. One, disband the Imperial Army so it could not become a weapon of counter-revolution. Two, maintain the army to defend Russia's true revolution. The third option, reforming a more politically acceptable army, was an impossibility in the time available. What was to be done? For the next few weeks and months the new government tried to kick the problems around, like autumn leaves, in the hope they would go away.

On 22 November Lenin ordered the Commander-in-Chief, Dukhonin, to begin peace negotiations with Germany immediately. His refusal led to his replacement by Krylenko, the assault on *Stavka* and the lynching of Dukhonin but no peace negotiations. On 10 December

Lenin was still drafting a peace programme following the line of 'no annexations or indemnities'. However, real peace negotiations were getting nowhere and the German Army was picking away at a collapsing front. At this point Lenin not only considered continuing the war but, on 21 December, even consulted with the US representative, Colonel Robins, about bringing in American specialists to bolster Russia's war effort. Ten days later the bellicose tone remained in a Sovnarkom (Council of People's Commissars) draft resolution submitted by Lenin which called for 'intensified agitation against the annexationist policy of the Germans' and 'Greater efforts to reorganize the army'. [CW 26 397] During much of this time fighting had been intermittent because Trotsky had been at the front-line town of Brest-Litovsk conducting negotiations with the enemy. His brief, as much as anything, was to stall and wait to see what turned up. However, German patience was not interminable. On 15 January 1918 Lenin called him and suggested breaking off negotiations. The previous day, apart from being shot at in his car, an attack which wounded his old friend and organizer of the return from Switzerland, Fritz Platten, Lenin had formally sent off the first detachments of the socialist army and had encouraged the overcoming of 'every obstacle on the way to world revolution'. [CW 26 420]

Despite this apparent dalliance with war, Lenin, on 21 January, dropped one of his greatest bombshells in the form of theses on what he called the 'immediate conclusion' of peace. In them he proposed accepting the draconian terms offered by Germany. The ensuing debate was immensely illustrative of the standing of Lenin in the Party and the difficulties he had come to face. Of the sixty-three Bolsheviks at the Conference, thirty-two voted against Lenin's proposal and only fifteen supported him. The thirty-two supported the policy of revolutionary war. For Lenin, this would only be viable in the event of the German revolution breaking out in three to four months, otherwise one would risk the whole revolution in Russia on the mere possibility of a future German revolution. Trotsky tried to compromise calling for a policy of 'neither war nor peace' which only attracted sixteen votes. Lenin moved on to the next battleground. Addressing a meeting of Bolsheviks on 24 January during the Third Congress of Soviets, he outlined the three strategies – immediate peace (the one he continued to support); revolutionary war and neither peace nor war – but again could not command a majority. Calling, instead, for a delay in signing the peace he won the vote twelve to one and the proposal for revolutionary war was thrown out by eleven to two. Trotsky's compromise was then supported by nine votes to seven.

However, everyone seemed to have forgotten Lenin's earlier injunction that war cannot be ended by a refusal. The Germans simply advanced against the faltering Russian Army and presented ever more onerous peace terms. On 17 February the Central Committee narrowly rejected Lenin's call for immediate peace by six votes to five. Despite this, the following day he radioed his acceptance of terms to the German command. Only on 23 February did he get the Central Committee to accept the increasingly inevitable. Even though the Germans were advancing and resistance was apparently impossible Lenin's proposal hardly received a ringing endorsement. Seven voted in favour, four against and four abstained. Lenin was under no illusion that the decision was serious. 'We have signed *a Tilsit peace*' he said on 3 March alluding to the disastrous peace made by Alexander I in July 1807 as Napoleon advanced after subduing the continent at the battle of Austerlitz in December 1805 and in the campaign which followed. A Fourth Extraordinary Congress of Soviets was called to ratify the Treaty which it did by 784 votes to 261 with 116 abstentions. Clearly there was still a major opposition to Lenin and a strong faction, calling itself the Left Communists, which wanted to continue what they saw as the proactive revolutionary policies of 1917, in this case revolutionary war which, they rightly argued, had been part and parcel of Bolshevik thinking throughout the war. They were soon to clash with him on other apparent u-turns.

For the moment, however, the peace was signed and the disastrous terms made known. Not only did Lenin face pressure from within the Party, the entire Left SR group, which was still in coalition, favoured revolutionary war. They left the government complaining that it was German-dominated. For them, not to mention enemies on the right, the Treaty of Brest-Litovsk was the clearest proof of the Bolsheviks being 'German agents'. Indeed, on 6 July, they began an insurrection in Moscow against the Soviet government by assassinating the German ambassador, Count von Mirbach, whom they denounced as the real dictator of Russia. Such accusations were false. Lenin had feared they would be made but his reasons for signing the peace simply arose from the need to face up to the inevitable consequences of his policies. Having wrecked Russia's already-declining defence capability, unconditional surrender, which is what it virtually was, remained the only way out.

Lenin had, however, based his decision on two other closely related calculations. First, he believed that any price was worth paying in the short run for the revolution to survive. To last out the year, in whatever form, would be a victory from which they could consolidate and move on. Second, he believed the terms would be short-lived because the party with which he agreed them, Imperial Germany, was on its last legs. The latter point was more accurate than the former in that one could argue that the cost of survival was the stifling of the revolution. However, before turning to Lenin's policies after Brest-Litovsk we need to look at the Soviet government's early attempts at the transition to socialism in the crucial area of the economy.

Bread

The nineteenth century provides many examples of socialist utopias. As well as Marx's communism, socialists from Fourrier and Robert Owen to Chernyshevsky painted visions of a perfect future society. While such dreams might be inspirational they left a practical void. How did one get from the confused conditions of today to the beauty of tomorrow? One could easily distinguish journey's end on a distant sunlit peak, but what was the first step to take, then the second and so on? There were no route maps for the voyage. Indeed, Marx had scoffed at other forms of socialism precisely because they were 'utopian' whereas his and Engels' version was 'scientific', by which they meant that they had identified the mechanisms which would bring communism into existence. What were those mechanisms? Capitalism itself – through the pursuit of profit, the ensuing competition, declining surplus value available and consequently increasing level of exploitation – would force proletarians, having nothing to lose but their chains, to unite to overthrow the system and use its potential to fulfil the needs of the many rather than the whims of the rich. But how did this apply on 26 October 1917?

Lenin knew Russia was 'backward' in terms of capitalist development and had not been very explicit about how the economy should be reformed and made to catch up. Given that Marxism was understood at the time largely though not exclusively as a form of economic materialism – that is that economic relations were the basis of political, social and cultural relations – it is surprising that, as we have already remarked, Lenin had little to say about economics. What he did say was wrapped up in political prescriptions. Can we piece together his first plan for the transition to socialism?

First, the key writings of the time – *April Theses* and *State and Revolution* above all – showed a preoccupation with institutions. First, banks were to be seen as the key to the first stage of economic control. Amalgamate the banks into a single bank and then nationalize it. Since managers rather than owners of capital controlled investment flows the banks could continue to function without a glitch under their new state controllers. Second, a political revolution would have brought the soviets to power in order for this to have happened in the first place, so the soviets would become the supervisors of the banks. Lenin had also said on several occasions and continued to do so after October, that socialism could not be 'introduced'. He usually used the inverted commas himself. He meant it had to grow organically out of the revolution, through the multiple action of a creative working class and so on. It could not be artificially decreed from above. It would take time to evolve, though the actual scale of the time needed was never explicit, varying at different times from what looked like months or years to intimations that the task would not be completed for a whole epoch, that 'we of the older generation may not live to see the decisive battles of the coming revolution.' [SW 1 802] In the words of the *April Theses*, the first task was 'to bring social production and the distribution of products at once under the *control* [i.e. supervision] of the Soviets of Workers' Deputies.' [SW 2 14]

The model implied seems to be one of political supervision exercised by soviets over a slowly transforming capitalist and market economy, since there are no proposals whatsoever to make private investment illegal or to replace the market immediately by an alternative. Indeed, the model sounds a reasonable one. The capitalists and their institutions would be nudged bit by bit towards socially beneficial rather than privately beneficial policies by the constant pressure of the soviets, which he later called the dictatorship of the proletariat. Any resistance would be dealt with ruthlessly. A few exemplary arrests and occasionally even executions of speculators, Lenin thought, and the rest would soon accept the hopelessness of attempting to thwart the will of the vast majority.[8] It was absolutely crucial to Lenin's strategy that the majority would hold very firm against the recalcitrant minority in the early days and quickly break the remnants of its power. It explains the uncharacteristic ferocity and, occasionally, near-hysterical bloodthirstiness, apparent in a few of his statements of the early months.

In the last weeks before the revolution a further refinement was added to the model. The soviets must take over to *avert* approaching economic catastrophe and they 'would soon learn' how to supervise the collection and distribution of key goods.

Practice can be cruel to even the most elegant theories and here was no exception. Confronted with the declining situation of the real world, the optimistic gloss of the 'gradual, peaceful and smooth' transition was soon ripped away. The model collapsed at all of its major points. Resistance to Bolshevik proposals grew rather than diminished. Capitalists would not carry on as best they could for the sake of the revolution. The civil servants and groups such as the managers and employees of banks, who were supposed to move transparently to working for the new controllers, in fact resisted bitterly, bringing the financial system to its knees. Finally, the dependence of a complex modern economy on a mass of small groups of educated and trained personnel was brought into focus. Not only engineers and managers but accountants, cost analysts, quantity surveyors, quality controllers and all the rest were needed for a modern, complex factory, let alone economy, to operate. Deep opposition within this petty-bourgeois class of clerks and white-collar workers sabotaged many crucial economic enterprises. Add to that political opposition, even from some workers such as the railwaymen, and the vast implosion of transition model number one becomes clear.

Far from improving supplies of bread or anything else the economy went into a tail-spin. A strike of public employees in November 1917 paralysed government itself. At the same time, bank employees also struck in protest against amalgamation and nationalization. Factory owners made off with any movable assets they could get their hands on. Very quickly technical personnel, managers and clerks were in conflict with the blue-collar-dominated factory committees and soviets. Many left to try to find better conditions elsewhere. Some sought the protection of White enclaves as they developed. The result was a downward spiral. Difficulties with production and decreasing co-operation between management and workers led to workers being forced to take over more managerial and technical functions. The more they did that, the more they alienated the technicians and managers and drove them away. The more they drove them away, the deeper they were sucked in to taking their place and so on. Sadly, the workers lacked the skills needed, and so layer upon layer of chaos evolved.

In priority areas, such as the railways, direct involvement by the new authorities prevented total collapse and, though it was also failing, the war effort was maintained in part. However, by the end of the year Russia's cities and urban, industrial economy were in chaos. Chaos promoted shock moves by workers to try and preserve their jobs. Various methods were tried. One was so-called workers' control, which would be better translated as 'workers' supervision', which appeared to correspond with Lenin's plans for transition. However, Lenin quickly turned against the movement because it usually meant the takeover of individual factories by their individual workforce. This then turned factories into support networks for their workers, not efficient production units. It promoted what Lenin feared to be a process of subdividing and sectionalizing the working class into competing micro-units rather than drawing them together as a whole. Workers also nationalized factories without permission from the centre. It was only several months into the revolution that the centre itself promoted nationalization, not because it believed in it at that moment but because no alternative presented itself.

Conditions in towns and cities became worse and worse. Jobs were disappearing fast. Urban populations began to collapse as workers returned to the countryside to seek survival and join in the redistribution of land. As the war wound down even the armaments workers of Petrograd began to suffer. A combination of economic desperation and patriotic disgust fuelled a protest in the city just after the signing of the Treaty of Brest-Litovsk. It appeared that Lenin's critics might be proved right and there would be an extensive backlash against the unequivocal surrender to the Germans. In fact the protest is more notable for its eloquence than for its impact.

> The new regime calls itself *Soviet* … In reality, however, the most important matters in the life of the state are decided without the participation of the Soviets … They promised us immediate *peace* … In fact, they have given us a shameful capitulation to the German

> imperialists ... They promised us *bread*. In fact, they have given us a
> famine of unparalleled dimensions. ... They promised us *freedom* ...
> All have been trampled by the heels of the police and crushed by the
> force of arms.[9]

However, many other workers' groups were protesting. Having apparently secured its immediate position through victory in what was
thought to have been the Civil War and having ended the war with
Germany, the new authorities turned more and more to the critical state
of the home front. The industrial economy had to be restored. The
unbridled transfer of land to the peasants, though initially sanctioned
by the Soviet government, was stoking up potential problems for the
future. Though it was not yet clear, the handing over of vast territories
to the Germans provided a much more threatening renewal of the Civil
War. Abandonment of the concept of revolutionary war, not to mention
steps being taken to restore factory discipline such as one-person management, were provoking resistance from the left of the Party. The
shambolic situation called imperatively for a reappraisal. The first
model of transition was definitively dead. Lenin was surrounded only by
the wreckage of his initial hopes and expectations. What could be done?

7

REVOLUTIONARY WAR

The period from early 1918 to 1920/1 is often described as the Civil War, but it was much more than that. Minority nationalities conducted their own revolutions. Within them smaller but no less bitter civil wars were fought out. Social conflicts within the civil wars added to the complexity. Wars and revolutions were inextricably entwined. It is beyond the scope of a biography to trace the narrative of these chaotic years. In any case it has been expertly done already. What has been less remarked upon, and which is crucial to our project, is the strategy, or to be more precise the series of three strategies pursued by Lenin. As we have seen, the first, naive, strategy for transition had already collapsed by spring 1918. It was to be followed by two more, discussed in depth in the next two chapters. However, these strategies did not exist in a vacuum and it is necessary to make a number of remarks about the flood of events which they were intended to contain and transform.

From late spring 1918 the new government was fighting on numerous fronts. The conflict against the Whites flared up again after a revolt by Czech former war prisoners who were returning home. This opened up new political vacuums that right-wing enemies of the regime could exploit. From summer 1918 into the crucial year of 1919 anti-Bolshevik armies composed of remnants of the tsarist Army, mostly from the officer class, battled to overthrow the usurpers. They also contained contradictions both within the separate armies – the main ones being Denikin's Volunteer Army in South Russia, Kolchak's force in

Siberia and Yudenich's troops in the now independent Baltic States – as well as between them as they sought eventual supremacy after a victory they considered inevitable. Despite considerable support from other countries, both direct and indirect, the anticipated victory was no more than illusory. They never had the personnel to win the war but even more problematically, they did not have a political strategy to light a fire under the Bolsheviks. Their confused, stale, contradictory principles of restoration, Great Russian nationalism and proto-fascism, including sickening bouts of anti-semitism, set few hearts racing. They were, in the end, only able to hold the ground on which they stood. When they moved away from a place the inhabitants were mostly glad to see them go and forgot all about them. Even so, in 1919 the three forces all advanced sufficiently to scare the Bolsheviks. By the end of the year, however, they were in headlong retreat and remained peripheral thereafter.

In fact, their existence was, on balance, a great help to the Bolsheviks because it sowed massive confusion in the minds of non-Bolsheviks, including most of the peasants and workers, who were growing restive at the developing Bolshevik dictatorship and armed requisitioning of grain, but were reluctant to take steps to undermine them while they provided the only protection against the Whites. As we shall see, Bolshevik internal problems multiplied as the White threat was replaced in 1920–1 by serious internal rebellions which could only be controlled by the abandonment of Lenin's second strategy for transition, usually referred to as War Communism. It was replaced by his third attempt, the New Economic Policy as a result of economic defeat at the hands of the masses. While there is much debate about the degree of improvisation and pragmatism in Bolshevik policies at this time the focus below is mainly on Lenin's attempted strategies to go beyond the everyday problems and get on with the implementation of his project, encapsulated in his statement of October, turned into a political poster cliché, that 'we will now proceed to construct the socialist order'.

For Lenin, the first six months or so of the Revolution were a mixture of exhilaration and exhaustion. The dizziness he felt on the morrow of seizing power barely dissipated. Hardly any character in history had undergone such a precipitate rise. Up to 25 October Lenin had lived like a hermit crab, moving from shell to shell as appropriate, possessing nothing, accumulating no material goods whatsoever. He had been driven by revolutionary energy of extraordinary depth and conviction.

From this perspective his inner drive, to change the metaphor, was more like a volcano. Ideas, letters, articles, pamphlets, books, projects, alliances exploded from his mind. The energy and power of his intellectual creativity accounted for his pre-eminence. It was the feature which attracted his supporters and repelled his opponents. He was supported throughout by close family ties, especially to his mother and his sisters, Anna and Maria. Nadezhda and Inessa were extensions of this loving group. Friends, notably the Zinovievs, often moved around with them. A wider circle of friends, including Gorky who had become extremely critical of what he saw as Bolshevik adventures in 1917, and Bonch-Bruevich, were on hand to provide crucial support at decisive moments. Within this framework he had lived his life, partly as a professor holding seminars and defending his tumult of theses, partly as a stop-at-nothing politico, driven to get his way by a morality of revolutionary expediency and class warfare.

His incredible self-belief was at the core of his political personality. Lenin was not the sort of person to sit with his head in his hands wondering if he was doing the right thing. It was not a question that arose to him, even privately, it seems. It was both his greatest strength and greatest weakness. The greatest strength in giving him the dynamism to achieve what he did. The greatest weakness in leading him to impose his own views at times when compromise and co-operation would have been beneficial. Arising from this was his failure to accept opposition. As we have seen, from early in his career, and increasingly from 1903, Lenin was almost pathological in attacking opponents. He not only refuted their ideas but questioned their motives, their class affiliations, their opinions. All opponents were automatically deemed to be mouthpieces of class enemies of the Revolution. They were at best mistaken, at worst malevolently undermining the true faith. In Lenin's simple universe of ideas there were only believers and heretics.

In exile, the two Lenins – the intellectual-professorial and the political – had tended to live side by side, or perhaps more precisely, in alternating sequences with the bulk of the time Lenin being the quintessential intellectual, reading and writing his way to his goals. Intermittently, during Party meetings and conferences, the political Lenin took over to attempt the complete victory of his ideas and the political annihilation of his opponents. After the struggle, Krupskaya took him to the mountains, the forest or the beach to recover his equilibrium and resurrect the intellectual from the politician with shattered nerves. The transition to power did not kill off either of the Lenins. The intellectual survived. Lenin even referred to Central Committee meetings as gatherings of great minds which were conducted like professorial seminars. But the balance was changed forever. For slightly more than four years, from October 1917 onwards, the political Lenin came to the fore. Only severe illness undermined both Lenins from 1921 onwards, leaving him as only a shadow of his former self in his last years.

In the early months after the Revolution, Lenin was deeply conscious of the fragility of the forces which had brought him to power, but also of the epochal significance of what was happening, or so he thought. The Russian revolution was, as the title of his first newspaper had put it, the spark (*iskra*) to light the prairie fire of world revolution. In his morality of revolutionary expediency almost anything could be justified if it brought success. In the middle of the First World War, at that time the most massive human blood-letting ever, refinements of morality seemed not only constricting but obscene. A few sacrifices, a moment of ruthlessness, was not only justified but demanded if millions could be saved from death at the front and from the worldwide tentacles of imperialist exploitation. To lay the foundations of a new world, a more perfect, classless and human world, it was the revolutionary's duty to have dirty hands. The morality of Leninism and Stalinism began from this premise. It was a morality of war – not of a disgusting national war that misled the many into serving the needs of the few, but a class war of the multitude against the exploiting minority. Soldiers, and increasingly civilians, suffered and died in war, that was inevitable. It was not desirable but that was the way it had to be.

It was in this frame of mind that Lenin, in the early months and beyond, was at his most violent. He never rejoiced in violence but he was convinced it was necessary in self-defence. As he had said several times in 1917, the Bolsheviks would refrain from violence until it was used against them. The struggle would necessarily become violent at some point because the repressive instruments of the state would have to be confronted and smashed. However, Lenin argued that there would be a short, sharp, shock and the enemy would see sense. They could not coerce a rampant, armed, revolutionary majority.

At first, it was the Military Revolutionary Committees (MRCs) which conducted the ruthless repression. By December, a new, supposedly temporary institution, the Cheka, the first Soviet secret police, was set up. Its full title expressed its function. It was 'The All-Russian Extraordinary Commission for Combating Counter-Revolution and Sabotage'. Though it was by no means the first such organization – the tsars had made extensive use of secret police as had the Jacobins in the French Revolution – the Cheka had a peculiarly and characteristically Leninist aura. It embodied the complexities and contradictions of Lenin's approach to revolution. In essence, the argument for its existence was unanswerable. A highly effective agent of revolutionary enforcement was needed against the resistance of the old ruling class. It needed, however, like the French Revolution, an 'incorruptible' leader imbued with the correct revolutionary consciousness. In choosing Dzerzhinsky to lead it Lenin had found such a person. He was intelligent, loyal and determined, and he knew what Lenin wanted. He would create a weapon in the same image. It would dispense revolutionary justice swiftly and sharply. Once resistance died down it could be disbanded.

One cannot underestimate the Cheka's importance as an embodiment of correct revolutionary consciousness. For Lenin, the success and failure of the Revolution lay in its ability to nurture political consciousness, to persuade Russia, and then the world, of the correctness of the Marxist revolutionary path as mapped out by Lenin himself. The Party was supposed to be such an instrument. Only with the aid of people of the right consciousness could the Revolution be constructed. In this sense, the intellectual Lenin lurked in the depths of the political Lenin.

However, a key problem was quickly emerging. In 1917 Lenin had claimed that if the old elite could govern through 130,000 landowners then the Revolution could do the same. In *Can the Bolsheviks Retain State Power?*, written in September 1917, Lenin had claimed:

Since the 1905 revolution, Russia has been governed by 130,000 landowners, who have perpetrated endless violence against 150,000,000 people, heaped unconstrained abuse upon them, and condemned the vast majority to inhuman toil.

Yet we are told that the 240,000 members of the Bolshevik Party will not be able to govern Russia, govern her in the interests of the poor against the rich. These 240,000 are already backed by no less than a million votes of the adult population. ... We therefore already have a 'state apparatus' of *one million* people devoted to the socialist state for the sake of high ideals and not for the sake of a fat sum received on the 20th of every month. [SW 2 402]

As Bolshevik Party membership had risen in 1917 from about 25,000 to about 250,000, Lenin seemed to have the material to hand. However, the events of 1917 had 'deBolshevized' the Party. People flocked to it to establish soviet, rather than Bolshevik, power and to overthrow the Provisional Government, end the war and take over the economy. They were not imbued with Marxist ideas and had no idea of Lenin's deeper agenda, the 'maximum' as opposed to the 'minimum' programme. In reality, only a small number of really conscious Bolsheviks existed. In the early years many efforts were made to expand their number but it was an uphill struggle, as we shall see.

For the moment, however, Dzerzhinsky was in charge of an institution whose fate resembled that of many other similar attempts to embody the elusive consciousness, the key ingredient of Leninist revolution. In place of high-minded, intelligent and well-informed people like himself, the Cheka had to rely on whoever would work for it. That increasingly meant a sizeable minority of unreliables who might even have served in the tsarist police. True, many determined revolutionaries, especially from the minority nationalities, above all Jews as White pogroms hit their communities in Ukraine, joined the Cheka to become the avenging arm of revolutionary justice. Unfortunately, neither they nor the scanty judicial authorities had the wisdom of Solomon to keep the enterprise within bounds. It became increasingly arbitrary though devastatingly effective in defending the regime.

In recent years, there has been much more attention given to this violent and repressive Lenin. There is no doubt that he sanctioned executions of several categories of active counter-revolutionaries. Asked how to deal with speculators who were exploiting shortages to make money he proposed arresting some to warn off the rest. Other parasitic and exploiting groups, as Lenin viewed them, from prostitutes to priests, were put on the list for arrest and, in extreme cases, execution. In the morality of the class war, the sacrifice of even hundreds, perhaps thousands, of resisters would, it was hoped, open the way to save the lives of millions.

However, only perfect justice could have guaranteed the success of such a policy. Lenin and the leadership took no delight in it, but, like generals who think they see an opportunity, they were prepared to call a barrage of fire down on the enemy's weak spot and hasten the end of the war.

The Cheka, then, embodies the complexities of Lenin's philosophy perhaps better than any other institution of the early months of the Revolution. Where the Party had become less 'Leninist' this new, as yet small, but armed and supposedly conscious elite, took up where the Party left off. But the crucial shortage of personnel in this sphere added to the woes of Lenin and the setbacks his earliest revolutionary enterprises had met with.

No one had expected the Revolution to be easy but it was an even greater struggle than expected. The constant effort of the early stages took its toll on Lenin's health. Eventually, Krupskaya, ever protective of her husband, was able to persuade him to take a holiday around the Russian Christmas and New Year, the latter being celebrated for the last time ever under the old date (14 January) as Russia was due to adopt the western calendar on the 1/14 February 1918. They withdrew to Finland. Once again Krupskaya records the occasion. 'The marked Finnish cleanliness, the white curtains on the windows, everything reminded Il'ich of his illegal stay in Helsinki in 1907 and 1917, before the October Revolution, when he was working on *State and Revolution*.' However, the break did not bring the customary restoration of Lenin's equilibrium. 'The holiday did us little good, Il'ich at times even spoke sotto voce, as during the days when he was in hiding. We went for daily walks but without really enjoying them. Il'ich was too taken up with his thoughts and wrote practically the whole time.' [Weber 143]

It is not in the least surprising that Lenin found it impossible to break away from his work. The war question, above all, was pressing in. Conflict was mounting. Indeed, the day he returned to Petrograd, 14 January, was the day his car had been shot at and his Swiss friend Fritz Platten slightly wounded. It seems to have been a robbery attempt rather than a political act. However, the ongoing collapse of the first transition plan, the approaching end of the war with the Central Powers and the growing hostility from the left of the Party led to the need, in early 1918, for a further reappraisal. By February, Lenin was moving, in a piecemeal fashion, to a second model of transition.

THE SECOND MODEL OF TRANSITION – 'IRON PROLETARIAN DISCIPLINE'

On 10–11 March 1918 the Soviet government moved out of Petrograd to Moscow, mainly on account of the German threat. Lenin and Krupskaya had shared a small flat in the Smolnyi since October. Now, after an initial sojourn at the Hotel Natsional, Lenin, Krupskaya and Maria Ulyanova moved into the Kremlin. Lenin had a modest office at his disposal and the three of them had a small suite of four rooms altogether. Living in the centre of Moscow did not preclude some continued communion with nature. The Kremlin has a garden and a footpath which follow the line of the Moscow river. It is one of the most beautiful walks in the city, situated inside the beautifully crenellated Kremlin wall and the brilliant white, golden-domed churches at the heart of the complex. Lenin and Krupskaya frequently took the air along the footpath. The irony of Russia's great atheist and modernizer settling in the quintessentially medieval, tsarist and ecclesiastical heart of traditional Russia did not go unnoticed. Later, a small mansion outside the city, in the village of Gorky, was also put at his disposal. From spring 1918 until his death Lenin's life revolved around these two places. He rarely spent time anywhere else.

He had plenty to think about in his new surroundings. On 26 October Lenin had made two historic statements. In one, for which he had removed his disguise in order to reveal himself to the Second Congress of Soviets, he said the new authorities would now proceed to construct the socialist order.[1] In the second, he said the new government would allow complete creative freedom for the masses. [SW 2 470] As time went on, a fatal contradiction between the two opened up. Given freedom the masses did not build the socialism Lenin expected of them. It brought into focus the quintessential problem of Lenin's way of thinking. If the masses chose something different from Lenin they were wrong and had to be corrected. Ideally, this would be done patiently and gently, as with a beloved child. However, continued bad behaviour would, unfortunately, require necessary chastisement. Lenin, as we have seen time and time again, could not assimilate opposition. It could only be overcome and destroyed. In place of complete creative freedom Lenin turned to a new discourse based on a completely opposite theme – iron proletarian discipline.

The emphasis on discipline began to appear in his writings and speeches in February and March of 1918 and reached its most sustained exposition in his most important theoretical pronouncement since he had come to power, the pamphlet *The Immediate Tasks of the Soviet Government*, written in mid-April and published, to underline its importance, simultaneously in *Pravda* and *Izvestiia*, the main Party and government newspapers respectively, on 28 April. Like most of his writings of the period it was still signed with his full conspiratorial name N. Lenin, the N. standing for Nikolai.

What was it about? Starting from an analysis of key problems facing the Revolution, Lenin laid down certain principles for dealing with them. The breathing space purchased at Brest-Litovsk meant there was now 'an opportunity to concentrate efforts for a while on the most important and most difficult aspect of the socialist revolution, namely, the task of organization'. [SW 2 645] His injunctions seem curiously mundane and undramatic: 'Keep regular and honest accounts of money, manage economically, do not be lazy, do not steal, observe the strictest labour discipline.' He was well aware that many in the Party would bridle at the return of formulae which were 'justly scorned by the revolutionary proletariat when the bourgeoisie used them to conceal its rule as an exploiting class'. However, he insisted that practical application of these '"hackneyed" and "trivial" slogans' was 'a necessary and *sufficient* condition for the final victory of socialism'. [SW 2 651] 'The decisive thing', he went on to argue, 'is the organization of the strictest country-wide accounting and control of production and distribution of goods.' Why was such a mundane proposition so important? Because 'without this there can be no thought of achieving the second and equally essential material condition for introducing socialism, namely, raising the productivity of labour on a national scale.' [SW 2 652]

What did Lenin mean? In these few, apparently banal, words he was laying a new foundation for the Soviet system. Note first that these were not aspects of socialism but preliminary steps enabling the country to move on to the introduction of socialism. Setting aside the inconsistency of language, Lenin, having stated many times that socialism could not be 'introduced', was pointing to the fundamental problem of the Revolution from the Marxist point of view – it had occurred in an economically 'backward' country. What Lenin was saying was that backwardness – measured as labour productivity – had to be overcome before the serious construction of socialism could begin. Indeed, it was even necessary to suspend the offensive against capital. [SW 2 652–3] In this respect, his formulae were not inconsistent with *The April Theses*.

However, the further development of his ideas opened up new perspectives. One aspect of the assault on capital – the 'expropriation of the expropriators' as he put it – had been successful, but the question of running the newly acquired system lagged behind. Having broken the capitalist opposition politically, the Revolution could afford to take what he acknowledged to be a step backward and call upon specialists from the old system to work for the construction of the new, even at higher salaries than workers, with all the consequences such a compromise would entail. There should also be a new form of competition between different factories. In addition, industrial production implied nationwide discipline in order to function. At a national level, the government too should become more disciplinary, more dictatorial. 'Dictatorship, however, is a big word, and big words should not be thrown about carelessly. Dictatorship is iron rule, government that is revolutionarily bold, swift and ruthless in suppressing both exploiters and hooligans. But our government is excessively mild, very often it resembles jelly more than iron.' [SW 2 670]

Every unit also had to be disciplined. Lenin also wanted not only the return of one-person management to ensure this, but that managers should be the dictators of every factory, instantly obeyed by their workforces.

> Given ideal class-consciousness and discipline on the part of those participating in the common work, this subordination would be something like the mild leadership of a conductor of an orchestra. It may assume the sharp forms of a dictatorship if ideal discipline and class-consciousness are lacking. But, be that as it may, *unquestioning subordination* to a single will is absolutely necessary for the success of the processes organized on the pattern of large-scale industry. [SW 2 673]

There is no better example of Lenin indicating that dictatorship takes up where ideal class-consciousness leaves off.

He went on to stress even more clearly, perhaps because he realized how much opposition it would cause, 'that the people *unquestioningly obey the single will* of the leaders of labour.' [SW 2 673] Lenin well knew that workers and Party activists prized the democratic freedoms workers had won and they would cling to them. He had to at least tacitly acknowledge their existence in the face of the emphasis on discipline. 'We must learn to combine the "public meeting" democracy of the working people – turbulent, surging, overflowing its banks like a spring flood – with *iron* discipline while at work, with *unquestioning obedience* to the will of a single person, the Soviet leader, while at work.' Unsurprisingly, Lenin did not suggest how this particular circle might be squared. 'We have not yet learned to do this. We shall learn it' was all he could add. [SW 2 675] In a set of theses codifying the contents of the article, Lenin emphasized the need for piece-work, the Taylor system of scientific management, competition between factories and sectors, 'unquestioning obedience during work to the one-man decisions of Soviet directors, of the dictators elected or appointed by Soviet institutions, vested with dictatorial powers' and 'the general and summarising slogan of the moment' which was 'iron discipline and the thorough exercise of proletarian dictatorship against petty-bourgeois vacillations'. [SW 2 683]

There was no subtlety or ambiguity in Lenin's prescription. 'Complete creative freedom' was no longer an option. Central and local dictatorship were the order of the day. In the eyes of his supporters Lenin was facing the realities of the situation in a bold and necessary way. He was pointing out a realistic path forwards. The 'gradual, peaceful and smooth' transition expected in October had given way to a quite different law of revolution discovered for current purposes. 'Every great revolution, and a socialist revolution in particular, even if there is no external war, is inconceivable without internal war, and involves thousands and millions of cases of wavering and desertion from one side to another. It implies a state of extreme indefiniteness, lack of equilibrium and chaos.' [SW 2 669]

However, to his critics inside and outside the Party the whole thing promised a nightmare. Once again, if the local and national dictators possessed the wisdom of a socialist Solomon all might be well, but in the absence of such ideal personalities the workers were being thrown, unprotected since they could no longer organize for themselves, into a maelstrom of managerial dictators. Practice, however, modified the ferocity of theory and workers tended to vote with their feet. If they were dissatisfied they left jobs and continued to leave cities. Flight to the countryside continued. This gave ammunition to Lenin's increasing array of critics, including the growing band of Left Communists who objected to compromise, especially when the workers had to pay its costs.

Many other issues of dispute were building up but, before turning to them, there are two more crucial points to make about these first stirrings of a new model of transition. First, despite its many ringing phrases as a document the original article/pamphlet is very complex and was probably understood in its entirety and put into practice by very few people despite its mass circulation. Even the theses that accompanied the article a few days later require some considerable effort to understand. As in earlier writings, such as *One Step Forward: Two Steps Back*, Lenin continued to show faith in the efficacy of the written word as an agent of social change. He expected his principles to be acted upon by the Party and its agencies who would pass them on to the masses. Words were acts for Lenin. In this respect, the intellectual still existed alongside the politician. He was still the dispenser of doctrine as well as its implementer.

Second, implicit in this complicated little article was the whole orientation of the Soviet system practically throughout its life. Lenin emphasized that backwardness had to be overcome and the efficiency of capitalism replicated and superseded before socialism could be embarked upon. In other words, the Soviet system had to outproduce capitalism as a preliminary to socialism. This became known as productionism. For the rest of its life productionism – maximizing economic output for ideological as well as practical reasons – was the *raison d'être* of the Soviet system.

Productionism was not the only area in which one-man management and a stress on discipline and consciousness-raising were taking over from earlier assumptions. Though Trotsky was more directly responsible than Lenin, the Red Army was going through a comparable revision of expectations. There could hardly have been a concept more deeply embedded in Lenin's thinking in 1917 than that of turning the standing army into a militia. 'Abolish the army' along with the state and the bureaucracy was clearly stated in *The April Theses*. However, another u-turn had begun. Militias, like the Red Guards, were being broken up and a regular army formed. By early 1919 the Party Congress even stated that, in current conditions, 'the slogan "people's militia" is deprived of its meaning … and becomes a weapon of the reaction.' 'To preach the doctrine of guerilla forces is tantamount to recommending a return from large-scale to cottage industry.' Election of officers was deemed inappropriate in the 'class-based workers' and peasants' Red Army'.[2]

The developing army had three other characteristics distinguishing it. First, the doctrine of specialists had great force and between a third and half of all officers had previously served in the Imperial Army. To counterbalance their potentially harmful ideological influence and to capitalize on the army as a point of political contact between the Party and the mass of the population, political commissars were attached to military units. Their task was to uphold ideological rectitude and educate, especially peasants, in the fundamentals of the Bolshevik cause. However, as in all comparable spheres, it was not easy to find people with the right consciousness. By December 1918 the Red Army had nearly 7,000 commissars. Astonishingly, many of them were not communists! This is one of the most striking examples of the shortage of 'conscious' supporters of the cause. Third, the Party was largely enrolled in the army as the Civil War flared up again. In March 1919 there were 60,000 communists in the army. By March 1920 the figure was 280,000 constituting about half the entire membership of the Party, though only comprising 8 per cent of the personnel of the army itself. None the less, it does indicate that, far from being a freely elected and participative militia, the Red Army was becoming a key instrument, not of soviet, but of Bolshevik power and influence.[3] One-man management and iron discipline, enforced by the reintroduction of the hated death penalty – the abolition of which had brought the Bolsheviks their first majorities in the key soviets – were firmly entrenched in the Red Army.

Could the principles of the second transition be extended into the village? Here Lenin was more directly involved in policy-making which bore a distinctly Leninist imprint. At the heart of Lenin's view of the peasantry, as we have seen, was the assumption that there were class divisions within it corresponding to wealth and status. We have already mentioned that this might be seen as wishful thinking in that it provided a respectable Marxist excuse for enrolling a chunk of the peasantry, which might otherwise be thought to be hostile to the proletarian revolution, into the proletarian camp. Lenin had made a great deal of the need to demarcate the poor peasants and labourers from the middle peasants and so-called kulaks. In June 1918 he was instrumental in setting up committees of poor peasants (*kombedy*). The ostensible aim was to cement the expected alliance between the Party and the most exploited part of the peasantry. In practice it turned the commune peasants as a whole against the non-commune rural population, such as small traders and incomers, who opposed the commune because it denied them land. The result was rural chaos and the committees were, in effect, disbanded in December 1918 because, Lenin said, they had become 'so well established we found it possible to replace them with properly elected soviets'.[4] In fact it was the first sign of yet another transformation in Lenin's policies towards the peasants, referred to as 'the turn towards the middle peasant'. The new line, which evolved through the militarily critical year of 1919, was intended to heal the breach between the Party and the majority of the peasantry who, Lenin now argued, should be won over to the socialist cause. He even went so far as to say, in his article 'Economics and Politics in the Era of the Dictatorship of the Proletariat' written in October 1919, that 'In this demarcation, lies the *whole essence* of socialism.' [SW 3 279] Why was the divide growing?

The setting up of *kombedy* was not Lenin's only initiative. Approaching civil war and urban disruption brought two new initiatives, conscription and food requisitioning. The peasants were not enthusiastic about the former but, as White advances happened in 1918 and 1919, they began to see the need for it to protect themselves from returning landlords. By and large, perhaps also because it was an accepted aspect of peasant life, conscription worked fairly smoothly. However, when it came to giving up their produce, they believed workers in the cities were, by comparison, being feather-bedded and resented their supposed privileged position. Peasants perceived workers as shirkers protected from conscription in defence industries and idle recipients of requisitioned food, since, in the peasants' eyes, the workers were not producing the goods the peasants were promised in exchange for their produce. Throughout the period from 1918 to 1920 grain requisitioning provoked deep peasant resentment and, more than anything, drove a wedge between the Party and the peasantry. They evaded it in every possible way and under-delivered, especially to the resented cities, which brought famine to Petrograd and Moscow. Eventually, as we shall see, peasant resistance to the requisitioning of produce brought the collapse of Lenin's second model of transition in late 1920.

INTO THE STORM – THE CRISIS OF 1918–21

If Lenin thought the situation up to late spring 1918 was complicated that which followed was infinitely more difficult. Let us take a look at the interacting factors that made the next three years incredibly complex.

Conventionally these are often seen as years of civil war and related war communism. To put the focus in that direction is misleading. True the Civil War, which reignited in June and July 1918, was a major component of the crisis. Soviet Russia was threatened by advancing White armies backed up diplomatically, financially and militarily by Britain, France and the United States. Other neighbouring countries joined in the attempt to seize territory – Turkey, Germany, Austria, Poland and Japan all mounted attacks at various points. Finland, Estonia, Latvia and Lithuania all became independent while Ukraine almost did as well. In mid-1919, Lenin's writ ran in only some 10 per cent of the territory of the former Russian Empire. However, the Soviet government still controlled the majority of the population, the industrial (though not the food) resources and, crucially, the hub of the railway network. By the end of 1919 it had put most of its enemies to flight.

But beneath this conflict there were other serious historical processes taking place. The underlying one was that the Communist Party (as the Bolsheviks renamed themselves in March 1918) was doing its best to deepen the revolutionary transformation of Russian society. This meant continuing to pressurize the peasantry but also to turn the industrial economy into something worthy of being called socialist and the Russian worker, whom Lenin frequently upbraided for being backward, into a true, advanced, conscious proletarian. To do this involved coercion of the population on a massive scale, and this aspect of events is often overlooked in traditional views of the period. In fact, the Whites' inability to find a secure political and ideological base in the population meant that, despite the military advances, they were a paper tiger.

By comparison, the threat to the Leninist project presented by recalcitrant workers and peasants was much greater than has been traditionally thought. Ironically, it was perhaps the existence of the Whites which saved the Soviet regime. How so? In many ways their actions, especially the atrocities they committed including the massacre of tens of thousands of Jews and their hostility to the separatist aspirations of the peripheral populations like the Cossacks among whom they were forced to establish their bases, undermined their cause. Whatever their differences with the Communists, the workers, peasants and the national minorities had even more issues with the Whites who threatened the reversal of the land settlement, the return of capitalist exploitation and the return of 'Russia one and indivisible'.

True, Bolshevik promises of federalism for the minorities were vague and for workers the Revolution had brought very little but it still promised some kind of better future. In fact, the very meagreness of their gains could be explained as a consequence of the White challenge. As a result, the White advance served to discipline the population and cause most of them to turn to the Reds for protection. Only small numbers looked to the Whites. The corollary of this is that, as the White threat receded, the opposition of peasants and workers to the Bolsheviks would become more overt. In 1920 and 1921 this is exactly what happened with a series of anti-Communist uprisings in West Siberia, Tambov and Kronstadt. Strikes also threatened the authorities in Petrograd and elsewhere. However, by 1920, the population was exhausted by war and social upheaval and there was insufficient energy left in the popular movement to prevail against an ever-more organized and self-defensive soviet system. Had the uprisings happened in 1918, the outcome might have been very different.

It should also be added that the twists and turns of policy to deal with these issues created tensions within the Party. As early as Brest-Litovsk and the turn to 'iron proletarian discipline' in spring 1918 a substantial proportion of the longest-serving members of the Party began to criticize the leadership for abandoning the fundamental principles of the Revolution. Workers were not being liberated, they argued, but merely fitted with new harnesses. Given that the right wing of the Party had objected to the actions of October and the establishment of a purely Bolshevik rather than soviet system, one can see how the threat to Party unity was a real one. Lenin had to look to pacify both right and left oppositions.

There was also another, more deadly, dimension to the crisis of these years. Social and economic collapse led to famine. Famine brought death to hundreds of thousands. Even those who survived might suffer physical weakness which made bodies vulnerable to illness and infection. Social breakdown multiplied the sources of infection, especially bad water. As a result, cholera, typhoid, typhus and influenza mowed down great swathes of the population. It has been calculated that the associated traumas of these years brought about 10 million premature deaths. The vast majority of these, even in the fighting armies, were the result of disease rather than of violence and repression.

As if all this were not sufficient, Soviet Russia was trying to spark off world revolution, without which it did not expect to survive. In practice, this element had little major impact on the crisis of 1918–21. It did help marginally in organizing overseas sympathizers in Britain, France and elsewhere to conduct campaigns against intervention. In Britain, the 'Hands off Russia' campaign was, perhaps, the last straw which broke the camel's back when the government finally came to wind down the policy of intervention instead of build it up as Churchill suggested. The war with Poland in 1920 was also a point at which the spread of the revolution impinged on the crisis but it was not the decisive factor in causing the war. Conversely, eventual failure in the war with Poland was decisive in undermining optimistic expectations of a rapid spread of revolution to Germany and beyond. Even so, spreading the Revolution played a huge part in Lenin's thinking: it was the revolution as a whole, not just the Russian Revolution, which occupied his mind. Russia's was never more than a second-rank revolution in Lenin's eyes. Famously, in a message sent to 'American comrades' via Albert Rhys Williams in May 1918, he said he was 'absolutely convinced that the social revolution will finally prove victorious in all civilized countries. When it begins in America it will surpass the Russian revolution by far.' [Weber 149] None the less it was with the realities of the Russian Revolution that Lenin had to deal.

Such was the massively complex set of interacting processes with which Lenin was confronted from spring 1918 onwards. Our present purpose is not to focus on the general historical picture of these years.[5] Instead, we will concentrate on how Lenin responded to the multiple challenges. From his point of view, military, internal and even foreign policies were only threads in a holistic cloth of carrying out a revolution. However, it is easier to understand what he was doing if we separate out some of the sub-areas. In particular, we need to look at the evolution of his socio-political policies and then turn to the sometimes marginalized but actually crucial sphere of cultural revolution. Also, the stress will be on the evolution of Lenin's strategic thinking rather than the morass of everyday decisions he had to make.

LENIN'S REVOLUTIONARY STRATEGY 1918–20 – THE ROAD MAP

From 1918 to about 1920, when its shortcomings were too great to be ignored any longer, Lenin was preoccupied with implementing his new model of revolutionary transformation. Combating the White enemy was, to some extent, subsumed in the struggle against class enemies – notably the bourgeoisie – as well as the struggle against 'backward' parts of the working class and the mass of the peasantry, the petty-bourgeoisie. Lenin was working at the levels of theory and practice and it is easier for us to follow what he was trying to do if we divide our analysis into the same two categories. The first section will look at his revolutionary road map, the second at the vehicles he was using to travel along his chosen route.

In the field of theory a number of themes dominated Lenin's think-ing. The foundation of his outlook was the world revolution. Lenin still saw it as the main *raison d'être* of the Revolution. Without it the Russian Revolution would not be able to follow the path he believed it should. Beyond that there were the practical problems of transition, how to run the economy to support the population and to transform it at the same time. This produced a hybrid, based on productionism, which Lenin increasingly referred to as state capitalism. The term most frequently used in western discourse is 'war communism' but that term was only coined after the phenomena to which it referred had been radically altered and was applied in retrospect. Productionism affected Lenin's thinking on a wide variety of social issues, from the role of trades unions to women's rights. Let us look at these two aspects of Lenin's road map.

WORLD REVOLUTION

One might expect that, given the great weight of practical problems pressing in on him, Lenin would have become preoccupied with the mundane. This was not the case. The 'intellectual with vision' survived in the soul of the everyday decision-maker and the larger picture was never far from the centre of Lenin's attention. In particular, the international revolution was a major preoccupation even though its immediate practical impact on events in Russia was minimal, not least because the desired revolution never materialized. However, its mythical significance for the leadership was very great. Lenin put it starkly on 7 March 1918: 'At all events and under all conceivable circumstances, if the German revolution does not come we are doomed.' [SW 2 583] Trotsky had said the same at the Second Congress of Soviets on 26 October 1917: 'Our whole hope is that our revolution will kindle a European revolution. If the rising of the people does not crush imperialism, then we will surely be crushed. There is no doubt about that. The Russian Revolution will either cause a revolution in the West, or the capitalists of all countries will strangle ours.'[6] In Lenin's mind there was an intimate connection between events inside and outside Russia. He was still working in the framework of a European, even worldwide, civil war. He followed radical developments in Europe and later in the colonies with great optimism, though little hard information. He also saw foreign intervention in Russia as part of counter-revolution. The result was a very complex discourse in Lenin's mind. World revolution must happen because theory said it should. At times, he appeared to propose Bolshevism as a worldwide model for such a revolution – in the Comintern for example – while at others he emphasized that not only every country but even minority nationalities within them, including Russia's minorities, would have to find their own ways to socialism. As far as capitalist governments were concerned he also had a complex attitude. Do what you can to overthrow them but do not hesitate to do beneficial trade and diplomatic deals with them if you can in the meantime. It was an area in which the strengths and weaknesses of Lenin's analytical powers were brought out. The overall framework set up a dogmatic discourse of the inevitability of revolution which interacted with his pragmatism and often brilliant assessments of particular conjunctures, such as having to sign the Treaty of Brest-Litovsk.

His most constant theme was reiteration of the basic point about survival. He returned to it time and time again. In May 1918, in his article '"Left-wing" Childishness and the Petty-Bourgeois Mentality' he affirmed that the victory of socialism requires 'the revolutionary co-operation of the proletarians of all countries'. [CW 27 323–54] In a

Report on Foreign Policy to the All-Russian Central Executive Committee of the Soviet and the Moscow Soviet he said the same thing – final victory can come only through the efforts of the workers of all countries – but opened up a crucial nuance. It was vital to 'preserve our socialist island in the middle of stormy seas'. [CW 27 368–71] The seed of 'socialism in one country' was beginning to germinate. Thereafter, Lenin's discourse developed both themes. The final victory depended on world revolution but the world revolution depended on the survival of the Russian Revolution.

It was clear, however, that Lenin did not believe the Russian Revolution could survive long without help from abroad. He believed that it was only the contradictions within imperialism, mainly expressed in the fact the imperialists were at each other's throats, which meant they had less time to do what they should do, as he had oddly predicted in 1917, namely, settle their differences and mount a consolidated joint assault on the real threat to them all posed by the Russian Revolution. [Letter to Shaumyan 14 May 1918, CW 35 332] When such help would come, was, however, another question. In August 1918 he wrote that, while world revolution was inevitable, 'only a fool can answer when revolution will break out in the West. Revolution can never be forecast; it cannot be foretold; it comes of itself. Revolution is brewing and is bound to flare up.' [CW 28 79–84, *Address at a Meeting in the Polytechnic Museum*]

Only a few weeks later the revolutionary temperature began to rise. It appeared, from events in Germany, that the process had begun. Writing to Sverdlov and Trotsky on 1 October, while convalescing from a serious assassination attempt on 30 August, he said that world revolution has 'come so close in *one week* that it has to be reckoned with as an event of the *next few years* ... We are all ready to die to help the German workers to advance the revolution which has begun in Germany.' [CW 35 364–5] His enthusiasm continued to get the better of him through the autumn. On 3 November he waxed lyrical about the revolution in Austria-Hungary: 'The time is near when the first day of the world revolution will be celebrated everywhere. Our labour and sufferings have not been in vain.' [CW 28 131] Three days later, at an All-Russian Congress of Soviets, he said the complete victory of the revolution 'in our country alone is inconceivable and demands the most active co-operation of at least several advanced countries, which do not include Russia.'

This was a point he had made many times before and was to do again. On 23 April 1918 he had said unequivocally that Russia was in the forefront of world revolution 'not because the Russian proletariat is superior to the working class of other countries, but solely because we were one of the most backward countries in the world.' [CW 27 229–33]

Nonetheless, he went on to say at the Soviet Congress that 'We have never been so near to world proletarian revolution as we are now', though he warned 'the situation is more dangerous than ever before.' [CW 28 135–64] Lenin's realism and optimism were in close combat at that moment! Even after the decline of the post-war revolutionary wave his point remained the same. In one of his last writings, *Notes of a Publicist* of February 1922, he said: 'we have always urged and reiterated the elementary truth – that the joint efforts of the workers of several advanced countries are needed for the victory of socialism.' [CW 33 204–11]

By the end of 1918 Lenin believed the time was ripe for implementing yet another point from *The April Theses*, the establishment of a new International. It should, he wrote on 31 December, be 'based on the programme of the Spartacus League and the All-Russian Communist Party'. [Weber 154] Just a couple of weeks later the Spartacist leaders, Rosa Luxemburg and Karl Liebknecht, were murdered and the German revolution was on its way to destruction. It was, however, one of the few occasions when Lenin appeared to be ready to cede at least a fraction of his supremacy to another party or group. When the Comintern finally became established it had an indubitably Bolshevik feel about it.

The First Comintern Conference in 1919 was not a very grand affair. Because of the blockade and other post-war travel restrictions, it was largely composed of foreign sympathizers who were already in Russia. It may have had some effect, however, in calling on workers of western Europe to oppose their governments' policy of intervention in Russia. However, it was only in 1920 that a more substantial organization was set up. By then, in France and elsewhere, communist parties had already begun to get off the ground. There were over 200 delegates from sixty-seven organizations in thirty-two different countries. The main focus of the meeting, apart from propagandistic boasting of the coming export of revolution via Warsaw, the Russo–Polish war being in progress at the same time, was the establishment of conditions of entry. Lenin listed nineteen, the meeting finally approved twenty-one. Key provisions committed adherent parties to support Soviet Russia, call themselves communist parties and fight an unrelenting struggle against centrist social democrats. The last point was obsessive. A majority of the conditions referred, directly or indirectly, into splitting parties to obtain purity of doctrine and unity of purpose. Purges were required to maintain standards.

No better model of 'Bolshevizing' the international movement could have been thought up, even though Lenin continued to insist on separate roads to socialism. Even in areas of Soviet influence which were to be incorporated in the Soviet Union when it was finally formed Lenin held to the principle. Back in March 1919 he had chided Bukharin for overlooking the right of national self-determination. In Lenin's view, although each nation is travelling 'in the same historical direction' each one does so 'by very different zigzags and bypaths'. 'The more cultured nations are obviously proceeding in a way that differs from that of the less cultured nations. Finland advanced in a different way. Germany is advancing in a different way.' [CW 29 97–140]

Two years later he made the same point. He wrote to communists in the Transcaucasus that they should 'refrain from copying our tactics but thoroughly vary them and adapt them to the differing concrete conditions.' [CW 32 316–18] He even appeared miffed when critics claimed the Russian model was being imposed. He accused the Italian communist, Serrati, of telling tales that the Russians wanted to impose a model. 'We want the very opposite.' Principles 'must be adapted to the specific conditions of various countries. The revolution in Italy will run a different course from that in Russia. It will start in a different way. How? Neither you nor we know.' The Comintern will never require that others 'slavishly imitate the Russians'. [CW 32 451–96] The accusation remained, however, and in November 1922, at the Fourth Comintern Congress, Lenin was at pains to refute it again. According to an American observer he told foreign communists 'not to hang Russian experience in a corner like an icon and pray to it.'[7]

Lenin's outlook on international revolution remained complex to the end. He hovered between the need for Soviet Russia to survive and the need for revolutions to occur elsewhere. Yet, at the same time, he continually castigated the left inside and outside Russia for putting too much stress on the international revolution. Unlike them, Lenin would not mobilize serious forces to back foreign revolutions. Revolution would be exported only by example and by nurturing friendly communist parties elsewhere, not at the point of Red Army bayonets. There was also a crucial gap through which Stalin was eventually able to drive the doctrine of 'socialism in one country' in that, for Lenin, protection of the Soviet Revolution was a major duty of all communists from wherever they came and survival of the Russian Revolution was the first prerequisite for international revolution. Indeed, Lenin might have followed the same path since practical prospects for revolution were thin by the mid-1920s. There was also a related ambiguity. World revolution was always, in Lenin's mind, needed before the 'final', 'complete' or 'total' victory of socialism was possible. However, what constituted its ultimate victory? How far could one go in the interim? This was another area that Lenin did not resolve. Nor could he. He was not a clairvoyant. His principle continued to be, as he put it in 1917, quoting Napoleon: *'On s'engage, et puis, on voit'* meaning roughly, get on with it and see what happens. What Lenin was getting on with, above all, was building the internal structures for socialism within Russia.

PRODUCTIONISM

World revolution was an essential part of Lenin's revolutionary discourse. For a Marxist it could not be otherwise. This was doubly so for a Russian Marxist. Only by seeing the Russian Revolution as an essential component of something larger could one possibly promote a Marxist revolution in a Russia Lenin frequently acknowledged to be backward and with a proletariat he also described on numerous occasions as backward. It followed that, internally, the first duty of a Russian Marxist was to overcome backwardness. Ironically, the first step of the Revolution in Russia was to build its own prerequisites. It had to establish the conditions which were theoretically required for it to have come to power in the first place! In a word, we have already termed this productionism – putting every effort into developing the economy to a high level of output consistent with constructing socialism. Lenin made it clear many times that what was being built in Soviet Russia could not be called socialism: that was further down the line. Lenin eventually settled on state capitalism as the term to best describe what existed. What did he mean by the term?

The clearest expression of its essence came in June and July of 1919 in the pamphlet *A Great Beginning*. Lenin argued that 'in the last analysis labour productivity is the most important, the principal thing for the victory of the new social system.' It had also been the key to the capitalist revolution: 'Capitalism created a productivity of labour unknown under serfdom. Capitalism can only be utterly vanquished by socialism creating a new and much higher productivity of labour.' [SW 3 219] He had already made similar statements in 1918 at the time of adoption of the new line in the draft and final versions of *The Immediate Tasks of the Soviet Government*. But how was it to be achieved? In this light the hated Taylor system of scientific management was transformed from the most advanced capitalist tool for the exploitation of labour into a key weapon in the liberation of labour. However, for the worker in question the daily grind of work would not be much different under either dispensation, and intensive labour and associated systems like piecework remained highly unpopular with workers. Other ways to achieve it were equally unpopular. Paying engineers and managers high wages was one. The new emphasis on discipline and one-man management was another. Lenin also set great store by voluntary labour days known as *subbotniki* or subbotniks. The word derives from the Russian for Saturday because it usually involved giving up part of a Saturday to do work voluntarily. This might mean an extra day in the factory to produce a locomotive or a boiler without being paid or it might involve volunteering for communal work such as cleaning streets. As an example to his countrymen and women Lenin himself participated on 1 May 1920, helping to move lumber in the Kremlin. He had great praise for the system, though from an interesting angle. The point, he argued, once again in *A Great Beginning*, was that, although no one knew if subbotniks would work, they were of 'enormous historical significance precisely because they demonstrate the conscious and voluntary initiative of the workers in developing the productivity of labour, in adopting a new labour discipline, in creating socialist conditions of economy and life.' [SW 3 216] Lenin was perceptive enough to understand that voluntary labour alone would never enable the Soviet system to catch up with the capitalists and achieve 'scientific American efficiency of labour'. [CW 42 68–84] What other strategies were there?

Echoing the original relationship foreshadowed in *The April Theses* he went on to say 'The possibility of building socialism depends exactly upon our success in combining the Soviet power and the Soviet organization of administration with the up-to-date achievements of capitalism. We must organize in Russia the study and teaching of the Taylor system and systematically try it out and adapt it to our own ends.' [SW 2 664 *Immediate Tasks of the Soviet Government*] Although Lenin had many 'most important', 'vital', 'essential' and 'all that is needed' formulae and the use of such terms has to be understood rhetorically rather than literally, the theme of Soviet power and disciplined labour remained strong throughout the rest of his life. In *A Great Beginning* he expressed it most fully:

> In order to achieve victory, in order to build and consolidate socialism, the proletariat must fulfil a twofold or dual task: first, it must, by its supreme heroism in the revolutionary struggle against capital, win over the entire mass of the working and exploited people; it must win them over, organize them and lead them in the struggle to overthrow the bourgeoisie and utterly suppress their resistance. Secondly, it must lead the whole mass of the working and exploited people, as well as all the petty-bourgeois groups, on the road of new economic development, towards the creation of a new social bond, a new labour discipline, a new organization of labour, which will combine the last word in science and capitalist technology with the mass association of class-conscious workers creating large-scale socialist industry. [SW 3 215]

If one also adds their prescriptive nature, far removed from the once-promised 'complete creative freedom for the masses', most of what Lenin was about when in power can be found encapsulated in those words.

'The last word in science and capitalist technology.' Lenin was extremely interested in technological fixes to Russia's problems. He was fascinated by the liberating potential of modern technology. Even during the war scientific research establishments remained operative. Although he was not a radical, the world-renowned psychologist Pavlov was protected and, to discourage him from emigrating, Lenin ordered he should be given 'more or less decent conditions'. Some scientists, like Timiriazev, came to sympathize with the Revolution but most were neutral or hostile. Even so, one of the most remarkable features of the early Soviet years is that the Academy of Sciences, Russia's leading research institution which covered sciences and humanities (social sciences not yet having developed independently), was allowed to continue with a high degree of autonomy until 1928. Lenin always assumed that science and socialism enjoyed a special relationship and would reinforce one another. He also assumed that science was the refutation of religion. The thought that they might be compatible seems never to have crossed his mind.

In the grim years of the Civil War, resources for scientific and technical research were sparse. Basic conditions, like heating and lighting let alone salaries and rations, were poor. None the less, Lenin did encourage key projects. In particular, electrification came to be seen as a priority national goal. For Lenin it had obvious practical significance but beyond that it was also symbolic. It embodied the Promethean myth. Electricity was the new fire of the gods and man was stealing it to extend his own life chances. It would provide a portable system of power to take on heavy tasks as well as provide illumination all over the country and in the countryside. In one of the most famous photos of the 1920s, a peasant stares almost worshipfully at a light bulb in his hut. Not only would electricity transform the town it would also be a powerful factor in showing the peasantry the advantages of socialism, the task Lenin believed from mid-1919 onwards to be one of the most crucial if the Revolution was to survive. Rural application of electricity was thus a high priority, though that did not in itself guarantee success. Lenin was very enthusiastic about developing an electric plough and put considerable funds into its development though, in the end, it turned out not to be practicable. None the less electricity was the ultimate symbol of progress and Lenin developed a project of nationwide electrification by 1920. The well-known slogan of the period, displayed along the banks of the River Moskva opposite the Kremlin right up to the end of the Soviet era, famously quoted Lenin: 'Communism equals Soviet power plus the electrification of the whole country.' The whole country. The rural areas were not to be overlooked.

The electrification project was a forerunner of another key Leninist approach to economic advance, planning. Even as civil war raged Lenin was promoting the reconstruction of the Russian economy. A first step was the convening of a group of scientists, non-communist almost entirely, for the task of making an inventory of national resources and suggestions as to how they might best be exploited. It was called the

Academy of Sciences Commission for the Study of Scientific Productive Forces, or KEPS from the Russian initials. Many scientists and engineers, while they were not communist, accepted its Promethean vision. One of them, I.P. Bardin, recounted in his memoirs that his pre-Revolutionary dreams of turning Russia into 'a fairy-tale country of technical marvels, where everything was mechanized, blast-furnaces ran like clockwork and people in mines did not have to fear anything unexpected' appeared to be coming closer through the Bolsheviks.[8] Indeed, Lenin was the product of and was able to plug into a deep vein of Prometheanism in the Russian intelligentsia tradition which made it easy to promote KEPS and other scientific-productive endeavours.

Planning was soon incorporated into the economic fabric with the setting up of the Supreme Council of the National Economy in 1918 which had a scientific and technical section from late 1918 onwards. In part, it had been forced on Lenin by circumstance in that direct allocation of key products, which requires extensive planning, was the only kind of nationwide distribution there was after the collapse of money and markets (apart from the fast-growing local black markets). It was also partly a conscious imitation of the direction the great European economies, especially Germany, had taken during the war and, finally, it was the embodiment of the socialist aim of promoting a rational economy adjusted to needs rather than the irrational capitalist economy adjusted to maximizing profits. However, it must be said that what was meant by planning fell far short of the experience of the 1930s and beyond. Most obviously, in the trying times of revolutionary war, there were no resources for serious planning. None the less, it held promise for the future as the socialist alternative to the anarchy and unpredictability of the market. In an article of 21 February 1921, entitled 'An Integrated Economic Plan', Lenin praised the pioneering work of the electrification commission (GOELRO). It had succeeded in 'mobilizing hundreds of specialists and producing an integrated economic plan on scientific lines within ten months (and not two, of course, as we had originally planned). We have every right to be proud of this work.' Lenin described the plan as modest and indeed it was in that it only involved the task of electrification, but he praised it highly, quoting the Eighth Congress of Soviets, which described it as *the first step in a great economic endeavour* and saw its propagandist significance and called for *the most extensive popularization* of this plan', even stipulating that 'a study of this plan must be an item in the curricula of *all educational establishments of the Republic, without exception*.' [SW 3 552] Lenin's praise for the plan, ironically coming a month before the adoption of the New Economic Policy (known as NEP) which partially reinstated the market, was also tied up with another issue that had begun to attract his attention, the poor quality of Party and state officials compared to the specialists who had drawn it up.

Productionism had many other ramifications but labour productivity, technological advance and embryonic planning were the most important. There were a number of others. If labour productivity was to be raised how would the workers take it? The issue of worker representation and trades unions in the early Soviet days is very tangled. What rights did workers have to protest against the Workers' State? Wouldn't state capitalism exploit them as much as capitalism itself? Certainly many thought so. Lenin's early assumption, that their chief protector was the state and Party itself, was largely unshaken. But there was an even more sinister edge to the question. If the state was the expression of the best interests of the workers why should its power over them be limited at all? As far back as January 1918 the Declaration of Rights of Working and Exploited People had talked about the introduction of universal labour conscription. In other words, it opened up the possibility that labour could become analogous to military service. Workers would be enrolled and posted wherever they were needed. Initially, the idea had been to enact a universal duty to work in order to force the bourgeoisie into forms of socially useful labour. However, as the Civil War wound down and troops were being demobilized, Trotsky was once again taken by the incontrovertible logic. If the state could demand your life in battle, why could it not demand your labour in the revolutionary struggle on the economic front? In his words it was 'the right of the workers' state to send each working man and woman to the place where they are needed for the fulfilment of economic tasks.'[9]

Such a move would have turned workers into state pawns. If carried out it would have been disruptive beyond measure. How would families be handled? Mothers might be sent to one place, fathers to another. It was the gradual dawning of the practical implications that sank the project though there was some opposition. Lenin, however, remained somewhat equivocal, claiming that 'labour must be organized in a new way, new forms of incentives to work, of submission to labour discipline must be created.'[10] He also talked about 'more labour discipline' working 'with military determination' and 'sacrificing all private interests'. [CW 30 502–15] Clearly Lenin's vision was not far removed from Trotsky's, though his sense of what was possible was more acute and it held him back from the more extreme position.

Other issues where productionism impinged on everyday life in Lenin's outlook include diverse questions such as women's rights and education and culture. While women's rights were always part of the socialist project Lenin linked them closely with releasing mothers into the labour force. By collectivizing traditional family tasks, such as cooking, laundry, child-minding and so on, women would be able to spend more time at work. The link was captured at a conference on 19 November 1918 where Lenin stated that the Revolution would 'abolish all restrictions on women's rights' and that previously, women had been in the position 'of a slave; women have been tied to the home and only socialism can save them from this', the implication being they would join the workforce on an equal basis with men. [CW 28 180–2]

As far as culture and education was concerned Lenin's thoughts on this continued to develop but as far as his attitude to workers was concerned two elements predominated. One was the need to overcome the backwardness of the majority of Russian workers through practical measures such as abolishing illiteracy. Only a better educated worker would serve the productionist cause to the full. One step beyond that was the development of political consciousness in the workers. Only a politicized worker would be able to play a full part in the project of socialist construction. However, setting aside mass expansion of the desired consciousness, Lenin was having problems with his supposedly advanced workers and others gathered in the Party. The Party as a whole was not fulfilling Lenin's expectations and a multitude of problems were emerging. At this point we need to switch from Lenin's ideas about what productionism and state capitalism were to examining the agencies he was using to implement those ideas.

LENIN'S REVOLUTIONARY STRATEGY 1918–20 – AGENCIES FOR IMPLEMENTING TRANSFORMATION

To a Marxist, theory was no good without practice. For some Marxists, possibly Marx himself to some degree, there was a sense that the laws of history would work themselves out regardless. For Marx this approach was summed up in his crucial assumption that the liberation of the workers would be the task of the workers themselves. Through their everyday experiences they would come to realize that the roots of the problems they faced – low wages, poor conditions, harsh discipline, unemployment – were not the result of the whims of employers but were integral to the capitalist system itself. Through everyday labourist struggles over such issues they would come to see that only revolution in the realm of property relations would enable them to be free and have a reasonable share of the wealth modern industry and technology could create. In other words, they would raise their revolutionary consciousness through everyday struggle.

As we have seen, from its origin, Bolshevism took a different line. Summarizing what we examined earlier, we can reiterate the following. Starting from the question facing all Marxists at the time, 'Why has there not been a revolution?', Lenin had pinpointed the need for a party, an agency, to speed up the process. In that sense, Leninism was Marxism in a hurry. The model of agency with which he was familiar was the populist movement in the service of which his brother had given his life. So Leninism, in its struggle against tsarism, combined Marxist theory with elements of populist practice, and, perhaps, some theoretical influences from the latter as well. The question now was, how would this model sustain the leap from opposition to government? Should completely new structures be set up? What problems would the chosen model encounter? There were a myriad other implications. What was Lenin's answer?

Consciousness, culture and religion

Any analysis of Lenin's practice has to start at the point where theory and practice meet, with the quality of consciousness. Consciousness was as vital, perhaps more so, in building a new system as it had been in bringing down the old. In any case, the positive consciousness needed for construction required more imagination and was infinitely more complex than the negative consciousness needed to oppose a tyranny. Some Bolsheviks were more interested in these issues than others but for Lenin, although he spent relatively little time on it, consciousness was crucial. Socialism could not be built unless it succeeded in winning over the minds and hearts of the population. This did not have to be very sophisticated at the lowest level. The promise of a new and better life based on science, medicine and technology was enough. However, that could only be a first step. It was necessary to reveal the whole Bolshevik mission and win support. This led to a multitude of problems. At one level, the Bolshevik mission was not coherently thought out in the long term. At the immediate practical level Russia was one of the most traditionally religious countries in the world and scientific Marxism fitted the cultural outlook of only a few educated intellectuals. Arising from these was the devastating shortage of missionaries. Things did not look promising on the cultural front. It put a number of priority tasks before Lenin and the Party. First, work out just what the mission was, produce what today would be called a mission statement. Second, develop a strategy for converting the religious-minded masses. Third, find the personnel to achieve these. Since the Party was the association which, in Lenin's mind, brought the conscious parts of the population together in order to lead the rest of their fellow beings to Leninist enlightenment, we will look at it, and the problems of leadership and personnel, in the next section. Here, we will look at how Lenin dealt with the other two issues.

Before that, however, we should note that Bolshevik success and survival were built on both mobilization of support and on coercion. Supporters of Lenin have concentrated more on the former and have often overestimated it. Critics have concentrated on coercion, particularly by the Cheka, and have often overestimated it. The point is that there was a balance between the two. Lenin could not have survived by either of them alone. Here we will look at how he raised the crucial support he needed to survive, even though he failed to gain all the support needed to build a new world.

Lenin had always put the role of the newspaper in the first rank of Party tasks while in the underground. With the whole state mechanism at his disposal, ramshackle though it now was, he had even wider scope for creating instruments of propaganda. In an appropriate phrase the Soviet state has been called a 'propaganda state'.[11] By the time of the turn to 'iron proletarian discipline' in early 1918, Lenin had not only encouraged the flourishing of a vast array of official newspapers and journals, he had supervised the destruction of almost all those which were independent. Starting with the 'counter-revolutionary' liberal and conservative press the government had moved on to ban left-wing papers published by its opponents. In the process, Lenin had alienated one of his former key friends and associates, Maxim Gorky, whose independent paper, *Novaia zhizn'* (*New Life*), was forced into closure. It was also in the debate over press closures that Trotsky made his famous remark that the Bolshevik policy of freedom of the press was part of its minimum programme, closure of the counter-revolutionary press its maximum programme. In addition to newspapers, all print media and eventually all means of artistic expression, including film (in which Lenin was to show increasing interest), theatre and music, were under the supervision of a censorship apparatus which began to formalize itself from 1918 onwards. In the early years the control functions were exercised largely by the newly formed (December 1917) State Publishing House (*Gosizdat*) which was charged with 'regulating and supervising' the 'publishing activities of all scholarly and literary societies and equally of all other publishers'.[12] In 1922 a specialized censorship apparatus was set up known as *Glavlit*.[13]

Taking over the media was only one aspect of mobilization. Paper shortages and economic and distribution problems, not to mention illiteracy, meant that many key targets of propaganda were out of reach, especially in rural areas. In the early days, Lenin conducted what he called propaganda by decree and this was an especially important area. From the outset the Declaration of Soviet Power and the Decrees on Land and Peace of the Second Congress had a major propaganda role in building support for Bolshevik initiatives. The Decree on Peace, for example, was never even seriously communicated to foreign powers but was widely circulated within Soviet Russia. Similarly, the Declaration of Rights of the Exploited and Working People, produced as a Party riposte to the Constituent Assembly in January 1918, was widely circulated and, in an innovation arising in part from Krupskaya's early experiences in workers' circles and Lenin's admiration of London's newspaper reading rooms, the texts were put up in public places and their contents discussed through Party, trade union and factory committee bodies. The most important example of propaganda by decree was the Party programme of 1919 – its mission statement at last – and the associated publication by Bukharin and Preobrazhensky of an official commentary on it entitled the *ABC of Communism*. It laid out Party policy and aspirations in all areas from political power to finance, from religion to social policy. As such, it is the best guide to Bolshevik aims of the period. It was widely circulated and, although much of it and of the Party programme were written in an inaccessible intellectual style, it was used as the basic text for a wide range of reading groups especially in factories above all.

Lenin encouraged these developments, though, apart from closely supervising the production of the new Party programme (fulfilment, incidentally, of another of *The April Theses*), he was not always directly involved. He was, however, more taken up with issues of the content of the new, socialist culture. From questions of sexual behaviour to styles of painting, Lenin's personal views were conservative. On sexual matters, for instance, he wrote in January 1915 to Inessa Armand, commenting on her pamphlet on women's rights. Lenin chided her: 'I advise you to throw out paragraph 3 altogether – the "demand (women's) for freedom of love". That is not really a proletarian but a bourgeois demand.' [CW 35 180–1] A week later he wrote again suggesting that she should 'contrast philistine-intellectual-peasant ... vulgar and dirty marriage without love to proletarian civil marriage with love'. [CW 35 182–5] In November 1920 Clara Zetkin recalls that he dismissed 'Freudian theory as fashionable folly' saying he was 'always distrustful of those who concentrate on the sexual aspect'. He continued, referring to the fashionable view among some Party members that having sex was as natural and as insignificant as drinking a glass of water, that he was 'a Philistine to some extent, although I find philistinism repugnant. But I also hold the famous glass of water theory to be completely unmarxist and moreover unsocial. Sexual life is more than the purely physical, there is also the impact of culture.' [Weber 175] For Lenin, civil marriage based on love was the proper context for sexual relations.[14]

Sexuality was not the only sphere where he found himself in conflict with the avant-garde which sprang up so powerfully in early revolutionary Russia. In artistic and cultural matters in general Lenin preferred traditional forms of theatre, concert music and opera. Abstract artists like Chagall and El Lissitsky, the futurists and other brilliant schools which emerged were not at all to Lenin's taste. Even artists who claimed to be supporters of the Bolsheviks were not approved of. In May 1922, for example, he opposed the voting of funds to print 5,000 copies of Mayakovsky's avant-garde poem *150,000,000* describing it as 'nonsense, stupidity, double-dyed stupidity and affectation'. [CW 45 138] He also wrote to the Bolshevik historian and cultural commissar M.N. Pokrovsky requesting his help to 'fight futurism'. [CW 45 139]

Given Lenin's own brand of 'futurism', namely his stress on the technological utopia, his views seem unexpected. However, the key to them lies in his constant awareness of the outlook and life of the ordinary people who, he believed, had no truck with bohemian intellectual pretentiousness. In this respect he was not wrong to identify himself as, in some ways, a philistine. It was only in the 1930s that one of the foundations of the official artistic and cultural doctrine of socialist realism was defined as *narodnost'*, meaning art that was accessible to and focused on the ordinary people. This was a bedrock of Lenin's outlook. He preferred traditional artistic styles because they were more immediately comprehensible. In the early years, when many artists were incorporated into the propaganda apparatus at various levels, it was the less experimental ones who were retained. By 1921, the avant-garde was more or less dispersed by emigration, starvation or 'internal exile' (i.e. abandoning their art, or at least not showing it in public). A few were caught up in repression and executed. Many were forcibly deported. A mass expulsion of over 200 intellectuals, many of whom were not avant-garde but were certainly non-Bolshevik, took place in the summer of 1922. Most of them were university teachers. In their place, the educational and propaganda apparatus recruited people whose message was more consistent with that of the Bolsheviks and whose style was more easily accessible via posters, cartoons and so on.

One focus of poster campaigns was religion, an area in which Lenin had complex views. Personally, he developed a deep antipathy to all forms of religion as his attacks on the Godbuilders had shown before the war. He was aware, however, that direct confrontation risked deepening what he considered to be the prejudices of religious believers. Party pronouncements emphasized 'helping the toiling masses to liberate their minds from religious prejudices' without 'offending the religious susceptibilities of believers, which leads only to the hardening of religious fanaticism'.[15] This reflected Lenin's own opinion. For instance, in 1921, in a letter to Molotov, he complained of what he called tactless propaganda claiming to 'expose the falsehood of religion'. It was, he wrote, '*absolutely*' necessary to '*avoid any affront to religion*'. [CW 45 119–20] On another occasion, on 2 April 1919, he supported a plea from a group of artisans to be able to complete the building of a church in

Cherepovets. [Weber 158] At the same time, Lenin had been uncompromising from the first with any attempt to allow believers to join the Party. Unlike Social Democrats elsewhere Lenin was firmly opposed. On occasions he contravened his more 'liberal' assertions about not offending religious people by approving, even encouraging, harsh measures including shooting clerical personnel, albeit ones who had actively supported the Whites.

Finally, Lenin also participated directly in a major dispute within the Party over cultural issues. A group, under the influence of Lenin's former friend and then opponent A.A. Bogdanov, had attempted to define proletarian culture and to assign it a major role in revolutionary transformation. The group became known as Proletkul't, derived from the Russian abbreviation of The Proletarian Cultural Educational Association. In their view, successful classes could only take power if they possessed a powerful culture. The classic example was the bourgeois revolution which, in Britain, France, Italy, Germany and elsewhere, had been preceded by centuries of preparation of bourgeois-individualist as opposed to clerical-feudal culture. To assert itself, the proletariat, they argued, needed to do the same.

The principle opened up a whole set of issues, not least: what did proletarian culture consist of?[16] The debate brought Lenin's views on the subject to a head. For him, there was no developed proletarian culture and, for the time being, the point was to absorb the basics of bourgeois culture. Lenin was not thinking of its individualist values but its vast store of knowledge, technique and science. He was particularly critical of the view that there was such a thing as a distinctively proletarian science. Here he clashed not only with Proletkul'tists but senior Party members like Bukharin who took more than a passing interest in problems of cultural revolution. In 1921 Lenin drafted a decree severely restricting the activities of Proletkul't. The main statements were that 'the Marxist world outlook is the only true expression of the interests, the viewpoint and the culture of the revolutionary proletariat' and it had won this position because, 'far from rejecting the most valuable achievements of the bourgeois epoch, it has, on the contrary, assimilated and refashioned everything of value.' [SW 3 476–7] In fact, Proletkul't had not rejected the achievements of the past. Lenin, deliberately or not, was confusing their principles with those of the futurists. Perhaps Lenin's real objection came in the final paragraph of the draft where he rejected Proletkul't's claim to autonomy and called for it to be placed firmly under the direction of the Education Ministry. Needless to say, that is what happened and it became a sub-department of the ministry largely occupied with conventional adult education, an activity Nadezhda Krupskaya increasingly occupied herself with.

Be that as it may, Lenin's assertion that the first task was to assimilate real bourgeois culture reflected a major concern that was growing throughout the later years of the revolutionary war. Social and economic chaos and collapse called for activists rather than theoreticians. Lenin increasingly complained about the tendency of communists to argue and debate forever, in the good old Russian intelligentsia style, without getting anything done. The time, Lenin increasingly argued, was one where the doers rather than the thinkers must come to the fore. Apart from being a clarion call to the likes of Stalin, who had barely touched Lenin's life until then (though the reverse is not true in that Lenin had already profoundly influenced Stalin's life), it was the basis of a degree of soul-searching and breast-beating about bureaucracy on Lenin's part.

The Party and state apparatus

Before the October Revolution, and especially in the months between February and October, Lenin's theory of the Party was ceasing to be an accurate description of its practice. Rather, Sukhanov's view, of a party where slogans had one meaning for the masses and another for the leadership, seems much closer to reality. The cascade of members into the Party in 1917 had burst its theory-imposed confines. After October the expansion continued apace. In March 1919 membership stood at 313,000, rising to 611,000 in March 1920 and 732,000 in March 1921. This continued to be a mixed blessing. Lenin needed all the supporters he could get but mass admission to the Party threatened to dilute its revolutionary resolve by admitting members whose revolutionary consciousness was weak or even non-existent. Before discussing Lenin's response to the problem we need to look briefly at the processes affecting the ruling apparatus as the revolutionary war unfolded.

In the first place, the fundamental stance of the Party changed from destruction of an old order to construction of the new, something Lenin had no experience of whatsoever. In reality, the break was not a clean one. Throughout the years of revolutionary war both aspects ran in parallel, though the imperative of construction was always increasing while the problem of replacing the old was constantly diminishing as the new authorities increased their grip on power. Second, the distinction between Party and state became increasingly blurred. Small, dominant Party cells, commissars and so on had been attached to state institutions ranging from local soviets to major ministries. At the top, the overlapping personnel of the Politburo and Sovnarkom put the state apparatus firmly under the thumb of the Party. The state was becoming the Party's errand boy. As such, it makes little sense for us to examine the two components separately. Many of the growing problems Lenin identified were common to both. Some arose from the relationship that was emerging. Third, the scope of leadership action was widening enormously at an immensely rapid pace. Traditional state activities up to 1914 had largely comprised foreign and military policy, maintaining law and order at home and raising the cash needed for the other two. Slight dabbling in education and social insurance had also crept in during the latter part of the previous century. During the war the British, French and German states expanded their responsibilities to include supervision of military-related industries and problems. Famously, in Britain, licensing laws, the remnants of which survived into the twenty-first century, were introduced to force pubs to close in the afternoon to ensure armaments workers would return to their factories. The quality of weapons they built after a pub session doesn't appear to have worried the legislators. In Russia, total prohibition was introduced on the grounds that a sober manhood would make better fighting material than a drunken one. In terms of front-line fighting most evidence suggests the reverse is the case. There were other drawbacks in the Russian legislation. Prohibition cut government tax income by a massive amount and in any case the population turned to illegal distilling for their vodka, an even more frightening prospect.

By comparison, the scope of the early Soviet state expanded exponentially in the early months. By mid-1918, not only was it responsible for the war but it had taken over most major industries through nationalization. It ran whatever transport networks remained open. It had taken over all schools including religious and private ones. It sponsored all scientific research. It subsidized all artistic enterprises including publishing, theatre, opera, art galleries, museums and cinema, becoming effectively the sole patron for the arts in general. It also, through rationing, took on the task of replacing the market for food and other essential products. It could not, of course, take on all these tasks efficiently in such a short time and under the chaotic conditions of war and revolution. Rations, as a prime example, had to be supplemented through a vast black market for the population to reach even survival level in the great cities. Once again, of course, the Bolsheviks had been criticized by others on the left precisely because the critics foresaw these difficulties. Lenin, however, had continued to believe in *'On s'engage et puis, on voit.'* What was his reaction to these developments?

Not surprisingly, the double-edged nature of Lenin's views affected this area along with many others. Ideally, self-administration by the masses who 'would soon learn' the necessary skills was his core belief. In practice, of course, the dream did not work out. One could not kick down an economy and society and expect ordinary people to rebuild them simply out of some kind of instinct. They needed infrastructure, knowledge and resources. Lenin's refusal to acknowledge this could be breathtakingly naive. For example, law is one of the most complex and organically evolved aspects of any civilized society. One of the chief problems facing a revolution is what to do about law. It is impossible to maintain the old law, yet there is no time or personnel to devise a whole new law code to replace it quickly. Like all other aspects of transition, time and expertise were needed. However, in his *Report on the Party Programme* at the Eighth Party Congress on 19 March 1919, Lenin mentioned he had found a short cut. 'Take, for example, the courts. Here it is true, the task was easier; we did not have to create a new apparatus, because anybody can act as a judge basing himself on the revolutionary sense of justice of the working class.' [SW 3 160] An 'easier' task which 'anybody' can do! The Party programme itself left the judgment of crimes, where there was as yet no Soviet law, to 'socialist conscience'.[17]

Ironically, the happy dreams of a self-administered society, functioning like the German post office, as Lenin had argued in *State and Revolution*, were evaporating, just as the pamphlet was published for the first time. Grimmer realities of collapse, incompetence and administrative confusion were to replace them.

Lenin knew exactly what he expected of Party members. They should be paragons of revolutionary virtue. They should know what they were doing and why, be ever-obedient to Party orders and their duty should come first. They should lead by example, never by force, which should be reserved for the enemy. It was up to them to win over the rest of the working people to the communist cause. They must never abuse their position for personal gain. They should be the first in self-sacrifice, last in self-interest. In fact, though Lenin would not relish the comparison, the women and men in the Party should be a secular, revolutionary version of a disciplined religious order. In the words of a decree of the Eighth Party Congress 'membership in the Russian Communist Party accords no privileges whatsoever, but merely puts heavier responsibilities on them.'[18] The heroism of Party members should be expressed not only in fighting the enemy but also at work. As well as increasing output, subbotniks were an opportunity to show the fruits of heroic leadership at work. Lenin himself quoted many examples of labour heroism from the Soviet press. Here is one example from *Pravda* of 17 May 1919:

> The enthusiasm and team spirit displayed during the work were extraordinary. When the workers, clerks and head office employees, without even an oath or an argument, caught hold of the half-ton wheel tire of a passenger locomotive and, like industrious ants, rolled it into place, one's heart was filled with fervent joy at the sight of this collective effort, and one's conviction was strengthened that the victory of the working class was unshakable … When the work was finished those present witnessed an unprecedented scene: a hundred Communists, weary, but with the light of joy in their eyes, greeted their success with the solemn strains of the *Internationale*. [*A Great Beginning*, SW 3 207–8]

The atmosphere of a religious meeting was clearly conveyed. While one might doubt the heroic simplicity of such tales, the point is that they defined the ideal.

However, by 1919 problems had begun to emerge. Lenin and the rest of the leadership were increasingly concerned about the quality of recruits to the Party. Far from embodying the much-vaunted ideals of communist morality, they appeared to have joined the Party for personal advantage. In the deadly conditions of 1919, survival was more likely within the Party than without, provided, of course, one stayed out of the army where many thousands of communists were heroically sacrificing their lives to lead the struggle for the workers' cause. Those with less honourable intentions were infiltrating leadership roles and divert-ing the few perks of office towards themselves. The state administration, if anything, was even worse in that most of its members were not even nominally committed to communist morality. It was the task of tiny communist cells, often less than three per cent of the workforce, to supervise the growing state administration. Bribery and corruption were rife. A cosmopolitan leftist and sympathizer with the Revolution, Victor Serge, who eventually joined Trotsky's group in exile, has left a vivid vignette of the atmosphere generated:

> Committees were piled on top of Councils, and Managements on top of Commissions. Of this apparatus, which seemed to me to function largely in a void, wasting three-quarters of its time on unrealisable projects, I at once formed the worst impression. Already, in the midst of general misery, it was nurturing a multitude of bureaucrats who were responsible for more fuss than honest work.[19]

The Party left picked on the issue of the decline in Party morality and state administration as major themes to attack Lenin's policies. Allowing non-Party people into important posts was, they said, dilut-ing the proletarian purity of the revolutionary leadership. The terms 'careerism' and 'bureaucratism' began to be tossed around in Party debates. Careerism identified groups of Party members who were more interested in their own careers and advancement than in the Revolution. Bureaucratism was the tendency among administrators to do what was easiest for them rather than fulfil the needs of those whom they admin-istered. The Party Congress of 1919 had pointed out the twin evils. The resolution on organization opened unequivocally. 'Numerical growth of the party is progressive only to the extent that healthy proletarian ele-ments of town and countryside are brought into the party ... The party must constantly follow with care the changes occurring in its social composition ... Expansion of the numerical base must in no case be con-ducted at the cost of worsening their qualitative composition.'[20] On bureaucratism it was equally forthright: 'Many of the party members assigned to state tasks are becoming cut off from the masses to a consid-erable extent and are becoming infected with bureaucratism.'[21]

The problem was much easier to identify than to deal with. In the first place the vastly expanded scope of Party and state activities put colossal strain on its human resources. There simply were not enough members to do all the jobs that needed doing. Lenin commented that, when the future historians try to discover who administered Russia during the last seventeen months, 'nobody will believe that it was done by so few people. The number was small because there were so few intelligent, educated and capable political leaders in Russia.' [CW 29 146–64]

The first response, purging, in some ways made matters worse because it reduced the number of members. From 250,000 the total fell to 150,000 as a result of the first Party purge in 1919.[22] The idea of the purge was to throw out those who were unworthy of Party membership. As such, purging was, in various ways, a common practice in elite institutions. Anyone who fell short of the standards had to be eliminated from the organization, whether it was the British Cabinet, a gentleman's club or a political party. However, when there was a desperate shortage of personnel its effectiveness was severely undermined. Lenin was aware of the consequences, complaining in his *Report on the Party Programme* to the Eighth Party Congress on 19 March 1919 that unwanted members 'have been thrown out of the door but they creep back in through the window'. [SW 3 160] The Party needed vastly more members, not fewer. Indeed, it was constantly recruiting. Lenin, for example, waxed lyrical over the 'huge, quite unexpected success' of Party Week in Moscow in autumn 1919 when 13,600 new recruits joined the Party. In the Party as a whole some 200,000 were recruited.[23] Revealingly, Lenin, giving *The Results of Party Week in Moscow and Our Tasks*, went on to discuss what to do with them. 'They must be *more boldly* given the most varied kinds of state work, they must be tested in practice as rapidly as possible.' [SW 3 272]

Let us pause for a moment to digest the implications. First, the statement reveals the relationship between Party and state. Even raw recruits can be thrown into the fray of controlling state institutions immediately. Second, as raw recruits, what did they know of Party objectives? Well, Lenin says, give them the job and then we will see. In Leninist terms their responsibilities were awesome. First was '*supervision* over office workers, officials and specialists by new members who are well acquainted with the condition of the people, their needs and requirements'. They were to 'check up on the conscientiousness with which old officials perform their tasks' and 'be placed so as to renovate and refresh the intermediary links between the mass of workers and peasants on one hand and the state apparatus on the other'. The problem was that 'In our industrial "chief administrations and central boards", in our agricultural "state farms" there are still too many, far too many, saboteurs, landowners and capitalists in hiding, who harm Soviet power in every way' – words with an unmistakably Stalinist ring to them. Indeed, Stalin was in the course of becoming the member of the leadership group with the greatest responsibility for supervising the supervisors and rooting out bad apples, a habit he retained throughout his life. Lenin did not envisage Stalinist sanctions at this time, however. Rather, old Leninist illusions, for example that the new Party members would 'quickly learn the job themselves', re-emerged. [SW 3 272]

By 1920, no real solution had been found to the evils of bureaucratism and careerism. The issue remained a running sore throughout Soviet history. Trotsky made it the chief plank of his critique of 'Stalinism' from the 1920s until his death. Panaceas were sought by Khrushchev and Brezhnev. The bureaucracy – the 'administrative-command system' – was the central target of Gorbachev's reforms. Arguably, it was the bureaucracy which survived the Soviet system and grabbed Russia's assets for itself after the fall of communism. Even though Stalin added to the bureaucratization of the Revolution there can be little doubt that it was an endemic feature of the Soviet, Leninist, system from the beginning. Lenin became increasingly aware of it and, in the reorientation of 1920–2, tried to deal with it again. However, before we turn to that last transformation we need to look at one other crucial agency of Leninism at this point and also examine how Lenin personally was bearing up to the pressures of governance.

Coercion and terror

The Soviet system was not built on force alone. Mobilization was as important. In the propaganda sphere, mobilization was uppermost. In the Party and administrative sphere mobilization and coercion existed side by side. At times, however, pure coercion – terror – was undoubtedly a crucial instrument. No aspect of Lenin's rule has generated more heat and less light in recent years than this one. Increasingly tied up with cold war and post-cold war propaganda the issue has, since the collapse of communism, eclipsed most other aspects of Lenin's work and life.

The end result is that he has been bracketed with a job lot of dictators – for instance, by US Defense Secretary Donald Rumsfeld who said, on 9 April 2003, 'Saddam Hussein is now taking his rightful place alongside Hitler, Stalin, Lenin, Ceauşescu in the pantheon of failed brutal dictators.'[24] Arbitrary as such lists are, does Lenin deserve to be on them?

Some people are born violent; some achieve violence; some have violence thrust upon them. Lenin was not a violent person, he did not relish violence and would, like any civilized person, have preferred to live without it. In 1917 he said the workers should refrain from using violence unless it was used against them first. He did not participate directly in violence. Neither Lenin nor his party shared the fashionable ideas derived from Nietzsche (though Nietzsche himself might well have bridled at them) and some futurists and taken up by fascists in Italy first of all that violence was cleansing, that it was a positive force that tested the mettle of a man (sic) and brought out his most noble and heroic qualities. Although under Stalin there was praise for the armed forces, Communism did not develop a fascist-style warrior cult. Even in Stalin's time soldiers were not portrayed as killers but as husbands and fathers defending their women and children. Unlike many other dictators who followed him, including Stalin, Lenin never wore a military or any other kind of uniform. He remained the irascible professor, the tutor of his unruly and ill-disciplined people. So where did the violence fit in?

In the communist morality to which Lenin subscribed the greatest good was the good of the Revolution. Whatever served revolution was right. There were no qualms about whether ends justified means, it was a given that the end of revolution justified almost any means. Lenin frequently said that one could not make an omelette without breaking eggs. There would have to be a necessary amount of suffering for the cause to triumph. For Lenin, to argue along these lines was not a matter of principle alone, it was simply reality. Revolution would be a violent act, like its cousin, war. It has been pointed out that the degree of violence in a revolution is, in many cases, directly proportional to the resistance offered by the old elites.[25] Lenin made the same connection. The violence of revolution arose from the resisters, the former possessors of power and property, struggling to hold on to their ill-gotten gains and privileges. For Lenin the Revolution was a fight for justice, the resistance to it a fight for injustice. At some point, almost any revolution would have to use force to dispossess the exploiters, the ruling class, because it would not give in without a fight. From this point of view, it was the counter-revolution that defined the necessity or otherwise of violence and its degree.

Associated with this was the morality of class struggle. Again from the Marxist point of view, class struggle was not something invented by Marxists or the proletariat. All Marx had done was to identify the practice of ruling classes from time immemorial. Their everyday reality was to practise class struggle against their own people, even though many of them would deny it. Starting from this assumption, liberating the masses from class struggle meant waging class struggle back, defending the masses against the myriad weapons of class struggle, notably law, the state with its armed forces, religions which preached submission, the media and so on. Class struggle was a kind of war the tactics of which changed according to the situation. Peaceful skirmishing through strikes might be appropriate at times but in a revolutionary crisis the morality of national war and the reality of class war would fuse. What difference was there between a general sending people to their death on both sides of the conflict and a revolutionary leader doing the same? Didn't the end of victory justify the means of violence in both cases? To refuse this fight was simply to allow exploitation to continue forever, to surrender to the vicious war waged by the elites. Another favourite expression of Lenin's was '*Kto kogo?*', roughly, who will do whom in? Class struggle was a fight to the finish. The Revolution did not invent the rules, it simply tried to turn them to the advantage of the poor.

Going beyond these theoretical considerations Lenin's outlook on violence was, of course, deeply affected by the brutality going on around him. 1914–17 were the bloodiest years in human history. No previous bloodletting had matched the ghastly pace of the First World War. Tens of thousands destroyed in minutes, hundreds of thousands in weeks. The death toll made the worst previous historical atrocities pale by comparison. In Lenin's view the ruling classes were responsible for this slaughter. In order to prevent it, even to eliminate war from human affairs, some violence was fully justified. Lenin could only snort with derision when bourgeois commentators accused his government of being violent. Imperialist violence, for the material advantage of the elite, using the masses as cannon fodder, was, he argued, infinitely worse than the violence of the masses trying to put an end to imperialist and nationalist ambition.

Lenin was also prepared to condone further forms of violence, including hostage-taking, retaliation and exemplary punishment. In the former cases Lenin believed the morality of revolution justified what 'needed' to be done. As far as exemplary punishment was concerned his practice differed little from that of European generals. Lenin expressed on numerous occasions that numbers of exploiters, swindlers and racketeers should be shot in order to send a message to others that such behaviour should not be tolerated. Deserters were also in danger of summary justice, including execution. On the western front French and British generals were also carrying out executions to quell simmering unrest among wavering armies. They also had a tradition of ruthless repression of colonial rebellions, using summary execution to control unrest, such as the Boxer Rebellion in China and the exactly contemporaneous Amritsar Massacre of 1919 in India. The scale was different, the practice identical. Like Amritsar, many tragedies arose from one man on the spot taking matters into his own hands. Lenin and his supporters tended to see criticism of their policies from the right as purely hypocritical. In their eyes they were giving the ruling class a taste of its own medicine.

Of course, two wrongs do not make a right and to understand Lenin's position is not to condone it. Each reader can make up her or his own mind. However, it is worth weighing up these considerations in a world where imperialist, military and civil violence is rarely dwelt on compared to revolutionary violence. Whatever one's view of the morality of Lenin's use of violence, it is time to look at some examples.

In the first half of 1918 Lenin's exhortations to terror tended to be related to so-called economic crimes and 'sabotage'. Food supply was the main issue. Fearful that famine might take hold Lenin resorted to ultimate measures. In January he told food supply officials that 'we can't expect to get anywhere unless we resort to terrorism: speculators must be shot on the spot. Moreover bandits must be dealt with just as resolutely: they must be shot on the spot.' [CW 26 501–2] The following day, 28 January, he sent letters to two subordinates urging them 'Take the *most* decisive and *revolutionary* measures and send *grain*, *grain* and again *grain*!! Otherwise Petrograd will starve to death.' [Weber 144] In May he returned to the same theme. In the 'war for grain' he urged the declaration of martial law and 'shooting for indiscipline'. [*Theses on the Current Situation*, 26 May 1918, CW 27 406–7] His rationale was, as he put it in a letter, that the whole enterprise was at stake: 'For *obviously* we shall perish and ruin the *whole* revolution if we do not conquer famine in the next few months.' (By 'whole' he probably meant the international revolution.) [Letter to Shliapnikov, 28 May 1918, CW 44 95.] Incidentally, there is no known direct correlation between rhetoric of this kind and actual violence. Shootings and terror were endemic whether or not Lenin commented on it.

His discourse of 'iron discipline' and the so-far 'excessively mild' dictatorship had important repercussions for coercion, but it was the events of the summer which spiralled the issue out of control. The threshold was raised by the renewal of armed resistance by the Czech Legion in June and the Left SRs in July, plus the shooting of Lenin himself on 30 August, as a result of an assassination attempt by Fanya Kaplan, a disaffected SR. Lenin, unsurprisingly, called for the Left SR uprising to be 'mercilessly suppressed'. [Weber 150] In early August he called on the authorities in Nizhnii Novgorod to take extreme steps to pre-empt a supposed White Guard insurrection. He called for 'Mass searches. Executions for concealing arms. Mass deportations.' [CW 35 349] Ironically, in the wake of his own shooting he was too ill to advise retaliatory measures. However, that did not make any difference. The Cheka was ready to step up its actions and in August and September organized terror really took off. According to official Cheka figures in 1918, there were 6,300 executions, 2,431 of which were for participation in revolts. 1,000 were shot for embezzlement. In 1919 there were 3,456 executions (excluding Ukraine). In 1918, 1,150 people died on the Red side fighting against these 'uprisings' and the like. However, the full scale of terror was much greater. It was certainly on a scale greater than anything seen under tsarism and may have reached 500,000 victims though the grounds for such a conclusion are unclear. There was also massive anti-Red terror and appalling pogroms which may have brought about comparable death rates. According to one estimate, 115,000 Ukrainian Jews were killed in 1919 alone.[26]

Unsurprisingly the desperate situation of 1919 brought further expressions of the need for summary violence from Lenin. Like those of 1918 they were directed against outsider individuals and groups trying to enrich themselves from the common misery. Former bureaucrats disrupting Soviet administration were a 'scum' that must be fought against. [CW 29 19–37] On 31 May he co-signed Dzerzhinsky's article on the danger of spies as the Whites approached Moscow and Petrograd. Again unsurprisingly the article called for 'Death to Spies'.[27] The same crisis caused Lenin to urge another subordinate that 'More hostages from the ranks of the bourgeoisie and the families of officers must be seized because of the increasing incidence of treason.' [Weber 160] In August he declared peasants must be protected in bringing in the harvest and 'robbery, violence and illegal procurement of grain by soldiers are to be ruthlessly punished by execution by a firing squad.' [Weber 162] Later in the year, replying to Gorky who was trying to keep alight the wan flame of intellectual freedom in the dark night of 1919, Lenin claimed that 'there was no harm' in making intellectuals 'spend some weeks or so in prison, if this *has* to be done to *prevent* plots ... and the deaths of tens of thousands.' [CW 44 283–5] As the situation improved, in December, at the Eighth Party Conference, he was able to announce that 'our main difficulty is now behind us'. Terror was forced on Soviet power but now Soviet Russia wants to live in peace with its neighbours and concentrate on internal development. [CW 30 167–94 and Weber 164] From 1920 onwards the resort to terror was much reduced and disappeared from Lenin's mainstream discourses and practices.

All the above quotes are from works of Lenin published long ago so it seems odd to talk of an *Unknown Lenin*[28] who resorted to terror and other kinds of chicanery. There are no aspects of Lenin's outlook which cannot be figured out from long-published sources. However, a veil of secrecy was drawn over certain aspects. Violence against the church in 1922 was a major example. Lenin took advantage of the famine in 1922 to campaign to remove valuables from the churches. In some places, notably Shuia, the actions provoked major resistance. Prior to that, during the Revolutionary War, many clerics had been killed, some in support of the Whites, some executed by the Cheka, some as a result of the spontaneous violence endemic in the power vacuum of war and revolution. According to church figures, by 1920 322 bishops and priests had been executed during the Revolution. Another calculation put the figure at twenty-eight bishops and 1,000 priests who had died by 1923.[29] Soviet sources remained very reticent about this and the most infamous quotation from Lenin supporting it was suppressed. In a letter to the Politburo of 19 March 1922 Lenin, as prone as his protégé Stalin to find conspiracies, interpreted the resistance at Shuia as part of a co-ordinated campaign against the Party led by Patriarch Tikhon, who had earlier anathematized the Bolsheviks. Referring to Machiavelli on the need to make brutalities short and sharp if they were necessary, he urged taking advantage of the famine to press home a Bolshevik counter-attack 'because no other moment except that of desperate hunger will guarantee us the sympathy of these masses or at least their neutrality.' He wanted to give 'battle to the Black Hundred clergy in the most decisive and merciless manner and crush its resistance with such brutality that it will not forget it for decades to come.' The most infamous passage reads: 'The greater the number of representatives of the reactionary clergy and reactionary bourgeoisie we succeed in executing for this reason [i.e. resisting the confiscations], the better.' As far as quantifying these vague figures are concerned the only specific reference to numbers in the document is that 'no fewer than several dozen' clergy and associates should be arrested and tried. Needless to say, Lenin specified that the whole operation of confiscation required the appointment of 'the best [Party] workers'.[30] This example, like most of the others, fits Mayer's interpretation of the close relationship between revolutionary and counter-revolutionary violence.

While the debate about terror has been the more prominent, perhaps the deeper issue was use of coercion in general because it was born of structural problems of Lenin's project itself. European left-wing critics were among the first to point out the democratic deficit in Lenin's 'democratic centralism', one-party state, resort to censorship and abandonment of freedom of speech and total inability to tolerate opposition. Kautsky launched a major attack in a pamphlet entitled *The Dictatorship of the Proletariat* published in Vienna in 1918.

Lenin's response was characteristically forthright. In a pamphlet entitled *Proletarian Revolution and the Renegade Kautsky* (October–November 1918) he accused his old foe of being 'a lackey of the bourgeoisie' [SW 3 55 and 119] and indistinguishable from 'a counter-revolutionary bourgeois' [SW 3 121]. He said Kautsky was 'chewing rags in his sleep' [SW 3 46] and 'like a blind puppy sniffing at random first in one direction and then in another'. [SW 3 49] There were many such insults. Lenin's main point of defence was that Kautsky wanted 'a revolution without revolution, without fierce struggle, without violence'. [SW 3 120] He had underestimated the significance of the transitional dictatorship of the proletariat. 'The proletarian revolution is impossible without the forcible destruction of the bourgeois state machine and the substitution for it of a *new one* which, in the words of Engels, is "no longer a state in the proper sense of the word."' [SW 3 50] 'The Soviets are the direct organization of the working and exploited peoples themselves' and, as a result, 'proletarian democracy is a *million times* more democratic than any bourgeois democracy.' [SW 3 59] For nearly one hundred pages Lenin raged at Kautsky and used all kinds of insults, traded quotes from Marx and Engels and generally engaged in massive academic polemic. The extraordinary thing is that Lenin, pressed on all sides as the Civil War developed, recovering from the attempted assassination and returning to his round of meetings, conferences and so on, believed it worthwhile to spend so much mental energy on such a target and in such a format. In fact, only his convalescence really opened up the space for him to do it. The professorial Lenin took advantage of the moment to re-emerge at the expense of the revolutionary activist who was, for the moment, on the injured list.

Whatever one might think of his polemic with Kautsky it was another, more radical, figure from the German left, Rosa Luxemburg, who made a more telling critique of Soviet reality as far as she could discern it from Berlin. In his dispute with Kautsky, Lenin had indicated that formal democracy was an extra which would emerge later. In 1921 he was to confirm this mind-set by stating to the delegates at the Tenth Party Congress that, in the conditions of the time, discussion in the Party was an 'amazing luxury'. [SW 3 560] Rosa Luxemburg had already detected the problem nearly two years earlier. Freedom and democracy were not luxuries, they were essentials. 'The whole mass of the people must take part ... otherwise socialism will be decreed from behind a few official desks by a dozen intellectuals.' Lenin was 'completely mistaken in the means he employs. Decree, dictatorial force of the factory overseer, draconic penalties, rule by terror.' It was this last, 'rule by terror, which demoralizes'. It opened up an unhealthy cycle:

> In place of the representative bodies created by general, popular elections, Lenin and Trotsky have laid down the soviets as the only true representation of the labouring masses. But with the repression of political life in the land as a whole, life in the soviets must also become more crippled. Without general elections, without unrestricted freedom of the press and assembly, without a free struggle of

opinion, life dies out in every public institution, becomes a mere semblance of life, in which bureaucracy remains as the active element.[31]

Whether or not it was the case, as Clara Zetkin later claimed, that Rosa Luxemburg had admitted her critique was 'wrong' [Weber 184], her words were brilliantly prophetic and, had she lived longer, might well have seen that she had been correct in the first place. Indeed, the essence of her criticisms go back to 1905 when she had accused Lenin of trying to 'bind' the creativity of the working class.

Be that as it may, Lenin did not respond to Luxemburg in the way he did to Kautsky and, indeed, until her murder in a Berlin prison, kept her in the forefront of his mind as a key player in the German revolution. Afterwards she was elevated to iconic, martyr status. Lenin remained convinced of the necessity of doing things his way, the revolutionary way. 'Europe's greatest misfortune and danger,' he lamented, 'is that it has *no* revolutionary party.' It would need 'world Bolshevism' to 'conquer the world bourgeoisie'. [CW 28 105–13] It required an altogether tougher stance. The Soviet outlook started from a different premise: 'The Soviet Republic is besieged by the enemy. It must become a single military camp, not in word but in deed.' [*All Out for the Fight Against Denikin!*, 9 July 1919, SW 3 227] The habit survived the defeat of the White enemy. In April 1920 Lenin reiterated in a speech to a miners' conference that 'we continue to be a besieged fortress towards which the world's workers are turned, for they know their freedom will come from here; and in this besieged fortress we must act with military ruthlessness, with military discipline and self-sacrifice.' [CW 30 495–501] Protests about 'formal democracy' were laughed aside. In *'Democracy' and Dictatorship* (December 1919) Lenin wrote that the democratic republic is 'in practice the dictatorship of the bourgeoisie'. [CW 28 368–72] There were only the two dictatorships to chose from, bourgeois or proletarian. In August 1922, in a letter to Myasnikov, who was demanding complete freedom of the press, Lenin put his position bluntly: 'We laugh at "pure democracy" ... We do not wish to commit suicide and we will not do this.' [CW 32 504–9]

Here was a central dilemma of Leninism. Was Lenin correct? Was it just sentimental to believe that there were democratic norms beyond direct class rule? His supporters would claim any relaxation would only allow the counter-revolution, capitalism, with its enormous worldwide resources, to get leverage on the situation and begin to undermine it. Critics would say that the very absence of democracy was a feature which did more to discredit the Revolution than anything the capitalists could do. In Lenin's dismissive laughter, they could hear the death knell of true revolution.

8

RE-EVALUATION, SUCCESSION AND TESTAMENT

The years of warfare, internal struggle and attempted construction against a background of ever-more unbelievable social and economic collapse had taken their toll on Lenin. He had been shot at twice and still had a bullet lodged in his body. He had maintained a fearsome schedule of meetings, writings and speech-making. 1920 had brought a watershed in the flow of history. How did Lenin deal with it? How had he handled the personal transition from revolutionary conspirator to ruler of Russia?

LENIN'S LIFE IN THE YEARS OF REVOLUTION

Lenin had never been lazy but the maelstrom of work into which he threw himself in 1918 was unprecedented. The core of his activity was chairing meetings of Sovnarkom (Soviet of People's Commissars), the Soviet 'cabinet'.[1] At first it tended to meet three or four times a week, though over the years the number of meetings slowly declined. Equally important though less frequent were meetings of the Party Central Committee. More important were meetings of the sub-committees and steering committees of these two. From November 1918, as the Civil War gathered pace, the main government organ became the Defence Soviet (renamed the Labour and Defence Committee in April 1920) composed of Lenin, Trotsky, Stalin and others. Annual events like Party conferences and congresses were very demanding and Lenin often had to be at his best to win over doubting delegates. Until 1921, at least, these fora were scenes of real discussion within the Party. They were also places where the professorial Lenin met up with the politician. As we have seen, he once compared early meetings of the Central Committee to an academic seminar at which all the great minds of the country exchanged ideas. By 1920 he was fed up with the exchange of ideas and, as we have seen and will see again, he put a premium on action rather than words.

The relentless pace left little room for the breaks that had kept him together in exile. Even his 1918 New Year break in Finland had not allowed him to recuperate. Theatre visits and similar pleasures and relaxations continued but were few and far between. Ironically, the assassination attempt in August 1918 brought a little relief. Immediately after the shooting Lenin had been pessimistic. Krupskaya interpreted his demeanour, as he lay pale and silent on the hospital bed, to be saying 'It is almost over.' [Weber 131] A week later, however, he sent a telegram to Trotsky saying his recovery was proceeding excellently. [CW 35 359] Another week and he was back chairing Sovnarkom. However, to aid his recovery he retired to the estate at Gorky, where he found the peace, tranquillity and contact with nature that had meant so much to him before. Usually, it was only snatched weekends but later he spent longer vacations there. Gorky was the greatest personal pleasure of his last years and he was keen to invite friends. In July 1919 his brother Dmitrii and sister Anna stayed with him. He wrote to Nadezhda, whose own responsibilities contributed to keeping them apart more than ever, that 'The limes are in bloom. We had a good rest. I embrace you fondly and kiss you. Please rest more and work less.' [CW 37 546] A few days later he invited Maxim Gorky: 'Come here for a rest – I often go away for two days to the country where I can put you up splendidly.' [CW 35 409]

However, Gorky was not enough. The pace of work was taking its toll. Lenin continued to fall ill when under pressure and the cycle continued. He complained more and more frequently. On 10 August 1919, 'I am unwell. I have had to go to bed.' On 30 May 1920 he complained of being 'exhausted'. From then on the frequency increases fast. In November 1920 Clara Zetkin painted a grim picture of him: 'his face before me was all shrivelled up. Countless wrinkles, great and small, furrowed deep into it. And every wrinkle spoke of a heavy sorrow or a gnawing pain. A picture of inexpressible suffering was visible on Lenin's face.' [Weber 175] In December he mentioned his insomnia in a letter. After the Tenth Party Congress (March 1921) he said he was 'very tired and ill'. In April he said he was overworked. Retreat to Gorky in July for a holiday was not enough to arrest the decline. In August he was worse. In October he was 'too ill to write'. He was given increasing periods of sick leave in late 1921 and early 1922. He was barely able to attend the Party Congress in March 1922. The following month it was decided things were so bad that it was worth undertaking a risky opera-tion to remove a bullet from the August 1918 assassination attempt. However, a month later he had his first stroke, on 26 May 1922. After that, the hope that he might recover was slim indeed.

The years from 1918 to April 1922 were tough on Lenin in many ways. The pain observed by Clara Zetkin had many sources beyond the physical shortcomings of his own body. According to Gorky, the meth-ods of rule he was forced into caused him great anguish. In an article, he wrote that for Lenin 'the terror is unbearable and is very painful even though this is very skilfully concealed.'[2] There was nothing in Lenin's background to suggest it might have been otherwise. It was also the case that the rigours of the period touched those close to him. In addi-tion to colleagues like Sverdlov who died in 1919 at the age of 34, members of his close family also died. His brother-in-law Mark Elizarov, with whom he and Krupskaya had lodged in 1917, died in March 1919. More poignantly, Inessa Armand went to the south to try and recover her health in August 1920. Lenin wrote asking the regional sanatoria administration to do everything to look after her and her son. Not con-tent with that, he charged Sergo Ordzhonokidze, the leading Bolshevik in the Caucasus, with supervising their care and, in the event of capture by the Whites, Lenin asked him to execute them! Sadly, she caught cholera en route and died on 24 September 1920. Angelica Balabanoff described Lenin at Inessa's funeral in Moscow on 12 October: 'Not only his face but his whole body expressed so much sorrow that I dare not greet him, not even with the slightest gesture. It was clear he wanted to be alone with his grief ... his eyes seemed drowned in tears held back with effort. As our circle moved, following the movement of the people, he too moved without offering resistance, as if he were grateful for being brought nearer to the dead comrade.'[3] That was not the end of the touching story. Lenin discovered six months later that the grave was being neglected. No one had taken responsibility for looking after it. Lenin wrote to Kamenev asking him to arrange for flowers to be put on it and for a stone slab or gravestone to be set up. [Weber 181]

Lenin's critics have suggested that, in the words of Richard Pipes, 'as far as his personality is concerned, we note first and foremost, his utter disregard for human life, except where his own family and closest associates were concerned. Of them he was very solicitous' and again 'For humankind at large Lenin had nothing but scorn'.[4] Lenin may have had many faults but it is hard to see how one could reach such a conclusion. We have already seen many occasions on which Lenin expressed concern for individuals as well as for groups, not least the victims of the war. The fact that Leninist historiography painted an over-rosy picture of his concerns doesn't mean the opposite is true. Stories of him meeting and discussing with workers are not all fiction. Before adopting the New Economic Policy (NEP) he had several informal meetings with groups of peasants in the Gorky area, for instance, and he also consulted locals while he was on a rare hunting trip in September 1920. He frequently diverted gifts sent to him by soldiers and workers' delegations, to children's hospitals and sanatoria. On several occasions he asked for special consideration to be afforded to 'defective adolescents' as he called them, or special-needs teenagers as we would call them today. He even, on one occasion, called for an individual's commandeered bicycle to be returned to its rightful owner! While one would not want to set too much store by acts of 'official' generosity, there is nothing in Lenin's background to suggest he was as misanthropic as he is sometimes painted. All was done within the stern confines of Bolshevik morality, of course, which required duty before sentimentality, but there are no grounds to charge Lenin with utter disregard for human life.

There were two other outstanding aspects of his personality which came to the fore in these years. First, any sign of what was later called a cult of personality was knocked on the head; and second, he developed a characteristic way of handling relations with colleagues.

During Lenin's life the trappings of a cult of personality – ubiquitous posters; constant quoting of the great leader's thoughts; flattering speeches and ceremonies organized by sycophantic courtiers; claims of near-supernatural powers – none of these existed. Only a few photos of Lenin were published. He hardly ever appeared on the propaganda posters of the day. In fact, when he heard that a woman named

Valentina Pershikova had been imprisoned in Tsaritsyn for defacing one of the relatively infrequent portraits of him Lenin ordered her release saying 'Nobody should be arrested for defacing a picture.' Indeed, the cult of Lenin only really took off with his funeral and associated rituals – lying-in-state; processions; preservation of his body in the mausoleum – largely masterminded by Stalin. Stalin also gave a series of lectures entitled *Problems of Leninism*, to all intents and purposes inventing the term. Lenin would have been nauseated by it all. He never promoted himself and did not like others doing so. On one occasion on 31 July 1920, he even had Gorky censured by the Politburo for being too glowing in his praise of Lenin. He called Lenin a saint which no doubt sparked off Lenin's visceral dislike of Gorky's tendency towards 'Godbuilding'. [Weber 172] He was, of course, well known in the Party and received cult-of-personality-style standing ovations on major occasions like Party congresses, but then so do many politicians.

It is, however, a moot point as to the degree of what would today be called 'face recognition' that he enjoyed. Certainly, he was not a familiar figure, to the embarrassment of some Red Guards who shot at his car and a patrol of young communists who arrested him by mistake in July 1918 during the uprising. Upon showing his identity card as V. Ulyanov, Chairman of the Council of People's Commissars, the patrol reacted with scepticism. Only when the group arrived at the police station was Lenin recognized and released. [Krupskaya 533] He was somewhat better known by January 1919 when, on the way to spend the Russian Christmas (6/7 January) with Krupskaya, his car was stopped by bandits who were somewhat taken aback when they discovered who was in it. They none the less jumped in and stole it, leaving Lenin, his sister Maria, the chauffeur and the bodyguard, who never let go of the jug of milk he was carrying, to get help. Once again, the unlikely band of 'bedraggled' crime victims was not immediately recognized when they tried to raise the alarm. [Krupskaya 533] Incidentally, the name on the identity card mentioned above, V. Ulyanov, reminds us that the name by which we know him, Vladimir Lenin, was a hybrid he rarely used. It was a mixture of his most frequently used conspiratorial name, Nikolai Lenin, which he used right to the end to sign most of his articles and pamphlets, often in the form N. Lenin, and his real name, Vladimir Ulyanov.

Lenin was the kind of person who would not have enjoyed surprise parties in his honour. On his fiftieth birthday he received many letters and telegrams of congratulation and, at a celebration on the following day, 23 April 1920, he thanked the organizers for sparing him congratulatory speeches. He refused a proposal to open a museum in his honour and confided to a colleague, M.S. Olminsky: 'You have no idea how unpleasant I find the constant promotion of my person.' [Weber 169] He also described Kamenev's proposal to collect and reprint Lenin's works as 'completely superfluous' and only changed his mind when he was asked if he preferred the young to read Menshevik and Economist authors instead. Incidentally, later, when some items were published, Karl Radek mentioned to Lenin that he had been reading his writings of 1903, Lenin replied mockingly with a crafty smile: 'It's interesting to read now how stupid we were then!' On another occasion he claimed that, in exile, his thought had been too left-wing, a characteristic he believed to be typical of émigré thought in general. [Weber 168] One could speculate endlessly over the implications of such throwaway remarks!

Finally, it is worth saying a few words about the principles Lenin kept to in dealing with colleagues, since the issue looms very large in his last years and we will have to return to the question. The fundamental point remains, as we have seen earlier, that political expediency dominated Lenin's relations. The extreme examples of Martov, a friend for whom he retained feelings throughout his life but cut off ruthlessly for political reasons, and Trotsky, whom he welcomed back unconditionally after a decade of bitter political enmity, still held true. In January 1918, for example, Lenin refused to meet an old friend from Paris, Charles Dumas, because of political differences. Even close friends, like Vladimir Bonch-Bruevich, were not beyond being scolded, as Lenin did when, without warning, he raised Lenin's salary from 500 to 800 roubles a month, one of the few cases of an official being reprimanded by someone for giving that person a pay rise. The same principles held for his main associates, like Trotsky, Stalin, Bukharin, Kamenev and Zinoviev. None was above criticism and everyone was supposed to take it with discipline. In 1919, Lenin supported Trotsky against Stalin over the incorporation of a military specialist with Stalin's staff. Discipline was paramount. It also became a regular Party practice that a leading figure in a defeated group would be called upon to draft the finally agreed resolution or equivalent. Despite being a prominent figure in the Left Communist group Bukharin, along with another leftist,

Preobrazhensky, was entrusted with the task of producing the vital propaganda piece *The ABC of Communism* in 1919 which was supposed to reflect consensual rather than leftist views of the Party programme. In any case, by 1919, Lenin was getting fed up with the multitude of arguers in the Party and beginning to put a premium on the doers, of whom Stalin was his ideal type, who could be entrusted to get a job done with the minimum of discussion.

Incidentally, Lenin was personally beyond challenge as leader of the Party. Everyone saw him as the senior figure. While they might mumble behind his back or argue for different courses of action in meetings, it was unthinkable that anyone would criticize Lenin personally in the terms he used to reprimand others. He did not fully accept the truth of this himself, however, and when a leftist critic, A.A. Ioffe, claimed that Lenin was the Central Committee Lenin denied it exclaiming it was an *'absolutely, impossible, absolutely impossible* thing' which could only have been proposed by someone 'in a state of nervous irritation and overwork'. He claimed, somewhat unconvincingly since no one has been able to identify the reference, that he had been defeated in the Central Committee 'on one of the vastly important questions'. [CW 45 99–100] Lenin was a prophet among disciples: reprimands only went in one direction.

Altogether, by 1920 Lenin had made himself into a kind of philosopher king. He was not simply administering a country, still less milking it in his own interest. There can hardly be any modern ruler who personally benefited less than Lenin from his period in office. Rather, he was conducting a nationwide seminar and practical based on hypotheses which Lenin took as undeniable axioms. Indeed, the legitimacy he claimed for himself and his government did not arise from a clear popular mandate – no serious elections were ever held in these years – but from his philosophical claim to possess the correct policies and consciousness of the ruled, even if the ruled themselves did not see things that way. He was, in this respect a secular equivalent of theocratic leaders who derive their legitimacy from the truth of their doctrines, not popular mandates.

Such were the qualities and personal assets and liabilities which Lenin brought to the situation of 1920. The ending of the struggle against the Whites did not bring unalloyed joy but a new set of problems on which Lenin was, in reality, defeated by the indirect forces of the working class and, even more so, of the peasants.

THE EMERGENCE OF NEP; TRANSITION MODEL NUMBER THREE

In January 1921 Lenin came up with a phrase that encapsulates a great deal of what he stood for: 'Politics must take precedence over economics. To argue otherwise is to forget the ABC of Marxism'. He also claimed 'that politics is a concentrated expression of economics'. [*Once again on the Trade Unions, the Current Situation and the Mistakes of Trotsky and Bukharin*, 25 January, SW 3 527.] In these words lie the strength and weakness of Leninism in practice. By 1921 Lenin had, in a sense, got the politics right in that his party was unchallenged in its governing position. All other political parties had been reduced to nothing. However, political victory had been bought at a terrible social and economic price. The cost of concentrating on politics had been neglect of the economy. Even worse, the economy had been subjected to ill-thought-out experiments arising from minds in which the political had been overwhelmingly dominant. As we saw even in *The April Theses*, economic proposals were almost entirely lacking and those that were present were reduced to political and institutional measures. In the eyes of Marxist critics of Bolshevism, notably most Mensheviks, to put such stress on politics was to put the cart before the horse. Marxism was about economic conditions giving rise to political outcomes, not the other way round.

In practice, there was much in the situation of 1920/1 to enable both sides to claim to have been right. In a self-justificatory piece entitled *Our Revolution: A Propos of N.N. Sukhanov's Notes* written later, Lenin defended his approach against Menshevik criticism. Who could say that it was impossible to take power first and then build the necessary level of civilization later and 'proceed to overtake the other nations'? [SW 3 767] In productionism Lenin had developed a tool he hoped would do exactly this. For Mensheviks, however, the complete collapse of Russia's society and economy confirmed the mistake of the Bolsheviks in taking power prematurely. In their view, the cost of seizing and holding power was to destroy the vital life forces of the popular revolution and substitute a hungry and desperate mass of people.

Lenin's stance is all the more complicated in that, on 22 December 1920, in the same speech to the Eighth Congress of Soviets in which he coined the ultimate productionist slogan – 'Communism is Soviet

Power plus the Electrification of the Whole Country' – he also commented that 'We have, no doubt, learned politics; here we stand firm as a rock. But things are bad as far as economic matters are concerned.' [SW 3 510] In fact, even the political situation was not as rosy as Lenin implied. The decline of the Whites had opened up the prospect of the masses airing their grievances against the Bolsheviks, and this is exactly what many of them were doing. Major peasant uprisings in West Siberia and Tambov were echoed by many smaller acts of opposition. Workers were protesting against worsening conditions and the approaching threat of labour conscription. As Lenin spoke, in December, one of the heartlands of popular revolution, the Kronstadt naval base, was seething with discontent arising mainly from the continuation of armed grain requisition and suppression of its liberties. In March 1921 open revolt broke out.

The main driving force behind the opposition was economic. The industrial economy had collapsed. Lenin's grandiose schemes for covering Russia 'with a dense network of electric power stations and powerful technical installations' so that 'our communist economic development will become a model for a future socialist Europe and Asia' [SW 3 514] seemed very distant. The constant references in the speech to state compulsion of labour were menacing. The end of the war; the collapse of the industrial economy; the unpopularity of continued forcible extraction of grain from the peasants; the uprisings – all demanded a major overall rethink of strategy. Transition model number two, war communism, was dead in the water. Lenin had to think up yet another transition model. In early 1921 it emerged in the form of the New Economic Policy (NEP).

NEP was born out of failure and defeat. Since 1919 Lenin had been attempting to win over the middle peasants. The uprisings showed he had failed. He had failed because the peasants were not prepared, once the war was ended, to put up with forced grain requisitioning. Although their active revolts were savagely suppressed they none the less defeated the Party economically. By responding to requisitioning by growing less they posed a major threat to the remnants of industry, the cities and the army. 'Political' methods had failed. In its place Lenin turned, for once, to an economic solution. Replace requisitioning by a tax in kind which was officially endorsed at the Tenth Party Congress in March 1921. The new system meant that the more the peasants grew, the more they could keep, so they had an incentive. The more the peasants grew the more they would hand over to the state in tax, so the community also gained. Lenin believed the measures would create a positive dynamic. The peasants would grow more, the state could take more and use it to industrialize. The increasingly wealthy peasants would provide a market for the new industries so the industrial sector would also be stimulated. Under NEP, Lenin believed, the prosperity of the peasant would grow hand-in-hand with the development of industry. Not only that. Seeing the potential benefits industry could bring to the rural economy, especially machinery, peasants would realize they could enrich themselves better through amalgamating their holdings than in sticking with household-based smallholdings. They would, thereby, be won over to superior socialist forms of agriculture.

It is not our present task to trace the long-term problems of this system and join in the fascinating debate about its potential since the longer-term implications were not clear to Lenin before he died. The main problem was maintaining a satisfactory (to the Party) balance between agriculture, which the authorities wanted to downplay, and industry, which they wanted to expand as quickly as possible to 'catch up other nations'. Arguably, by the time of Lenin's death, the problems of NEP were already emerging. It was much easier to restore farms over two or three years than industry which was much more complex and interrelated so that progress could only advance at the speed permitted by the slowest bottleneck. Agricultural recovery provided a better supply of food products. Better supply caused prices to fall. Continuing industrial scarcity kept prices for manufactured goods high. The danger was that the combination of low prices for the produce they sold and high prices for the goods they wanted to buy would discourage the peasants from maximizing output.

The attempt to directly control industry was also abandoned as impractical. Output was at something like 20 per cent of pre-war norms in 1920 so failure was visible here too. In the event, factories were de-linked from the centre. A new system of 'economic accounting' (*khozraschet*) was introduced which gave larger enterprises their independence and required them to sink or swim by their own resources. It was not universally popular because, under this system, even though the larger elements remained state-owned, they could still face bankruptcy. They also tried to improve productivity and this ended the featherbedding of workers, many of whom were made redundant. Unemployment was a rising problem by the mid-1920s. Some space for small private workshops and co-operative restaurants, shops and other small services was also opened up. The state retained control of the 'commanding heights' of the economy – large factories, transport, taxation, foreign trade and so on – but a greater degree of independence characterized the new conditions.

However, in the short term, NEP allowed the economy and society gradually to recover. By about 1927/8 pre-war levels of agrarian and industrial output had been achieved. By laying off excessive 'political' direction from above, the economy had considerably improved. Interestingly, it was not foreordained that the change would be towards the state taking one step back. True to form, Lenin, and even more so Trotsky, retained the instinct of maximum direction and control from above. It has been argued that, between 'war communism' and NEP, there was an attempt to impose a more dirigiste model based on labour conscription.[5] Certainly, the demobilization of the army presented a tempting opportunity. If five million peasants could join up to fight for the Soviet state, why could they not be retained to work for it in priority sectors? And if that could be done why not extend it to workers in general?

The breathtaking leap from worker liberation to complete worker servitude was being contemplated. Even in December 1920, only a few weeks before the adoption of NEP, in his already mentioned address to the Eighth Congress of Soviets, Lenin was still playing with the idea of greater central control as the solution to the crisis. 'The dictatorship of the proletariat has been successful because it has been able to combine compulsion with persuasion. The dictatorship of the proletariat does not fear any resort to compulsion and to the most severe, decisive and ruthless forms of coercion by the state.' [SW 3 495] In their unprecedented response to the military struggle, Lenin argued, the non-Party peasants 'did really come to the conclusion that the exploiters are ruthless enemies and that a ruthless state power is required to crush them. We succeeded in rousing unprecedented numbers of people to display an intelligent attitude towards the war, and to support it actively.' [SW 3 496] While people were accustomed to such methods to fight a war, the task was to persuade peasants and trade unionists that comparable discipline and what he referred to as 'new methods', which clearly incorporated detailed direction from above, were still needed. [SW 3 497–9] 'We must convince both workers and peasants that, without a new combination of forces, new forms of state amalgamation, and the forms associated with compulsion, we shall not escape the abyss of economic collapse on the brink of which we are standing'. [SW 3 500] 'To accomplish this transition', Lenin continued, 'the peasants' participation in it must be ten times as much as in the war. The war could demand, and was bound to demand, part of the adult male population. However, our country, a land of peasants which is still in a state of exhaustion, has to mobilize the entire male and female population of workers and peasants without exception. It is not difficult to convince us Communists, workers in the Land Departments, that state labour conscription is necessary.' [SW 3 500–1] In sentences reminiscent of the collectivization drive of 1929 Lenin argued:

Comrades, here is what I particularly want to bring home to you now that we have turned from the phase of war to economic development. In a country of small peasants, our chief and basic task is to be able to resort to state compulsion in order to raise the level of peasant farming ... We shall be able to achieve this only when we are able to convince millions more people who are not yet ready for it. We must devote all our forces to this and see to it that the apparatus of compulsion, activated and reinforced, shall be adapted and developed for a new drive of persuasion. [SW 3 502]

Once again, with disarming naivety, Lenin reveals interlocking strength and weakness, the strength of conviction to push ahead, the weakness that 'compulsion' and 'persuasion' are considered siblings not opposites. The besetting problem of Leninism was that the greater the compulsion used, the greater the resentment aroused and consequently the lesser the desired effect of persuasion. The fact that Lenin's lengthy speech ended with a peroration to electrification and future technical marvels merely coated the pill. The machine of productionism was in full swing and labour conscription was one of its proposed weapons. Politics was certainly not giving way to economics at this point. In fact, when the moment came to enact measures to carry out the above policies, labour conscription had disappeared from the agenda. Opposition to it had been too great and, in combination with the fragile state of the working class and industry and the need to improve food supply, it had inflicted another, unacknowledged, defeat on Lenin. Economic compulsion took a back seat until one of its master organizers came to power at the end of the decade. Even Stalin, however, did not contemplate universal labour conscription although the gulag has sometimes been seen to incorporate elements of it.

If Lenin had been blown off course at the last minute over labour compulsion it did not mean he had abandoned authoritarianism. In other areas it began to strike deep roots and flourish. By the time he came to address the Tenth Party Congress, in March 1921, his last major point of direct impact on Soviet history, it was still in the forefront of much of his thinking.

One of the factors that appears to have led Lenin to change course was the existence of a large 'Workers' Opposition' which was claiming that the working class had already been too tightly bound by the bonds of bureaucracy and that it needed greater freedom of self-expression in order to develop the Revolution. Any suggestion of ultimate bureaucratic bonds – labour conscription – was anathema to them. Lenin's strategy was to concede on the issue but, at the same time, to obliterate the opposition itself. Alongside the 'liberalization' of the economy represented by the adoption of the tax in kind, Lenin was tightening the political and intellectual screws on society and Party. From the Marxist point of view, the processes were inter-related. Economic concessions to 'capitalism' presented the danger that pro-capitalist elements might take advantage of the new conditions to organize themselves politically and seek the means to spread their ideas. At the Congress Lenin made it clear that one of its tasks would be, in his phrase, to put the lid on opposition, both within the Party and without.

In his speech opening the Congress, Lenin said the Party had indulged itself in the 'amazing luxury' of discussions and disputes. Enemies, 'their name is legion', would take advantage of what they perceived as Communist weakness. In the face of this and the fact that, having been defeated on the battlefield, their enemies' 'warfare against us has taken a form that is less military but is in some respects more severe and more dangerous', he called for 'our efforts' to be 'more united and harmonious than ever before'. [SW 3 559–61] The key measures taken at the Congress put these remarks into effect. A ban on factions, presented as a resolution 'On Party Unity', made it clear that the Party would not tolerate organized opposition groups within. The Workers' Opposition was condemned as an 'Anarcho-Syndicalist deviation'. They had wanted to do the opposite of the labour conscription Trotsky and Lenin had called for. They wanted trades unions to be independent of Party control. The outcome, which partly emerged before the Congress, was that Lenin took a centre position between the extremes. Trades unions became 'schools of communism' and 'a school of economic management'.[6] Their task, implicitly, was to present the priorities of the workers' state to the workers, not the other way round. The resolution 'On the Tax in Kind' was also accepted. As the Congress drew to a close, volunteers left the debating chamber and headed to Petrograd and the Gulf of Finland, to participate in the suppression of the Kronstadt revolt which took place on 17 March.

In the year following the Congress some complementary measures were taken, notably the reorganization of censorship functions around a single institution, *Glavlit*; the 'temporary' Cheka turning itself into the permanent GPU and a show trial of members of the SR Party. Taken together, the reorientation of 1921–2 constituted Lenin's last formula for transition. The restoration of partial market relations for agriculture and industry; the rejection of extreme compulsion of labour but a tightening of political and intellectual control and surveillance provided a new balance. Lenin had time to develop his views on the new system but not to see it through. After the Tenth Party Congress Lenin's personal story became one of diminishing powers, of illness and, on 21 January 1924, of death at his estate in Gorky. His withdrawal from active day-to-day involvement in running the Revolution gave him an opportunity to look at some of the deeper problems. For better or worse, Lenin was unable to resolve any of the remaining issues before his death.

UNRESOLVED PROBLEMS

Lenin spent most of his last years wrestling with three inter-related aspects of the Revolution: how to deal with the increasingly bureaucratic aspects of the system, the way NEP should go and an effort to pre-empt the predictable future crisis of the succession. Taken together his response to these problems represents Lenin's last attempt to influence, or even control, the way the Revolution was to develop. In dealing with them he reverted to his professorial mode. Lenin the activist had not survived the first stroke.

Bureaucracy

The bureaucratization of the Russian Revolution is one of its great ironies and one of its great weaknesses. From the outset the Revolution, particularly in its Leninist form, targeted bureaucracy as a key enemy. 'Abolish the police, the army and bureaucracy' in *The April Theses*; smash the state, not take it over was the message of *State and Revolution*. Of course it was the tsarist bureaucracy that was to be smashed but there is no doubt Lenin believed that, by following the principles of the Paris Commune such as limiting salaries of officials, instituting the principle of election and recall and organizing rotation of administrative duties, he had found a democratic antidote that would prevent a new parasitic bureaucracy from congealing. As we have seen, as early as 1918 and 1919 bureaucratism, careerism and opportunism had been remarked on by the Party. In a way, bringing them together put those who wanted to deal with the problem on the wrong track. If bureaucratic deformation was caused by a significant minority of individuals in it for their own gain, that is careerists, then the problem could be solved by kicking them out. In other words there appeared to be a handy scapegoat. Lenin was ready to seize on it. On 12 March 1919, a week before the issue came up at the Party Congress, he said at a session of the Petrograd Soviet that 'We threw out the old bureaucrats but they have come back, they call themselves "commonists" when they can't bear to say the word "Communist" and they wear a red ribbon in their button-holes and creep into warm corners. What to do about it? We must fight this scum again and again.' [CW 29 32–3]

The first purges did not, as we have already seen, solve the problem. Instead, the influence of bureaucratism appeared to be spreading from the state institutions to the Party itself. Within a year Lenin was identifying 'communist arrogance' (*komchvanstvo*) as a major deformation in the Party. It referred to an increasing heavy-handedness some Party members were showing in dealing with non-Party people. In late November 1920 he told a Party meeting in Moscow that 'It was only to be expected that red tape in the Soviet apparatus would penetrate into the Party apparatus.' [CW 31 434–6] In October 1921 he announced

'Our enemies are communist arrogance, illiteracy and bribery.' [CW 33 60–79 and Weber 185] At the Eleventh Party Congress in March/April 1922, he went so far as to suggest that the Party was being swamped by the bureaucracy it had created. He even compared the process to a vanquished nation imposing its culture on its conquerors. [CW 33 259–326 and Weber 189]

Lenin, not least because he was constantly prodded by various oppositions over the issue, spent a great deal of time pondering the problem of bureaucratization in his last years. He had no doubt what the administration should look like. In March 1918 Lenin said: 'Socialism cannot be implemented by a minority, by the Party. It can be implemented only by tens of millions when they have learnt to do it themselves. We regard it as a point in our favour that we are trying to help the masses themselves set about it immediately.' [CW 27 135] In the original version of *Immediate Tasks of the Soviet Government* he wrote: 'There is nothing more mistaken than confusing democratic centralism with bureaucracy and routinism.' [CW 27 209] To combat these last requires that 'co-operative organizations spread throughout society'. [CW 27 215] In January 1919 he looked forward to a time when there will be 'universal training of the working people in the art of governing the state'. [CW 28 393] and, later in the month at the Second All-Russian Trade Union Congress, that 'the tasks of trades unions are to build a new life and train millions and tens of millions who will learn by experience not to make mistakes and will discard the old prejudices, who will learn by their own experiences how to run state and industry.' [CW 28 428]

He clearly was aware of how far away from such dreams the actual situation was. In January 1919 he declared: 'Our enemy today is bureaucracy and profiteering.' [CW 28 405] In December 1920, with the workers' opposition coming to a head, he stated that 'ours is a workers' state *with a bureaucratic twist to it*' [CW 32 24] and again, at the Party Congress in March 'we do have a bureaucratic ulcer'. [CW 32 190]

The debate heated up from 1920 onwards and remained thereafter at the forefront of Lenin's soon-to-be-declining attention. In explaining why things were not working out and bureaucratic deformations remained Lenin was still not above reaching for the simplistic excuse of looking for obvious scapegoats. In December 1922 he described the state apparatus as something 'which, in effect, we took over ... from the tsar'. [Weber 194] Astonishingly, in his last but one article, 'How to Re-organize the Workers' and Peasants' Inspection', he stated that, apart from the Foreign Ministry, 'our state apparatus is to a considerable extent a survival of the past and has undergone hardly any serious change. It has only been slightly touched up on the surface.' [SW 3 769] A week or so earlier he had written that the state apparatus was something 'which is utterly useless, and which we took over in its entirety from the preceding epoch'. [*On Co-operation*, SW 3 764] This quotation suggests Lenin's concern was deepening in that he was now calling the state apparatus 'utterly useless'. Elsewhere he made the same point. In a letter of 21 February 1922 he had written, unequivocally: 'The departments are shit; decrees are shit.' [CW 36 566] Purges and selection of personnel were a favoured solution for Party and state. The Party must be purged of 'rascals, of bureaucratic, dishonest and wavering communists and of Mensheviks'.[7] In connection with the comment about decrees and departments he also said 'the centre of gravity' should shift 'from writing decrees to *selection of people* and *checking fulfilment* ... To find men and check up on their work – that is the whole point.' [CW 36 566] To do this he proposed further development of the system of what one might call superinstitutions which were developing. In the absence of reliable, that is politically conscious, personnel to fulfil the required tasks, it was necessary to create supervisory institutions which embodied that consciousness in order to check on the rest. Not the rest of the masses but the rest of the supervisors.[8] Institutions like the Cheka and political commissars had arisen from the same problem, one is tempted to say contradiction, of the Revolution.

Around 1920 and 1921 Party Control Commissions, and a Worker Peasant Inspectorate to supervise the state apparatus, were set up. It was in these waters that Stalin learned to swim so adeptly that he was made General Secretary of the Party in 1922, the leading organizational post in the Party. An interesting feature of the Control Commissions, illustrating the point about consciousness, was that different Party generations were defined with different degrees of trust. The Central Control Commission needed members who had been in the Party before 1917 and lower ones required 1917 members and only at the lowest level were post-1917 members accepted. Such definitions were the closest the Party could come to an objective measure of consciousness. It worked on the not unreasonable assumption that those who had been in the Party longest were the most reliable.[9] From this time onwards Party *stazh'* (length of service) was an increasingly important feature of a Party member's personal profile.

Lenin's last years produced a number of reshuffles of the same worn out pack of cards. They seem astonishingly inadequate to the problem even as Lenin defined it. He suggested that 60 per cent of members of the Soviet Central Executive Committee should be 'workers and peasants not occupying any official posts in government bodies'. [CW 42 420] He said 'we are convinced that our machinery of state, which suffers from many defects, is inflated to twice the size we need', but offered no solution except further study of the problem. [CW 33 394] In *Letter to the Congress* he proposed that the Central Committee should be vastly expanded from 27 to '50 or 100' members. [SW 3 737] The State Planning Commission should be granted legislative functions. [SW 3 742–5] The Central Control Commission should be enlarged and amalgamated with the Worker Peasant Inspectorate. Members of it should be present at Politburo meetings. [SW 3 769–70 and 772] His final article, 'Better Fewer but Better', showed a continuing preoccupation with tinkering with control mechanisms. His suggestions were to ensure the Control Commission was staffed with 'irreproachable communists' [SW 3 777] and, poignantly, almost his last published words were that 'only by thoroughly purging our government machine, by reducing to the utmost everything that is not absolutely essential in it, shall we be certain of being able to keep going.' [SW 3 786]

The deeper problems giving rise to bureaucracy were never recognized and yet Lenin's discourse on bureaucracy frequently came close to identifying them. For instance, in calling for the selection of 'irreproachable communists' for control duties, he said, without the slightest realization of the irony, that 'a great deal has yet to be done to teach them the methods and objects of their work.' [SW 3 777] Even the supervisors of the supervisors needed supervising! Here was the unrecognized core of the problem. Everything had to come from the centre. All Lenin's reforms were simply ways of trying to make the centre's grip more effective. To start out with such a requirement was bound to lead to 'bureaucratism'. In another revealing comment, at the Eleventh Party Congress, Lenin had complained that, although the Party had 'quite enough political power' and adequate 'economic power … to ensure the transition to communism' there was one vital ingredient lacking, 'culture among the stratum of communists who perform administrative functions'. The result was that 'if we take Moscow, with its 4700 Communists in responsible positions, and if we take that huge bureaucratic machine [that is the political-economic apparatus], that gigantic heap, we must ask: who is directing whom? I doubt very much if it can be truthfully said that the Communists are directing that heap. To tell the truth, they are not directing, they are being directed.' [*Political Report of the Central Committee of the RCP(B)*, Eleventh Party Congress, 27 March 1922, SW 3 692]

Lenin refused to recognize that although the quality of communists was part of the problem, the implications of the task they were being called upon to perform was far more important. In the dispute on trades unions of 1920–1, Lenin had coined a phrase which later became integral to the Soviet system. To follow the 'anarcho-syndicalist' plans of the oppositions would mean 'repudiating the Party's leading role in relation to the non-Party masses'.[10] [CW 32 43–53] In October 1920 he had cut down Proletkul't for insisting that it should be autonomous. [SW 3 477] He had, in a letter of 11 October, made his position clear to Bukharin. '1. Proletarian culture = communism. 2. The Communist Party takes the lead. 3. The proletarian class = the Communist Party = *Soviet Power*.' [CW 51 298–9]

Here was the crux of the problem. The Party insisted on playing a leading role in all spheres. From that all the other consequences followed. It simply did not have the resources to perform the task as Lenin wanted it to. From this perspective the antidote to bureaucratism was not purging, amalgamating committees, setting up new committees or raising the cultural level of Party members. The antidote was greater democracy, greater self-activity by the masses as called for by leftists in the Party, the Kronstadt rebels and others. However, to retract Party control would be to cease to be Leninist. The fundamental contradiction of Leninism becomes clear. Leninism needed politically conscious people to implement it. In its absence the steps taken to substitute for it were repressive and centralizing. Centralization and repression made it harder to 'win over' the masses to the necessary political consciousness, so central control became ever-greater. Lenin's 'solutions' to the bureaucratic problem were really attempts to square a vicious circle. Once again the incompatibility of Lenin's two great aspirations of 26 October 1917 –

'we shall now proceed to construct the socialist order' and allowing 'complete creative freedom for the masses' – could not have been clearer. The former ambition was stifling the latter.

The final panacea Lenin toyed with to deal with the problem and to establish the future of the Revolution was cultural revolution. As we have already seen, several of the comments about bureaucratism blamed the low cultural level of the country for shortcomings. It became a more frequent theme in Lenin's final years right up until his last work, 'Better Fewer but Better', where he wrote that 'we lack enough civilization to enable us to pass straight on to socialism.' [SW 3 785] He had a low opinion of the capabilities of Russians. In exile he had warned against Russian doctors for their incompetence and the theme continued after the Revolution. In 1921 he tried to arrange for key personnel to go abroad for medical checks rather than face Russian doctors. He advised Gorky to seek help in a foreign sanatorium because 'over here we have neither treatment, nor work – nothing but hustle. *Plain, empty* hustle' [CW 45 249] and he had the psychological state of leading figures checked when a German specialist in nervous diseases visited Moscow in March 1922.[11] He had also expressed a low opinion of Russian capabilities on other occasions. He complained to V.V. Vorovsky, the head of the State Publishing House in October 1919, that the published version of the report on the Comintern Congress was 'A slovenly mess ... Some idiot or sloven, evidently an illiterate, has lumped together, as though he were drunk, all the "material", little articles, speeches, and printed them *out of sequence* ... an unheard of disgrace.' [CW 35 427–8] The experience still rankled months later when he asked Chicherin to supervise the collection of all available materials of foreign socialist, anarchist and communist movements in all languages. He specified that he should find a foreigner to handle the task because 'Russians are slovenly and will *never* do this meticulously'. [CW 44 325–6] Such comments were the obverse of his point about Soviet Russia having 'so few intelligent, educated and capable political leaders'. [Weber 157]

The evils of bureaucratization continued to haunt the Soviet system throughout its life. Both Trotsky and Lenin spent enormous time and energy on supposedly combating it but their responses were feeble. What neither of them would recognize was that bureaucracy was not an accidental deformation of the system, it was a structural consequence of Lenin's (and Trotsky's for that matter) approach to revolution. It arose from Leninism as surely as, for a Marxist, squeezing surplus value gave rise to exploitation. It was central to the whole enterprise. Lenin had expanded the concerns of the state in all directions. He was determined that state and Party developments should be controlled firmly from the centre by a tiny group of trustworthy, conscious communists. A military model of command from the top and obedience among the lower ranks was evolving across the whole system. The obvious result of all these factors was bureaucratization. Lenin's failure to see this simple truth is not, perhaps, surprising in that it would force him to acknowledge a massive faultline in the entire project, but it was fatal.

'All that is necessary to build a complete socialist society'

In one of his last works, *On Co-operation*, Lenin defended NEP as the road ahead providing certain modifications were made. These were that the importance of co-operatives should be recognized.

> All we actually need under NEP is to organize the population of Russia in co-operative societies on a sufficiently large scale, for we have now found that degree of combination of private interest, of private commercial interest, with state supervision and control of this interest, that degree of its subordination to the common interests which was formerly the stumbling block for very many socialists. Indeed, the power of the state over all large-scale means of production, political power in the hands of the proletariat, the alliance of the proletariat with the many millions of small and very small peasants, the assured proletarian leadership over the peasantry, etc. – is that not all that is necessary to build a complete socialist society out of co-operatives, out of co-operatives alone? ... Is that not all that is necessary to build a complete socialist society? It is still not the building of socialist society, but it is all that is necessary and sufficient for it. [SW 3 758–9]

To make them work meant spreading the idea of co-operatives. It therefore followed that 'strictly speaking there is "*only*" one thing left to do and that is to make our people so "enlightened" that they understand all the advantages of everybody participating in the work of the co-operatives, and organize this participation. "*Only*" that.' It would take 'a whole historical epoch to get the entire population into the work of the co-operatives through NEP. At best we can achieve this in one or two decades.' [SW 3 760] 'Given social ownership of the means of production, given the class victory of the proletariat over the bourgeoisie, the system of civilized co-operators is the system of socialism.' [SW 3 761]

Two tasks (Lenin seems to have overlooked the earlier point that there was only one thing left to do) confronted the Party. One was 'to re-organize our machinery of state', the second was 'educational work among the peasants', the aim of which was to persuade them to organize in co-operative societies. His conclusion fused many Leninist motifs:

> Our opponents repeatedly told us that we were rash in undertaking to implant socialism in an insufficiently cultured country. But they were misled by our having started from the opposite end to that prescribed by theory (the theory of pedants of all kinds), because, in our country the political and social revolution preceded the cultural revolution, that very cultural revolution that now confronts us.
>
> This cultural revolution would now suffice to make our country a completely socialist country; but it presents immense difficulties of a purely cultural (for we are now illiterate) and material character (for to be cultured we must achieve a certain development of the material means of production, must have a certain material base). [SW 3 764]

On Co-operation was Lenin's last survey of the Revolution in general. His last two articles dealt, as we have seen, with the problems of the state and Party machines but the scope of *On Co-operation* was much wider. In these final paragraphs we catch many echoes of Leninist motifs. Clearly, he anticipated the balance discovered in NEP would last for 'an entire historical epoch' defined as 'at best one or two decades'. Whether this would turn out to be the case depended on many things, not least the politician's nightmare as defined by British Prime Minister Harold Macmillan – 'Events, dear boy, events' – but also who would succeed the ailing Lenin. Here, too, Lenin left the problem unresolved.

The succession

The question of Lenin's succession has been turned into one of the great 'if only' myths of modern history. Trotsky's interpretation, that Lenin was about to make a decisive move against Stalin in March 1923 when he was struck down by his third stroke, has gained widespread currency.[12] There are certainly some facts to support it. In late 1922 Lenin, for more or less the first time in his career, had serious differences with Stalin. As we said earlier, Stalin had not made much impact on Lenin's life up to around 1920 though Lenin had had a major impact on Stalin. It may be that Stalin, back around 1908, had even chosen the name by which he is now known because it sounded like 'Lenin'. He certainly admired and followed Lenin from around 1906 and became increasingly useful to Lenin as time went by. Lenin called him his 'splendid Georgian' but also had to be reminded during the war of what his name was, so one might conclude Stalin was still a marginal figure. Sverdlov's premature death at the age of 34 had deprived the Party not only of a leading light but also of its filing system which, so the joke went, Sverdlov carried around in his head. Stalin moved into the administrative space Sverdlov had left and, coinciding with the moment that Lenin was turning to doers rather than thinkers, his timing could not have been better. Lenin used him increasingly for practical things, not least packing the Tenth Party Congress to ensure a Leninist majority over the oppositions. Stalin's reward was to be promoted to the post of General Secretary of the Party in 1922.

The story of how Stalin turned the administrative power this post gave him into political power does not directly concern us here. What we do need to note, however, is that up to this point differences between Lenin and Stalin had been on a small scale, including Stalin taking a conciliatory position when Lenin was raving against Kamenev and Zinoviev in October and November 1917 and the moment when Lenin sided with Trotsky over the appointment of a military specialist, Sytin, to command alongside Stalin at Tsaritsyn in 1919. Stalin was, on this occasion, recalled but no grudges were held, at least not between Stalin and Lenin. Between Stalin and Trotsky was another thing altogether.

The case for Stalin being on the verge of losing Lenin's favour has three components. The first is that, in his so-called 'Testament', officially entitled *Letter to the Congress*, Lenin, on 24 December 1922, described Stalin as having 'unlimited authority concentrated in his hands, and I am not sure whether he will always be capable of using that authority with sufficient caution.' [SW 3 738] However, on 4 January 1923 he added a special note about Stalin.

Stalin is too rude and this defect, though quite tolerable in our midst and in dealings among us Communists, becomes intolerable in a General Secretary. That is why I suggest that the comrades think of a way of removing Stalin from that post and appointing another man in his stead who in all other respects differs from Comrade Stalin in having only one advantage, namely that of being more tolerant, more loyal, more polite and more considerate to the comrades, less capricious etc. This circumstance may appear to be a negligible detail. But I think that from the standpoint of safeguards against a split and from the standpoint of what I wrote above about the relationship between Stalin and Trotsky it is not a detail, or it is a detail which can assume decisive importance. [SW 3 739]

Unknown to Lenin, on 22 December 1922, Stalin, who had been appointed to liaise between the Politburo and Lenin, discovered that, contrary to Politburo and Central Committee instructions, Krupskaya had been discussing politics with Lenin at greater length than the doctors allowed. Stalin swore at her in a manner only a Georgian can. Krupskaya was deeply insulted but did not tell Lenin of the incident. He only found out about it in March, when he was already disgusted with Ordzhonikidze and Stalin for engaging in crude bullying of Georgian Communists. Although, ironically, Ordzhonikidze and Stalin were both Georgians themselves, Lenin equated their behaviour with that of typical, heavy-handed 'Great Russian chauvinists' against whom he had been warning for several years. The revelation about Stalin's rudeness was a last straw. On 5 March 1923 Lenin wrote to Stalin demanding a complete apology. Were it not forthcoming Lenin threatened to break all relations with him. Stalin eventually made a fulsome apology. However, by the time he made it Lenin had taken a severe turn for the worse, on 9 March, and was in no condition to receive it. Lenin was confined to bed and, as soon as he was well enough, on 22 May, was removed to Gorky where he lived out his remaining days.

The case that all this adds up to a decisive turn against Stalin appears strong but there are a number of mitigating circumstances. First, Lenin did not suggest removing Stalin from all his posts only that of General Secretary. Over the years, Lenin had quarrelled seriously with many other leaders, for example, Kamenev and Zinoviev in October 1917, Trotsky from 1906 to 1917. More recently he had had very open and bitter disputes with Trotsky and Bukharin over the trade union issue in 1920 and 1921. His criticisms of them were far deeper and more public than his criticism of Stalin and they went on for several weeks. Lenin, on 7 December, even found himself in a minority on the Central Committee (seven votes to eight) against their view of the role of trades unions. He accused them of bureaucratic excesses and of factionalism, perhaps the most severe accusation that could be made against a fellow Party member. Lenin simply steamrollered the Party into supporting him and took no further action against Trotsky and Bukharin.

Second, though the additional note on Stalin was more damning, the testament itself was not very flattering about any of the other leadership candidates. Trotsky, although he was 'personally perhaps the most capable man in the present Central Committee', was said to exhibit 'excessive self-assurance' and to be 'too preoccupied with the administrative side of affairs'. Bukharin was an outstanding figure among the younger members and was 'rightly considered the favourite of the whole Party' but he was also 'scholastic' and had not properly understood dialectics. [SW 3 738–9] In the end, Lenin made no decisive choice between them. It was a dangerous document to all and it is hardly surprising that, when Volodicheva, the secretary who had taken Lenin's dictation, showed it to Stalin he ordered her to burn it. The following day Lenin, not knowing what had happened, asked her to keep the document secret. Volodicheva retyped a copy to replace the one she had burned.

When Stalin saw Lenin's demand for an apology in March 1923 his immediate reaction was that it was not Lenin that was speaking but his illness.[13] The same criticism has been made of the whole issue. Lenin's sister, Maria, played down its significance in later years for this reason. Others, too, have said Lenin's judgement was impaired by his illness. Post-Soviet revelations, not to mention photos of Lenin in his last months and years, have underlined the severity of his condition. Indeed, from late 1922 onwards the Central Committee had been at pains to control Lenin politically. They were afraid that he still retained sufficient prestige to embarrass them and that he was a potential loose cannon capable of going off in any direction. That is why Stalin was appointed to liaise with him. Stalin was chosen precisely because Lenin trusted him most to do his will, including asking him to keep a cyanide capsule available in case Lenin thought it was time to make his exit. In this case, Stalin was forbidden by the Central Committee to do what

Lenin asked. The Central Committee, in consultation with doctors, had ordered Lenin to restrict his political reading and activity to protect him against overexertion. It was for violating this provision that Stalin had sworn at Krupskaya on 22 December. Despite the attempts to protect him Lenin suffered a series of turns for the worse in December which were disabling him to the extent that he could only dictate for five or ten minutes a day. It is only too likely that his judgement was also not at its best. In fact, the testament in the broad sense, including the last articles, was un-Leninlike. The wide perspective on problems which it revealed was not matched by incisive solutions. Lenin was uncharacteristically tentative. Perhaps his own awareness of the impact of his illness meant that he too only half-believed in what he was doing in these troubled months. Lenin had succeeded only in complicating the resolution of these final problems.

THE FINAL MONTHS

On 9/10 March 1923 Lenin suffered a major medical crisis, a third and hopelessly disabling stroke. He was paralysed down one side and barely able to speak. The frustrations of anyone in this condition, let alone a strong-minded and determined revolutionary, are insupportable. Lenin presented a pathetic figure. It was several weeks before he was even well enough to be removed from the Kremlin and on 15 May he was taken to Gorky. As ever, the support of Krupskaya and his sisters Maria and Anna was essential. They made the household as comfortable as possible. Lenin's abilities came and went. At times he was able to speak a little better. He even managed to walk with a stick at one point. He discovered another convalescent at Gorky was an old friend from Alakaevka and they had discussions that lasted for two days. The old pleasures, walks (in his wheelchair now) in the forest, mushroom hunting, sleigh rides in the snow, provided his last moments of joy. The presence of children delighted him as did visits from Party leaders including Zinoviev, Kamenev, Bukharin and Preobrazhensky. In October he even felt well enough to demand an emotional trip to his office in the Kremlin in his Rolls Royce. As his sisters had predicted, the guard would not even allow him in at first because he did not have an up-to-date pass, but he eventually succeeded, spending the night there because he was too exhausted to return home. It was his last trip out of Gorky. On several occasions he demanded poison capsules but no one would agree to his request. He was kept in the dark about the bitter feud that had arisen, as he predicted, in the Party between the Trotsky left and the Stalin centre. In November and December he had a further series of crises. Even so, the end came suddenly. In the late afternoon of 21 January 1924 he suffered his final attack out of the blue. Krupskaya and Maria were with him. Bukharin, who was visiting, rushed over. Lenin died in their presence just over an hour after the attack had struck, at 6.50 p.m.

CONCLUSION: LENIN LIVED! LENIN LIVES! LENIN WILL LIVE FOREVER!

LENIN AS ICON

The death of Vladimir Ulyanov was by no means the end of Lenin. In many ways it was only the beginning. From being the increasingly revered, sometimes hated but by no means personally well-known or physically recognized leader of Soviet Russia, Lenin became one of the most widespread, universally recognizable icons of the twentieth century. Leninism, or to be more precise, Marxism-Leninism, became the basic ingredient of the twentieth century's most potent revolutionary cocktail. With certain, often locally added mixers – Stalinism, Maoism, the *juche* idea in North Korea, Castroism, Ho Chi Minh thought – it was adapted to many of the most prominent revolutionary movements of the century. Despite endemic sectarian differences in the communist movement, the idealized figure of Lenin was revered by everyone who adhered to it and his revolution was acknowledged as the model for all those that followed, even though most of them, in China, Vietnam, North Korea, Eastern Europe, Cuba and so on, actually occurred under very different conditions. Portraits of him were carried at the head of the largest political processions ever organized. His works were reprinted *ad nauseam* and he became the most widely published author in human history. Copies of his writings outnumbered copies of holy books like the Bible or the Q'uran. Indeed, the canonical core of his work – eventually established as his pamphlets *What is to be Done?*;

Imperialism: The Highest Stage of Capitalism; and *State and Revolution* – became the texts of the new revolutionary faith. At the same time, those who were sceptical about communist revolutions – ranging from democratic socialists and anarchists on the left to conservatives and fascists on the right – tended to demonize Lenin as much as the communists idolized him. In this way Lenin became a touchstone of the twentieth century. Tell me what you think about Lenin and I will tell you who you are!

Lenin himself abhorred the idea of a cult of his personality. As we have seen he was dismissive about republishing his works and about the value of digging up early polemics which only showed 'how stupid we were then'. [Weber 168] In his active lifetime the cult barely existed. It was his successor, Stalin, who was primarily responsible for building it up. He could be said to have invented, or at least established, 'Leninism' as a mode of thought. In 1924, shortly after Lenin's death, he gave a series of lectures, later published as a pamphlet, entitled *Problems of Leninism*. One of the most potent weapons bringing him to power was his assertion of himself as the chief priest of the burgeoning Lenin cult. He gave an oration at Lenin's funeral. It was his opinion that was decisive in preserving Lenin's body and setting up the mausoleum on Red Square which remained a place of pilgrimage long after the Soviet system itself had collapsed. Indeed, though it is not our direct concern here, it is likely that Stalin saw himself as Lenin's most faithful disciple. Be that as it may, the cult spread rapidly in the communist movement. It very quickly took on quasi-religious overtones, not only in Stalin's solemn intonation at Lenin's funeral of vows to fight for Lenin's principles, but also in, for example, Mayakovsky's adaptation of Christian liturgy 'Lenin lived! Lenin lives! Lenin will live forever!'.[1]

Not everyone was drawn into it. In the non-communist world the figure of Lenin was eventually demonized as thoroughly as he was deified among his disciples. While, in many ways, the cold war dated from the Revolution itself and cast a long shadow over the peace negotiations at Versailles in 1919, it was only in its latter stages and in the wake of the Soviet system's collapse that Lenin's reputation in the outside world reached its lowest point. Many of his critics as well as his followers met Lenin in his years as Soviet leader and, although there was a tendency on the visitor's part to encounter the Lenin they were predisposed to expect, so that actually meeting him often confirmed pre-existing notions rather than providing real insights into his character, the reports nonetheless portrayed a person rather than a god or demon. A recent study of British left-wing connections with Lenin's Russia provides examples. George Lansbury 'praised Lenin's "far-reaching ability, downright straightforwardness and the wholehearted enthusiasm and devotion to the cause of humanity."' Lansbury 'believed that he was "absolutely indifferent both to love and hatred – I do not mean that he has no feeling, because I am confident that he loved little children."' As if that wasn't enough 'Lansbury also refused to believe stories of violence that were reported in the British press could be attributed to Lenin. "While talking with him it is impossible to imagine that such a man would love or care for violence or butchery, torture or any of the other horrors which are laid to his charge. He is too big in his outlook and much too wide in his sympathies to want to kill anyone."' Ethel Snowden came to a different conclusion. In her view Lenin possessed 'a firm belief in the necessity of violence for the establishment throughout the world of his ideals [which] makes one doubt miserably.' Interestingly, Snowden also remarked that Lenin was a 'keen-brained, dogmatic professor in politics'.[2] The professorial comparison also occurred to Bertrand Russell when he met Lenin. He wrote that 'The materialist conception of history, one feels, is his life-blood. He resembles a professor in his desire to have the theory understood and in his fury with those who misunderstand or disagree.' For Russell it was 'obvious that he has no love of luxury or even comfort. He is very friendly, and apparently simple, entirely without a trace of *hauteur*. ... I have never met a personage so destitute of self-importance.'[3]

As the cold war deepened after 1945 the figure of Lenin and the debate around him was a central battleground of the ideological struggle. The Soviet cult of Lenin became as increasingly mechanical and formalistic as the Soviet system itself. With increasing speed after 1956, the leadership of the USSR began to distance itself from its founding ideas. Surprisingly, in the non-communist world, views of Lenin still showed a certain respect for his ideas and personality. Revisionists from the late 1960s to the 1980s, often associated with the New Left, tried to present a 'good' Lenin, a democrat blown off course by Russian backwardness and the exigencies of the Civil War, as opposed to a 'bad' Stalin.

It was not only the left that showed a certain respect for Lenin. While they had no time for his ideas, some of Lenin's most powerful critics had a more human and nuanced view of their adversary than was often the case later. In his formidable history *The Russian Empire 1801–1917*, Hugh Seton-Watson pointed out that 'Lenin was, of course, no more exclusively inspired by personal ambition or arrogance than were his rivals.' He described *Two Tactics of Social Democracy in the Democratic Revolution* as 'one of his most brilliant works' concluding that its 'preference for partnership between highly sophisticated professional revolutionaries and primitive masses ... was characteristic of Lenin's later career and greatness.'[4] Leonard Schapiro surmised that 'it was perhaps because he was a revolutionary of genius that Lenin was a failure as a statesman.' Lenin was a 'strange and troubled genius, whose personal impact on events may well have been greater than that of any other individual in this century'. The historian, Schapiro concluded, 'is left with the choice between two alternatives'. One sees 'Lenin as a giant labouring under the unavoidable difficulties not of his own making, which were inherent in the gigantic task which he undertook.' Alternatively his 'stature must be measured in terms of his determination, his strength of will, his certainty of purpose and his qualities of leadership. But his obsessional character must then also be seen as one of the elements which led to the chaos of 1917 out of which bolshevik victory emerged ... And yet, Lenin's actions and their consequences will always, for some at any rate, be redeemed by his integrity, his lack of vanity, and his single-minded devotion to a cause in which he believed.' Schapiro ended by quoting a nineteenth-century Russian thinker: 'Great actors in history ... bear responsibility only for the purity of their intentions, and for their zeal in carrying them into effect, and not for the remote consequences of the labour which they perform.'[5]

By the 1980s and 1990s the tone had changed radically. Schapiro's subtlety was lost on Norman Stone. Writing in a popular British newspaper, in an article entitled 'The monster who sired the greatest evils of our century', Stone seemed determined to pile responsibility for exceedingly remote consequences onto Lenin. He claimed that 'Lenin and his twisted ideology gave rise to the evil that was Nazism. ... When Mussolini triumphed in Italy, or Hitler in Germany, it was because of two things, both to do with Lenin. The first was that fascism was a reaction to him, and the second was that it learned from him everything that it did.'[6] One of the first post-Soviet biographies, written by Dmitrii Volkogonov, a former believer in the system, was equally unsubtle. 'Bolshevism destroyed everything in Russia.'[7] Characteristics of Pipes' *Unknown Lenin* included 'utter disregard for human life except where his own family and closest associates were concerned'; 'nothing but scorn' for 'humankind at large'; 'thoroughgoing misanthrop[y]'; a 'policeman's mentality' and a tendency to 'treat his vast realm like a private estate'.[8]

RETRIEVING THE HISTORICAL LENIN

After such an assault it is no wonder that in 2003 Lars Lih pointed out the need to embark on 'the quest for the historical Lenin'.[9] In Lih's view the central position of *What is to be Done?* developed relatively late in the Leninist canon and did not fully support the widespread assumptions that Lenin founded a 'party of a new type' in 1903, nor did he preach permanent intelligentsia hegemony over workers. Some of these nuances are shared by the present work but there are also a variety of other recent works helping in the quest to retrieve the historical Lenin. Biographies by Service, White and Williams plus articles by Anna Krylova and Leopold Haimson, not to mention two new books by Haimson, have laid down parameters for a new interpretation of Lenin which is less in thrall to cold war ideological influences.[10]

The new approach to Lenin has a long way to go but as far as the present study is concerned, a number of issues have already become prominent. First, the myth that the Party 'split' in 1903, in the sense that there was a clean break into two competing factions with clearly opposed, well-defined and unchanging views, has to be abandoned. For many years, the fluid groups manoeuvred around each other both in the Russian arena and, very important to all concerned, also in the Second International. The dispute was acknowledged to be within one and the same family and it was in no one's interest to completely break up what was in any case a small party. Rather, the groups worked to control the Party and unite it around their particular principles. Associated with this, it is also necessary to define more clearly where and when 'Leninism' or Bolshevism stepped outside the broad framework of European social democracy. While many would say it was only for tactical reasons, it is none the less the case that Lenin did not push the break to the limit or consciously accept he had stepped outside the accepted tenets of social-democratic tradition until much later than 1903. It is hard to identify a precise moment of fracture. While it could be argued that in 1910 to 1912 Lenin was establishing his own separate camp it is still the case that, until the debacle of summer 1914, Lenin worked within the framework of the Second International. Had the Party already split, in the way which has long been assumed, 1914 would not have been so dramatic and painful. In any case, it should be noted that even at this juncture, in his own eyes, Lenin was following the true path of social democracy – that of class rather than nation, of internationalism rather than defensism – which he believed the majority leaders had betrayed. The division could be said to have become an unbridgeable gulf as late as July 1914. It was only during the war, and as one of the controversial *April Theses*, that Lenin proposed renaming his party and adopting a new programme completely separate from that of earlier Russian social democracy and the Mensheviks. This was done in 1918. Incidentally, even after the disaster of July 1914 the new division in the socialist movement, into internationalists and defensists, cut across factional ties. In 1917, Left Mensheviks like Martov and Sukhanov shared key points of view with Lenin and Left SRs joined the Bolsheviks in government for the first six months of Soviet power.

A number of other features also point the way to a more realistic, balanced, rounded, human portrayal of Lenin. Some of the most important arise from the fact that, although he was himself reluctant to face up to its implications, Lenin was, first and foremost, an intellectual and an integral member of a particular, long-established branch of the Russian intelligentsia. While attempts have long been made to associate him with extreme 'Jacobinism', once again it is not so simple. Lenin is and remained much more mainstream. He worked in the open – to the extent his major works and thoughts were all in the public domain via his vast writings and speeches – and he was not conspiratorial in the Nechaev sense, portrayed by Dostoevsky in *The Devils*, even though such characteristics were sometimes attributed to him. While his ideas were, as we have seen, sometimes Bakuninist, his personal activity never was. In fact, the picture that emerges from studying the historical Lenin leads to the emphasis being put on the 'professorial' Lenin rather than the on the street activist.

This in turn opens up a number of further points for reinterpretation. For example, if Lenin was an intellectual, living essentially the life of a café revolutionary, what was his relationship to actual workers? As we have seen, in London he was an observer of working-class life who made occasional forays into working-class districts but who, apart from a few lectures here and there, did not have much direct contact with them. He lived a typically middle-class life rarely participating in proletarian activities and cultures. Even in Russia, in 1905–6, when he increasingly admired the outburst of working-class activity, he did so from a distance, observing demonstrations and offering guidance and analysis but without participating. He did not follow Trotsky's example and become a Soviet activist (nor did he in 1917). He encouraged the Moscow uprising but, unlike Bakunin, who, one might surmise, would have thrown himself into the thick of the action, Lenin watched it unfold to its tragic conclusion from St Petersburg. Thus, the relationship in Lenin's ideas between workers, consciousness and intellectuals can no longer be reduced to simple formulae.

Seeing Lenin in this light also puts a spotlight on what has often been seen as the crucial difference between the Revolution of 1905 and that of 1917 – the presence in the latter of the leadership provided by Lenin and the Bolsheviks. For the present writer the key difference lies elsewhere, notably in the fact that the 1917 Revolution was set off by the virtual collapse of the state in February prompted by divisions within the elite and a collapse of its support for Nicholas II. These fissures opened the way for social revolution to develop with relatively little hindrance in the following months. In contrast, in 1905, the state remained strong and, after the publication of the October Manifesto, the propertied elite remained united behind the tsar. Be that as it may, the question of how Lenin could have 'led' the Revolution needs to be examined, not least because he was away in hiding for the crucial months and had difficulty leading his party let alone the Revolution. Insofar as the Bolsheviks came to exert 'leadership' it arose from them concealing their own long-term aims and picking up the immediate aims of the popular movement – peace, bread, land and all power to the Soviets – and treating them as though they were their own. While this might be considered great tactics, in practice it was closer to what Lenin scoffed at as 'tailism' in 1905 – that is hanging on to the tail of the mass movement – rather than leadership. The Party, in the short term, adapted to the masses. It did not, at this point, lead the masses to Bolshevik conceptions of socialism and revolution. That task only began seriously after 25 October.[11]

Finally, Lenin's intelligentsia style also affects our understanding of how he governed. While he was undoubtedly involved in a wide range of decision making, some of it at a surprisingly low level, he was not himself a nuts-and-bolts activist but relied on close supporters, especially Sverdlov and later Stalin, who were the ones who got things done. Lenin himself, with his continuing cycle of stress-related illnesses, remained the analyst, the strategist and the tactician of the Soviet government, attempting to treat the business of government to some extent like the running of a seminar. It followed from his understanding of the role of consciousness, that genuine reflection would lead to harmonious action to sustain the Revolution. Honest discussion would lead to conclusions with which only the benighted would disagree.

Taking the last two points together, that is Lenin's distance from day-to-day government and the Bolshevik tactic of following not leading the masses, opens up the issue of exactly when, if at all, Lenin really began to get a grip on events instead of following them. Arguably, during the Civil War the torrent of events was too rapid for anyone to master and it was only in 1921, around the time of the Tenth Party Congress, that Lenin began to impose himself and his party on the population after their 'defeat' at the hands of the masses had forced a last, massive concession, the abandonment of war communism and grain requisitioning and the adoption of the New Economic Policy. Without doubt, 1921 was a moment of decision and a moment of truth in that, for the first time since October 1917, Lenin had clear choices before him. His selection of a combination of political and cultural repression, which increased as the years went by, alongside a measure of restoration of market relations in place of doomed efforts to centrally plan the economy and coerce the peasantry, defines Lenin more than any other of his policy options. He expected the compromise embodied in NEP to be a dynamic system leading Russia ineluctably to socialism. After his death, the Party right, led by Bukharin and Rykov, struggled to preserve NEP because they perceived it as Lenin's last testament. A more impatient and vociferous Party left turned back to the policies of 1918 and 1919. The victory of the latter group, with Stalin at its head, shaped the Revolution for the rest of its life.

How much the outcome had to do with Lenin is still hotly debated. What one can say is that two 'Leninist' models were in conflict. On one hand, there was the disbanded system of war communism, on the other the NEP system for which Lenin had such high hopes in his last years. While Stalin's leftist policies of 1928–32 clearly violated Lenin's injunction to preserve the alliance between workers and peasants at all costs, it has to be said that Lenin took this position only because he believed the Party and state apparatus was too weak to enforce its policies and the Revolution would face defeat once more. However, would he, like Stalin and his supporters, be tempted by coercion if he thought it would be successful? One could make out a plausible case on both sides of this argument. A crucial consideration here is that NEP embodied a cultural element and Lenin was well aware that changing the cultural environment of traditional Russia would be a long job. Quick fixes were not possible in this scenario. Opposed to that, however, is the view that, by 1928, NEP had, in any case, become unworkable. The scissors crisis was so acute that the system could not survive without endless concessions to the market and property orientation of the peasantry. Bukharin believed Lenin would have stuck to NEP. The Stalinists believed it had to be abandoned.

Complex though it is, the argument does not even stop there. One could also surmise that, even if Lenin had been around to choose a Stalinist path, he might well have conducted it in a less crude and less needlessly violent manner. There is no way that any definitive conclusion can be drawn. Leonard Schapiro's formulation of the relationship of Lenin to Stalin remains as relevant as ever. In his words 'It was Lenin who provided Stalin with the weapons and set him on his path.' That is not the same as saying there was no difference between them or that Stalinism was the one and only potential outcome of Leninism. There was nothing inevitable about the emergence of Stalin or of the policies associated with him.[12] One thing that is inevitable, however, is that the debate about Lenin will go on for a long time yet. The influence of and interest in one of the most important figures of the twentieth century is far from exhausted. Lenin's future may hold as many surprises as his past.

NOTES

INTRODUCTION

1 Susan Sontag, 'Cases of the Comrades: Why Victor Serge Should be as Famous as Koestler and Orwell', *Times Literary Supplement*, 9 April 2004, p. 13. The essay has also appeared as the Introduction to V. Serge, *The Case of Comrade Tulyaev* (New York, 2004).

1 CHOOSING REVOLUTION

1 Nikolai Chernyshevsky, *What is to be Done?* (ed. Michael R. Katz, trans. William G. Wagner) (Ithaca, NY and London, 1989).
2 N. Valentinov, *The Early Years of Lenin* (Ann Arbor, 1969), p. 135.
3 See e.g. Vladimir C. Nahirny, *The Russian Intelligentsia: From Torment to Silence* (New Brunswick, N.J. and London, 1983).
4 See James White, *Lenin* (London, 2001), pp. 44–5.
5 I.N. Wolper, *Pseudonyme Lenins* (Berlin, 1970), p. 38.

2 LAYING THE FOUNDATIONS OF LENINISM (1896–1902)

1 M. Gorky, 'Vladimir Lenin', *Russkii sovremennik*, no. 1, 1924, pp. 229–44. Quoted in B. Wolfe, *The Bridge and the Abyss: The Troubled Friendship of Maxim Gorky and V.I. Lenin* (London, 1967), p. 157.
2 Quoted in R. Pipes, *Struve: Liberal on the Left* (Cambridge, Mass., 1970), p. 195.
3 For a discussion of theories arising from this, see the Introduction to Christopher Read, *The Stalin Years: A Reader* (London, 2003) and Abbott Gleason, *Totalitarianism: The Inner History of the Cold War* (New York and Oxford, 1995). The founding texts arguing that Lenin's conception of the Party was at the root of Soviet totalitarianism are: H. Arendt, *The Origins of Totalitarianism* (New York, 1951); J.L. Talmon, *The Origins of Totalitarian Democracy* (London, 1952); idem, *Political Messianism: The Romantic Phase* (London, 1960); idem, *The Myth of the Nation and the Vision of Revolution* (London, 1980); Karl Popper, *The Open Society and its Enemies* (Princeton,

1950); F.A. Hayek, *The Road to Serfdom* (London, 1944); C. Friedrich (ed.), *Totalitarianism* (Cambridge, Mass., 1954); Carl Friedrich and Zbygniew Brzezinski, *Totalitarian Dictatorship and Autocracy* (New York, 1956); and Zbygniew Brzezinski, *The Permanent Purge: Politics in Soviet Totalitarianism* (Cambridge, Mass., 1956).

4 For a cogent and convincing statement of the argument that *What is to be Done?* was 'a restatement of the principles of Russian Marxist orthodoxy', see Neil Harding, *Lenin's Political Thought*, 2 vols (London, 1977 and 1981), vol. 1, ch. 7 ('The Reaffirmation of Orthodoxy'). The quotation is from p. 189.

3   CONSTRUCTING LENINISM

1 R. Luxemburg, 'The Organisational Question of Russian Social Democracy'. There is an English translation in Mary-Alice Waters (ed.), *Rosa Luxemburg Speaks* (New York, 1970), pp. 114–30. The quotation is on p. 122.

2 Quoted in L. Kochan, *Russia in Revolution* (London, 1970), p. 47.

3 There are many works on aspects of the revolution of 1905 but only one relatively recent general history, Abraham Ascher, *The Revolution of 1905*, 2 vols (Stanford, 1988). For a discussion of the historiography of autocratic 'liberalization' after 1905, see Christopher Read, 'In Search of Liberal Tsarism: The Historiography of Autocratic Decline', *The Historical Journal*, 45, 1 (2002), pp. 195–210.

4 Quoted in R. Pipes, *Struve: Liberal on the Left* (Cambridge, Mass., 1970), p. 195.

5 K. Marx, *Contribution to the Critique of Hegel's Philosophy of Right: Introduction* (1844) in Karl Marx and Friedrich Engels, *Collected Works*, vol. 3 (London, 1975), p. 175.

6 For a fuller account of Lenin's role in party meetings and congresses at this time, see Christopher Read, 'Lenin in 1905', in A. Heywood and J. Smele (eds), *The Russian Revolution of 1905: Centenary Perspectives* (London, 2005).

7 See Weber 52 for 26–27 January but also elsewhere.

8 Miliukov claimed he could not recall using the phrase but agreed it represented his opinion. P. Miliukov, *Political Memoirs: 1905–17* (Ann Arbor, 1967), p. 66.

9 This has been suggested in James White, *Lenin* (London, 2001), p. 70.

10 Bogdanov evolved into one of the most interesting and original thinkers to emerge from the Bolshevik movement. After he was

sidelined in the party by Lenin he spent more time on refining his ideas about proletarian culture, coupled with concepts of a proletarian encyclopedia to encapsulate it and a proletarian university to promote it. Later on he developed ideas on organization theory and was an accomplished writer of science fiction. He was also a doctor and conducted medical experiments on himself including a fatal blood transfusion in 1928. Among his disciples was the prominent Italian Marxist theorist Antonio Gramsci. There is a growing literature on him; see Christopher Read, *Religion, Revolution and the Russian Intelligentsia: The Vekhi Debate and its Intellectual Background* (London, 1979); Christopher Read, *Culture and Power in Revolutionary Russia* (London, 1990); Lynn Mally, *Culture of the Future: The Proletkult Movement in Revolutionary Russia* (Berkeley, 1992); John Biggart (ed.), *Bogdanov and His Work: A Guide to the Published and Unpublished Works of Alexander A. Bogdanov (Malinovsky), 1873–1928* (Aldershot, 1998); and John Biggart (ed.), *Alexander Bogdanov and the Origins of Systems Thinking in Russia* (Aldershot, 1998).

4   IMPERIALISM, WAR AND REVOLUTION

1 James Joll, *Europe Since 1870: An International History* (London, 1976), pp. 186–7.
2 Ibid., p. 186.
3 Ibid., p. 187.
4 For an excellent account, see Jonathan Schneer, *London 1900: The Imperial Metropolis* (New Haven and London, 1999) and, with a focus on the financial centres, David Kynaston, *The City of London*, vol. 2: *Golden Years, 1890–1914* (London, 1995).
5 All quotes are from extracts in D.K. Fieldhouse, *The Theory of Capitalist Imperialism* (London, 1967), pp. 84 and 85.
6 It was finished in 1915 at which time Lenin read it and wrote a supportive preface. However, the book was not actually published until 1917.
7 See Robert Service, *Lenin: A Biography* (London, 2000), p. 158.

5   FROM THE FINLAND STATION TO THE WINTER PALACE

1 For a survey of such activities, see Christopher Read, *From Tsar to Soviets: The Russian People and Their Revolution, 1917–21* (London, 1996), pp. 61–142.

2 N.N. Sukhanov, *The Russian Revolution: An Eyewitness Account* (trans. and ed. J. Carmichael), 2 vols (New York, 1962), vol. 2, p. 441.

3 The fullest study of the July Days is still A. Rabinowitch, *Prelude to Revolution* (Bloomington, N.Y., 1968).

4 The myths have been most successfully rebutted in S. Lyandres, 'The Bolsheviks' "German Gold" Revisited: An Inquiry into the 1917 Accusations', in *The Carl Beck Papers in Russian and East European Studies*, no. 1106 (Centre for Russian and East European Studies, Pittsburgh, Penn., 1995).

5 See J. White, 'Lenin, Trotskii and the Arts of Insurrection: The Congress of Soviets of the Northern Region, 11–13 October 1917', *Slavonic and East European Review*, 77(1), 1999, pp. 117–39.

6 *The Bolsheviks and the October Revolution: Minutes of the Central Committee of the Russian Social-Democratic Labour Party (Bolsheviks) August 1917–February 1918* (trans. Anne Bone) (London, 1976), p. 107.

7 Sukhanov (1962), vol. 2, p. 524.

6 FROM CLASSROOM TO LABORATORY – EARLY EXPERIMENTS

1 Lenin's campaign is discussed at greater length in Christopher Read, *From Tsar to Soviets: The Russian People and Their Revolution, 1917–21* (London, 1996), pp. 161–76. There is a useful compilation of Lenin's writings of 1917 – V.I. Lenin, *Between the Two Revolutions: Articles and Speeches of 1917* (Moscow, 1971).

2 W.H. Chamberlin, *The Russian Revolution*, vol. 1 (New York, 1965), p. 320.

3 *The Bolsheviks and the October Revolution: Minutes of the Central Committee of the Russian Social-Democratic Labour Party (Bolsheviks) August 1917–February 1918* (trans. Anne Bone) (London, 1976), pp. 141–2.

4 Ibid., p. 145.

5 Ibid., p. 137.

6 Ibid.

7 Read (1996), pp. 228–30.

8 Ibid., p. 203. See *V.I. Lenin i VChK: sbornik dokumentov (1917–1922 gg.)* (Moscow, 1987) for examples.

9 'Extraordinary Meeting of delegates of Factories and Plants in the City of Petrograd', in *Kontinent 2: The Alternative Voice of Russia and Eastern Europe* (London, 1978), pp. 238–40.

7   REVOLUTIONARY WAR

1 The scene is described, with slightly different words, by David Shub in *Lenin* (Harmondsworth, 1966), p. 285.

2 R.H. McNeal (ed.), *Resolutions and Decisions of the Communist Party of the Soviet Union* (Toronto, Buffalo, 1970), pp. 74 and 76.

3 See Christopher Read, *From Tsar to Soviets: The Russian People and Their Revolution, 1917–21* (London, 1996), pp. 209–11.

4 E.H. Carr, *The Bolshevik Revolution*, vol. 2 (Harmondsworth, 1968), p. 163.

5 An account which follows the lines of this interpretation can be found in Read (1996), chs 8–12, pp. 177–282.

6 J. Bunyan and H.H. Fisher (eds), *The Bolshevik Revolution 1917–18 – Documents*, 3 vols, vol. 1 (Stanford, 1961), p. 136.

7 Louis Fischer, *The Life of Lenin* (London, 1965), p. 619.

8 I.P. Bardin, *Zhizn' inzhenera* (Moscow, 1957), p. 46.

9 Carr (1968), p. 217.

10 Ibid., p. 216.

11 Peter Kenez, *The Birth of the Propaganda State: Soviet Methods of Mass Mobilization, 1917–29* (Cambridge, 1985).

12 Christopher Read, *Culture and Power in Revolutionary Russia* (London, 1990), p. 173.

13 For the emergence of Bolshevik policy in this area, see Read (1990) and Kenez (1985).

14 See the discussion of these issues in Robert Service, *Lenin: A Biography* (London, 2000), pp. 218–20 and 231–2.

15 R.H. McNeal (ed.), *Resolutions and Decisions of the Communist Party of the Soviet Union*, 4 vols, vol. 2 (Toronto, Buffalo, 1974), pp. 63–5.

16 See Read (1990) as a starting point for this discussion. It includes references to many other works on the topic.

17 McNeal, vol. 2, p. 63.

18 On the Organizational Question, see ibid., p. 89.

19 Victor Serge, *Memoirs of a Revolutionary 1901–41* (London, Oxford and New York, 1963), p. 74.

20 McNeal, vol. 2, pp.83–4.

21 Ibid., p. 84.

22 Leonard Schapiro, *The Communist Party of the Soviet Union*, 2nd edn (London, 1979), p. 235.

23 By March 1920 the membership stood at 611,978; Schapiro, p. 235.

24 www.defenselink.mil/news/apr2003/. Note the significant absence of Mao Zedong.

25 Arno Mayer, *The Furies: Violence and Terror in the French and Russian Revolutions* (Princeton, 2000), p. 4.

26 These figures come from Read (1996), pp. 206–8 where a fuller discussion can be found.

27 *Pravda*, no. 116, 31 May 1919.

28 R. Pipes, *The Unknown Lenin* (Princeton, 1996).

29 Read (1996), p. 207.

30 Quotations taken from Pipes, pp. 153–5.

31 R. Luxemburg, 'The Russian Revolution', in *The Russian Revolution and Leninism or Marxism* (Ann Arbor, 1961), p. 71.

8   RE-EVALUATION, SUCCESSION AND TESTAMENT

1 The best account of Lenin's day-to-day administrative routine is still T.H. Rigby, *Lenin's Government: Sovnarkom (1917–22)* (Cambridge, 1979).

2 The article can be found in *Communist International*, no. 12, 1920, pp. 7–8.

3 Angelica Balabanoff, *Impressions of Lenin* (Ann Arbor, 1968), p. 15.

4 R. Pipes, *The Unknown Lenin* (Princeton, 1996), pp. 8 and 10.

5 Vladimir Brovkin suggests this in *Behind the Front Lines of the Civil War: Political Parties and Social Movements in Russia, 1918–22* (Princeton, 1994).

6 R. McNeal (ed.), *Resolutions and Decisions of the Communist Party of the Soviet Union*, 4 vols, vol. 2 (Toronto, Buffalo, 1974), pp. 126–7.

7 'Purging the Party', *Pravda*, no. 210, 1 September 1921.

8 Christopher Read, 'Values, Substitutes, and Institutions: The Cultural Dimension of the Bolshevik Dictatorship', in Vladimir Brovkin (ed.), *The Bolsheviks in Russian Society: The Revolution and the Civil Wars* (New Haven and London, 1997), pp. 308–12.

9 More detail on these developments can be found in Christopher Read, *From Tsar to Soviets: The Russian People and Their Revolution, 1917–21* (London, 1996), pp. 211–23; and Christopher Read, *The Making and Breaking of the Soviet System* (Basingstoke and New York, 2001), pp. 41–7.

10 First published as 'The Party Crisis', in *Pravda*, no. 13, 21 January 1921.

11 Pipes (1996), pp. 156–7.

12 The seminal account of this argument is to be found in Moshe Lewin, *Lenin's Last Struggle* (New York, 1968).

13 Robert Service, *Lenin: A Biography* (London, 2000), p. 474.

CONCLUSION: LENIN LIVED! LENIN LIVES! LENIN WILL LIVE FOREVER!

1 For an excellent survey, see N. Tumarkin, *Lenin Lives! The Lenin Cult in Soviet Russia* (Cambridge, Mass., 1983).

2 I am indebted to Jonathan Davis for these references taken from his forthcoming article, 'Left out in the Cold: British Labour Witnesses the Russian Revolution' and from his Ph.D. thesis, *Altered Images: The Labour Party and the Soviet Union in the 1930s* (De Montfort University, Leicester, 2002). The comments were originally published in G. Lansbury, *What I Saw in Russia* (London, 1920), pp. 22 and 26 and Ethel Snowden, *Through Bolshevik Russia* (London, 1920), p. 117.

3 Bertrand Russell, *The Practice and Theory of Bolshevism* (London, 1962), pp. 26–7. The book was first published in 1920.

4 H. Seton-Watson, *The Russian Empire 1801–1917* (Oxford, 1967), pp. 605 and 606.

5 Leonard Schapiro, 'Lenin after Fifty Years', in L. Schapiro and P. Reddaway (eds), *Lenin: Man, Theorist and Leader* (London, 1967), pp. 8 and 19–20.

6 *Daily Mail*, 22 January 1994.

7 D. Volkogonov, *Lenin: Life and Legacy* (London, 1995), p. 326.

8 R. Pipes, *The Unknown Lenin: From the Secret Archives* (New Haven and London, 1998), pp. 8, 10, 12 and 13.

9 Lars Lih, 'How a Founding Document Was Found, or One Hundred Years of Lenin's *What is to be Done?*', *Kritika: Explorations in Russian and Eurasian History*, 4(1), Winter 2003, pp. 5–49. The phrase quoted occurs on pp. 41 and 49.

10 Important recent accounts of Lenin, in addition to those mentioned above, include: R. Service, *Lenin: A Political Life*, 3 vols (London, 1985; 1991; 1994); R. Service, *Lenin: A Biography* (London, 2000); B. Williams, *Lenin* (London, 2000); J. White, *Lenin: The Practice and Theory of Revolution* (London, 2001); Anna Krylova, 'Beyond the Spontaneity-Consciousness Paradigm: Class Instinct as a Promising Category of Historical Analysis', *Slavic Review*, 62(1), 2003, pp. 1–23; Leopold Haimson, 'Lenin's Revolutionary Career Revisited: Some Observations on Recent Discussions', *Kritika: Explorations in Russian and Eurasian History*, 5(1), Winter 2004, pp. 55–80; R. Zelnik (ed.), *Workers and Intelligentsia in Late Imperial Russia* (Berkeley, 1999); R. Zelnik, 'A Paradigm Lost? A Response to Anna Krylova', *Slavic Review*, 62(1), 2003, pp. 24–30; L. Haimson, *Russia's*

Revolutionary Experience and the Issue of Power (1905–1917) (New York, 2004); L. Haimson, *Political Struggles and Social Conflicts in Early Twentieth-Century Russia (1900–1917)* (forthcoming).

11 Some of these considerations are raised in C. Read, 'Lenin and Mass Action in the Russian Revolutionary War' (paper presented at the *History Under Debate* conference, July 2004, Santiago de Compostela. Publication forthcoming. (Abstract available on the *History Under Debate* website, www.h-debate.com/congresos/3/)

12 These issues are explored more fully in C. Read, *The Making and Breaking of the Soviet System* (Basingstoke and New York, 2001), chs 1–5.

FURTHER READING

The best way to get to understand Lenin is to read some of his works. This is a very easy proposition since the forty-seven volumes of his *Collected Works* are gradually being transferred to the Web at www.marxists.org. This American site also has biographical and other information and an excellent collection of photos of Lenin. For those who prefer traditional print there are useful collections of his works which have been mentioned in the text, notably *Collected Works*, 47 vols (Moscow, 1960–70) (English edition) and the three-volume *Selected Works* (Moscow, 1963–4).

Books about Lenin are legion. In the forefront of recent scholarship is Robert Service whose political and personal biographies are the starting point for all explorations of Lenin's life and works. They are R. Service, *Lenin: A Political Life*, 3 vols (London, 1985; 1991; 1994) and R. Service, *Lenin: A Biography* (London, 2000). Other excellent recent biographies include Beryl Williams, *Lenin* (London, 2000) and James White, *Lenin: The Practice and Theory of Revolution* (London, 2001). Notable as the leading Russian contribution to the literature is D. Volkogonov, *Lenin: Life and Legacy* (London, 1995).

In addition to these there are a number of older biographies which still retain much interest. These include: L. Schapiro and P. Reddaway (eds), *Lenin: Man, Theorist and Leader* (London, 1967); David Shub, *Lenin* (New York, 1948; revised edition, Harmondsworth, 1966); Adam Ulam, *Lenin and the Bolsheviks* (London, 1969); Harold Shukman, *Lenin and the Russian Revolution* (London, 1967). Christopher Hill's *Lenin and the Russian Revolution* (London, 1947) is a curiosity both because it reflects the period in which it was written and because of the person who wrote it rather than the person written about. Leon Trotsky, *The Young Lenin* (New York and London, 1972), Rolf Theen, *Lenin: Genesis and Development of a Revolutionary* (Philadelphia and New York, 1973) and Isaac Deutscher, *Lenin's Childhood* (Oxford, 1970) all seek to show the child as father of the man.

There are numerous accounts by people who knew Lenin. The following are all flawed in various ways but are still stimulating and valuable if used with discrimination and critical intelligence. They are Nadezhda Krupskaya, *Memories of Lenin* (London, 1970), Angelica Balabanoff, *Impressions of Lenin* (Ann Arbor, 1968) and N. Valentinov, *Encounters with Lenin* (Oxford, 1968).

There are a number of important books on aspects of Lenin's life and thought. Neil Harding's two-volume *Lenin's Political Thought* (London, 1977 and 1981) was pathbreaking. A very readable guide to Lenin's thought illustrated with many, extensive quotations from his work is E. Fischer and F. Marek (eds), *The Essential Lenin* (New York, 1972). Carmen Claudin-Urondo has written about *Lenin and the Cultural Revolution* (Hassocks, 1977). The hypothesis that there is really a democratic Lenin is scrutinized from different angles by Marcel Liebman, *Leninism under Lenin* (London, 1975) and Samuel Farber, *Before Stalinism: The Rise and Fall of Soviet Democracy* (New York, 1990). Moshe Lewin, *Lenin's Last Struggle* (New York, 1968) is a classic account of Lenin's attempt to censure Stalin in 1922–3. Tamara Deutscher, *Not by Politics Alone: The Other Lenin* (London, 1973) focuses on the emotional and cultural side of Lenin's life he was so at pains to keep under control.

Recent items focusing on specific questions include: Richard Pipes, *The Unknown Lenin: From the Secret Archives* (New Haven and London, 1998); Lars Lih, 'How a Founding Document Was Found, or One Hundred Years of Lenin's *What is to be Done?*', *Kritika: Explorations in Russian and Eurasian History*, 4(1), Winter 2003; Anna Krylova, 'Beyond the Spontaneity-Consciousness Paradigm: Class Instinct as a Promising Category of Historical Analysis', *Slavic Review*, 62(1), 2003, pp. 1–23; and Leopold Haimson, 'Lenin's Revolutionary Career Revisited: Some Observations on Recent Discussions', *Kritika: Explorations in Russian and Eurasian History*, 5(1), Winter 2004, pp. 55–80.

There is an exhaustive chronology of Lenin's life in one of the supplementary volumes of his *Collected Works*. A really excellent and more manageable chronology which incorporates key selected phrases from many of his works is G. and H. Weber, *Lenin: Life and Works* (London and Basingstoke, 1980).

The reader looking to put Lenin into his political context could do worse than to start with Christopher Read, *From Tsar to Soviets: The Russian People and Their Revolution, 1917–21* (London, 1996) or Rex

Wade, *The Russian Revolution 1917* (Cambridge, 2000). Also in this category are the rather idiosyncratic but very interesting and readable Richard Pipes, *The Russian Revolution 1899–1918* (New York, 1990) and *Russia under the Bolshevik Regime 1918–24* (New York, 1995) and Orlando Figes, *A People's Tragedy* (London, 1996).

INDEX

ABC of Communism 236, 262
Abo 85
Academy of Sciences 238; Committee
    for the Study of Scientific
    Productive Forces (KEPS) 231
Adler, Victor 185,127
Alakaevka 17, 281
Aleksinsky, Grigorii 85, 94, 161
Alexander II, Tsar 9–10
Alexander III, Tsar 10
Alexandra, Tsarina 138
Alexeev, General 187
American revolution 221
Amritsar massacre 249
Aristotle 127
Armand, Inessa 95, 103, 129–30,
    131, 134, 207, 237, 258–9
August 1915 crisis 138
Avenarius, Richard 89
Axel'rod, Pavel 11, 43, 72

Bakunin, Mikhail 13, 167, 288
Balabanoff, Angelica 129, 258
Baltic Fleet 159, 179
Baltic States 205
Bebel, August 58, 93, 118
Bednyi, Demian 96
Beethoven, Ludwig van 36
Berne 127, 129, 130, 131, 132, 151
Bernhardt, Sarah 65
Bernstein, Eduard 40–1, 67, 121
Bible 283
Blanquism 154, 167
Bloody Sunday (1905) 75
Bogdanov, A.A. 65, 78, 88–91, 92, 93,
    94, 95, 102, 125, 164, 180, 239

Bolshevik (Communist) Party 161,
    163, 178–82, 192, 210, 225,
    240–6; seventh All-Russian
    Conference (April–May 1917)
    154; Tenth Congress March 1921
    253, 258, 264, 268–9, 278, 290;
    Central Committee 154, 160, 165,
    175, 178–82, 188, 190, 199, 256,
    257, 262 changes name to
    Communist Party (March 1918)
    219; purging 245, 272–3
Bolshevism 59, 66, 70, 72, 73, 87,
    88, 149, 155, 160, 174–5, 184–6,
    190, 206, 234, 252–5, 263, 287
    and split in party 60–2, 83–4,
    92–7
Bonch-Bruevich, Vladimir 157, 182,
    287, 261
Bosh, Evgeniia 129
Boxer rebellion 249
Brest-Litovsk 187
Brest-Litovsk, treaty of 124, 193,
    198,–9, 200, 203, 213, 228,
    223
Brezhnev, L.I. 246
Britain 43, 46–8, 116, 121, 124, 140,
    143, 144, 219
British Museum 90
Brussels 102
Bukharin, N.I. 96, 125, 236, 239,
    261, 280–2
Bund see Jewish Workers' Party
bureaucracy 243–6, 270–6

Capri Party School 91, 93
careerism 243–6, 278–1

Castroism 283

Ceausescu, N 247

Chagall, Marc 237

Cheka 97, 186, 209–11, 235, 250, 269, 272

Chernov, Victor 160, 193, 194–5

Chernyshevsky, Nikolai 12, 18, 33, 52, 103, 200, *What is to be Done?* 12–13, 18, 33

China 171, 249

Chudivise 135

Churchill, Winston 221

civil war 205–6, 219–20, 290 'first' (1917–18) 187, 204

Comintern (Communist International) 223, 225–6, 275

committees of poor peasants (*kombedy*) 217–9

communist arrogance 270–1

Communist Party *see* Bolshevik Party

Constituent Assembly 176, 177, 192–3, 194, 236

Constitutional Democratic (Kadet) Party 60, 71, 83, 84, 85, 142, 192

Control Commission, Party 272, 273

Copenhagen 81, 102

cossacks Don 187

Crimean War 8

Cuba 283

cult of Lenin's personality 283–4

cultural revolution 234–40

Czech Legion 205

Danielson, N.F. 37

Danton, Georges-Jacques 189

Defence Soviet (Labour and Defence Committee) 256–7

Denikin, General 205

dialectics 128

Dostoevsky, Fyodor 288, *The Devils* 288

Dukhonin, Admiral 186, 197

Duma 152, 176 First (1906) 84; Second (1906) 76, 85; Third (1907–12) 85, 86–7, 92; Fourth (1912–17) 92–3, 106–7, 138–9

Dzerzhinsky, Feliks 209, 250

Economism 14, 41–2, 53–6, 57, 59, 61, 66, 261

Eisenhower, Dwight 120

Ekaterinodar 187

electrification 230, 231; electrification commission (GOELRO) 231

Elizarov, Mark 161, 164, 258

Engelhardt, Alexander 39

Engels, Frederick 18, 40, 54, 90, 168, 172, 200, *The Condition of the Working Class in England* 18; *The Origins of Family, Private Property and the State* 23

Estonia 219

fascism 247

February revolution (1917) 129, 138–41, 142, 143–4, 145

Finland 81, 100–1, 219, 226, 257

Finland Station 141, 142, 147

First International 109

First Machine Gun Regiment 159

Flakserman, Galina 179

Fofanova, Marguerita Vasilevna 179

Fourrier, Charles 200

France 43, 47–8, 66, 116, 119, 124, 132, 140, 143, 144, 219

French Revolution 188

Gapon, Fr Georgii 75

Geneva 64–6, 88, 101, 104, 131

Geneva, Lake 11, 68, 76

Germany 100, 110, 116, 119, 121, 161, 184, 219, 221, 226

Gestapo 122

Girondins 188

Glavlit (censorship) 236, 269

Gorbachev, Mikhail 246

Gorky (village) 212, 257, 258, 269, 281–2

Gorky, Maxim 36, 68, 72, 81, 88–9, 91, 92, 93, 94, 97, 101, 102, 136, 179, 207, 236, 251, 257, 258, 260

Grey, Sir Edward 127

Guchkov, A. 143

Hegel, Friedrich 33, 127

Helsinki 85, 165–6, 179

Hilferding, Rudolf 118–26, 169–71; *Finance Capital* 118–25

Hitler, Adolf 247

Ho Chi Minh 283

Hobson, J.A. 117–8, 123

India 249

International Socialist Bureau 78, 85, 92

Iskra (*The Spark*) 43, 52, 55, 60, 63–4, 71, 78

Izvestiia 213

Jacobins 188, 189, 288

Japan 75, 219

Jaurès, Jean 93

Jewish Workers' Party (Bund) 60, 61

juche idea 283

July Days 159–64, 172

Kadet Party *see* Constitutional Democratic Party

Kalinin, M 152

Kamenev, L 94, 96, 101, 129, 152, 163, 167, 179–80, 189, 190, 259, 260, 278, 279, 281

Kant, Immanuel 33

Kaplan, F 250

Kautsky, Karl 58, 72, 93, 122, 142, 149, 252–3, *Dictatorship of the Proletariat* 252

Kerensky, Alexander Fyodorovich 9, 107, 144, 160–1, 162, 173, 174, 175, 194–5

Kerensky, Fyodor 9

Keynes, John Maynard 124

Khrushchev, N.S. 246

Kienthal conference 110, 133–4

Kiev 187

Kokushkino 7, 17

Kolchak, Admiral 205

Kollontai, Alexandra 129, 142

Korea, North 283

Kornilov, General Lavr 162, 173–4, 175, 176, 181, 184, 187, 194

Krakow 104–5, 107, 127

Kremer, Arkadii 23; *On Agitation* 23

Kremlin 186, 212, 230, 281

Kronstadt 84, 159, 160, 179, 220, 264, 269

Krupskaya Nadezhda 14, 17, 19, 20–1, 55, 63, 81, 83, 91, 117, 157, 158, 161, 164–6, 207, 211, 212, 240, 257, 260; meets Lenin 20; with Lenin in Siberia 30–36; marries Lenin 30; joins Lenin abroad in 1901 44–5; in Geneva with Lenin (1903–5) 64; in Geneva, Paris and Krakow with Lenin (1907–14) 101–5; and dispute with Stalin 1922–3 279; in Switzerland with Lenin 126–30,132–7; death of her mother 130; with Lenin at Gorky 257, 281–2

Kshesinskaya mansion 151, 158, 159, 161

Kuban 187
Kuokkala 81, 88
Kuskova, E. 41

labour conscription 232–3, 266–8
Lafargue, Paul 93
Lahti 165
Lansbury, George 285
Latvia 219
Latvian Rifle Regiment 186
Lausanne 129, 131
Lena massacre 106
Lenin, Vladimir Il'ich (Ulyanov) birth
    and family background 4–7;
    school record 9; and execution of
    brother 11, 14, 67; and populism
    11, 13–14, 21–2, 25, 58–9 ,182;
    influence of Bakunin on 13, 23,
    24, 41, 167; at Kazan University
    15, 16; as student of St Petersburg
    University 15, 18; first visit to
    western Europe 20, 25–6; meets
    Nadezhda Krupskaya 20; knowl-
    edge of conspiratorial techniques
    21; early contacts with workers
    22; nicknamed 'starik' (the old
    man) 27; exile in Siberia 29–42;
    marries Nadezhda Krupskaya 30;
    returns from Siberian exile 42;
    leaves Russia (1900) 43; in
    Munich 1901–2 44–6; in London
    1902–3 46–8; and party building
    1901–3 49–62; in Geneva 1903–5
    64–6, 77–81; and 1905 revolution
    74–6, 77–86; and party in 1905
    77–9, 83; and tactics in 1905
    79–81; in Russia and Finland
    1905–7 81–6; and violence 80,
    208–11, 246–55; returns to
    western Europe 1907 85–6; and
    philosophy 88–91; and party

organization 1909–12 92–7; on
    imperialism 98–9, 123–6; on
    reforms 99; on Taylorism 100; in
    Geneva, Paris and Krakow 100–5;
    in Switzerland 1914–17 105–41;
    and outbreak of war 1914 107–9,
    111–16; and dialectics 128;
    returns to Russia April 1917
    140–1; in Petrograd April–July
    1917 142–164; in Finland
    July–October 1917 162–179;
    campaign for insurrection 175–82,
    188–9; and bureaucracy 187,
    270–6; and land policy 1917
    193–5; and Decree on Peace 1917
    196; and peace treaty March 1918
    198–9; and policies for transition
    to socialism 200–2, 212–19,
    263–8, 276–7; mental framework
    and morality of 206–8; 247–9,
    259–60; in Finland with
    Krupskaya Jan 1918 211; car shot
    at Jan 1918 211; on dictatorship
    214–5; and 'turn towards the
    middle peasant' 218; importance of
    consciousness to 234–40, 274–5;
    on sex 237; dismisses freudianism
    237; on religion 238–9, on
    Defence Committee 256–7;
    illnesses worsen 258; and cult of
    personality 259–61, 283–4; and
    relations with colleagues 261–2; as
    philosopher-king 262; at Tenth
    Party Congress 268–9; on leading
    role of party 274; and question of
    succession 277–81; and final
    dispute with Stalin 278–81; last
    visit to Kremlin 281; dies at
    Gorky 282
Leninism 72, 208, 275–6, 284, 287
Liebknecht, Karl 58, 225

liquidators 92–7, 102
Lissitsky, El 237
Lithuania 219
London 46–8, 60–1, 63, 67, 78, 81, 102, 104, 117, 126, 157, 289
Loyola, Ignatius 96
Lunacharsky, A.V. 72, 88, 89, 93, 102, 159, 186
Luxemburg, Rosa 72, 91, 100, 114, 125, 225, 253–4

Macchiavelli, Niccolo 252
Mach, Ernst 89
Malinovsky, Roman 93, 96
Mao Zedong 171; Maoism 283
Marne, river 127
Martov, Iulii 45, 50, 52, 60–2, 63, 70, 71, 72, 93, 94, 129, 131, 164, 180, 261, 288
Marx, Karl 11–12, 13, 14, 18, 36, 39, 40, 53, 54, 61, 64, 82, 88, 90, 155, 167, 168, 169, 170, 172, 186, 200, 233–4, 248; *Communist Manifesto* 12, 18, 40; *Das Kapital* 18, 23; *The German Ideology* 90; *Anti-Duhring* 90
Marxism 36, 49, 50, 59, 72, 88, 99, 166–9, 227, 233–4, 235, 239, 248, 263
Masurian Lakes 127
Mayakovsky, V 237, 284
Menshevism 14, 59, 73, 84, 92–7, 131, 147, 149, 150, 163, 174, 176, 177, 180, 181, 182, 183, 186, 188, 192, 261, 263, 288
Miliukov Note 158
Miliukov, Pavel 86, 142, 143, 175
Mirbach, Count von 199
Mogilev 186
Molotov, V.M. 96

Moscow 68, 75, 83, 179, 186, 251, 274, 289; Soviet government moves to 212
Moscow State Conference 173
Moscow uprising (1905) 76, 84, 219
motor cycles 100
Munich 43, 45, 166; Fasching in 43

Narodnaya volya (The Peoples Will) 23, 58
Nechaev, Sergei 13, 288
Neivola 157
New Economic Policy 206, 232, 259, 264–6, 276–7, 290–1
Nicholas I, Tsar 8
Nicholas II 75, 76, 86, 138, 139, 289
Nietzsche, Friedrich 247
Nizhnii Novgorod 250
Novaia zhizn'i (New Life) (1905) 64, 81; (1917) 236
NovoCherkassk 187

October Manifesto 76, 77, 78, 86
October Revolution 159, 172, 184, 188, 189, 197, 206
Ordzhonikidze, S 96, 258, 279
otzovists 92–7, 102
Owen, Robert 200

Paris 63, 88, 91, 101–4, 126, 155
Paris Commune 155, 167–9
Passchendaele 127
Pershikova, Valentina 260
Petrograd Soviet 144, 152, 156, 173, 179, 182–3, 105; Military Revolutionary Committee 182–3, 185, 189
planning, economic 231–2
Plato 89
Platten, Fritz 140–1, 198, 211

Plekhanov, George 11, 26, 38, 43, 52, 58, 61, 62, 70, 71, 72,77,78, 85, 92, 93, 129, 131, 164, 180; *Our Differences* 38
Pobedonostsev, Konstantin 10
pogroms 210
Pokrovsky, M.N. 238
Poland 104–5, 219, 221
populism 11, 24, 25, 37, 49, 99
Poronin 105
Port Arthur 75
Potemkin mutiny 75
Potresov, N 61
Prague 44, 95, 166
Pravda 95, 152, 163, 165, 192, 213, 243
Preobrazhensky, E 236, 262, 281
productionism 216, 227–33
Progressive Bloc 138
Prokopovich, S 41; *Credo* 41
Proletarii (Proletarians) 64, 78, 88, 93
Proletkul't 239–40, 274
Provisional Government 138, 142, 147, 153, 154, 156, 162, 174, 175, 180, 182, 192
Pyatakov, G 129

Q'uran 283
Quelch, Harry 51

Radek, K 96, 261
Rasputin 138
Razliv 165
recallists 92–7, 102
Red Army 186, 217; political commissars 217, 272; communists in 217
Red Guards 186, 216
red terror 1918–19 250
Revel 179
revolutionary war 205–55

Robins, Colonel J 198
Rostov 187
Rothorn 132–3
Rozmirovich, Elena 96, 129
Rumsfeld, Donald 247
Russell, Bertrand 285
Russian Social-Democratic Labour Party (RSDLP) founded 1898 42; Second Congress 42, 60–2, 66; Third Congress 77–8, 79; central committee 94
Rykov, A 96

Saddam Hussein 247
Second International 109, 128, 142, 149, 288; and outbreak of war in 1914 109–110
Serge, Victor 244
Shklovsky, V 129
Shlyapnikov, Alexander 129
Shmidt inheritance 95
Shuia 251
Shushenskoe 31–6
Siberia 206
Simbirsk 4, 187
Skaldin (Alenev, Fyodor) 39
Smith, Adam 39
Smolny Institute 102
Snowden, Ethel 285
socialism in one country 227
Socialist Revolutionary Party (SRs) 71, 74, 83, 150, 153, 163, 174, 176, 180, 181, 182, 183, 186, 188, 192, 194–5, 269; left SRs 193, 288; left SR uprising (July 1918) 199–200
Soerenberg 132–3
Somme, battle of 127
Sotsial Demokrat 127
soviets 144, 148–9, 153, 170, 201, 202; First All-Russian Soviet

Congress (June 1917) 156–7, 188;
    Second All-Russian Congress
    (October 1917) 183, 185, 189,
    190, 194, 195–6, 212, 223; Third
    All-Russian Congress (Jan 1918)
    193; Fourth (Extraordinary) All-
    Russian Congress (March 1918)
    193, 199; Congress of Soviets of
    the Northern Region 179
Sovnarkom (Council of People's
    Commissars) 183, 198, 256,
    257
Spartacus League 225
Spiridonova, Maria 193
SRs *see* Socialist Revolutionary Party
St Petersburg (Petrograd) 74, 75, 81,
    126, 141, 146–7, 156, 179, 203,
    219, 249, 250, 289; Soviet gov-
    ernment moves from 212
St Petersburg Soviet 83
St Petersburg, University of 8–9, 15,
    18
Stalin I.V. 96, 129, 152, 162, 247,
    251, 256, 260, 261, 268, 272,
    278–81, 284, 290, 291; *Problems of
    Leninism* 284
Stalinism 208, 246, 283
State Publishing House (*Gosizdat*)
    236, 275
Stavka (General Staff
    Headquarters)186, 187, 197
Stockholm 81, 102
Stolypin, P 76, 86, 87
Struve, Peter 50, 53, 87
Stuttgart 81, 85
Styrs Udde (Stjernsund) 81, 100
subbotniks 228, 243
Supreme Council of the National
    Economy (*Vesenkha*) 231
Sveaborg 84
Sweden 140–1, 142

Switzerland 20, 43, 64–6, 88, 101,
    104, 126–41, 142, 146

Tallin *see* Revel
Tambov uprising 228, 264
Tauride palace 152, 160
Tikhon, Patriarch 251–2
Timiriazev, K 229
Tolstoy, Leo 17, 33, 88; *Anna
    Karenina* 17
Trotsky, Leon 26–7, 28, 29, 48, 51,
    76, 91, 94, 129, 162, 164, 182–3,
    190, 198–9, 223, 224, 232, 236,
    244, 246, 256, 261, 275, 277,
    279, 280, 288
Turgenev, Ivan 17
Turkey 219

Ukraine 187, 210, 219
ultimatumists 92–7
Ulyanov, Alexander 8–9, 10, 11, 67
Ulyanov, Dmitrii 66, 257
Ulyanov, Ilya Nikolaevich 4, 5, 6, 7,
    8, 9, 17
Ulyanova, Anna 9, 41, 66, 88, 93,
    101, 103, 151, 161, 207, 257,
    281
Ulyanova Mariia (Lenin's sister) 9, 51,
    66, 102–3, 151, 207, 280, 281–2
Ulyanova, Mariia Alexandrovna
    (Lenin's mother) 4, 5, 19, 20, 66,
    151; in Stockholm 102–3; dies
    130
Ulyanova, Olga 9, 18, 19, 20, 130,
    151
United States 115, 124

Vandervelde, Emile 109
Verdun 127
Versailles, treaty of 124, 284
Vienna 44

Vietnam 283
Volunteer Army 187, 205
Vpered (Forward) 64, 74, 78, 79, 94
Vyborg 179

War Communism 206, 290
West Siberian Uprising 220, 264
Whites 205–6, 218, 219–20, 222, 250, 251, 264
Williams, Albert Rhys 221
Wilson, Woodrow 115
Winter Palace 182
Witte, Sergei 86
women's rights 233, 237
Worker Peasant Inspectorate 272, 273
workers' control 203
Workers' Opposition 268–9
world revolution 184, 221, 222–7
writings of Lenin (in chronological order) *Development of Capitalism in Russia* 34, 39–40; *The Heritage we Renounce* 38; *Urgent Tasks of our Movement* 39; *What is to Be Done* 52–60, 69, 73, 88, 283, 287; *Letter to a Comrade* 68; *One Step Forward, Two Steps Back* 68–74, 82, 85, 88, 216; *The Revolutionary-Democratic Dictatorship of the Proletariat and Peasantry* 79; *Two Tactics of Social-Democracy in the Democratic Revolution* 79–80, 82, 85, 286; *The Reorganization of the Party* 81–2; *Party Organization and Party Literature* 82; *Socialism and Religion* 82–3; *The Attitude of the Workers' Party Towards Religion* 81–2; *Lessons of the Moscow Uprising* 84; *Materialism and Empiriocriticism* 90, 91, 93, 97; *Towards Unity* 94; *On Unity* 95; *The War and Russian Social Democracy* 111–14;

Imperialism the Latest {Highest} Stage of Capitalism 115, 123–6, 284; *State and Revolution* 123, 137, 145, 166–72, 200, 242, 270, 284; *Philosophical Notebooks* 127–8; *Lecture on the 1905 revolution* 139 *Letters From Afar* 142–6,166; *Farewell Letter to the Swiss Workers* 146; *The Tasks of the Proletariat in the Present Revolution {The April Theses}* 143, 146–50, 151, 166, 168, 169, 181, 196, 200, 214, 216, 225, 228–9, 237, 263, 270, 288; *Letter on Tactics* 152, 155; *The Dual Power* 154; *The Political Situation: Four Theses* 162–3; *On Compromises* 176; *The Tasks of the Revolution* 176–7; *The Impending Catastrophe and How to Combat It* 177; *The Bolsheviks Must Assume Power* 188; *Can the Bolsheviks Retain State Power* 188, 209–10; *Immediate Tasks of the Soviet Government* 213–5, 228, 271; *Economics and Politics in the Era of the Dictatorship of the Proletariat* 218; *"Left-wing" childishness and the petty-bourgeois mentality* 223–4; *Notes of a Publicist* 225; *A Great Beginning* 228, 229, 243; *Report on the Party Programme at Eighth Party Congress* 242, 245; *Proletarian Revolution and the Renegade Kautsky* 252; *Letter to the Congress (Testament)* 273, 278–9; *Better Fewer but Better* 275; *On Co-operation* 276–7

Yudenich, General 206

Zakopane 105
Zarya (The Dawn) 52, 60

Zasulich, Vera 72
Zemlya i volya (*Land and Liberty*) 58
Zetkin, Klara 237, 254, 257–8
Zimmerwald Conference 110,
    132–3
Zinoviev, Grigorii 91, 96, 101, 104,
    129, 134, 140, 162, 163, 165,
179–80, 189, 190, 207, 278,
    279, 281
Zinovieva, Lilina 104, 129, 131, 140,
    207
Zubatov, P 75
Zurich 132, 134, 135–6, 140, 151
Zurichberg 136